WOMEN AND REVOLUTION

WOMEN AND REVOLUTION

A DISCUSSION OF THE UNHAPPY MARRIAGE OF MARXISM AND FEMINISM

edited by
Lydia Sargent

SOUTH END PRESS

First printing
Cover design by Lydia Sargent
Typeset at Carrier Pigeon, Boston
Production at South End Press
Printed in the U.S.A.
Library of Congress number: 80-54829
ISBN 0-89608-061-7 paper
ISBN 0-89608-062-5 cloth

SOUTH END PRESS/BOX 68 ASTOR STA/BOSTON MA 02123

CONTENTS

EXTENSIONS OF PATRIARCHY

REFOCUSING THE DISCUSSION

REJOINDER

PREFACE

WHY A CONTROVERSIES SERIES?

South End Press is a publishing collective committed to furthering the socialist movement in the United States. We are concerned with the totality of oppressions, especially those based on race, sex, and class; and we are striving for a world in which all people are directly and collectively in control of their lives.

Women and Revolution is the second volume in the South End Press political controversies series. This series is designed as a forum for discussing contemporary political issues facing socially concerned people around the world. Beyond being a forum, it is our hope that the debate provoked by this series will lead to a theory and practice that can assist in the creation of genuinely democratic and liberating societies.

Although controversies series formats will vary, most of them will consist of a lead article which develops a position on a particular political issue, various responses to the lead article, and possibly a rejoinder by the author of the lead piece. Lead essays are chosen on the basis of the strength of their arguments, and their ability to stir controversy and raise strategical considerations. Responses will be both supportive and critical.

The political controversies series stems from the belief that a powerful, democratic, and united movement for socialism requires a process of vigorous discussion. There is not "one road to socialism." This series will open debates, air positions, and pull together people's experiences and theories, eventually contributing to programs for social change.

Between Labor and Capital, the first volume in this series focuses on the class position and consciousness of those poeple who work in jobs located between labor and capital, "the middle class." This second volume, *Women and Revolution,* focuses on the interaction between marxist and feminist theory and their respective positions on the importance of patriarchy and class, the role of women in revolution, and the importance of sexism as a revolutionary issue.

We would like the political controveries series to be a means through which people who do theoretical work will feel compelled to root that work in experience and to present it in understandable terms. At the same time, we want this series to attract contributions from people who have not previously done theoretical work, but who have considerable organizing skills and experience. We also see the series as a means of publishing people who have never before been published or who do not have the time and the means to write long books. As these kinds of contributions begin to merge, our controversies series will come closer to the ambitious goal of the further development of an integrated theory and program relevant to social change.

Other proposed topics for the political controversies series are: race and revolution, socialism and internationalism, radical american history, reform and revolution, unions and revolution, high culture and people's culture, gay/lesbian liberation and socialism, socialist sexuality, and ecology and capitalism.

We encourage our readers to participate in this series by suggesting other series books, by writing essays for them, and by helping find other lead essays and contributions.

—The South End Press Collective

NEW LEFT WOMEN AND MEN: THE HONEYMOON IS OVER

by Lydia Sargent

Lydia Sargent has been a member of South End Press since it began in 1976. She is also playwright, director, and actor with The Newbury Street Theater and a member of The Living Newspaper, a radical newstheater collective. She has adapted women's fiction and oral histories into a show called FOOTHOLDS, has scripted a full length play based on Daughter of Earth by Agnes Smedley, and written an original feminist mystery comedy, The Long Sigh.

THE UNHAPPY MARRIAGE

In the opening paragraph of "The Unhappy Marriage of Marxism and Feminism" Heidi Hartmann states:

> The marriage of marxism and feminism has been like the marriage of husband and wife depicted in English common law: marxism and feminism are one, and that one is marxism. Recent attempts to integrate marxism and feminism are unsatisfactory to us as feminists because they subsume the feminist struggle into the "larger" struggle against capital. To continue the simile further, either we need a healthier marriage or we need a divorce. (Hartmann, p. 2.)

That unhappy marriage of marxism and feminism is what this book is about. Can we as radical, socialist, marxist, lesbian, anarchist, and black feminists achieve equality in a left/progressive movement whose dominant ideology is marxism and can we achieve equality in a future society which is organized around marxist theory and practice? In this book, thirteen women from different politics, theoretical perspectives, and experiences discuss Hartmann's unhappy marriage of marxism and feminism in an attempt to clarify and expand on current feminist theory and practice.

REASONS WHY

The immediate impetus for this discussion of the "failed" marriage of marxism and feminism came out of the experiences of women in the civil rights, new left, and women's movement of the 1960s and 1970s. As the new left debated, marched, organized, and eventually developed an analysis of U.S. capitalism and imperialism, new left activists, more often than not, identified themselves within a marxist leninist tradition of thought and revolutionary practice. While rejecting the "old left" and the tradition of communist and socialist parties with their attachment to the politics of the soviet union, the new left, nonetheless, identified itself with one or another of the socialist countries in the world and with all countries struggling for national liberation from neo-colonial powers: Cuba, Vietnam, Zimbabwe, Chile...It was a new kind of marxism, to be sure, a marxism that attempted to integrate the student and youth culture concept that capitalist/imperialist ideology permeated every aspect of daily life: schools, work, music, television, film, community, environment, and expecially sexual/social relations. But within this "expanded" new left politics the bottom line for women in the U.S movement was always limited to: "men will make the revolution and make their chicks."[1] Women working in new left and civil rights organizations were faced more and more with two main problems: (1) the problem of day-to-day work (who cleans the office/who messes it up, who writes the leaflets/who types them, who talks in meetings/who takes notes, who gains status through sexual relations/who gives status through sexual relations) and; (2) the problem of theory (who leads the revolution, who makes it, who is liberated by it, and who keeps the home fires burning during it).

It didn't take long for new left women to discover the answers to the problems of theory and day-to-day work. Marxism defined the answer to the first question; sexist males the answer to the second. That is, workers at the point of production (read white working class males) will make the revolution led by revolutionary cadre of politicos (read middle class white males steeped in marxist economic theory). Women (mostly white) would keep the home fires burning during it, functioning as revolutionary nurturers/secretaries: typing, filing, phoning, feeding, healing, supporting, loving, and occasionally even participating on the front lines as quasi revolutionary cheerleaders.

It became crucial, given this vision (nightmare), for women to define the nature and extent of their oppression if they were to become more than sex-objects for their revolutionary "brothers."

THE PROBLEM OF WHO CLEANS THE OFFICE: DEFINING OUR OPPRESSION

Betty Friedan writes about the "problem with no name" in her book *The Feminine Mystique:*

> The problem lay buried, unspoken, for many years in the minds of American women. It was a strange stirring, a sense of disatisfaction, a yearning that women suffered in the middle of the twentieth century United States. Each suburban wife struggled with it alone. As she made the beds, shopped for groceries, matched slipcover material, ate peanut butter sandwiches with her children, chauffered Cub Scouts and Brownies, lay beside her husband at night—she was afraid to ask even the silent question—"Is this all?"[2]

At the same time that suburban women read and identified with Friedan's "problem with no name," women in the new left were busy cleaning and decorating movement offices, cooking movement dinners, handling daycare, chauffering activists to demonstrations, typing letters and leaflets, answering phones, and lying beside their movement lovers and husbands at night also afraid to ask the silent question—"Is this all?"

Although Simone de Beauvoir didn't give this "problem" of women's alienation and sense of valuelessness a name, she did attempt to define it as early as 1949 in her book *The Second Sex:*

> Thus, humanity is male and man defines woman not in herself but as relative to him; she is not regarded as an autonomous being...And she is simply what man decrees; thus she is called "the sex," by which is meant that she appears essentially to the male as a sexual being. For him she is sex—absolute sex, no less. She is defined and differentiated with reference to man and not he with reference to her; she is incidental, the inessential as opposed to the essential. He is the Subject, he is Absolute—she is the Other.[3]

In the new left, to be "the Other" extended to all aspects of daily work but the focus, as de Beauvoir's analysis predicts, was sexuality. Sara Evans recounts in her book *Personal Politics:*

> Fucking a staff into existence is only the extreme form of what passes for common practice in many places. A man can bring a woman into an organization by sleeping with her and remove her by ceasing to do so. A man can purge a woman for no other reason than he has tired of her, knocked her up, or is after someone else; and that purge is accepted without a ripple.[4]

Women in the movement were confronted, then, with a painful and frustrating situation. On the one hand, they knew their was a qualitative difference between being part of the movement and being outside it. They were doing important, valuable work: stopping a war, fighting for civil rights; they were taking risks, learning and growing. They had rejected the rigid roles of the authoritarian 1950s. On the other hand, they also knew that the men in the movement (and in some cases the women) saw women's function and legitimacy primarily through their participation in traditionally "feminine" ways i.e., as movement wives, mothers, sisters, mistresses, secretaries, maids, waitresses, nurses, and sex objects.

Early attempts to confront sexism were met with derisive sexual name-calling: "bitch, lesbian, castrator." Early attempts to speak about sexism at meetings or demonstrations were turned into circuses by men catcalling, whistling, and shouting for women to get off the stage and "have a good fuck." Early attempts to write about sexist behavior were written anonymously by women and ignored by men. Later when men saw they could no longer engage in the more blatant forms of sexism because women pushed for continual consciousness raising around sexism and even developed many structural solutions to inequalities, men developed an intricate set of more subtle, sexist behavior. So, in addition to putting their energy into defining and eliminating sexism, women also had to spend a great deal of time proving that there was sexist behavior going on at all. The following is a description of some of the endless ways women's attempts to name and eliminate sexist behavior were coopted and used.*

Women's Caucuses

This practice, used mainly at conferences and large meetings, provided a forum for women to voice their feelings about sexism, sexual politics, and other topics in an atmosphere free of power-tripping by men. Successful for women, they were often viewed by the men as something separate and unequal. Since men did not spend time discussing their roles as sexist oppressors but rather in discussing "important political issues," women had to choose between women's caucuses and other political issue meetings happening at the same time.

Women as Chair

Designed to give women leadership and experience talking in front of large groups, women as chair became a means for men to control the direction of the meeting. Powerful men would pick certain women to be chair (often a woman they were interested in sleeping with or already sleeping with) and sit next to them in meetings. During the meeting these men would whisper agenda items to the woman chair, suggest who to call on, often ridicule her when the decision wasn't going their way, making the woman feel that she

---

*It is difficult to put a chronology to the behavior that follows. It occurred in early new left and civil rights organizations and later on in all mixed organizations even after women split to form autonomous women's groups. Although many men struggled with their sexism, the conscious and unconscious ways that men circumvented and sabotaged women's attempts to eliminate sexism predominated the movement throughout the sixties, seventies, and on into the eighties.

wasn't handling the meeting correctly. Often other men would assist in making the woman chair feel totally incompetent by laughing, and talking, speaking out of order, and ignoring her entirely thereby giving strength to their argument that a male chair (read strong) was necessary for "really important meetings."

Women as MC

Attempts to involve women on the speaker's platform at large local and national demonstrations resulted in women as mc. Women would act as announcer for a long list of mostly male speakers. So women as mc became women as movement hostess who gave glowing introductions to thirty or more male speakers who would proceed to speak on the war, poverty, injustice, racism, imperialism, the draft, the government, the environment and on and on interrupted by a woman's voice introducing the next male speaker.

Women as Speakers

Men were enthusiastic about women speaking as long as they spoke about two things: events and women's issues. Concretely, this meant that at any given large meeting or demonstration, women would mc as mentioned above, announce events (marches, meetings etc.), and speak about sexism after the twenty-second male speaker. At this point, many people would have left already, the men in the crowd would fall asleep or talk during the woman speaker.

Women as Strategists

There were a number of different ways that this tactic was used. Women staff or steering committee members would be singled out by certain men who wanted to effect a decision regarding policy or tactics for a march or demonstration. Usually they picked women who were new or inexperienced. Under the guise (sometimes sincere) of friendship or sharing of knowledge, men would discuss certain strategies with the women. Then they would encourage them to argue for those strategies in meetings. Women, then, were used as "conveyors" of male strategies. Often the men were not involved in that particular meeting so the women would be acting as proxy. If the men were present, the effect of this conveyor relationship was for men to gain votes while at the same time avoiding being attacked as "heavies" who were dominating the group. A conveyor relationship could also be the beginnings of a sexual relationship.

Women as Staff Leaders

Many movement organizations were composed of staffs who did the day to day work and steering committees who made the decisions. In many cases the day-to-day staff was composed largely of women and the steering committee of men. The result was that while women were doing a lot of important day-to-day work as staff members, they were also receiving direction and policy from a male-led steering committee. In some cases, this was irrelevant since the people doing the work often guided policy more than the steering committee. But in many cases, the dynamic resembled that of a regular office: men (bosses) defining the work for women (secretaries).

Taking Turns Cleaning the Office

Probably the cause of the most conflict in mixed organizations, this tactic involved elaborate rotation systems to ensure that men participated in cleaning, cooking, and neatening movement offices (also political collective households). To this day, every strategy has been a failure. First, men pretended they didn't know what clean was. Women typed out cleaning instructions which were followed for one week and then ignored. Another tack was "when it's your turn (women) to clean, you clean; when it's our turn (men), we'll clean for five minutes. This was followed by "when it's your turn to clean, you clean; when it's our turn, we won't." After that, men began to accuse women of nagging them to clean, causing them to block out the cleaning issue because they were reminded of their mothers. So it was actually women's fault that men did not do any cleaning. Variations on this were team cleaning in which women did the cleaning while men developed a sudden interest in answering the constantly ringing phone. If challenged men would pretend they had already finished their part of the team effort. Then, there was the buy-them-off-by-doing-a-big-cleaning-job-once-in-a-great-while strategy in which men did something REALLY BIG like washing windows or painting rooms (which usually caused more mess than they cleaned up) while ignoring the garbage, the food lying around, the boxes of leaflets blocking the doorway, and so on. After the REALLY BIG job was done, men felt they had proven that they could clean as well as or better than women.

Women Talking in Meetings

Many tactics were used to insure that women spoke equally in meetings: the chair calling on women who hadn't spoken on various issues and encouraging them to speak; chip systems,* time limits, women speaking first before men spoke etc. Men's response to these tactics could be described as "the pause that refreshes" or "women can speak but we don't have to listen." Concretely, this meant that in meetings whenever a woman spoke, men would either cough, mumble, read, or simply tune out while they gathered together their next argument to refute the previous male speaker. Women speaking in meetings became a refreshing pause for men.

Selective Listening

A variation of the above, men would listen to women only when they wanted to. This meant that when a woman spoke about design, they might listen to her but not when she spoke about politics. Or if they were interested in developing a relationship with a woman, men would "listen attentively" and nod approval. Or if a woman was attractive, they would listen when she spoke about office decoration but not when she spoke about imperialism. An assertive women would be called a lesbian and discounted totally. A woman known to be a lesbian would not be listened to at all.

When women continued to fight for equality in movement organizations, men turned to what they thought was the final crushing blow: "the important political struggle is to stop U.S. imperialism; the important struggle is the struggle of the working class to overthrow the capitalist class. And so, the problem of theory arose. If, after all the efforts made in the arena of day-to-day work, women were simply going to be quoted chapter and verse of Marx, Lenin and Mao, or fraternally/paternally encouraged to go read their *Communist Manifesto,* their *Eighteenth Brumaire,* their *On Contradiction,* their three volumes of *Capital,* their *Imperialism: the Highest Stage of Capitalism,* and subsequent works by the Habermas, Marcuse, Weber, Althusser, Sweezey, Magdoff, Braverman contingent, then the importance of the politics involved in the "who cleans the office" question had to be struggled over at a theoretical as well as a practical level.

THE PROBLEM OF THEORY

When attempts by women in the new left to define

---

*Everyone in a meeting had the same number of chips or slips of paper. When a person talked, they threw in a chip. When your chips were gone, you couldn't talk anymore.

sexism as a legitimate theoretical issue were met by statements similar to "the best position for women is horizontal," women were faced with three possible responses to male new left sexism. They could stay and struggle it out; they could split and struggle it out in autonomous women's organizations; or they could do both: stay and go. Staying meant, as Sheila Rowbotham describes in *Women, Resistance, and Revolution,* "letting go of the explicitly female consciousness and pretending that the specific oppression of women does not exist."[5]; going meant possibly isolating female consciousness from any other movement for liberation; and doing both meant a split personality, split loyalties, split meeting time, split political analysis. Whichever path women chose, there was a point at which a greater portion of women separated from the male-dominated new left and began to define their own politics, theory, and culture. The vitality of this new autonomous women's movement of the late 1960s and early 70s was in large part characterized by its process—small non-hierarchical conscious-ness raising groups; by the politics of "the personal is political"; and by a theoretical analysis of patriarchy. Charlotte Bunch states in *Personal Politics* that "there is no private domain of a person's life that is not political and there is no political issue that is not personal. The old barriers had fallen."[6] And Ann Popkin describes women's theoretical task:

"By male supremacy we meant the institutional, all-encom-passing power that men have as a group over women, the systematic exclusion of women from power in the society, and the systematic devaluation of all roles and traits which society has assigned to women. Slowly we came to realize that we had to confront and attack male supremacy as a whole system.[7]

Within this period of development and definition, women's practice was enormous. Thousands of consciousness raising groups sprang up on campuses, in communities, and workplaces. Women's centers were demanded and fought for. Building occupations on campuses were sometimes the only way to get colleges to provide places for women to work and study. And a major emphasis was placed on organizing daycare, self-help programs, and health care centers. Pro-abortion campaigns which gave women control over their reproductive processes became a central focus of activity. Barbara Ehrenreich and Deirdre English explained the tremendous importance the women's movement placed on taking back control of their bodies from a sexist medical profession:

Medical science has been one of the most powerful sources of sexist ideology in our culture. Justifications for sexual discrimination—in education, in jobs, in public life—must ultimately rest on the one thing that differentiates women from men: their bodies. Theories of male superiority ultimately rest on biology.[8]

The work done to give theoretical underpinnings to women's practice and to understanding sexism as a legitimate issue in the "larger struggle against capital" was also enormous. Women's theoretical task was defined by the questions: how can women understand their particular oppression in a way that can confront the narrowness of marxist terminology (as used by the men in the movement) which focuses on work and economic relations as the primary (sometimes only) area of importance; and how can they develop a new theory which understands the importance of reproduction, family, and sexuality as central to current analyses and future visions?

Which brings us back to this book, *Women and Revolution.* The discussion here details and extends those early theoretical questions. For what developed were three *predominant* feminist theories: radical, socialist, and marxist feminism. There were many variations within each of these. Lesbianism emerged as an integral part of radical feminist analysis and lesbian separatism of radical feminist practice. Anarchism influenced process and structure. Racism, while part of the discussion, was never successfully integrated into feminist theory and practice resulting in a strong black feminist protest against the racism (and classism) implicit in a white feminist movement, theory, and practice. Black feminists eventually formulated their own position on the importance of uniting racism and sexism in feminist theoretical analyses.

The relationships between these three feminist theories were sometimes strained, often antagonistic. At other times each clearly influenced and drew support from the others. And there were similarities among them. The influence of psychology is evident in all of them. The concern over reproduction and the sexual division of labor is evident throughout. But the basic theoretical and strategic conflicts often seemed irreconcilable.

Radical feminists believed that the primary oppression was the patriarchal sex oppression. For them the division of labor by sex preceeded and gave birth to the division of labor by class and race. Strategically, then, the elimination of sex oppression would bring about the elimination of all other oppressions. Women were the key revolutionary group and for many this meant working separately from their male oppressors.

Marxist feminists believed in the importance of women in the struggle against capital as "workers" but not as "women." They began to define women's role in reproduction (domestic labor) in terms that gave women an importance in marxist analysis and which extended marxist categories. Strategically, marxist feminists continued to work primarily in mixed organizations although many joined with women working on autonomous projects.

Socialist feminists agreed with radical feminists that there was a system of oppression called patriarchy, and they agreed with marxist feminists that there was a class oppression defining the situation for all workers. They attempted to combine the two approaches in their analysis of society. Strategically, most socialist feminists ended up working in both the male-dominated new left and in autonomous women's organizations.

These three predominant approaches defined the contours of the debate. Marxist feminists criticized radical and socialist feminists for being insufficiently materialist and therefore oblivious to class oppression and the class nature of the feminist movement. Radical feminists criticized marxists and socialists for ignoring the importance of patriarchy as part of the formation of people's consciousness and for ignoring the importance of people's psychological need to maintain sexist behavior. Socialist feminists criticized marxist and radical feminists—the former for being overly economistic, the latter for being overly subjective and therefore ahistorical. Black feminists criticized all three for being racist and posed a theory which incorporated race as part of feminist analysis. Lesbian feminists in all three areas argued for consciousness raising around heterosexuality as an institution and for the importance of lesbianism as part of feminist analysis and strategy.

As women studied, read, talked, marched, organized, and developed their own culture and institutions the contours of the feminist theory discussion became more clear. It was essentially a time for discovering what questions needed to be answered. Were women the true revolutionary class whose liberation would end all other oppressions? Could marxist and feminist analyses be used together and have equal weight? Were economic categories sufficient for understanding women's oppression or was there an ingrained socialization process that caused people to hold sexist attitudes even as people's relations to the economic system changed?

What was the importance of sex/gender or kinship in the formation of consciousness? What areas should be studied to shed light on why women throughout history have almost always filled the same roles?

Within political differences and the strategic questions raised by them, there was a common thread. Women developed a consciousness of their shared culture and history. They took inspiration, thoughts, and strategies from women who had marched, written, and organized before them. A common language, a shared past, a shared present were all important parts of a developing feminist movement. Women read about other times, other social systems, and the personal lives of other women and knew that it had happened before—over and over. Alexandra Kollontai, a leading woman in the communist party in Russia wrote in 1926:

> I still want to say a few words about my personal life. The question whether in the middle of all these manifold, exciting labors and party assignments [she complained frequently that the party never concerned itself with the particular situation of women], I could still find time for intimate experiences, for the pangs and joys of love. Unfortunately, yes! I say unfortunately because ordinarily these experiences entailed all too many cares, disappointments, and pain, and because all too many energies were pointlessly consumed through them. Yet the longing to be understood by a man down to the deepest most secret recesses of one's soul, to be recognized by him as a striving human being repeatedly decided matters. And repeatedly disappointment ensued all too swiftly, since the friend saw in me only the feminine element which he tried to mold into a willing sounding board for his own ego. So repeatedly the moment inevitably arrived in which I had to shake off the chains of community with an aching heart but with a sovereign, un-influenced will. Then I was again alone.[9]

But unlike Kollontai, we are not alone. We have a movement. We have the beginnings of a theory and practice. Never again will the "woman question" be described as "the problem with no name." We have a name. But for many, as we begin the 1980s, we seem to be floating. We need motion. The discussion that follows in this book will, we hope, contribute to the work and writing that is currently being done. And we hope, too, that it will contribute to that necessary motion.

THE UNHAPPY MARRIAGE DISCUSSION

You will be reading in the following pages, thirteen theoretical essays arguing about the role and importance of women in revolution and a future liberated society. The first essay, quoted earlier, "The Unhappy Marriage of Marxism and Feminism" by Heidi Hartmann, sets the contours of the discussion for the other twelve contributing essays. Some women agree with Hartmann, some do not, some elaborate on her thesis, and some present alternative formulations. The following is an outline of these essyas. It will help guide you through the various political perspectives in the pages to come.

THE LEAD ESSAY

"The Unhappy Marriage" essay states that "marxism and feminism are one and that one is marxism"; that we need a "healthier marriage or we need a divorce"; that while marxist analysis provides insights into laws concerning history and the economy, it fails to understand the dynamics of sexism. Marxism is sex-blind. Only specific feminist analysis, according to Hartmann, can reveal the systemic character of relations between men and women. Yet feminist analysis alone is inadequate because it is blind to history and "insufficiently materialist." Therefore, Hartmann argues, we must use marxist analysis for its strength in understanding economic laws of motion and feminist analysis for its strength in understanding the particular predicament of women. Hartmann argues for a more "progressive union between marxism and feminism" which requires not only improved intellectual understanding of relations between class and sex but a practice of equality in left politics as well.

DIASGREEMENTS: SOCIALIST, BLACK, ANARCHIST, AND MARXIST FEMINIST PERSPECTIVES

In "Beyond the Unhappy Marriage: A Critique of the Dual Systems Theory," Iris Young argues that the framework proposed by Hartmann still gives the marxist theory of production relations predominance over the feminist theory of gender relations. Young argues against the thesis that the situation of women is best understood as conditioned by two distinct systems of social relations, capitalism and patriarchy, which have distinct structures, movement, and histories. Rather, according to Young, the project of socialist feminism should be to combine the insights of marxism and feminism into a unified theory which can understand capitalist patriarchy as a single system in which the oppression of women is a core attribute. Young proposes that such a theory would take gender division of labor as a central category through which a marxist feminist theory can analyze production relations in a gender differentiated fashion. In a brief analysis of capitalist patriarchy specifically, Young argues that the defining of women as secondary labor is an essential and fundamental characteristic of that system.

Christine Riddiough argues in "Socialism, Feminism, Gay/Lesbian Liberation" that Hartmann's definition of patriarchy fails to explain why it is *women* who are oppressed and *men* who dominate. An expanded definition of feminism must, according to Riddiough, be aimed at the liberation and sexual self-determination of all people: women, gays, lesbians. Riddiough uses Antonio Gramsci's concept of "civil society" as a way of understanding all the various institutionalized methods that the ruling class uses to establish and maintain its ideological hegemony. Trade unions, schools, churches, families; and their value systems, attitudes, beliefs, and morality all support the established order and the interests of those in power. Controlling sexuality is an important part of maintaining political hegemony. The struggle for sexual self-determination is, then, an important struggle. Riddiough argues that a civil society analysis allows us to see the links between family, the oppression of gays and women, and capitalism more clearly; and points the way to a true union of socialism and feminism.

In the "Incompatible Menage à Trois: Marxism, Feminism, and Racism," Gloria Joseph laments the absence of an analysis of Black women as a "member of the wedding." Hartmann and other feminists, Joseph states, continually fail to integrate racism into marxist and feminist analysis. Joseph argues that the categories of marxism are not only sex-blind, they are race-blind. And similarly, the categories of feminism are race-blind (and often class-blind as well). Hartmann, Joseph continues, defines patriarchy by lumping all men into one group united in their shared dominance of women, dependent on each other to maintain that dominance. But Joseph questions Black men's supremacy over any female. There is more solidarity, Joseph maintains, between white males and females than between white males and Black males or between white females and Black females. The vast majority of whites are more likely to bond together on the basis of their whiteness than on their biological sex.

Finally, Joseph feels that a viable feminist movement must give full consideration to Black and white women; it must understand the particular situation of Black women vis-a-vis patriarchy; and it must unite developments in Black feminist theory with white feminist analysis.

In "The Unhappy Marriage of Marxism and Feminism: Can It Be Saved?" Carol Ehrlich argues that it is impossible to build a feminist theory and practice that will be an equal partner in the marriage of marxism and feminism. The task for feminists, Ehrlich argues, should be to use categories which can explain the complexities of class, race, sex, nation, age, and sex orientation. A theory that can unite all of the above without abstracting away from any one of them, must be a theory that sees power relationships as the root of all institutionalized inequality. Ehrlich defines power relationships as those in which one has the ability to compel another's obedience or control another's actions. Ehrlich argues for a union of social anarchism and radical feminism which can see the inherent coercive and hierarchical nature of power relationships as key to class, race, and sex inequality alike. Strategically, anarchist feminists would work to break down all forms of centralized hierarchical organization.

Sandra Harding argues for what she calls the "radical solution" to the problem of the unhappy marriage of marxism and feminism. In the "First Division of Labor Maintains Patriarchy and Capital," Harding criticizes Hartmann for failing to show the "real material base of patriarchy and capital." Harding argues that not only is marxism sex-blind, it is also sexist. The material base of patriarchy and capital, Harding states, is not only rooted in the economic aspects of the division of labor by gender in the family. It is also rooted in the biological and psychological birth of a social person. Harding states that social structures of infant care produce gendered social animals. Once the roots of the partnership of patriarchy and capital are understood as a "pact between genetic siblings," then we can see that women cannot expect men to liberate anyone from class and sex oppression. Women must lead the way not only in the struggle against patriarchy but also in the struggle against all other oppressions as well.

In "Capitalism Is An Advanced Stage of Patriarchy: But Marxism Is Not Feminism," Azizah Al-Hibri argues that Hartmann's thesis leaves the door open for the argument that it is not altogether impossible for women to be liberated in a capitalist society as "women," although not as "workers" because Hartmann argues that it is the superimposition of the patriarchal gender hierarchy on the capitalist hierarchy that instructs the capitalist as to who fills the empty places in his hierarchy. Al-Hibri defines the root of the relationship as one in which capitalism is an advanced stage of patriarchy. The original patriarchal impetus can be found in the male's perception of his exclusion from reproduction and his consequent need to establish his immortality and importance in the cycle of life through his control of the female who, in contrast, can reproduce and nourish life. Al-Hibri describes the male's desire for immortality through the works of Aristotle, Socrates, Sartre, and Nietzsche. She describes man's change in thinking from a desire to control reproduction through control of the female to a desire to control production as a means of reproducing himself. Viewed in this light, Al-Hibri argues, marxism is an improvement over capitalism because it liberates some men from exploitation by other men. But marxism is not feminism because it does not liberate women. Strategically, the struggle against capitalism, racism, imperialism and all other oppressions must be based on an understanding of their basic patriarchal nature.

In contrast, Lise Vogel believes in "Marxism and Feminism: Unhappy Marriage, Trial Separation, or Something Else?" that the marxist tradition has proven itself powerful and flexible. The real problem, she argues, is that theorists have been working with too limited an understanding of marxism and too little awareness of the real advances made in expanding and incorporating a feminist analysis with marxist categories. Vogel takes another look at the work of many of the theorists that Hartmann criticizes and concludes that they represent an important contribution to the breadth and value of the marxist tradition. Whether or not socialist-feminist theorists have utilized basic marxist categories, Vogel asserts, they have made substantial gains in developing a materialist theory of women's oppression, in critiquing the weaknesses of Engels' work, in exploring women's double relationship to wage labor as both paid and unpaid workers, and in describing women's activity as consumer and domestic laborer. The present task for socialist feminist theorists, she believes, is to transcend the dualism between marxism and feminism that is inherent in much of socialist feminist writings. To accomplish this task, Vogel recommends that socialist feminist theories examine and develop the marxist theoretical tradition itself.

In her essay, "Cultural Marxism: Nonsynchrony and Feminist Practice," Emily Hicks argues that the marriage of marxism and feminism leads to a narrow formulation of their respective oppressions and a narrow understanding of the dynamics of society. Hicks states that a cultural marxism is needed to reach and incorporate broader groups of people into a socialist movement: people who do not all have the same politics or the same political needs. Nor the same socialist vision. A marxism that cannot reach more people with its theory and practice will become irrelevant. With an analysis of current political and economic trends viewed through the concept of nonsynchrony, Hicks shows why it is that despite a huge disatisfaction with capitalism among certain sectors of the population (gays, working women, blacks), there is not necessarily a huge outpouring of support for a radical alternative. Hicks discusses why some women will make radical demands for childcare, birth control, equal pay but will also feel a tremendous antagonism towards the women's movement claiming forcefully that they are not "women's libbers." Hicks argues strategically for the need to build broad non-exclusive organizations struggling for progressive change.

EXPANDING OUR CONCEPT OF PATRIARCHY

Carol Brown describes current changes in the nature of patriarchy in her essay "Mothers, Fathers, and Children: From Private to Public Patriarchy." Brown sees a development in the last century from private to public patriarchy. Focusing on the changes in laws relating to child custody, divorce, and father right/mother right, she concludes that children have become a costly family burden in monopoly capital and therefore that male-headed families are no longer essential for the maintenance of patriarchy and capitalism. The state now controls more of the reproduction of labor power through legal abolishment of the rights of individual men over individual women. This change to public patriarchy implies, Brown states, certain strategic contradictions. If we make demands on public patriarchy for more support for female-headed families, we increase the scope of public patriarchy. If we do not make these demands, women-headed families will suffer an unjustified burden and all women will be forced (for lack of alternatives) into greater dependence on individual men and private patriarchy. Brown argues that women must struggle against patriarchy and capital or else they will achieve only an improvement in their position of subordination.

In "The Marriage of Capitalist and Patriarchal Ideologies: Meanings of Male Bonding and Male Ranking in U.S. Culture," Katie Stewart argues that a materialist theory of patriarchy such as Hartmann's is not sufficient if we are to understand the relationship between class and gender hierarchies. Stewart takes an exhaustive look at puritan, victorian, and contemporary meanings of gender and class in U.S. culture and finds that in each case, men's status-identities are formed in a dynamic tension between male-ranking and male dominance. Stewart details differences in status-identity and male dominance between men of different classes. Socialist feminists, Stewart concludes, need to dissolve the marxist dichotomy between objective and subjective reality so that they can identify the process "by which women and workers invest their identities in various existing statuses (e.g., the self-sacrificing mother, the strong man, the economic achiever)..." From this, we can understand why people support or oppose change and we can name the links between capitalist patriarchy and people's subjective experiences and interpretations of it.

Nancy Folbre and Ann Ferguson explore the contradictory relationship between patriarchy and capital in their essay "The Unhappy Marriage of Patriarchy and Capitalism." Where capitalist social relations, they argue, have incorporated many forms of patriarchal domination, they have also weakened many others. Feminists must expand, they feel, their concept of the role women play in production within capitalism. They define this role as sex-affective production: that is, the bearing and rearing of children, provision of affection, nurturance and sexual satisfaction. Sex-affective production, they argue, cannot be considered less important than other forms of labor. Strategically, then, women must continue to inform the left as a whole of feminist values and politics while at the same time building autonomous women's organizations across class, sex, and race lines. Along with these organizations they should build revolutionary feminist women's culture which can support women outside the patriarchy.

REFOCUSING THE DISCUSSION

In "Reform and/or Revolution: Toward a Unified Women's Movement," Zillah Eisenstein while agreeing with Hartmann's main theme, argues for the immediate need to refocus the theoretical discussion between radical, socialist, and liberal feminists who have as much, if not more, in common than socialist feminists and marxists. She believes that this is the first step in building a mass-based feminist movement. Socialist feminists and marxists share economic class concerns while radical, socialist and liberal feminists are concerned to dismantle the "most implicit, insidious, hierarchical relations known to civilization." Because the uncovering of sexual hierarchies will expose all other hierarchical forms as well, it becomes all the more crucial for radical women to try to reach the largest sector of the women's movement: liberal feminists. Confrontations with the state through ERA activity and other liberal feminist demands can increase left feminist awareness of the needs and politics of liberal feminists and can create possibilities for liberal feminists to become aware of the inherent patriarchal nature of the capitalist system. Eisenstein argues that without this work with liberal feminists, the left wing of the feminist movement will remain isolated from struggles with the state which is just what right wing elements of the state want.

STRATEGIC IMPLICATIONS

The essays described above focus some of the theoretical issues that have been filtering through the women's movement since what seemed to be the more active, vital, and visible years of the sixties and early seventies. The intention of this book is, in part, to contribute to that theoretical discussion but it is also to inspire a more focused, strategic, and visionary politics for the decade to come. Although thousands of women are currently working for progressive change, there is no unified organization and no unified strategy and goal. For many this isolation is dictated by practical reality. Making a living, supporting a family, finding ways to keep psychologically healthy in a sexist world make it difficult to do any political work at all. For others, there is a lack of clarity about what kinds of political work would make the most sense in this or any period of time. Numerous strategic questions remain unanswered. What can be gained by organizing for reproductive rights? Should we organize secretaries/office workers? Should we organize in factories, schools, or hospitals? How much can this mainstream work allow us to say about capitalism and socialism or about patriarchy? Will autonomous women's organizations be coopted? What is the effect of teaching women's studies programs when those programs are often defined and limited by school administrations? Finally, are theoretical and strategic differences too great to be overcome thereby preventing any possibility for mass left feminist organizations?

THE TONE OF THE TIMES:
IT'S THE ONLY GAME IN TOWN

This book does not answer the questions listed above. It does argue for the need to take some action in the coming years. The entire atmosphere of the eighties reeks of retrenchment, reaction, and cooptation. The ERA is losing ground, more and more books argue for women to accept their "god-given right to bear children." Abortion is attacked on all fronts. The head of the new right wing think tank, The Heritage Foundation even questions women's right to vote. Gains that were made as a result of sixties protests are disappearing. We are told that we were a fad, something to be tried for a while before we settle down to the serious business of marriage, family, and work in capitalist America. Our parents, schools, media, government all exude the message: "Look, you had your fun, you tried all those hippie and women's lib alternatives. You got divorced, explored open relationships, collective living, collective work and what did it get you? A lot of fighting, endless meetings, and loneliness. You did your thing in the streets. You did your thing about Vietnam, civil rights, and birth control and what did it get you? It's the same old world, same old people, same old oppressive relationships with a lover instead of a husband, same old environment."

The solution for the eighties can be summed up by a movie that happened to have been made in the sixties. It starred Warren Beatty and Elizabeth Taylor as two people who come together in Las Vegas. They both have dead end jobs and dead end lives and are coming from dead end marriages. They decide, for financial reasons, to share a small apartment together stating firmly that they've had it with long-term commitments of any kind. This will be an open relationship. No strings etc. During the course of the movie, they fall in love (but neither of them lets the other know this) and they both feel the old feelings for a permanent relationship coming over them. They have a fight, split up (Warren leaves). Of course, neither of them can stand it alone because they've developed this sensitive, warm feeling for each other, so what happens? Warren returns and argues for a commitment to each other. Liz refuses. They fight and throw things around the apartment and then, finally, Warren takes Liz by the shoulders and says, "Look, I love you. Marriage is the only game in town and we're going to play it." Love it or leave it becomes "stay and play."

Between the right wing and the stay and play types, the message for the eighties comes though loud and clear. History is being rewritten and replayed. College students never heard of Shulamith Firestone but they have heard of panty raids. The KKK is back in town (as if it ever left) and Vietnam is a vague memory of something we're supposed to forget while they write the version they'd like us to hear.

It becomes, then, all the more important to be visible and vital again. To the extent that theory informs practice, the discussion in this book makes important contributions to our understanding of patriarchy, the oppression of women through sex/gender systems, the sexual division of labor, the need to broaden our understandings of society and the nature of power, the need to clarify and overcome our differences. Perhaps there is a basis here for a coming together in the eighties.

FINAL NOTE

Time, availability, contact with organizations, past writings, personal relationships, academic affiliations have all, to a large extent, determined who is in this book. There are gaps. There are positions underrepresented here; positions not represented here. None of this is intentional—except the decision to have no male contributors. We hope that this book will be only the first in a series of works on women and revolution.

—Lydia Sargent
January 1981

FOOTNOTES

1. Robin Morgan, *Going Too Far* (New York: Random House, 1977), p. 127.
2. Betty Friedan, *The Feminine Mystique* (New York: Dell Publishing Co., 1963), p. 11.
3. Simone de Beauvoir, *The Second Sex* (New York: Bantam Books, 1961), p. xvi.
4. Sarah Evans, *Personal Politics* (New York: Vintage Books, 1979), p. 178.
5. Sheila Rowbotham, *Women, Resistance & Revolution* (New York: Vintage, 1974), p. 12.
6. Evans, *op.cit.*, p. 211.
7. Ann Popkin, "The Personal Is Political: The Women's Liberation Movement," in *They Should Have Served That Cup of Coffee*, ed. Dick Cluster (Boston: South End Press, 1979), pp. 199-200.
8. Barbara Ehrenreich and Deirdre English, "Complaints and Disorders" (New York: The Feminist Press Glass Mountain Pamphlet No. 2), p. 5.
9. Alexandra Kollontai, *The Autobiography of a Sexually Emancipated Woman* (New York: Herder and Herder, 1971), p. 22.

THE UNHAPPY MARRIAGE OF MARXISM AND FEMINISM: TOWARDS A MORE PROGRESSIVE UNION

Heidi Hartmann

Heidi Hartmann is an economist now working at the National Research Council/ National Academy of Sciences in the Assembly of Behavioral and Social Sciences. Recently she participated in a study of equal pay for jobs of equal value and continues to study issues of employment discrimination against women and minority males. She is also continuing research on technology and housework, and, in several groups, continues to discuss issues in marxist feminist theory. She is a member of the board of editors of Feminist Studies.

1

The "marriage" of marxism and feminism has been like the marriage of husband and wife depicted in English common law: marxism and feminism are one, and that one is marxism.[1] Recent attempts to integrate marxism and feminism are unsatisfactory to us as feminists because they subsume the feminist struggle into the "larger" struggle against capital. To continue our simile further, either we need a healthier marriage or we need a divorce.

The inequalities in this marriage, like most social phenomena, are no accident. Many marxists typically argue that feminism is at best less important than class conflict and at worst divisive of the working class. This political stance produces an analysis that absorbs feminism into the class struggle. Moreover, the analytic power of marxism with respect to capital has obscured its limitations with respect to sexism. We will argue here that while marxist analysis provides essential insight into the laws of historical development, and those of capital in particular, the categories of marxism are sex-blind. Only a specifically feminist analysis reveals the systemic character of relations between men and women. Yet feminist analysis by itself is inadequate because it has been blind to history and insufficiently materialist. Both marxist analysis, particularly its historical and materialist method, and feminist analysis, especially the identification of patriarchy as a social and historical structure,

---

Earlier drafts of this essay appeared in 1975 and 1977 coauthored with Amy B. Bridges. Unfortunately, because of the press of current commitments, Amy was unable to continue with this project, joint from its inception and throughout most of its long and controversial history. Over the years many indiviuals and groups offered us comments, debate, and support. Among them I would like to thank Marxist Feminist Group I, the Women's Studies College at SUNY Buffalo, the Women's Studies Program at the University of Michigan, various groups of the Union for Radical Political Economics, and Temma Kaplan, Anne Markusen, and Jane Flax for particularly careful, recent readings. A version substantially similar to the current one was published in *Capital and Class* in the summer of 1979. I would like to thank the editors of *Capital and Class*, Lydia Sargent, and other members of South End Press for their interest in this essay.

must be drawn upon if we are to understand the development of western capitalist societies and the predicament of women within them. In this essay we suggest a new direction for marxist feminist analysis.

Part I of our discussion examines several marxist approaches to the "woman question." We then turn, in Part II, to the work of radical feminists. After noting the limitations of radical feminist definitions of patriarchy, we offer our own. In Part III we try to use the strengths of both marxism and feminism to make suggestion both about the development of capitalist societies and about the present situation of women. We attempt to use marxist methodology to analyze feminist objectives, correcting the imbalance in recent socialist feminist work, and suggesting a more complete analysis of our present socioeconomic formation. We argue that a materialist analysis demonstrates that patriarchy is not simply a psychic, but also a social and economic structure. We suggest that our society can best be understood once it is recognized that it is organized both in capitalistic and in patriarchal ways. While pointing out tensions between patriarchal and capitalist interests, we argue that the accumulation of capital both accommodates itself to patriarchal social structure and helps to perpetuate it. We suggest in this context that sexist ideology has assumed a peculiarly capitalist form in the present, illustrating one way that patriarchal relations tend to bolster capitalism. We argue, in short, that a partnership of patriarchy and capitalism has evolved.

In the concluding section, Part IV, we argue that the *political* relations of marxism and feminism account for the dominance of marxism over feminism in the left's understanding of the woman question. A more progressive union of marxism and feminism, then, requires not only improved intellectual understanding of relations of class and sex, but also that alliance replace dominance and subordination in left politics.

1. MARXISM AND THE WOMAN QUESTION

The woman question has never been the "feminist question." The feminist question is directed at the causes of sexual inequality between women and men, of male dominance over women. Most marxist analyses of women's position take as their question the relationship of women to the economic system, rather than that of women to men, apparently assuming the latter will be explained in their discussion of the former. Marxist analysis of the woman question has taken three main forms. All see women's oppression in our connection (or lack of it) to production. Defining women as part of the working class, these analyses consistently subsume women's relation to men under workers' relation to capital. First, early marxists, including Marx, Engels, Kautsky, and Lenin, saw capitalism drawing all women into the wage labor force, and saw this process destroying the sexual division of labor. Second, contemporary marxists have incorporated women into an analysis of everyday life in capitalism. In this view, all aspects of our lives are seen to reproduce the capitalist system and we are all workers in the system. And third, marxist feminists have focussed on housework and its relation to capital, some arguing that housework produces surplus value and that houseworkers work directly for capitalists. These three approaches are examined in turn.

Engels, in *Origins of the Family, Private Property and the State*, recognized the inferior position of women and attributed it to the institution of private property.[2] In bourgeois families, Engels argued, women had to serve their masters, be monogamous, and produce heirs who would inherit the family's property and continue to increase it. Among proletarians, Engels argued, women were not oppressed, because there was no private property to be passed on. Engels argued further that as the extension of wage labor destroyed the small-holding peasantry, and women and children were incorporated into the wage labor force along with men, the authority of the male head of household was undermined, and patriarchal relations were destroyed.[3]

For Engels, then, women's participation in the labor force was the key to their emancipation. Capitalism would abolish sex differences and treat all workers equally. Women would become economically independent of men and would participate on an equal footing with men in bringing about the proletarian revolution. After the revolution, when all people would be workers and private property abolished, women would be emancipated from capital as well as from men. Marxists were aware of the hardships women's labor force participation meant for women and families, which resulted in women having two jobs, housework and wage work. Nevertheless, their emphasis was less on the continued subordination of women in the home than on the progressive character of capitalism's "erosion" of patriarchal relations. Under socialism housework too would be collectivized and women relieved of their double burden.

The political implications of this first marxist approach are clear. Women's liberation requires first, that women become wage workers like men, and second, that they join with men in the revolutionary struggle against capitalism. Capital and private property, the early marxists argued, are the cause of women's particular oppression just as capital is the cause of the exploitation of workers in general.

Though aware of the deplorable situation of women in their time the early marxists failed to focus on the *differences* between men's and women's experiences under capitalism. They did not focus on the feminist questions—how and why women are oppressed as women. They did not, therefore, recognize the vested interest men had in women's continued subordination. As we argue in Part III below, men benefited from not having to do housework, from having their wives and daughters serve them, and from having the better places in the labor market. Patriarchal relations, far from being atavistic leftovers, being rapidly outmoded by capitalism, as the early marxists suggested, have survived and thrived alongside it. And since capital and private property do not cause the oppression of women as *women*, their end alone will not result in the end of women's oppression.

Perhaps the most popular of the recent articles exemplifying the second marxist approach, the everyday life school, is the series by Eli Zaretsky in *Socialist Revolution.*[4] Although Zaretsky, in agreement with feminist analysis, argues that sexism is not a new phenomenon produced by capitalism, he stresses that the particular form sexism takes now has been shaped by capital. He focuses on the differential experiences of men and women under capitalism. Writing a century after Engels, once capitalism had matured, Zaretsky points out that capitalism has not incorporated all women into the labor force on equal terms with men. Rather capital has created a separation between the home, family, and personal life on the one hand and the workplace on the other.[5]

Sexism has become more virulent under capitalism, according to Zaretsky, because of this separation between wage work and home work. Women's increased oppression is caused by their exclusion from wage work. Zaretsky argues that while men are oppressed by having to do wage work, women are oppressed by not being allowed to do wage work. Women's exclusion from the wage labor force has been caused primarily by capitalism, because capitalism both creates wage work outside the home and requires women to work in the home in order to reproduce wage workers for the capitalist system. Women reproduce the labor force, provide psychological nurturance for workers, and provide an island of intimacy in a sea of alienation. In Zaretsky's view women are laboring for capital and not for men; it is only the separation of home from work place, and the privatization of housework brought about by capitalism, that creates the *appearance* that women are working for men privately in the home. The difference between the *appearance*, that women work for men, and the *reality*, that women work for capital, has caused a misdirection of the energies of the women's movement. Women should recognize that they, too, are part of the working class, even though they work at home.

In Zaretsky's view, "the housewife emerged, alongside the proletarian [as] the two characteristic laborers of developed capitalist society,"[6] and the segmentation of their lives oppresses both the husband-proletarian and the wife-housekeeper. Only a reconceptualization of "production" which includes women's work in the home and all other socially necessary activities will allow socialists to struggle to establish a society in which this destructive separation is overcome. According to Zaretsky, men and women together (or separately) should fight to reunite the divided spheres of their lives, to create a humane socialism that meets all our private as well as public needs. Recognizing capitalism as the root of their problem, men and women will fight capital and not each other. Since capitalism causes the separation of our private and public lives, the end of capitalism will end that separation, reunite our lives, and end the oppression of both men and women.

Zaretsky's analysis owes much to the feminist movement, but he ultimately argues for a redirection of that movement. Zaretsky has accepted the feminist argument that sexism predates capitalism; he has accepted much of the marxist feminist argument that housework is crucial to the reproduction of capital; he recognizes that housework is hard work and does not belittle it; and he uses the concepts of male supremacy and sexism. But his analysis ultimately rests on the notion of separation, on the concept of *division*, as the crux of the problem, a division attributable to capitalism. Like the "complementary spheres" argument of the early twentieth century, which held that women's and men's spheres were complementary, separate but equally important, Zaretsky largely denies the existence and importance of *inequality* between men and women. His focus is on the relationship of women, the family, and the private sphere to capitalism. Moreover, even if capitalism created the private sphere, as Zaretsky argues, why did it happen that *women* work there, and *men* in the labor force? Surely this cannot be explained without reference to patriarchy, the systemic dominance of men over women. From our point of view, the problem in the family, the labor market, economy, and society is not simply a division of labor between men and women, but a division that places men in a superior, and women in a subordinate, position.

Just as Engels sees private property as the capitalist contribution to women's oppression, so Zaretsky sees privacy. Because women are laboring privately at home they are oppressed. Zaretsky and Engels romanticize the preindustrial family and community— where men, women, adults, children worked together in family centered enterprise and all participated in community life. Zaretsky's humane socialism will reunite the family and recreate that ''happy workshop.''

While we argue that socialism *is* in the interest of both men and women, it is not at all clear that we are all fighting for the same kind of ''humane socialism,'' or that we have the same conception of the struggle required to get there, much less that capital alone is responsible for our current oppression. While Zaretsky thinks women's work *appears* to be for men but in reality is for capital, we think women's work in the family *really is* for men—though it clearly reproduces capitalism as well. Reconceptualizing production may help us think about the kind of society we want to create, but between now and its creation, the struggle between men and women will have to continue along with the struggle against capital.

Marxist feminists who have looked at housework have also subsumed the feminist struggle into the struggle against capital. Mariarosa Dalla Costa's theoretical analysis of housework is essentially an argument about the relation of housework to capital and the place of housework in capitalist society and not about the relations of men and women as exemplified in housework.[7] Nevertheless, Dalla Costa's political position, that women should demand wages for housework, has vastly increased consciousness of the importance of housework among women in the women's movement. The demand was and still is debated in women's groups all over the United States.[8] By making the claim that women at home not only provide essential services for capital by reproducing the labor force, but also create surplus value through that work,[9] Dalla Costa also vastly increased the left's consciousness of the importance of housework, and provoked a long debate on the relation of housework to capital.[10]

Dalla Costa uses the feminist understanding of housework as real work to claim legitimacy for it under capitalism by arguing that it should be waged work. Women should demand wages for housework rather than allow themselves to be forced into the traditional labor force, where, doing a "double day," women would still provide housework services to capital for free as well as wage labor. Dalla Costa suggests that women who receive wages for housework would be able to organize their housework collectively, providing community child care, meal preparation, and the like. Demanding wages and having wages would raise their consciousness of the importance of their work; they would see its *social* significance, as well as its private necessity, a necessary first step toward more comprehensive social change.

Dalla Costa argues that what is socially important about housework is its necessity to capital. In this lies the strategic importance of women. By demanding wages for housework and by refusing to participate in the labor market women can lead the struggle against capital. Women's community organizations can be subversive to capital and lay the basis not only for resistance to the encroachment of capital but also for the formation of a new society.

Dalla Costa recognizes that men will resist the liberation of women (that will occur as women organize in their communities) and that women will have to struggle against them, but this struggle is an auxiliary one that must be waged to bring about the ultimate goal of socialism. For Dalla Costa, women's struggles are revolutionary not because they are feminist, but because they are anticapitalist. Dalla Costa finds a place in the revolution for women's struggle by making women producers of surplus value, and as a consequence part of the working class. This legitimates women's political activity.[11]

The women's movement has never doubted the importance of women's struggle because for feminists the *object* is the liberation of women, which can only be brought about by women's struggles. Dalla Costa's contribution to increasing our understanding of the social nature of housework has been an incalculable advance. But like the other marxist approaches reviewed here her approach focuses on capital—not on relations between men and women. The fact that men and women have differences of interest, goals, and strategies is obscured by her analysis of how the capitalist system keeps us all down, and the important and perhaps strategic role of women's work in this system. The rhetoric of feminism is present in Dalla Costa's writing (the oppression of women, struggle with men) but the focus of feminism is not. If it were, Dalla Costa might argue for example, that the importance of housework as a social relation lies in its crucial role in perpetuating male supremacy. That women do housework, performing labor for men, is crucial to the maintenance of patriarchy.

Engels, Zaretsky, and Dalla Costa all fail to analyze the labor process within the family sufficiently. Who benefits from women's labor? Surely capitalists, but also surely men, who as husbands and fathers receive personalized services at home. The content and extent of the sevices may vary by class or ethnic or racial group, but the fact of their receipt does not. Men have a higher standard of living than women in terms of luxury consumption, leisure time, and personalized services.[12] A materialist approach ought not ignore this crucial point.[13] It follows that men have a material interest in women's continued oppression. In the long run this may be "false consciousness," since the majority of men could benefit from the abolition of hierarchy within the patriarchy. But in the short run this amounts to control over other people's labor, control which men are unwilling to relinquish voluntarily.

While the approach of the early marxists ignored housework and stressed women's labor force participation, the two more recent approaches emphasize housework to such an extent they ignore women's current role in the labor market. Nevertheless, all three attempt to include women in the category working class and to understand women's oppression as another aspect of class oppression. In doing so all give short shrift to the object of feminist analysis, the relations between women and men. While our "problems" have been elegantly analyzed, they have been misunderstood. The focus of marxist analysis has been class relations; the object of marxist analysis has been understanding the laws of motion of capitalist society. While we believe marxist methodology *can* be used to formulate feminist strategy, these marxist feminist approaches discussed above clearly do not do so; their marxism clearly dominates their feminism.

As we have already suggested, this is due in part to the analytical power of marxism itself. Marxism is a theory of the development of class society, of the accumulation process in capitalist societies, of the reproduction of class dominance, and of the development of contradictions and class struggle. Capitalist societies are driven by the demands of the accumulation process, most succinctly summarized by the fact that production is oriented to exchange, not use. In a capitalist system production is important only insofar as it contributes to the making of profits, and the use value of products is only an incidental consideration. Profits derive from the capitalists' ability to exploit labor power, to pay laborers less than the value of what they produce. The accumulation of profits systematically transforms social structure as it transforms the relations of production. The reserve army of labor, the poverty of great numbers of people and the near-poverty of still more, these human reproaches to capital are by-products of the accumulation process itself. From the capitalist's point of view, the reproduction of the working class may "safely be left to itself."[14] At the same time, capital creates an ideology, which grows up along side it, of individualism, competitiveness, domination, and in our time, consumption of a particular kind. Whatever one's theory of the genesis of ideology one must recognize these as the dominant values of capitalist societies.

Marxism enables us to understand many aspects of capitalist societies: the structure of production, the generation of a particular occupational structure, and the nature of the dominant ideology. Marx's theory of the development of capitalism is a theory of the development of "empty places." Marx predicted, for example, the growth of the proletariat and the demise of the petit bourgeoisie. More precisely and in more detail, Braverman among others has explained the creation of the "places" clerical worker and service worker in advanced capitalist societies.[15] Just as capital creates these places indifferent to the individuals who fill them, the categories of marxist analysis, class, reserve army of labor, wage-laborer, do not explain why particular people fill particular places. They give no clues about why *women* are subordinate to *men* inside and outside the family and why it is not the other way around. *Marxist categories, like capital itself, are sex-blind.* The categories of marxism cannot tell us who will fill the empty places. Marxist analysis of the woman question has suffered from this basic problem.

Towards More Useful Marxist Feminism

Marxism is also a *method* of social analysis, historical dialectical materialism. By putting this method to the service of feminist questions, Juliet Mitchell and Shulamith Firestone suggest new directions for marxist feminism. Mitchell says, we think correctly, that

> It is not "our relationship" to socialism that should *ever* be the question—it is the use of scientific socialism [what we call marxist method] as a method of analyzing the specific nature of our oppression and hence our revolutionary role. Such a method, I believe, needs to understand radical feminism, quite as much as previously developed socialist theories.[16]

As Engels wrote:

> According to the materialistic conception, the determining factor in history is, in the final instance, the production and reproduction of immediate life. This, again, is of a twofold character: on the one side, the production of the means of existence, of food, clothing, and shelter and the tools necessary for that production; on the other side, the production of human beings themselves, the propagation of the species. The social organization under which the people of a particular historical epoch live is determined by both kinds of production . . . [17]

This is the kind of analysis Mitchell has attempted. In her first essay, "Women: The Longest Revolution," Mitchell examines both market work and the work of reproduction, sexuality, and childrearing.[18]

Mitchell does not entirely succeed, perhaps because not all of women's work counts as production for her. Only market work is identified as production; the other spheres (loosely aggregated as the family) in which women work are identified as ideological. Patriarchy, which largely organizes reproduction, sexuality, and childrearing, has no material base for Mitchell. *Women's Estate*, Mitchell's expansion of this essay, focuses much more on developing the analysis of women's market work than it does on developing the analysis of women's work within the family. The book is much more concerned with women's relation to, and work for, capital than with women's relation to, and work for, men; more influenced by marxism than by radical feminism. In a later work, *Psychoanalysis and Feminism*, Mitchell explores an important area for studying the relations between women and men, namely the formation of different, gender-based personalities by women and men.[19] Patriarchy operates, Mitchell seems to be saying, primarily in the psychological realm, where female and male children learn to be women and men. Here Mitchell focuses on the spheres she initially slighted, reproduction, sexuality, and child rearing, but by placing them in the ideological realm, she continues the fundamental weakness of her earlier analysis. She clearly presents patriarchy as the fundamental ideological structure, just as capital is the fundamental economic structure:

> To put the matter schematically . . . we are . . . dealing with two autonomous areas: the economic mode of capitalism and the ideological mode of patriarchy.[20]

Although Mitchell discusses their interpenetration, her failure to give patriarchy a material base in the relation between women's and men's labor power, and her similar failure to note the material aspects of the process of personality formation and gender creation, limits the usefulness of her analysis.

Shulamith Firestone bridges marxism and feminism by bringing materialist anaysis to bear on patriarchy.[21] Her use of materialist analysis is not as ambivalent as Mitchell's. The dialectic of sex, she says, is the fundamental historical dialectic, and the material base of patriarchy is the work women do reproducing the species. The importance of Firestone's work in using marxism to analyze women's position, in asserting the existence of a material base to patriarchy, cannot be overestimated. But is suffers from an overemphasis on biology and reproduction. What we need to understand is how sex (a biological fact) becomes gender (a social phenomenon). It is necessary to place all of women's work in its social and historical context, not to focus only on reproduction. Although Firestone's work offers a new and feminist use of marxist methodology, her insistence on the primacy of men's dominance over women as the cornerstone on which all other oppression (class, age, race) rests, suggests that her book is more properly grouped with the radical feminists than with the marxist feminists. Her work remains the most complete statement of the radical feminist position.

Firestone's book has been all too happily dismissed by marxists. Zaretsky, for example, calls it a "plea for subjectivity." Yet what was so exciting to women about Firestone's book was her analysis of men's power over women, and her very healthy anger about this situation. Her chapter on love was central to our understanding of this, and still is. It is not just about "masculinist ideology," which marxists can deal with (just a question of attitudes), but an exposition of the subjective consequences of men's power over women, of what it feels like to live in a patriarchy. "The personal is political" is not, as Zaretsky would have it, a plea for subjectivity, for feeling better: it is a demand to recognize men's power and women's subordination as a social and political reality.

II. RADICAL FEMINISM AND PATRIARCHY

The great thrust of radical feminist writing has been directed to the documentation of the slogan "the personal is political." Women's discontent, radical feminists argued, is not the neurotic lament of the maladjusted, but a response to a social structure in which women are systematically dominated, exploited, and oppressed. Women's inferior position in the labor market, the male-centered emotional structure of middle class marriage, the use of women in advertising, the so-called understanding of women's psyche as neurotic—popularized by academic and clinical psychology—aspect after aspect of women's lives in advanced capitalist society was researched and analyzed. The radical feminist literature is enormous and defies easy summary. At the same time, its focus on psychology is consistent. The New York Radical Feminists' organizing document was "The Politics of the Ego." "The personal is political" means for radical feminists, that the original and basic class division is between the sexes, and that the motive force of history is the striving of men for power and domination over women, the dialectic of sex. [22]

Accordingly, Firestone rewrote Freud to understand the development of boys and girls into men and women in terms of power. [23] Her characterizations of what are "male" and "female" character traits are typical of radical feminist writing. The male seeks power and domination; he is egocentric and individualistic, competitive and pragmatic; the "technological mode," according to Firestone, is male. The female is nurturant, artistic, and philosophical; the "aesthetic mode" is female.

No doubt, the idea that the aesthetic mode is female would have come as quite a shock to the ancient Greeks. Here lies the error of radical feminist analysis: the dialectic of sex as radical feminists present it projects male and female characteristics as they appear in the present back into all of history. Radical feminist analysis has greatest strength in its insights into the present. Its greatest weakness is a focus on the psychological which blinds it to history.

The reason for this lies not only in radical feminist method, but also in the nature of patriarchy itself, for patriarchy is a strikingly resilient form of social organization. Radical feminists use patriarchy to refer to a social system characterized by male domination over women. Kate Millett's definition is classic:

> our society . . . is a patriarchy. The fact is evident at once if one recalls that the military, industry, technology, universities, science, political offices, finances—in short, every avenue of power within the society, including the coercive force of the police, is entirely in male hands.[24]

This radical feminist definition of patriarchy applies to most societies we know of and cannot distinguish among them. The use of history by radical feminists is typically limited to providing examples of the existence of patriarchy in all times and places.[25] For both marxist and mainstream social scientists before the women's movement, patriarchy referred to a system of relations between men, which formed the political and economic outlines of feudal and some pre-feudal societies, in which hierarchy followed ascribed characteristics. Capitalist societies are understood as meritocratic, bureaucratic, and impersonal by bourgeois social scientists; marxists see capitalist societies as systems of class domination.[26] For both kinds of social scientists neither the historical patriarchal societies nor today's western capitalist societies are understood as systems of relations between men that enable them to dominate women.

Towards a Definition of Patriarchy

We can usefully define patriarchy as a set of social relations between men, which have a material base, and which, though hierarchical, establish or create interdependence and solidarity among men that enable them to dominate women. Though patriarchy is hierarchical and men of different classes, races, or ethnic groups have different places in the patriarchy, they also are united in their shared relationship of dominance over their women; they are dependent on each other to maintain that domination. Hierarchies "work" at least in part because they create vested interests in the status quo. Those at the higher levels can "buy off" those at the lower levels by offering them power over those still lower. In the hierarchy of patriarchy, all men, whatever their rank in the patriarchy, are bought off by being able to control at least some women. There is some evidence to suggest that when patriarchy was first institutionalized in state societies, the ascending rulers literally made men the heads of their families (enforcing their control over their wives and children) in exchange for the men's ceding some of their tribal resources to the new rulers.[27] Men are dependent on one another (despite their hierarchical ordering) to maintain their control over women.

The material base upon which patriarchy rests lies most fundamentally in men's control over women's labor power. Men maintain this control by excluding women from access to some essential productive resources (in capitalist societies, for example, jobs that pay living wages) and by restricting women's sexuality.[28] Monogamous heterosexual marriage is one relatively recent and efficient form that seems to allow men to control both these areas. Controlling women's access to resources and their sexuality, in turn, allows men to control women's labor power, both for the purpose of serving men in many personal and sexual ways and for the purpose of rearing children. The services women render men, and which exonerate men from having to perform many unpleasant tasks (like cleaning toilets) occur outside as well as inside the family setting. Examples outside the family include the harrassment of women workers and students by male bosses and professors as well as the common use of secretaries to run personal errands, make coffee, and provide "sexy" surroundings. Rearing children, whether or not the children's labor power is of immediate benefit to their fathers, is nevertheless a crucial task in perpetuating patriarchy as a system. Just as class society must be reproduced by schools, work places, consumption norms, etc., so must patriarchal social relations. In our society children are generally reared by women at home, women socially defined and recognized as inferior to men, while men appear in the domestic picture only rarely. Children raised in this way generally learn their places in the gender hierarchy well. Central to this process, however, are the areas outside the home where patriarchal behaviors are taught and the inferior position of women enforced and reinforced: churches, schools, sports, clubs, unions, armies, factories, offices, health centers, the media, etc.

The material base of patriarchy, then, does not rest solely on childrearing in the family, but on all the social structures that enable men to control women's labor. The aspects of social structures that perpetuate patriarchy are theoretically identifiable, hence separable from their other aspects. Gayle Rubin has increased our ability to identify the patriarchal element of these social structures enormously by identifying "sex/gender systems":

> a "sex/gender system" is the set of arrangements by which a society transforms biological sexuality into products of human activity, and in which these transformed sexual needs are satisfied.[29]

We are born female and male, biological sexes, but we are created woman and man, socially recognized genders. *How* we are so created is that second aspect of the *mode* of production of which Engels spoke, "the production of human beings themselves, the propagation of the species."

How people propagate the species is socially determined. If, biologically, people are sexually polymorphous, and society were organized in such a way that all forms of sexual expression were equally permissible, reproduction would result only from some sexual encounters, the heterosexual ones. The strict division of labor by sex, a social invention common to all known societies, creates two very separate genders and a need for men and women to get together for economic reasons. It thus helps to direct their sexual needs toward heterosexual fulfillment, and helps to ensure biological reproduction. In more imaginative societies, biological reproduction might be ensured by other techniques, but the division of labor by sex appears to be the universal solution to date. Although it is theoretically possible that a sexual division of labor not imply inequality between the sexes, in most known societies, the socially acceptable division of labor by sex is one which accords lower status to women's work. The sexual division of labor is also the underpinning of sexual subcultures in which men and women experience life differently; it is the material base of male power which is exercised (in our society) not just in not doing housework and in securing superior employment, but psychologically as well.

How people meet their sexual needs, how they reproduce, how they inculcate social norms in new generations, how they learn gender, how it feels to be a man or a woman—all occur in the realm Rubin labels the sex/gender system. Rubin emphasizes the influence of kinship (which tells you with whom you can satisfy sexual needs) and the development of gender specific personalities via childrearing and the "oedipal machine." In addition, however, we can use the concept of the sex/gender system to examine all other social institutions for the roles they play in defining and reinforcing gender hierarchies. Rubin notes that theoretically a sex/gender system could be female dominant, male dominant, or egalitarian, but declines to label various known sex/gender systems or to periodize history accordingly. We choose to label our present sex/gender system patriarchy, because it appropriately captures the notion of hierarchy and male dominance which we see as central to the present system.

Economic production (what marxists are used to referring to as *the* mode of production) and the production of people in the sex/gender sphere both determine "the social organization under which the people of a particular historical epoch and a particular country live," according to Engels. The whole of society, then, can be understood by looking at both these types of production and reproduction, people and things.[30] There is no such thing as "pure capitalism," nor does "pure patriarchy" exist, for they must of necessity coexist. What exists is patriarchal capitalism, or patriarchal feudalism, or egalitarian hunting/gathering societies, or matriarchal horticultural societies, or patriarchal horticultural societies, and so on. There appears to be no necessary connection between *changes* in the one aspect of production and changes in the other. A society could undergo transition from capitalism to socialism, for example, and remain patriarchal.[31] Common sense, history, and our experience tell us, however, that these two aspects of production are so closely intertwined, that change in one ordinarily creates movement, tension, or contradiction in the other.

Racial hierarchies can also be understood in this context. Further elaboration may be possible along the lines of defining color/race systems, arenas of social life that take biological color and turn it into a social category, race. Racial hierarchies, like gender hierarchies, are aspects of our social organization, of how people are produced and reproduced. They are not fundamentally ideological; they constitute that second aspect of our mode of production, the production and reproduction of people. It might be most accurate then to refer to our societies not as, for example, simply capitalist, but as patriarchal capitalist white supremacist. In Part III below, we illustrate one case of capitalism adapting to and making use of racial orders and several examples of the interrelations between capitalism and patriarchy.

Capitalist development creates the places for a hierarchy of workers, but traditional marxist categories cannot tell us who will fill which places. Gender and racial hierarchies determine who fills the empty places. *Patriarchy is not simply hierarchical organization*, but hierarchy in which *particular* people fill *particular* places. It is in studying patriarchy that we learn why it is women who are dominated and how. While we believe that most known societies have been patriarchal, we do not view patriarchy as a universal, unchanging phenomenon. Rather patriarchy, the set of interrelations among men that allow men to dominate women, has changed in form and intensity over time. It is crucial that the hierarchy among men, and their differential access to patriarchal benefits, be examined. Surely, class, race, nationality, and even marital status and sexual orientation, as well as the obvious age, come into play here. And women of different class, race, national, marital status, or sexual orientation groups are subjected to different degrees of patriarchal power. Women may themselves exercise class, race, or national power, or even patriarchal power (through their family connections) over men lower in the patriarchal hierarchy than their own male kin.

To recapitulate, we define patriarchy as a set of social relations which has a material base and in which there are hierarchical relations between men and solidarity among them which enable them in turn to dominate women. The material base of patriarchy is men's control over women's labor power. That control is maintained by excluding women from access to necessary economically productive resources and by restricting women's sexuality. Men exercise their control in receiving personal service work from women, in not having to do housework or rear children, in having access to women's bodies for sex, and in feeling powerful and being powerful. The crucial elements of patriarchy as we *currently* experience them are: heterosexual marriage (and consequent homophobia), female childrearing and housework, women's economic dependence on men (enforced by arrangements in the labor market), the state, and numerous institutions based on social relations among men—clubs, sports, unions, professions, universities, churches, corporations, and armies. All of these elements need to be examined if we are to understand patriarchal capitalism.

Both hierarchy and interdependence among men and the subordination of women are *integral* to the functioning of our society; that is, these relationships are *systemic*. We leave aside the question of the creation of these relations and ask, can we recognize patriarchal relations in capitalist societies? Within capitalist societies we must discover those same bonds between men which both bourgeois and marxist social scientists claim no longer exist or are, at the most, unimportant leftovers. Can we understand how these relations among men are perpetuated in capitalist societies? Can we identify ways in which patriarchy has shaped the course of capitalist development?

III. THE PARTNERSHIP OF PATRIARCHY AND CAPITAL

How are we to recognize patriarchal social relations in capitalist societies? It appears as if each woman is oppressed by her own man alone; her oppression seems a private affair. Relationships among men and among families seem equally fragmented. It is hard to recognize relationships among men, and between men and women, as *systematically* patriarchal. We argue, however, that patriarchy as a system of relations between men and women exists in capitalism, and that in capitalist societies a healthy and strong partnership exists between patriarchy and capital. Yet if one begins with the concept of patriarchy and an understanding of the capitalist mode of production, one recognizes immediately that the partnership of patriarchy and capital was not inevitable; men and capitalists often have conflicting interests, particularly over the use of women's labor power. Here is one way in which this conflict might manifest itself: the vast majority of men might want their women at home to personally service them. A smaller number of men, who are capitalists, might want most women (not their own) to work in the wage labor market. In examining the tensions of this conflict over women's labor power historically, we will be able to identify the material base of patriarchal relations in capitalist societies, as well as the basis for the partnership between capital and patriarchy.

Industrialization and the Development of Family Wages

Marxists made quite logical inferences from a selection of the social phenomena they witnessed in the nineteenth century. But marxists ultimately underestimated the strength of the preexisting patriarchal social forces with which fledgling capital had to contend and the need for capital to adjust to these forces. The industrial revolution was drawing all people into the labor force, including women and children; in fact the first factories used child and female labor almost exclusively.[32] That women and children could earn wages separately from men both undermined authority relations (as discussed in Part I above) and kept wages low for everyone. Kautsky, writing in 1892, describe the process this way:

> [Then with] the wife and young children of the working-man . . . able to take care of themselves, the wages of the male worker can safely be reduced to the level of his own personal needs without the risk of stopping the fresh supply of labor power.
>
> The labor of women and children, moreover, affords the additional advantage that these are less capable of resistance than men [sic]; and their introduction into the ranks of the workers increases tremendously the quantity of labor that is offered for sale in the market.
>
> Accordingly, the labor of women and children . . . also diminishes [the] capacity [of the male worker] for resistance in that it overstocks the market; owning to both these circumstances it lowers the wages of the working-man.[33]

The terrible effects on working class family life of low wages and of forced participation of all family members in the labor force were recognized by marxists. Kautsky wrote:

> The capitalist system of production does not in most cases destroy the single household of the workingman, but robs it of all but its unpleasant features. The activity of woman today in industrial pursuits . . . means an increase of her former burden by a new one. *But one cannot serve two masters.* The household of the working-man suffers whenever his wife must help to earn the daily bread.[34]

Working men as well as Kautsky recognized the disadvantages of female wage labor. Not only were women "cheap competition" but working women were their very wives, who could not "serve two masters" well.

Male workers resisted the wholesale entrance of women and children into the labor force, and sought to exclude them from union membership and the labor force as well. In 1846 the *Ten-Hours' Advocate* stated:

> It is needless for us to say, that all attempts to improve the morals and physical condition of female factory workers will be abortive, unless their hours are materially reduced. Indeed we may go so far as to say, that married females would be much better occupied in performing the domestic duties of the household, than following the never-tiring motion of machinery. We therefore hope the day is not distant, when the husband will be able to provide for his wife and family, without sending the former to endure the drudgery of a cotton mill.[35]

In the United States in 1854 the National Typographical Union resolved not to "encourage by its act the employment of female compositors." Male unionists did not want to afford union protection to women workers; they tried to exclude them instead. In 1879 Adolph Strasser, president of the Cigarmakers International Union, said: "We cannot drive the females out of the trade, but we can restrict their daily quota of labor through factory laws."[36]

While the problem of cheap competition could have been solved by organizing the wage earning women and youths, the problem of disrupted family life could not be. Men reserved union protection for men and argued for protective labor laws for women and children.[37] Protective labor laws, while they may have ameliorated some of the worst abuses of female and child labor, also limited the participation of adult women in many "male" jobs.[38] Men sought to keep high wage jobs for themselves and to raise male wages generally. They argued for wages sufficient for their wage labor alone to support their families. This "family wage" system gradually came to be the norm for stable working class families at the end of the nineteenth century and the beginning of the twentieth.[39] Several observers have declared the non wage-working wife to be part of the standard of living of male workers.[40] Instead of fighting for equal wages for men and women, male workers sought the family wage, wanting to retain their wives' services at home. In the absence of patriarchy a unified working class might have confronted capitalism, but patriarchal social relations divided the working class, allowing one part (men) to be bought off at the expense of the other (women). Both the hierarchy between men and the solidarity among them were crucial in this process of resolution. Family wages may be understood as a resolution of the conflict over women's labor power which was occurring between patriarchal and capitalist interests at that time.

Family wages for most adult men imply men's acceptance, and collusion in, lower wages for others, young people, women and socially defined inferior men as well (Irish, blacks, etc., the lowest groups in the patriarchal hierarchy who are denied many of the patriarchal benefits). Lower wages for women and children and inferior men are enforced by job segregation in the labor market, in turn maintained by unions and management as well as by auxiliary institutions like schools, training programs, and even families. Job segregation by sex, by insuring that women have the lower paid jobs, both assures women's economic dependence on men and reinforces notions of appropriate spheres for women and men. For most men, then, the development of family wages, secured the material base of male domination in two ways. First, men have the better jobs in the labor market and earn higher wages than women. The lower pay women receive in the labor market both perpetuates men's material advantage over women and encourages women to choose wifery as a career. Second, then, women do housework, childcare, and perform other services at home which benefit men directly.[41] Women's home responsibilities in turn reinforce their inferior labor market position.[42]

The resolution that developed in the early twentieth century can be seen to benefit capitalist interests as well as patriarchal interests. Capitalists, it is often argued, recognized that in the extreme conditions which prevailed in the early nineteenth century industrialization, working class families could not adequately reproduce themselves. They realized that housewives produced and maintained healthier workers than wage-working wives and that educated children became better workers than noneducated ones. The bargain, paying family wages to men and keeping women home, suited the capitalists at the time as well as the male workers. Although the terms of the bargain have altered over time, it is still true that the family and women's work in the family serve capital by providing a labor force and serve men as the space in which they exercise their privilege. Women, working to serve men and their families, also serve capital as consumers.[43] The family is also the place where dominance and submission are learned, as Firestone, the Frankfurt School, and many others have explained.[44] Obedient children become obedient workers; girls and boys each learn their proper roles.

While the family wage shows that capitalism adjusts to patriarchy, the changing status of children shows that patriarchy adjusts to capital. Children, like women, came to be excluded from wage labor. As children's ability to earn money declined, their legal relationship to their parents changed. At the beginning of the industrial era in the United States, fulfilling children's need for their fathers was thought to be crucial, even primary, to their happy development; fathers had legal priority in cases of contested custody. As children's ability to contribute to the economic well-being of the family declined, mothers came increasingly to be viewed as crucial to the happy development of their children, and gained legal priority in cases of contested custody.[45] Here patriarchy adapted to the changing economic role of children: when children were productive, men claimed them; as children became unproductive, they were given to women.

The Partnership in the Twentieth Century

The prediction of nineteenth century marxists that patriarchy would wither away in the face of capitalism's need to proletarianize everyone has not come true. Not only did marxists underestimate the strength and flexibility of patriarchy, they also overestimated the strength of capital. They envisioned the new social force of capitalism, which had torn feudal relations apart, as virtually all powerful. Contemporary observers are in a better position to see the difference between the tendencies of "pure" capitalism and those of "actual" capitalism as it confronts historical forces in everyday practice. Discussions of the partnership between capital and racial orders and of labor market segmentation provide additional examples of how "pure" capitalist forces meet up with historical reality. Great flexibility has been displayed by capitalism in this process.

Marxists who have studied South Africa argue that although racial orders may not allow the equal proletarianization of everyone, this does not men that racial barriers prevent capital accumulation.[46] In the abstract, analysts could argue about which arrangements would allow capitalists to extract the most surplus value. Yet in a particular historical situation, capitalists must be concerned with social control, the resistance of groups of workers, and the intervention of the state. The state might intervene in order to reproduce society as a whole; it might be necessary to police some capitalists, to overcome the worst tendencies of capital. Taking these factors into account, capital*ists* maximize greatest *practicable* profits. If for purposes of social control, capitalists organize work in a particular way, nothing about capital itself determines who (that is, which individuals with which ascriptive characteristics) shall occupy the higher, and who the lower rungs of the wage labor force. It helps, of course, that capitalists themselves are likely to be the dominant social group and hence racist (and sexist). Capitalism inherits the ascribed characteristics of the dominant groups as well as of the subordinate ones.

Recent arguments about the tendency of monopoly capital to create labor market segmentation are consistent with this understanding.[47] Where capitalists purposely segment the labor force, using ascriptive characteristics to divide the working class, this clearly derives from the need for social control rather than accumulation needs in the narrow sense.[48] And over time, not all such divisive attempts are either successful (in dividing) or profitable. The ability of capital to shape the workforce depends both on the particular imperatives of accumulation in a narrow sense (for example, is production organized in a way that requires communication among a large number of workers? if so, they had better all speak the same language)[49] and on social forces within a society which may encourage/force capital to adapt (the maintenance of separate washroom facilities in South Africa for whites and blacks can only be understood as an economic cost to capitalists, but one less than the social cost of trying to force South African whites to wash up with blacks).

If the first element of our argument about the course of capitalist development is that capital is not all-powerful, the second is that capital is tremendously flexible. Capital accumulation encounters preexisting social forms, and both destroys them and adapts to them. The adaptation of capital can be seen as a reflection of the *strength* of these preexisting forms to persevere in new environments. Yet even as they persevere, they are not unchanged. The ideology with which race and sex are understood today, for example, is strongly shaped by the particular ways racial and sexual divisions are reinforced in the accumulation process.

The Family and the Family Wage Today

We argued above, that, with respect to capitalism and patriarchy, the adaptation, or mutual accommodation, took the form of the development of the family wage in the early twentieth century. The family wage cemented the partnership between patriarchy and capital. Despite women's increased labor force participation, particularly rapid since World War II, the family wage is still, we argue, the cornerstone of the present sexual division of labor—in which women are primarily responsible for housework and men primarily for wage work. Women's lower wages in the labor market (combined with the need for children to be reared by someone) assure the continued existence of the family as a necessary income pooling unit. The family, supported by the family wage, thus allows the control of women's labor by men both within and without the family.

Though women's increased wage work may cause stress for the family (similar to the stress Kautsky and Engels noted in the nineteenth century), it would be wrong to think that as a consequence, the concepts and the realities of the family and of the sexual division of labor will soon disappear. The sexual division of labor reappears in the labor market, where women work at women's jobs, often the very jobs they used to do only at home—food preparation and service, cleaning of all kinds, caring for people, and so on. As these jobs are low-status and low-paying patriarchal relations remain intact, though their material base shifts somewhat from the family to the wage differential, from family-based to industrially-based patriarchy.[50]

Industrially based patriarchal relations are enforced in a variety of ways. Union contracts which specify lower wages, lesser benefits, and fewer advancement opportunities for women are not just atavistic hangovers—a case of sexist attitudes or male supremacist ideology—they maintain the material base of the patriarchal system. While some would go so far as to argue that patriarchy is already absent from the family (see, for example, Stewart Ewen, *Captains of Consciousness*),[51] we would not. Although the terms of the compromise between capital and patriarchy are changing as additional tasks formerly located in the family are capitalized, and the location of the deployment of women's labor power shifts,[52] it is nevertheless true, as we have argued above, that the wage differential caused by extreme job segregation in the labor market reinforces the family, and, with it, the domestic division of labor, by encouraging women to marry. The "ideal" of the family wage—that a man can earn enough to support an entire family—may be giving way to a new ideal that both men and women contribute through wage earning to the cash income of the family. The wage differential, then, will become increasingly necessary in perpetuating patriarchy, the male control of women's labor power. The wage differential will aid in *defining* women's work as secondary to men's at the same time it necessitates women's actual continued economic dependence on men. The sexual division of labor in the labor market and elsewhere should be understood as a manifestation of patriarchy which serves to perpetuate it.

Many people have argued that though the partnership between capital and patriarchy exists now, it may *in the long run* prove intolerable to capitalism; capital may eventually destroy both familial relations and patriarchy. The argument proceeds logically that capitalist social relations (of which the family is not an example) tend to become universalized, that women will become increasingly able to earn money and will increasingly refuse to submit to subordination in the family, and that since the family is oppressive particularly to women and children, it will collapse as soon as people can support themselves outside it.

We do not think that the patriarchal relations embodied in the family can be destroyed so easily by capital, and we see little evidence that the family system is presently disintegrating. Although the increasing labor force participation of women has made divorce more feasible, the incentives to divorce are not overwhelming for women. Women's wages allow very few women to support themselves and their children independently and adequately. The evidence for the decay of the traditional family is weak at best. The divorce rate has not so much increased, as it has evened out among classes; moreover, the remarriage rate is also very high. Up until the 1970 census, the first-marriage age was continuing its historic decline. Since 1970 people seem to have been delaying marriage and childbearing, but most recently, the birth rate has begun to increase again. It is true that larger proportions of the population are now living outside traditional families. Young people, especially, are leaving their parents' homes and establishing their own households before they marry and start traditional families. Older people, especially women, are finding themselves alone in their own households, after their children are grown and they experience separation or death of a spouse. Nevertheless, trends indicate that the new generations of young people will form nuclear families at some time in their adult lives in higher proportions than ever before. The cohorts, or groups of people, born since 1930 have much higher rates of eventual marriage and childrearing than previous cohorts. The duration of marriage and childrearing may be shortening, but its incidence is still spreading.[53]

The argument that capital destroys the family also overlooks the social forces which make family life appealing. Despite critiques of nuclear families as psychologically destructive, in a competitive society the family still meets real needs for many people. This is true not only of long-term monogamy, but even more so for raising children. Single parents bear both financial and psychic burdens. For working class women, in particular, these burdens make the "independence" of labor force participation illusory. Single parent families have recently been seen by policy analysts as transitional family formations which become two-parent families upon remarriage.[54]

It could be that the effects of women's increasing labor force participation are found in a declining sexual division of labor within the family, rather than in more frequent divorce, but evidence for this is also lacking. Statistics on who does housework, even in families with wage-earning wives, show little change in recent years; women still do most of it.[55] The double day is a reality for wage-working women. This is hardly surprising since the sexual division of labor outside the family, in the labor market, keeps women financially dependent on men—even when they earn a wage themselves. The future of patriarchy does not, however, rest solely on the future of familial relations. For patriarchy, like capital, can be surprisingly flexible and adaptable.

Whether or not the patriarchal division of labor, inside the family and elsewhere, is "ultimately" intolerable to capital, it is shaping capitalism now. As we illustrate below, patriarchy both legitimates capitalist control and delegitimates certain forms of struggle against capital.

Ideology in the Twentieth Century

Patriarchy, by establishing and legitimating hierarchy among men (by allowing men of all groups to control at least some women), reinforces capitalist control, and capitalist values shape the definition of patriarchal good.

The psychological phenomena Shulamith Firestone identifies are particular examples of what happens in relationships of dependence and domination. They follow from the realities of men's social power—which women are denied—but they are shaped by the fact that they happen in the context of a capitalist society.[56] If we examine the characteristics of men as radical feminists describe them—competitive, rationalistic, dominating—they are much like our description of the dominant values of capitalist society.

This "coincidence" may be explained in two ways. In the first instance, men, as wage laborers, are absorbed in capitalist social relations at work, driven into the competition these relations prescribe, and absorb the corresponding values.[57] The radical feminist description of men was not altogether out of line for capitalist societies. Secondly, even when men and women do not actually behave in the way sexual norms prescribe, men *claim for themselves* those characteristics which are valued in the dominant ideology. So, for example, the authors of *Crestwood Heights* found that while the men, who were professionals, spent their days manipulating subordinates (often using techniques that appeal to fundamentally irrational motives to elicit the preferred behavior), men and women characterized men as "rational and pragmatic." And while the women devoted great energies to studying scientific methods of child-rearing and child development, men and women in Crestwood Heights characterized women as "irrational and emotional."[58]

This helps to account not only for "male" and "female" characteristics in capitalist societies, but for the particular form sexist ideology takes in capitalist societies. Just as women's work serves the dual purpose of perpetuating male domination and capitalist production, so sexist ideology serves the dual purpose of glorifying male characteristics/capitalist values, and denigrating female characteristics/social need. If women were degraded or powerless in other societies, the reasons (rationalizations) men had for this were different. Only in a capitalist society does it make sense to look down on women as emotional or irrational. As epithets, they would not have made sense in the renaissance. Only in a capitalist society does it make sense to look down on women as "dependent." "Dependent" as an epithet would not make sense in feudal societies. Since the division of labor ensures that women as wives and mothers in the family are largely concerned with the production of use values, the denigration of these activities obscures capital's inability to meet socially determined need at the same time that it degrades women in the eyes of men, providing a rationale for male dominance. An example of this may be seen in the peculiar ambivalance of television commercials. On one hand, they address themselves to the real obstacles to providing for socially determined needs: detergents that destroy clothes and irritate skin, shoddily made goods of all sorts. On the other hand, concern with these problems must be denigrated; this is accomplished by mocking women, the workers who must deal with these problems.

A parallel argument demonstrating the partnership of patriarchy and capitalism may be made about the sexual division of labor in the work force. The sexual division of labor places women in low-paying jobs, and in tasks thought to be appropriate to women's role. Women are teachers, welfare workers, and the great majority of workers in the health fields. The nurturant roles that women play in these jobs are of low status because capitalism emphasizes personal independence and the ability of private enterprise to meet social needs, emphases contradicted by the need for collectively provided social services. As long as the social importance of nurturant tasks can be denigrated because women perform them, the confrontation of capital's priority on exchange value by a demand for use values can be avoided. In this way, it is not feminism, but sexism that divides and debilitates the working class.

IV. TOWARDS A MORE PROGRESSIVE UNION

Many problems remain for us to explore. Patriarchy as we have used it here remains more a descriptive term than an analytic one. If we think marxism alone inadequate, and radical feminism itself insufficient, then we need to develop new categories. What makes our task a difficult one is that the same features, such as the division of labor, often reinforce both patriarchy and capitalism, and in a thoroughly patriarchal capitalist society, it is hard to isolate the mechanisms of patriarchy. Nevertheless, this is what we must do. We have pointed to some starting places: looking at who benefits from women's labor power, uncovering the material base of patriarchy, investigating the mechanisms of hierarchy and solidarity among men. The questions we must ask are endless.

Can we speak of the laws of motion of a patriarchal system? How does patriarchy generate feminist struggle? What kinds of sexual politics and struggle between the sexes can we see in societies other than advanced capitalist ones? What are the contradictions of the patriarchal system and what is their relation to the contradictions of capitalism? We know that patriarchal relations gave rise to the feminist movement, and that capital generates class struggle— but how has the relation of feminism to class struggle been played out in historical contexts? In this section we attempt to provide an answer to this last question.

Feminism and the Class Struggle

Historically and in the present, the relation of feminism and class struggle has been either that of fully separate paths ("'bourgeois'' feminism on one hand, class struggle on the other), or, within the left, the dominance of feminism by marxism. With respect to the latter, this has been a consequence both of the analytic power of marxism, and of the power of men within the left. These have produced both open struggles on the left, and a contradictory position for marxist feminists.

Most feminists who also see themselves as radicals (antisystem, anti-capitalist, anti-imperialist, socialist, communist, marxist, whatever) agree that the radical wing of the women's movement has lost momentum while the liberal sector seems to have seized the time and forged ahead. Our movement is no longer in that exciting, energetic period when no matter what we did, it worked—to raise consciousness, to bring more women (more even than could be easily incorporated) into the movement, to increase the visibility of women's issues in the society, often in ways fundamentally challenging to both the capitalist and patriarchal relations in society. Now we sense parts of the movement are being coopted and "feminism" is being used against women — for example, in court cases when judges argue that women coming out of long-term marriages in which they were housewives don't need alimony because we all know women are liberated now. The failure to date to secure the passage of the Equal Rights Amendment in the United States indicates the presence of legitimate fears among many women that feminism will continue to be used against women, and it indicates a real need for us to reassess our movement, to analyze why it has been coopted in this way. It is logical for us to turn to marxism for help in that reassessment because it is a developed theory of social change. Marxist theory is well developed compared to feminist theory, and in out attempt to use it, we have sometimes been sidetracked from feminist objectives.

The left has always been ambivalent about the women's movement, often viewing it as dangerous to the cause of socialist revolution. When left women espouse feminism, it may be personally threatening to left men. And of course many left organizations benefit from the labor of women. Therefore, many left analyses (both in progressive and traditional forms) are self-serving, both theoretically and politically. They seek to influence women to abandon attempts to develop an independent understanding of women's situation and to adopt the ''left's'' analyses of the situation. As for our response to this pressure, it is natural that, as we ourselves have turned to marxist analysis, we would try to join the ''fraternity'' using this paradigm, and we may end up trying to justify our struggle to the fraternity rather than trying to analyze the situation of women to improve our political practice. Finally, many marxists are satisfied with the traditional marxist analysis of the women question. They see class as the correct framework with which to understand women's position. Women should be understood as part of the working class; the working class's struggle against capitalism should take precedence over any conflict between men and women. Sex conflict must not be allowed to interfere with class solidarity.

As the economic situation in the United States has worsened in the last few years, traditional marxist analysis has reasserted itself. In the sixties the civil rights movement, the student free speech movement, the antiwar movement, the women's movement, the environmental movement, and the increased militancy of professional and white collar groups all raised new questions for marxists. But now the return of obvious economic problems such as inflation and unemployment had eclipsed the importance of these demands and the left has returned to the ''fundamentals''—working class (narrowly defined) politics. The growing ''marxist-leninist preparty'' sects are committed antifeminists, in both doctrine and practice. And there are signs that the presence of feminist issues in the academic left is declining as well. Day care is disappearing from left conferences. As marxism or political economy become intellectually acceptable, the ''old boys'' network of liberal academia is replicated in a sidekick "young boys" network of marxists and radicals, nonetheless male in membership and outlook despite its youth and radicalism.

The pressures on radical women to abandon this silly stuff and become "serious" revolutionaries have increased. Our work seems a waste of time compared to inflation and unemployment. It is symptomatic of male dominance that *our* unemployment was never considered in a crisis. In the last major economic crisis, the 1930s, the vast unemployment was partially dealt with by excluding women from many kinds of jobs — one wage job per family, and that job was the man's. Capitalism and patriarchy recovered — strengthened from the crisis. Just as economic crises serve a restorative function for capitalism by correcting imbalances, so they might serve patriarchy. The thirties put women back in their place.

The struggle against capital and patriarchy cannot be successful if the study and practice of the issues of feminism is abandoned. A struggle aimed only at capitalist relations of oppression will fail, since their underlying supports in patriarchal relations of oppression will be overlooked. And the analysis of patriarchy is essential to a definition of the kind of socialism useful to women. While men and women share a need to overthrow capitalism they retain interests particular to their gender group. It is not clear—from our sketch, from history, or from male socialists—that the socialism being struggled for is the same for both men and women. For a humane socialism would require not only consensus on what the new society should look like and what a healthy person should look like, but more concretely, it would require that men relinquish their privilege.

As women we must not allow ourselves to be talked out of the urgency and importance of our tasks, as we have so many times in the past. We must fight the attempted coercion, both subtle and not so subtle, to abandon feminist objectives.

This suggests two strategic considerations. First, a struggle to establish socialism must be a struggle in which groups with different interests form an alliance. Women should not trust men to liberate them after the revolution, in part, because there is no reason to think they would know how; in part, because there is no necessity for them to do so. In fact their immediate self-interest lies in our continued oppression. Instead we must have our own organizations and our own power base. Second, we think the sexual division of labor within capitalism has given women a practice in which we have learned to understand what human interdependence and needs are. While men have long struggled *against* capital, women know what to struggle *for*.[59] As a general rule, men's position in patriarchy and capitalism prevents them from recognizing both human needs for nurturance, sharing, and growth, and the potential for meeting those needs in a nonhierarchical, nonpatriarchal society. But even if we raise their consciousness, men might assess the potential gains against the potential losses and choose the status quo. Men have more to lose than their chains.

As feminist socialists, we must organize a practice which addresses both the struggle against patriarchy and the struggle against capitalism. We must insist that the society we want to create is a society in which recognition of interdependence is liberation rather than shame, nurturance is a universal, not an oppressive practice, and in which women do not continue to support the false as well as the concrete freedoms of men.

FOOTNOTES

1. Often paraphrased as "the husband and wife are one and that one is the husband," English law held the "by marriage, the husband and wife are one person in law: that is, the very being or legal existence of the women is suspended during the marriage, or at least is incorporated and consolidated into that of the Husband," I. Blackstone, *Commentaries*, 1965, pp. 442-445, cited in Kenneth M. Davidson, Ruth B. Ginsburg, and Herma H. Kay, *Sex Based Discrimination* (St. Paul, Minn.: West Publishing Co., 1974), p. 117.
2. Frederick Engels, *The Origin of the Family, Private Property and the State*, edited, with an introduction by Eleanor Burke Leacock (New York: International Publishers, 1972).
3. Frederick Engels, *The Condition of the Working Class in England* (Stanford, Calif.: Stanford University Press, 1958). See esp. pp. 162-66 and p. 296.
4. Eli Zaretsky, "Capitalism, the Family, and Personal Life," *Socialist Revolution,* Part I in No. 13-14 (January-April 1973), pp. 66-125, and Part II in No. 15 (May-June 1973), pp. 19-70. Also Zaretsky, "Socialist Politics and the Family," *Socialist Revolution (now Socialist Review).* No. 19 (January-March 1974), pp. 83-98, and *Capitalism, the Family and*

Personal Life (New York: Harper & Row, 1976). Insofar as they claim their analyses are relevant to women, Bruce Brown's *Marx, Freud, and the Critique of Everyday Life* (New York: Monthly Review Press, 1973) and Henri Lefebvre's *Everday Life in the Modern World* (New York: Harper & Row, 1971) may be grouped with Zaretsky.

5. In this Zaretsky is following Margaret Benston ("The Political Economy of Women's Liberation," *Monthly Review*, Vol. 21, No. 4 [September 1961], pp. 13-27), who made the cornerstone of her analysis that women have a different relation to capitalism than men. She argued that women at home produce use values, and that men in the labor market produce exchange values. She labeled women's work precapitalist (and found in women's common work the basis for their political unity.) Zaretsky builds on this essential difference in men's and women's work, but labels them both capitalist.

6. Zaretsky, "Personal Life," Part I, p. 114.

7. Mariarosa Dalla Costa, "Women and the Subversion of the Community," in *The Power of Women and the Subversion of the Community* by Mariarosa Dalla Costa and Selma James (Bristol, England: Falling Wall Press, 1973; second edition) pamphlet, 78 pps.

8. It is interesting to note that in the original article (cited in n. 7 above) Dalla Costa suggests that wages for housework would only further institutionalize woman's housewife role (pp. 32,34) but in a note (n. 16,pp. 52-52) she explains the demand's popularity and its use as a consciousness raising tool. Since then she has actively supported the demand. See Dalla Costa, "A General Strike," in *All Work and No Pay: Women, Housework, and the Wages Due*, ed. Wendy Edmond and Suzie Fleming (Bristol, England: Falling Wall Press, 1975).

9. The text of the article reads: "We have to make clear that, within the wage, domestic work produces not merely use values, but is essential to the production of surplus value" (p. 31). Note 12 reads: "What we mean precisely is that housework as work is *productive* in the Marxian sense, that is, producing surplus value" (p. 52, original emphasis). To our knowledge this claim has never been made more rigorously by the wages for housework group. Nevertheless marxists have responded to the claim copiously.

10. The literature of the debate includes Lise Vogel, "The Earthly Family," *Radical America*, Vol. 7, no. 4-5 (July-October 1973), pp. 9-50; Ira Gerstein, "Domestic Work and Capitalism," *Radical America*, Vol. 7, no.4-5 (July-October 1973, pp. 101-128; John Harrison, "Political Economy of Housework," *Bulletin of the Conference of Socialist Economists*, Vol. 3, no. 1 (1973); Wally Seccombe, "The Housewife and her Labour under Capitalism," *New Left Review*, no. 83 (January-February 1974), pp. 3-24; Margaret Coulson, Branka Magas,

and Hilary Wainwright, "'The Housewife and her Labour under Capitalism,' A Critique," *New Left Review*, no. 89 (January-February 1975), pp. 59-71; Jean Gardiner, "Women's Domestic Labour," *New Left Review*, no. 89 (January-February 1975), pp. 47-58; Ian Gough and John Harrison, "Unproductive Labour and Housework Again," *Bulletin of the Conference of Socialist Economists*, Vol. 4, no. 1 (1975); Jean Gardiner, Susan Himmelweit and Maureen Mackintosh, "Women's Domestic Labour," *Bulletin of the Conference of Socialist Economists*, Vol. 4, no. 2 (1975); Wally Seccombe, "Domestic Labour: Reply to Critics," *New Left Review*, no. 94 (November-December 1975), pp. 85-96; Terry Fee, "Domestic Labor: An Analysis of Housework and its Relation to the Production Process," *Review of Radical Political Economics*, Vol. 8, no. 1 (Spring 1976), pp. 1-8; Susan Himmelweit and Simon Mohun, "Domestic Labour and Capital," *Cambridge Journal of Economics*, Vol. 1, no. 1 (March 1977), pp. 15-31.

11. In the U.S., the most often heard political criticism of the wages for housework group has been its opportunism.

12. Laura Oren documents this for the working class in "Welfare of Women in Laboring Families: England, 1860-1950," *Feminist Studies*, Vol. 1, no. 3-4 (Winter-Spring 1973), pp. 107-25.

13. The late Stephen Hymer pointed out to us a basic weakness in Engels' analysis in *Origins*, a weakness that occurs because Engels fails to analyze the labor process within the family. Engels argues that men enforced monogamy because they wanted to leave their property to their own children. Hymer argued that far from being a 'gift,' among the petit bourgeoisie, possible inheritance is used as a club to get children to work for their fathers. One must look at the labor process and who benefits from the labor of which others.

14. This is a paraphrase. Karl Marx wrote: "The maintenance and reproduction of the working class is, and must ever be, a necessary condition to the reproduction of capital. But the capitalist may safely leave its fulfillment to the labourer's instincts of self-preservation and propagation." [*Capital* (New York: International Publishers, 1967), Vol. 1, p. 572.]

15. Harry Braverman, *Labor and Monopoly Capital* (New York: Monthly Review Press, 1975).

16. Juliet Mitchell, *Women's Estate* (New York: Vintage Books, 1973), p. 92.

17. Engels, *Origins*, "Preface to the First Edition," pp. 71-72. The continuation of this quotation reads, "...by the stage of development of labor on the one hand and of the family on the other." It is interesting that, by implication, labor is excluded from occurring within the family; this is precisely the blind spot we want to overcome in this essay.

18. Juliet Mitchell, "Women: The Longest Revolution," *New Left Review*, No. 40 (November-December 1966), pp. 11-37, also reprinted by

the New England Free Press.

19. Juliet Mitchell, *Psychoanalysis and Feminism* (New York: Pantheon Books, 1974).20.

20. Mitchell, *Psychoanalysis*, p. 412.

21. Shulamith Firestone, *The Dialectic of Sex* (New York: Bantam Books, 1971).

22. "Politics of Ego: A Manifesto for New York Radical Feminists," can be found in *Rebirth of Feminism*, ed. Judith Hole and Ellen Levine (New York: Quadrangle Books, 1971), pp. 440-443. "Radical feminists" are those feminists who argue that the most fundamental dynamic of history is men's striving to dominate women. 'Radical' in this context does *not* mean anti-capitalist, socialist, counter-cultural, etc., but has the specific meaning of this particular set of feminist beliefs or group of feminists. Additional writings of radical feminists, of whom the New York Radical Feminists are probably the most influential, can be found in *Radical Feminism*, ed. Ann Koedt (New York: Quadrangle Press, 1972).

23. Focusing on power was an important step forward in the feminist critique of Freud. Firestone argues, for example, that if little girls "envied" penises it was because they recognized that little boys grew up to be members of a powerful class and little girls grew up to be dominated by them. Powerlessness, not neurosis, was the heart of women's situation. More recently, feminists have criticized Firestone for rejecting the usefulness of the concept of the unconscious. In seeking to explain the strength and continuation of male dominance, recent feminist writing has emphasized the fundamental nature of gender-based personality differences, their origins in the unconscious, and the consequent difficulty of their eradication. See Dorothy Dinnerstein, *The Mermaid and the Minotaur* (New York: Harper Colophon Books, 1977), Nancy Chodorow, *The Reproduction of Mothering* (Berkeley: University of California Press, 1978), and Jane Flax, "The Conflict Between Nurturance and Autonomy in Mother-Daughter Relationships and Within Feminism," *Feminist Studies*, Vol. 4, no. 2 (June 1978), pp. 141-189.

24. Kate Millett, *Sexual Politics* (New York: Avon Books, 1971), p. 25.

25. One example of this type of radical feminist history is Susan Brownmiller's *Against Our Will, Men, Women, and Rape* (New York: Simon & Shuster, 1975).

26. For the bourgeois social science view of patriarchy, see, for example, Weber's distinction between traditional and legal authority, *Max Weber: The Theories of Social and Economic Organization*, ed. Talcott Parson (New York: The Free Press, 1964), pp. 328-357. These views are also discussed in Elizabeth Fee, "The Sexual Politics of Victorian Social Anthropology," *Feminist Studies*, Vol. 1, nos. 3-4 (Winter-Spring 1973), pp. 23-29, and in Robert A. Nisbet, *The Sociological Tradition* (New York: Basic Books, 1966), especially Chapter 3, "Community."

27. See Viana Muller, ''The Formation of the State and the Oppression of Women: Some Theoretical Considerations and a Case Study in England and Wales,'' *Review of Radical Political Economics*, Vol. 9, no. 3 (Fall 1977), pp. 7-21.

28. The particular ways in which men control women's access to important economic resources and restrict their sexuality vary enormously, both from society to society, from subgroup to subgroup, and across time. The examples we use to illustrate patriarchy in this section, however, are drawn primarily from the experience of whites in western capitalist countries. The diversity is shown in *Toward an Anthropology of Women*, ed. Rayna Rapp Reiter (New York: Monthly Review Press, 1975), *Woman, Culture and Society*, ed. Michelle Rosaldo and Louise Lamphere (Stanford, California: Stanford University Press, 1974), and *Females, Males, Families: A Biosocial Approach*, by Liba Leibowitz (North Scituate, Massachusetts: Duxbury Press, 1978). The control of women's sexuality is tightly linked to the place of children. An understanding of the demand (by men and capitalists) for children is crucial to understanding changes in women's subordination.

Where children are needed for their present or future labor power, women's sexuality will tend to be directed toward reproduction and childrearing. When children are seen as superfluous, women's sexuality for other than reproductive purposes is encouraged, but men will attempt to direct it towards satisfying male needs. The Cosmo girl is a good example of a woman ''liberated'' from childrearing only to find herself turning all her energies toward attracting and satisfying men. Capitalists can also use female sexuality to their own ends, as the success of Cosmo in advertising consumer products shows.

29. Gayle Rubin, ''The Traffic in Women,'' in *Anthropology of Women*, ed. Reiter, p. 159.

30. Himmelweit and Mohun point out that both aspects of production (people and things) are logically necessary to describe a mode of production because by definition a mode of production must be capable of reproducing itself. Either aspect alone is not self-sufficient. To put it simply the production of things requires people, and the production of people requires things. Marx, though recognizing capitalism's need for people did not concern himself with how they were produced or what the connections between the two aspects of production were. See Himmelweit and Mohun, ''Domestic Labour and Capital'' (note 10 above).

31. For an excellent discussion of one such transition to socialism, see Batya Weinbaum, ''Women in Transition to Socialism: Perspectives on the Chinese Case,'' *Review of Radical Political Economics*, Vol. 8, no. 1 (Spring 1976), pp. 34-58.

32. It is important to remember that in the preindustrial period, women contributed a large share to their families' subsistence—either by partic-

ipating in a family craft or by agricultural activities. The initiation of wage work for women both allowed and required this contribution to take place independently from the men in the family. The new departure, then, was not that women earned income, but that they did so beyond their husbands' or fathers' control. Alice Clark, *The Working Life of Women in the Seventeenth Century* (New York: Kelly, 1969) describes women's preindustrial economic roles and the changes that occurred as capitalism progressed. It seems to be the case that Marx, Engels, and Kautsky were not fully aware of women's economic role before capitalism.

33. Karl Kautsky, *The Class Struggle* (New York: Norton, 1971), pp. 25-26.

34. We might add, "outside the household," Kautsky, *Class Struggle*, p. 26, our emphasis.

35. Cited in Neil Smelser, *Social Change and the Industrial Revolution* (Chicago: University of Chicago Press, 1959), p. 301.

36. These examples are from Heidi I. Hartmann, "Capitalism, Patriarchy, and Job Segregation by Sex," *Signs: Journal of Women in Culture and Society*, Vol. 1, no. 3, pt. 2 (Spring 1976), pp. 162-163.

37. Just as the factory laws were enacted for the benefit of all capitalists against the protest of some, so too, protective legislation for women and children may have been enacted by the state with a view toward the reproduction of the working class. Only a completely instrumentalist view of the state would deny that the factory laws and protective legislation legitimate the state by providing concessions and are responses to the demands of the working class itself.

38. For a more complete discussion of protective labor legislation and women, see Ann C. Hill, "Protective Labor Legislation for Women: Its Origin and Effect," mimeographed (New Haven, Conn.: Yale Law School, 1970) parts of which have been published in Barbara A. Babcock, Ann E. Freedman, Eleanor H. Norton, and Susan C. Ross, *Sex Discrimination and the Law: Causes and Remedies* (Boston: Little, Brown & Co., 1975), an excellent law text. Also see Hartmann, "Job Segregation by Sex," pp. 164-166.

39. A reading of Alice Clark, *The Working Life of Women*, and Ivy Pinchbeck, *Women Workers*, suggests that the expropriation of production from the home was followed by a social adjustment process creating the social norm of the family wage. Heidi Hartmann, in *Capitalism and Women's Work in the Home, 1900-1930* (Unpublished Ph.D. dissertation, Yale University, 1974; forthcoming Temple University Press) argues, based on qualitative data, that this process occurred in the U.S. in the early 20th century. One should be able to test this hypothesis quantitatively by examining family budget studies for different years and noting the trend of the proportion of the family income for different

income groups, provided by the husband. However, this data is not available in comparable form for our period. The family wage resolution has probably been undermined in the post World War II period. Carolyn Shaw Bell, in "Working Women's Contribution to Family Income," *Eastern Economic Journal*, Vol. 1, no. 3 (July 1974), pp. 185-201, presents current data and argues that it is now incorrect to assume that the man is the primary earner of the family. Yet whatever the *actual* situation today or earlier in the century, we would argue that the social norm *was* and *is* that men should earn enough to support their families. To say it has been the norm is not to say it has been universally achieved. In fact, it is precisely the failure to achieve the norm that is noteworthy. Hence the observation that in the absence of sufficiently high wages, "normative" family patterns disappear, as for example, among immigrants in the nineteenth century and third world Americans today. Oscar Handlin, *Boston's Immigrants* (New York: Atheneum, 1968) discusses mid-nineteenth century Boston, where Irish women were employed in textiles; women constituted more than half of all wage laborers and often supported unemployed husbands. The debate about family structure among Black Americans today still rages; see Carol B. Stack, *All Our Kin: Strategies for Survival in a Black Community* (New York: Harper and Row, 1974), esp. Chap. 1. We would also argue (see below) that for most families the norm is upheld by the relative places men and women hold in the labor market.

40 Hartmann, *Women's Work*, argues that the non-working wife was generally regarded as part of the male standard of living in the early twentieth century (see p. 136, n. 6) and Gerstein, "Domestic Work," suggests that the norm of the working wife enters into the determination of the value of male labor power (see p. 121).

41. The importance of the fact that women perform labor services for men in the home cannot be overemphasized. As Pat Mainardi said in "The Politics of Housework," "[t]he measure of your oppression is his resistance" (in *Sisterhood is Powerful*, ed. Robin Morgan [New York: Vintage Books, 1970], p. 451). Her article, perhaps as important for us as Firestone on love, is an analysis of power relations between women and men as exemplified by housework.

42. Libby Zimmerman has explored the relation of membership in the primary and secondary labor markets to family patterns in New England. See her *Women in the Economy: A Case study of Lynn, Massachusetts, 1760-1974* (Unpublished Ph.D dissertation, Heller School, Brandeis, 1977). Batya Weinbaum is currently exploring the relationship between family roles and places in the labor market. See her "Redefining the Question of Revolution," *Review of Radical Political Economics,* Vol. 9, no. 3 (Fall 1977), pp. 54, 78, and *The Curious Courtship of Women's Liberation and Socialism* (Boston: South End Press, 1978). Additional

studies of the interaction of capitalism and patriarchy can be found in Zillah Eisenstein, ed., *Capitalist Patriarchy and the case for Socialist Feminism* (New York: Monthly Review Press, 1978).

43. See Batya Weinbaum and Amy Bridges, "The Other Side of the Paycheck: Monopoly Capital and the Structure of Consumption," *Monthly Review*, Vol. 28, no. 3 (July-August 1976), pp. 88-103, for a discussion of women's consumption work.

44. For the view of the Frankfurt School, see Max Horkheimer, "Authority and the Family," in *Critical Theory* (New York: Herder & Herder, 1972) and Frankfurt Institute of Social Research, "The Family," in *Aspects of Sociology* (Boston: Beacon, 1972).

45. Carol Brown, "Patriarchial Capitalism and the Female-Headed Family," *Social Scientist* (India); no. 40-41 (November-December 1975), pp. 28-39.

46. For more on racial orders, see Stanley Greenberg, "Business Enterprise in a Racial Order," *Politics and Society*, Vol. 6, no. 2 (1976), pp. 213-240, and Michael Burroway, *The Color of Class in the Copper Mines: From African Advancement to Zambianization* (Manchester, England: Manchester University Press, Zambia Papers No. 7, 1972).

47. See Michael Reich, David Gordon, and Richard Edwards, "A Theory of Labor Market Segmentation," *American Economic Review*, Vol. 63, no. 2 (May 1973), pp. 359-365, and the book they edited, *Labor Market Segmentation* (Lexington, Mass: D.C. Heath, 1975) for a discussion of labor market segmentation.

48. See David M. Gordon, "Capitalist Efficiency and Socialist Efficiency," *Monthly Review*, Vol. 28, no. 3 (July-August 1976), pp. 19-39, for a discussion of qualitative efficiency (social control needs) and quantitative efficiency (accumulation needs).

49. For example, Milwaukee manufacturers organized workers in production first according to ethnic groups, but later taught all workers to speak English, as technology and appropriate social control needs changed. See Gerd Korman, *Industrialization, Immigrants, and Americanizers, the View from Milwaukee, 1866-1921* (Madison: The State Historical Society of Wisconsin, 1967).

50. Carol Brown, in "Patriarchal Capitalism," argues, for example, that we are moving from "family based" to "industrially-based" patriarchy within capitalism.

51. Stewart Ewen, *Captains of Consciousness* (New York: Random House, 1976).

52. Jean Gardiner, in "Women's Domestic Labour" (see n. 10), clarifies the cause for the shift in location of women's labor, from capital's point of view. She examines what capital needs (in terms of the level of real wages, the supply of labor, and the size of markets) at various stages of growth and of the business cycle. She argues that in times of boom or

rapid growth it is likely that socializing housework (or more accurately capitalizing it) would be the dominant tendency, and that in times of recession, housework will be maintained in its traditional form. In attempting to assess the likely direction of the British economy, however, Gardiner does not assess the economic needs of patriarchy. We argue in this essay that unless one takes patriarchy as well as capital into account one cannot adequately assess the likely direction of the economic system.

53. For the proportion of people in nuclear families, see Peter Uhlenberg, "Cohort Variations in Family Life Cycle Experiences of U.S. Females," *Journal of Marriage and the Family*, Vol. 36, no. 5 (May 1974), pp. 284-92. For remarriage rates see Paul C. Glick and Arthur J. Norton, "Perspectives on the Recent Upturn in Divorce and Remarriage," *Demography*, Vol. 10 (1974), pp. 301-14. For divorce and income levels see Arthur J. Norton and Paul C. Glick, "Marital Instability: Past, Present, and Future," *Journal of Social Issues*, Vol. 32, no. 1 (1976), pp. 5-20. Also see Mary Jo Bane, *Here to Stay: American Families in the Twentieth Century* (New York: Basic Books, 1976).

54. Heather L. Ross and Isabel B. Sawhill, *Time of Transition: The Growth of Families Headed by Women* (Washington, D.C.: The Urban Institute, 1975).

55. See Kathryn E. Walker and Margaret E. Woods *Time Use: A Measure of Household Production of Family Goods and Services* (Washington D.C.: American Home Economics Association, 1976; and Heidi I. Hartmann, "The Family as the Locus of Gender, Class, and Political Struggle: The Example of Housework," *Signs: Journal of Women in Culture and Society*, Vol. 6, no. 3 (Spring 1981).

56. Richard Sennett's and Jonathan Cobb's *The Hidden Injuries of Class* (New York: Random House, 1973) examines similar kinds of psychological phenomena within hierarchical relationships between men at work.

57. This should provide some clues to class differences in sexism, which we cannot explore here.

58. See John R. Seeley, et al., *Crestwood Heights* (Toronto: University of Toronto Press, 1956), pp. 382-94. While men's place may be characterized as "in production" this does not mean that women's place is simply "not in production"—her tasks, too, are shaped by capital. Her non-wage work is the resolution, on a day-to-day basis, of production for exchange with socially determined need, the provision of use values in a capitalist society (this is the context of consumption). See Weinbaum and Bridges, "The Other Side of the Paycheck," for a more complete discussion of this argument. The fact that women provide "merely" use values in a society dominated by exchange values can be used to denigrate women.

59. Lise Vogel, "The Earthly Family" (see n. 10).

BEYOND THE UNHAPPY MARRIAGE: A CRITIQUE OF THE DUAL SYSTEMS THEORY

Iris Young

Iris Young has lived in several regions of the U.S. in the last several years, where she has been involved in various feminist activities. She presently lives in Northampton, Massachusetts, and teaches humanities at Worcester Polytechnic Institute.

Even in its title Hartmann's essay reflects what has been the specific project of socialist feminism: to "wed" the best aspects of the new wave of feminist theory developed in the sixties and seventies to marxian theory, thereby transforming marxian theory. Hartmann argues that this marriage has thus far not succeeded. She recommends that the marriage between marxism and feminism be put on a stonger footing by developing a theoretical account which gives as much weight to the system of patriarchy as to the system of capitalism. Rather than perceiving the particular situation of women as an effect of capitalism, as she believes Engels, Mitchell, Dalla Costa, and Zaretsky do, we should understand that the system of patriarchy is at least of equal importance for understanding the situation of women. Socialist feminist theory thus should seek the "laws of motion" of the system of patriarchy, the internal dynamic and contradictions of patriarchy, and articulate how these interact and perhaps conflict with the internal dynamic of capitalism.

Hartmann's essay is not the first to have proposed this dual systems theory for socialist feminism. On the contrary, the majority of socialist feminists espouse some version of the dual systems theory. I shall argue, however, that the dual systems theory will not patch up the unhappy marriage of marxism and feminism. There are good reasons for believing that the situation of women is not conditioned by two distinct systems of social relations which have distinct structures, movement, and histories. Feminist marxism cannot be content with a mere "wedding" of two theories, marxism and feminism, reflecting two systems, capitalism and patriarchy. Rather, the project of socialist feminism should be to develop a single theory out of the best insights of both marxism and radical feminism, which can comprehend capitalist patriarchy as one system in which the oppression of women is a *core* attribute.

THE DUAL SYSTEMS THEORY

As with most other proponents of the dual systems theory, dissatisfaction with both traditional marxism and radical feminism taken alone motivates Hartmann to develop her conception of the dual systems theory. She states that the categories of traditional marxism are essentially gender-blind and that therefore marxian analyses of women's situation under capitalism have failed to bring issues of gender differentiation and hierarchy explicitly into focus.

Feminist theory has corrected this failing by developing the concept of patriarchy to describe and analyze gender hierarchy. Radical feminist theory, however, according to Hartmann, has several problems. It focuses too exclusively on child rearing as determining women's situation. It tends to view patriarchy as merely a psychological or cultural phenomenon, rather than as a system having a material base in real social relations. Finally, the radical feminist account tends to view patriarchy as basically unchanging through most if not all of history.

Hartmann then proposes a dual systems theory to remedy the weaknesses both of traditional marxism and radical feminism. We must understand women's oppression in our society as an effect of *both* capitalism and patriarchy. Patriarchy is defined as

> a set of social relations between men, which have a material base, and which, though hierarchical, establish or create interdependence and solidarity among men that enable them to dominate women.(Hartmann, p. 14.)

Patriarchal relations are phenomena distinct from the economic relations of production analyzed by traditional marxism. Capital and patriarchy are distinct forms of social relations and distinct sets of interests which do not stand in any necessary relationship and even exist in potential conflict. Even though it is difficult to separate analytically the specific elements of society which belong to patriarchy and those which belong to capitalism, we must do so. We must isolate the specific "laws of motion" of patriarchy, distinct from the mode and relations of production, and understand the specific contradictions of the system of patriarchy in their relation to the specific contradictions the system of capitalism.[1]

All versions of the dual systems theory start from the premise that patriarchal relations designate a system of relations distinct from and independent of the relations of production described by traditional marxism. An account can take two possible directions in describing how patriarchy is separate from the economic system of production relations. On the one hand, one can retain the radical feminist concept of patriarchy as an ideological and psychological structure. The resulting dual systems theory will then attempt to give an account of the interaction of these ideological and psychological structures with the material relations of society. On the other hand, one can develop an account of patriarchy as itself a system of material social relations, existing independently of and interacting with the social relations of production.

Juliet Mitchell's approach in *Psychoanalysis and Feminism* represents an example of the first of these alternatives. She takes patriarchy as a universal and formal ideological structure. "Patriarchy describes the universal culture—however, each specific mode of production expresses this in different ideological forms."[2]

> Men enter into the class dominated structures of history while women (as women, whatever their work in actual production) remain defined by the kinship pattern of organization. Differences of class, historical epoch, specific social situation alter the expression of femininity; but in relation to the law of the father, women's position across the board is a comparable one.[3]

Mitchell's idea seems to be that the patriarchal structures which she claims freudian theory articulates exist as a pre- or nonhistorical ideological backdrop to changes in the mode of production. This ideological and psychological structure lying outside economic relations persists in the same form throughout. She does not deny, of course, that women's situations differ concretely in different social circumstances. We account for this variation in women's situation by the way in which the particular structures of a given mode of production interact with the universal structures of patriarchy.

This version of the dual systems theory inappropriately dehistoricizes and universalizes women's oppression. Representing patriarchy as a universal system having the same basic structure through history can lead to serious cultural, racial, and class biases.[4] Describing the differences in the form and character of women's situation in different social circumstances as merely different "expressions" of one and the same universal system of patriarchy, moreover, trivializes the depth and complexity of women's oppression.

The main problem with this version of the dual systems theory, however, is that it does not succeed in giving the alleged system of patriarchy equal weight with and independence from the system of a mode of production. It conceives of all concrete social relations as belonging to the economic system of production relations. Thus it leaves no material weight to the system of patriarchy, which it defines in its essence as independent of the system of production relations. Thus it ends by ceding to the traditional theory of production relations the primary role in giving an account of women's situation. The theory of patriarchy supplies the form of women's oppression, but traditional marxist theory supplies its content, specificity, differentiation, and motors of change. Thus this version of the dual systems theory fails in undermining traditional marxism because it cedes to that marxism theoretical hegemony over historically material social relations.[5]

Recognizing these weaknesses in the first option for a dual systems theory, Hartmann chooses the second. She emphasizes that patriarchy has a material base in the structure of concrete relations, and maintains that the system of patriarchy itself undergoes historical transformation. Precisely these strengths of Hartmann's account, however, weaken her argument for a dual systems theory which conceives of patriarchy as a system distinct from the relations of production. If, as Hartmann maintains, "the material base upon which patriarchy rests lies most fundamentally in men's control over women's labor power," and if "men maintain this control by excluding women from access to some essential productive resources" (Hartmann, p. 15), then it does not seem possible to separate patriarchy from a system of social relations of production even for analytical purposes. If, as Hartmann states, patriarchal social relations in contemporary capitalism are not confined to the family, but also exist in the capitalist workplace and other institutions outside the family, it is hard to see by what principle we can separate these patriarchal relations from the social relations of capitalism. Hartmann concedes that "the same features, such as division of labor, often reinforce both patriarchy and capitalism, and in a thoroughly patriarchal capitalist society, it is hard to isolate the mechanisms of patriarchy"(Hartmann, p. 29). Yet she insists that we must separate patriarchy. It seems reasonable, however, to admit that if patriarchy and capitalism are manifest in identical social and economic structures they belong to *one* system, not two.

Several dual systems theorists who take the second approach, conceiving of patriarchy as a set of distinct material relations, solve this problem by positing patriarchy as a system or mode of production itself, which exists alongside the mode of capitalist production. Ann Ferguson, for example, argues that the family through history is the locus of a particular type of production distinct from the production of material goods. She calls this type of production sex-affective production with its own relations of production distinct from capitalist relations. Men exploit women in the contemporary nuclear family by appropriating their sex-affective labor without reciprocation. Women thus constitute a distinct class in the traditional marxian sense. The interaction of patriarchy and capitalism in contemporary society consists in the mutual interaction of these two modes of production which both overlap and stand in tension with one another.[6] Socialist feminists who regard the family under capitalism as a vestige of the feudal mode of production[7] hold a similar position with regard to women's situation in contemporary society (that is: structured by the interaction of two modes of production) as do those who wish to distinguish mode of reproduction from mode of production.[8] Hartmann similarly distinguishes between two different "types" or "aspects" of production, the production of people and the production of things. She does not, however, posit the "production of people" as a distinct *mode* of production,[9] however, nor does she want to restrict this type of production to the family, though it is not clear where or how it takes place, nor how it can be distinguished from relations in which people produce things.

In order to have a dual systems theory which conceives patriarchy as a system of concrete relations as well as an ideological and psychological structure, it appears necessary to posit patriarchy in this fashion as a distinct system of production. Almost invariably, however, this approach relies on what Rosalind Petchesky calls a "model of separate spheres" which usually takes the form of distinguishing the family from the economy, and in locating the specific relations of patriarchy within the family.[10] There are, however, a number of problems with the model of separate spheres.

One of the defining characteristics of capitalism is the separation of productive activity from kinship relations, and thereby the creation of two spheres of social life. Making this point, and showing how this separation has created a historically unique situation for women, has been one of the main achievements of socialist feminist analysis.[11] The model of separate spheres presupposed by many dual systems theorists tends to hypostasize this division between family and economy specific to capitalism into a universal form.[12] Even within capitalism, moreover, this separation may be illusory. In their paper, "The Other Side of the Paycheck," Batya

Weinbaum and Amy Bridges argue, for example, that contemporary capitalism has not only rationalized and socialized production operations in accordance with its domination and profit needs, but that it has also rationalized and socialized the allegedly private work of consumption[13]

Because the model of separate spheres assumes the primary sphere of patriarchal relations is the family, it fails to bring into focus the character and degree of women's specific oppression as women outside the family. For example, it is difficult to view contemporary capitalism's use of women as sexual symbols to promote consumption as a function of some separate sphere distinct from the economic requirements of monopoly capitalism. More mundanely, a dual systems theory does not appear to have the theoretical equipment to identify and analyze the specific forms of sexist oppression which women suffer in the contemporary workplace. When more than half the women over sixteen in the U.S. are at work at any one time, and when over 90 percent work outside the home at some time in their lives, such a failing may serve the interests of contemporary capitalism itself.

This, more generally, is the ultimate objection to any dual systems theory. However one formulates it, the dual systems theory allows traditional marxism to maintain its theory of production relations, historical change, and analysis of the structure of capitalism in a basically unchanged form. That theory, as Hartmann points out, is completely gender-blind. The dual systems theory thus accepts this gender-blind analysis of the relations of production, wishing only to add onto it a separate conception of the relations of gender hierarchy. Thus, not unlike traditional marxism, the dual systems theory tends to see the question of women's oppression as merely an additive to the main questions of marxism.

As long as feminists are willing to cede the theory of material social relations arising out of laboring activity to traditional marxism, however, the marriage between feminism and marxism cannot be happy. If, as Hartmann claims, patriarchy's base is a control over women's labor that excludes women from access to productive resources, then patriarchal relations are internally related to production relations as a whole. Thus traditional marxian theory will continue to dominate feminism as long as feminism does not challenge the adequacy of the traditional theory of production relations itself. If traditional marxism has no theoretical place for analysis of gender relations and the oppression of women, then that theory is an inadequate theory of production relations. Our historical research coupled with our feminist intuitions tells us that the labor of women occupies a central place in any system of production, and that sexual hierarchy is a crucial element in any system of domination.[14] To correspond to these intuitions we need a theory of relations of production and the social relations which derive from and reinforce those relations which takes gender relations and the situation of women as *core* elements. Instead of marrying marxism, feminism must take over marxism and transform it into such a theory. We must develop an analytical framework which regards the material social relations of a particular historical social formation as one system in which gender differentiation is a core attribute.

DIVISION OF LABOR ANALYSIS

In this essay I will propose that gender division of labor must be a central category for such a theory, and I will sketch how that category might function in a feminist historical materialism. In my reading, many concrete socialist feminist analyses, including some propounding a dual systems theory, do not actually take patriarchy, but rather gender division of labor, as their central category. Thus in arguing for gender division of labor as a central category of feminist historical materialism I believe I am making explicit a characteristic of socialist feminist theory which already exists.

Traditional marxism takes class as its central category of analysis. Feminists have rightly claimed that this category does not aid the analysis of women's specific oppression, or even its identification. The concept of class is indeed gender-blind. Precisely this conceptual flaw of the category class helped bring about the dual systems theory. Since class functions as the core concept of the marxian theory of social relations, and since it provides no place for analysis of gender differentiation and gender hierarchy, there appears to be no alternative but to seek another category and another system in which gender relations can appear. I suggest that there is another alternative, however. Agreeing that the category of class is gender blind and hence incapable of exposing women's situation, we can nevertheless remain within the materialist framework by elevating the category of *division of labor* to a position as fundamental as, if not more fundamental than, that of class. This category *can* provide us with means of analyzing the social relations of laboring activity in a gender differentiated way.

The division of labor category appears in Marx's own work almost as often as the class category, and he uses both in an equally ambiguous and equivocal fashion. One wonders, then, why the category of class has been taken up, refined and developed by the marxist theoretical tradition, while the category of division of labor has remained undeveloped. In *The German Ideology* division of labor operates as a category broader and more fundamental than that of class.[15] Division of labor, moreover, accounts for specific cleavages and contradictions within a class.[16] The category of division of labor can not only refer to a set of phenomena broader than that of class, but also more concrete. It refers specifically to the activity of labor itself, and the specific social and institutional relations of that activity, rather than to a relation to the means of labor and the products of labor, as does class.[17] The specific place of individuals in the division of labor explains their consciousness and behavior, as well as the specific relations of cooperation and conflict in which different persons stand.[18]

These attributes of division of labor as a category both more concrete in its level of analysis and broader in extension than the category of class, make it an indispensible element in any analysis of the social relations involved in and arising from laboring activity. Each category entails a different level of abstraction. Class analysis aims to get a vision of a system of production as a whole, and thus asks about the broadest social divisions of ownership, control, and the appropriation of surplus product. At such a level of abstraction, however, much pertaining to the relations of production and the material bases of domination remains hidden. Division of labor analysis proceeds at the more concrete level of particular relations of interaction and interdependence in a society which differentiates it into a complex network. It describes the major structural divisions among the members of a society according to their position in laboring activity, and assesses the effect of these divisions on the functioning of the economy, the relations of domination, political and ideological structures.

I believe that raising division of labor to a level of precision and centrality as important as class can have implications for analysis of phenomena in addition to gender differentiation. For example, questions surrounding the role of professionals and state workers in contemporary capitalism might be better resolved through division of labor analysis than class analysis. Analysis of racial tension in the contemporary working class as well as in the society as a whole, to take another example, might benefit from inquiring into the correlations of race with aspects of the contemporary division of labor. Finally, the indubitable presence of relations of domination in existing socialist societies might be better analyzed in terms of division of labor than in terms of class.[19]

I am here concerned, however, with the implications of division of labor analysis for feminist theory. I have argued thus far that a complete analysis of the material relations of a social formation requires specific analysis of the division of labor and that this analysis neither derives from nor reduces to class analysis. A crucial aspect of the division of labor in every hitherto existing society is an elaborate gender division of labor that affects the entire society. Thus a complete analysis of the economic relations of production in a social formation requires specific attention to the gender division of labor.

GENDER DIVISION OF LABOR

With the term "gender division of labor" I intend to refer to all structured gender differentiation of labor in a society. Such traditional women's tasks as bearing and rearing children, caring for the sick, cleaning, cooking, etc., fall under the category of labor as much as the making of objects in a factory. Using the category of production or labor to designate only the making of concrete material objects in a modern factory has been one of the unnecessary tragedies of marxian theory.[20] "Relations of production" or "social relations arising from laboring activity" should mean the social relations involved in *any* task or activity which the society defines as necessary. Thus in our own society, for example, the relation between female prostitutes and the pimps or organizations they work for is a relation of production in this sense. Use of the gender division of labor category provides the means for analyzing the social relations arising from the laboring activity of a whole society along the axis of gender.[21]

At a minimum, it seems to me that a gender division of labor analysis would attempt to answer the following questions: What are the major lines of gender division of labor in a particular social formation, and what is the nature and social meaning of the gender specified tasks? How does gender division of labor underlie other aspects of economic organization, and how does it underlie relations of power and domination in society, including gender hierarchy? How does gender division of labor relate to the organization of sexual and kinship relations? What accounts for the origin and transformation in this particular structure of gender division of labor? How have transformations in gender division of labor led to changes in the relations of men and women, other economic relations, political relations, and ideological structures?

Gender division of labor analysis can have a number of advantages over the approach of the dual systems theory. It brings gender relations and the position of women to the center of historical materialist analysis. A marxian account of the social relations of production must bring women's specific situation into focus through gender division of labor analysis. Failure to do so results not merely in diminishing or ignoring the significance of male domination, which is bad enough, but also in missing crucial elements of the structure of economic and social relations as a whole. For example, it surely makes a difference to the economic organization of Greek and Roman society, and to the slave mode of production there, that women managed the households. Women thus had the most direct relationship with family slaves while men had mobility for trade and warfare, as well as leisure for the production of culture and participation in politics.[22] A similar point might be made about the women of the ruling class in medieval Europe.[23]

Gender division of labor analysis may provide a way of regarding gender relations as not merely a central aspect of relations of production, but as fundamental to their structure. For the gender division of labor is the first division of labor, and in so-called primitive societies it is the only institutionalized division of labor. The development of other forms of social division of labor, such as the division between mental and manual labor, may thus be explicable only by appeal to transformations in the gender division of labor and the effect such changes have on the relations between members of each sex, as well as potentialities such changes make available to them.

More importantly, serious empirical investigation may reveal that the radical feminist account of class as based on sex—an account which the dual system theory abandons—may turn out to be appropriate for historical materialist theory. To do so one would not argue that class domination derives from sex oppression, as Shulamith Firestone does is the *Dialectic of Sex*.[24] Rather one would give an account of the emergence of class society out of changes in the gender division of labor. Engels, in the *Origin of the Family, Private Property and the State,* suggests something along these lines though he fails to recognize its implications, a failure which biases the whole account. More recently, in *The Underside of History*, Elise Boulding has suggested a connection between the rise of class stratified society and the fact that at a certain point in early societies men began to specialize in one trade while women did not.[25]

Gender division of labor analysis can also explain the origins and maintenance of women's subordination in social structural terms. Neither a biological account nor a psychological account, for example, can show how men in a particular society occupy an institutionalized position of superiority in a particular society. Men can occupy such an institutionalized position of superiority only if the organization of social relations arising from laboring activity gives them a level of control over and access to resources that women do not have. Gender division of labor can help explain this differential access to the means of labor and control, and thus can help explain how the institutions of male domination originate, are maintained, and change.[26]

Biological and psychological elements have their place, of course, in an account of women's situation and oppression. One among many factors conditioning the gender division of labor in most societies, for example, is women's biological reproductive function. Any account of the gender division of labor, moreover, presupposes that there are genders—that is, socio-cultural division and classification of people according to their biological sex. Since any particular gender division of labor presupposes gender identification and symbolic elaboration, we need some account of gender. Such an account, I think, must be psychological. The best account we have thus far of the origins, symbolic and ideological significance, and implications of gender differentiation is the feminist appropriation of the freudian perspective in such works as Dorothy Dinnerstein's *The Mermaid and the Minotaur* and Nancy Chodorow's *The Reproduction of Mothering.* Such works have cogently argued that women's relation to young children determines the development of gender differentiation as we know it, and explains why women signify "the other" in most cultural ideologies.[27] One must not confuse such biological accounts of the origins of gender identity and its symbolic structure, however, with accounts of the social power men have over women and their position of relative privilege...While these different accounts may reinforce one another, they belong to different levels of analysis.

Hartmann herself appears to take the division of labor by sex as the foundation of male domination, perhaps even of gender itself.

> The strict division of labor by sex, a social invention common to all known societies, creates two very separate genders and a need for men and women to get together for economic reasons. . . . The sexual division of labor is also the underpinning of sexual subcultures in which men and women experience life differently; it is the material base of male power which is exercised (in our society) not just in not doing housework and in securing superior employment, but psychologically as well.(Hartmann, p. 16.)

Gender division of labor analysis allows us to do material analysis of the social relations of labor in gender specific terms without assuming that all women in general or all women in a particular society have a common and unified situation. I believe this to be one of the primary virtues of such an analysis. Because the dual systems theory posits a distinct system underlying the oppression of women, it tends to claim that *qua* women we are in an identical situation whatever our historical location or situation. Gender division of labor analysis, however, can avoid this false identification while still focusing on the gender specific situation and oppression of women. Gender division of labor analysis notices the broad axes of gender structuration of the relations of labor and distribution, and notices that certain tasks and functions in a particular society are always or usually performed by members of one sex. This does not necessarily commit it to any claims about the common situation of all members of that sex. In some societies every woman must perform some tasks, but in most societies the tasks and positions of women vary, even though they are gender specific.

Not only can gender division of labor analysis take account of specific variations in the situations of women in its descriptions, but it can better explain such variations than can the dual systems theory. In particular, explaining variations in the kind or degree of women's subordination in a society requires reference to what women concretely do in a society. For example, it is not surprising that women tend to stand in a more equal position to men when they have access to weapons and warfare than when men have a monopoly over these.[28] Gender division of labor analysis, moreover, may prove fruitful in giving an account of why in a few societies—the Iroquois, for example—women do not appear to occupy a subordinate position.[29]

In giving centrality to phenomena of gender division of labor I am not claiming that gender division of labor can explain all the aspects of women's situation in a particular society. I am claiming only that in giving an account or explanation of some particular phenomenon of women's situation one should articulate its relation to the gender division of labor. I conceive that gender division of labor should always be a *part*—but almost never the *only* part—of an explanation of some aspect of women's situation.[30]

In proposing gender division of labor analysis for a feminist historical materialism, moreover, I am claiming that understanding the economic structure and relations of domination of a social formation as a whole requires paying attention to the structure of the gender division of labor. Through this category socialist feminists can view phenomena of class, domination, relations of production and distribution, on the one hand, and phenomena of women's oppression, on the other hand, as aspects of the same socio-economic system. In this way we can demand of all marxists that they consider issues of women's situation and oppression as integral to their analysis of a social formation.

The major purpose of material in this section has been to suggest some directions for a feminist materialist theory which regards gender differentiation as a crucial element in an account of social relations of production in a society. The need for a theory that regards the position of women as crucial to the understanding of the system of capitalism should by now be clear. In the following section I will sketch a historical account of women's situation in capitalism which might correspond to such a theory.

GENDER DIVISION AND CAPITALIST PATRIARCHY

Any historical account is an interpretative reconstruction within a specific theoretical framework. This holds true for women's history as much as any other form of history. Since one's theoretical approach already influences the way one gives the historical account, that account cannot confirm or disconfirm the theory. Hartmann poses her account of the role of the family wage in the history of capitalism as though it were empirical evidence supporting the claim that patriarchy exists alongside capitalism as an independent structure, at times conflicting with capitalism. But her account actually presupposes the dual systems theory.

In her essay as well as her paper, "Capitalism, Patriarchy and Job Segregation by Sex,"[31] Hartmann has offered us incontrovertible evidence that women's oppression within the modern era is complex and pervasive. In her historical accounts she has carried marxist feminism forward by giving us solid accounts of the structures and changes in women's role in the labor process and the economy as a whole under capitalism. After this work no one would dare claim that women's oppression under capitalism either does not exist, is a mere epiphenomenon, or is withering away.

The issue rather is not whether the specific sexist oppression of women exists in capitalist society, but *how* we should construe women's special oppression. Hartmann and many others claim that women's oppression in capitalist society does not have its foundation in the structure and dynamic of capitalism, but in an independent set of structures and dynamic of patriarchy. Others, such as Ehrenreich and English in *For Her Own Good*, argue that the specific situation of women under capitalism is a function of the structure of the commodity economy and the needs of bourgeois ideology.[32] The issue turns on whether male dominance under capitalism should be understood as a separate system or as part of the internal structure of capitalism itself.

In her account of women's oppression within capitalist society, Hartmann assumes a model of the structure and dynamic of capitalism as gender-blind. In her view nothing about the logic of capitalism itself requires differentiation among workers along lines of ascribed characteristics like sex (or race). Indeed, Hartmann shares an assumption about the nature of capitalism held by liberal and marxist theorists alike: that capitalism's inherent tendency is to homogenize the workforce, reducing the significance of ascribed statuses based on sex, race, ethnic origin, and so on. She claims that the development of capitalism from the fifteenth to the eighteenth century undermined male dominance over women and threatened to make women independent from and equal to men. "The theoretical tendency of pure capitalism would have been to eradicate all arbitrary differences of status among laborers, making all laborers equal in the marketplace."[33] Given that the internal dynamic of capitalism tends toward such homogenization, she argues, only the operation of a separate system of patriarchy can explain women's continued subordination and unequal status.

I believe that abandoning the assumption of a gender-blind capitalism allows one to approach the history of women's status in capitalist society in a more revealing light. A gender division of labor analysis of capitalism, which asks how the system itself is structured along gender lines, can give an account of the situation of women under capitalism as a function of the structure and dynamic of capitalism itself. *My thesis is that marginalization of women and thereby our functioning as a secondary labor force is an essential and fundamental characteristic of capitalism.*

In her book, *Women in Class Society*, Heleieth Saffioti argues that the marginalization of women's labor is necessary to capitalism and is the key to understanding women's situation under capitalism. Capitalism emerges as the first economic system whose nature dictates that not all potentially productive people be employed, and which also requires a fluctuation in the proportion of the population employed. The existence of the system thus requires, she argues, that some criteria be found to distinguish the core of primary workers from marginal or secondary workers. The preexistence of patriarchal ideology, coupled with the necessity that women be near small children, operated to make sex the most natural criterion by which to divide the workforce.[34] Capitalism uses criteria of race and ethnicity as well, when these are present in the society, but the sex division is always the most obvious and permanent; women are not likely to be ''assimilated.''

Hartmann cites the indisputable fact that women's social subordination existed before capitalism as evidence that our subordination under capitalism has its source in a separate system of social relations that interacts with the capitalist system.[35] We need not draw this conclusion, however. A marxist would not assert that the existence of class society prior to capitalism demonstrates that all class societies have some common structure independent of the system of capitalism. Class societies undergo systemic historical transformation. The weakness of the ahistorical view of patriarchy which sees it as essentially the same through changes in other social relations has already been pointed out. Once we admit, with Hartmann, that the form and character of women's oppression have undergone fundamental historical transformation, then the existence of precapitalist patriarchy need no longer count as

evidence that male domination in capitalist society has its foundation in a structure of social relations independent of the system of
capitalism itself.

While women in precapitalist society were by no means the
social equals of men, all the evidence points to the conclusion that
our situation deteriorated with the development of capitalism. In
precapitalist society women dominated a number of crucial skills,
and thus their labor and their knowledge were indispensible to the
family, the manor, and the village. In many craft guilds of the six-
teenth and seventeenth centuries women were members on equal
terms with men, and even dominated some of them. Women
engaged in industry and trade. Precapitalist culture understood
marriage as a economic partnership; men did not expect to
"support" women. The law reflected this relative equality of
women by allowing them to make contracts in their own name and
retain their own property even in marriage.[36]

By the nineteenth century women's economic independence
had been almost entirely undermined and her legal rights were
nonexistent. Capitalism thrust women for the first time in history
to the margins of economic activity. This marginalizaiton of
women's labor by capitalism never meant that women's labor was
jettisoned entirely from the socialized economy. In 1866 in France,
for example, women comprised 30 percent of the total industrial
workforce.[37] Rather, women were defined as a secondary labor
force which served as a reserve of cheap labor.

Throughout the history of capitalism women have served the
classic functions Marx describes as those of the reserve army of
labor.[38] They have served as a pool of workers who can be drawn
into new areas of production without dislodging those already
employed, and as a pool which can be used to keep both the wages
and militancy of all workers low. Whenever in the history of capitalism large numbers of new workers have been needed in new and
expanding industries, it is women more often than not who fill the
need. The early textile mills in New England, for example, actively
recruited women, as did the printers.[39] Many of the occupations
which today are considered "women's jobs" were areas of employment which opened in huge numbers during the nineteenth
century and which required relatively skilled workers. This is true
of nursing, for example, as well as saleswork, telephone workers,
and clerical workers.[40]

Employers have always tended to exaggerate divisions among workers in order to keep wages low and to maintain worker docility. Women have been used consistently for such purposes. Throughout the history of capitalism women have served as a ready pool of strikebreakers. In the history of industrialization capitalists consistently replaced men with women and children when they mechanized the production process. Then once the will and expectations of the men had lowered, they rehired the men and removed the women and children.[41] A similar pattern seems to have operated during the depression of the 1930s. Employers replaced high priced men by lower priced women until the wage expectations of the men had fallen, at which point the employers once again replaced the women with men.[42] The literature on sex segregation of the contemporary labor force often suggests that sex segregated jobs are new to the twentieth century. A close look at the history of capitalism, however, reveals that a sexually mixed occupation has been rare. Those jobs in which women have dominated at any particular time, moreover, have usually been accorded less pay and prestige than male jobs of comparable skill.[43] In this way as well women have always served as a secondary labor force.

Preexistent patriarchal ideology and the traditional location of women's labor near the home initially made possible the marginalization of women's labor, according it secondary status. Bourgeois ideology, however, greatly expanded and romanticized, at the same time that it trivialized, women's association with a domestic sphere and dissociation with work outside the home. The ideology of femininity which defined women as nonworking emerged as a consequence of and justification for the process of marginalization of women that had already begun. Not until well into the nineteenth century did treatises appear arguing that the true vocation of women was motherhood, that women were too frail to engage in heavy work, that women's proper activity was to nurture and create an atmosphere of shelter and comfort for her family.[44]

Capitalists actively promoted, and continue to promote, the ideology of domestic womanhood to justify low wages for women, arguments for their indispensibility, and to keep women from organizing.[45] Because only the bourgeois or petty bourgeois woman could live a life that corresponded to the ideology of femi-

ninity, that ideology acted as a powerful force in the upwardly
mobile desires of the working class. Women internalized the image
of femininity and both men and women took the "nonworking"
wife as a sign of status. One should note here that among the working class a wife who was not a wage worker was freed to bring in
income through petty commodity production or to produce food
and clothing which would make buying less necessary.

Without question male workers had sexist motivations and
used sexist arguments in the struggle for the family wage which
Hartmann discusses and in the struggle for protective legislation
for women and children which occurred at about the same time.
Given the history of capitalism up until that time, however, one
can see these motives and arguments as an effect and consolidation
of the capitalist gender division of labor which accorded women a
marginal and secondary position. One can, that is, explain the sexism of male workers without appealing to a system of social relations independent of capitalism, by seeing the essentially patriarchal character of the system of capitalism itself. One explains it
by seeing how capitalism is an economic system in which a gender
division of labor having a historically specific form and structure
which by marginalizing women's labor gives men a specific kind of
privilege and status.

Capitalism does not merely use or adapt to gender hierarchy,
as most dual systems theorists suggest. From the beginning it was
founded on gender hierarchy which defined men as primary and
women as secondary. The specific forms of the oppression of
women which exist under capitalism are essential to its nature.[46]
This does not mean, of course, that gender hierarchy did not exist
prior to capitalism, nor does it mean that the development of capitalism's gender division of labor did not depend on the prior existence of sexist ideology and a feudal gender division of labor. Many
other aspects of capitalism developed out of feudal society, but at a
certain point these developments took a specifically new form.

If we could find one instance of a capitalist society in which
the marginalization of women's labor did not occur, we might be
entitled to consider it a characteristic external to the structure of
capitalism. We can find no such instance, however. In her book
Women's Role in Economic Development, Ester Boserup documents in detail that the situation of women in third world economies seems to worsen with the introduction of capitalist and
"modern" industrial methods. Even where capitalism enters a

society in which women's work is the center of the economy, it tends to effect the marginalization of women's labor.[47] In claiming that the capitalist economy requires the marginalization of women, I am not claiming that we cannot logically conceive of a capitalism in which the marginalization of women did not occur. I am claiming, rather, that given an initial gender differentiation and a preexisting sexist ideology, a patriarchal capitalism in which women function as a secondary labor force is the only *historical* possibility.

PRACTICAL IMPLICATIONS

A theory must be evaluated by standards of coherence, consistency, simplicity, explanatory power, etc. A social theory, however, in addition to these, should be judged according to its practical implications. A theory intended as part of a political movement should be judged according to how well it may be expected to further the goals of that movement. Thus in this concluding section I argue that the dual systems theory has some undesirable practical implications which further indicate the need for a feminist materialist theory which is an integral part of a revised marxism, rather than merely married to marxism.

The dual systems theory originally developed for a determinate practical reason. The left was male dominated, blatantly sexist and dismissed feminist concerns as merely bourgeois. Angry and frustrated socialist women began forming all women's groups and arguing for the need for an autonomous women's movement to correct the problems of the left and to develop the practice and theory of feminism. The dual systems theory arose in part as an element in this argument for an autonomous women's movement. If capitalism and patriarchy, classism and sexism, each have a source in distinct social systems, then the necessity for a women's movement autonomous from the mixed left follows most reasonably.

Let me make clear that I believe that an autonomous women's movement is absolutely necessary both for women and the left today, for all the practical reasons usually articulated by feminists. Women must have the space to develop positive relations with each other, apart from men. We can best learn to develop our own organizing, decision making, speaking and writing skills in a supportive environment free from male dominance or paternalism. An autonomous women's movement can best reach women who see the need for the struggle against sexism, but have not yet seen that struggle as integrated with the struggle for socialism. And so on.

The indubitable practical necessity of an autonomous women's movement, however, does not show the need for a dual systems theory. The different positions of men and women within the capitalist patriarchal gender division of labor creates the strategic necessity for women to organize separately so that we are in a position to develop our own skills, make our own decisions, and struggle against men and their sexism. One need not draw the conclusion from this necessity which many socialist feminists draw, namely that these are two separate struggles against two separate systems.

I have some trouble conceiving what struggle against patriarchy as distinct from the struggle against capitalism might mean at a practical level. The issues of women's reproductive rights, for example, are unquestionably on the front lines of the struggle for women's liberation. If any cluster of issues could be singled out as involving specifically the struggle against patriarchy as distinct from the struggle against capitalism, one would think this would be it. Yet the actual struggle has been and must be against the integrated and virulent *capitalist* patriarchy we live in. In light of the recent supreme court ruling on the Hyde Amendment we know more than ever that the reproductive rights of poor and Third World women are more seriously threatened than those of other women. Not recognizing this has in the past been a serious failing of the women's movement. In raising issues of women's reproductive freedom, women confront the reality of the capitalist patriarchal medical system. Current struggles for reproductive rights, morever, necessarily involve confronting the structures of the capitalist patriarchal state, which is presently in the midst of a fiscal crisis. From a practical perspective, then, it is simply not possible to separate this most central aspect of the struggle against patriarchal structures from the struggle against capitalist structures.

One might propose the feminist struggle against the sexual abuse of women as a struggle against patriarchal structures which does not entail struggle against capitalism. A few actions in this struggle need not have an explicitly anticapitalist thrust, such as rape counseling, or "take back the night" patrols. But sexual harrassment and abuse in the workplace, for example, cannot be separated from the total system of hierarchy and subordination essential to contemporary capitalist production relations. Sexual harrassment of one form or another is a routine way of dealing with women workers, and is an integral part of the superior-subordinate relation in many factory and office settings. The larger structure of the sexual objectification of women certainly cannot be separated from the capitalist sales effort which constantly exploits and exposes women's bodies as symbols of pleasure, luxury, and convenience.[48]

There are urgent practical reasons, in my opinion, for rejecting the notion that patriarchy and capitalism are separate systems entailing distinct political struggles. Such an approach continues to see feminist political action as over and above anticapitalist socialist political action. This puts a double burden on those who identify themselves as socialist feminists, while it fails to confront other socialists directly.

As a result of the influence of feminism, many socialist individuals and organizaitons have become more self-conscious about examining their own sexist prejudices and practices, and they are more aware of the need to organize women and deal with women's issues. *By and large, however, socialists do not consider fighting women's oppression as a central aspect of the struggle against capitalism itself.* The dual systems theory encourages this by insisting that women's specific oppression has its locus in a system other than capitalism. As a result, within the socialist movement women's issues remain segregated, generally dealt with only by women, and the mixed socialist movement as a whole fails to take issues related to women's oppression as seriously as others.

A theory of women's oppression under capitalism which showed capitalism as *essentially* patriarchal could change the relation between feminist political practice and the struggle to transform capitalist institutions and relations. If it is the case that the marginalization of women and our functioning as a secondary labor force are central to capitalism as it developed historically and as it exists today, then the struggle against the oppression of women and our marginalization in this society is itself anticapitalist.

Barbara Ehrenreich has defined a socialist feminist as a socialist who goes to twice as many meetings.[49] This definition is not entirely tongue in cheek, for the present understanding of socialist feminism still tends to see the feminist practice as additional to the socialist practice. In this marriage we are presently like the harried secretary who also has to do all the housework at home.

In my view what distinguishes the politics of socialist feminism is adherence to the principles that engaging in feminist organizing projects in itself counts as valid socialist political work, and that all socialist political work should have a feminist dimension at least to the extent that explicit questions have been raised about the implications of the work for women's oppression or women's relation to a socialist movement. The dual systems theory does not provide the theoretical basis for justifying this claim about the meaning of socialist feminist politics. Only a theory which regards the conditions of women's oppression as located in one system in which that oppression is a core element can give that basis.

FOOTNOTES

1. For some other statements of the dual systems theory, see Linda Phelps, "Patriarchy and Capitalism," *Quest*, Vol. II, no.2, Fall 1975; Zillah Eisenstein, "Developing a Theory of Capitalist Patriarchy," in Eisenstein, ed., *Capitalist Patriarchy and the Case for Socialist Feminism* (New York: Monthly Review Press, 1979), pp.5-40.
2. Juliet Mitchell, *Psychoanalysis and Feminism* (New York: Vintage Books, 1975), p.409.
3. *Ibid*, p.406.
4. See Mina Davis Caufield, "Universal Sex Oppression: A Critique from Marxist Anthropology," *Catalyst*, nos.10-11, Summer 1977, pp.60-77.
5. Compare McDonough and Harrison's criticism of Mitchell in "Patriarchy and Relations of Production," in Kuhn and Wolpe, ed., *Feminism and Materialism* (London: Routeledge and Kegan Paul, 1978), pp.12-25.
6. Ann Ferguson, "Women as a New Revolutionary Class," in Pat Walker, ed., *Between Labor and Capital* (Boston: South End Press, 1979), pp.279-312.
7. This is basically the position Mitchell articulates in *Women's Estate* (New York: Vintage Books, 1973); see also Sheila Rowbotham, *Women's Consciousness, Man's World* (Middlesex: Penguin Books, 1973), pp.61-63.
8. See Jane Flax, "Do Feminists Need Marxism?" *Quest*, Vol. III, no.1, Summer 1976, p.55.
9. There are clear problems with Ferguson's attempt to describe the nuclear family as a distinct *mode* of production, but I do not wish to take

up space in the paper analyzing them. Firstly, in her idea of sex-affective production it does not seem that any material goods are produced; it is difficult to grasp the notion of a mode of production, in the marxian sense, which does not produce any material goods. Second, her idea presupposes that sex-affective mode of production could have some kind of independent existence from the capitalist mode of production. Given that no material goods are produced in it, however, such independence is not viable.

10. See Rosalind Petchesky, "Dissolving the Hyphen: A Report on Marxist Feminist Groups 1-5," in Eisenstein, ed., *op. cit.*, pp.373-387.

11. See Eli Zaretsky, *Capitalism, the Family and Personal Life* (New York: Harper and Row, 1976); Ann Oakley, *Women's Work: The Housewife Past and Present* (New York: Vintage Books, 1974); Roberta Hamilton, *The Liberation of Women: A Study of Patriarchy and Capitalism* (London: George Allen and Unwin, 1978).

12. In his *Origin of the Family, Private Property and the State*, which is the starting point for many of these analyses, Engels manifests the same tendency. He divides all labor through all historical periods into private labor and public labor.

13. Batya Weinbaum and Amy Bridges, "The Other Side of the Paycheck: Monopoly Capital and the Structure of Consumption," in Eisenstein, ed., *op. cit.*, pp.190-205.

14. For an incisive and persuasive recent account of the basis of class society and the state in the patriarchal family, see Sherry B. Ortner, "The Virgin and the State," *Feminist Studies*, Vol. 4, no.3, October 1978, pp.19-36.

15. Karl Marx and Frederich Engels, *The German Ideology*, C.J. Arthur, ed. (New York: International Publishers, 1970), p.43; p.54.

16. *Ibid*, p.65.

17. *Ibid*, p.52.

18. *Ibid*, p.68. For more complete accounts of the meaning of the concept of division of labor in marxian theory, and especially in the *German Ideology*, see Andreas Hegedus, "The Division of Labor and the Social Structure of Socialism," in Peter Berger, ed., *Marxism and Sociology* (New York: Appleton-Century Crofts, 1979), pp.128-145; see also Bertell Ollman, *Alienation* (Cambridge: Cambridge University Press, 1971), Chapter 24.

19. See Hegedus, *op. cit.*.

20. See Raymond Williams, *Marxism and Literature* (Oxford University Press, 1977), pp. 75-95.

21. In previous versions of this paper I have designated this category "sexual division of labor," in conformity with common usage. I have since come to the conclusion, however, that "gender division of labor" better captures the phenomenon, because through the concept of "gender" it

focuses on the social meaning of the division, rather than a biological or "natural" division.

22. For an account of the economic and political implications of women's relation to the household in ancient Greek society, see Marilyn Arthur, "'Liberated' Women: The Classical Era," in Bridenthal and Koonz, ed., *Becoming Visible* (New York: Houghton Mifflin, 1977), pp.60-89; see also Elise Boulding, *The Underside of History* (Boulder, Colorado: Westview Press, 1976), pp.257-263.

23. See JoAnn McNamara and Suzanne F. Wemple, "Sanctity and Power: The Dual Pursuit of Medieval Women," in Bridenthal and Koonz, ed., *op. cit.*; see also Elizabeth Janeway, *Man's World, Woman's Place* (New York: Dell Publishing Company, 1971), pp.13-22.

24. In *The Dialectic of Sex* (New York: Bantam Books, 1970), Firestone took herself to be giving a materialist account of women's oppression. The problem with her account, I am suggesting, may not be this project of explaining class by sex, but the completely psychologistic manner in which she does so.

25. Boulding, *op. cit.*

26. There is much evidence, for example, that whether a society is matrifocal or patrifocal depends in large measure on the gender division of labor. See Bette S. Denich, "Sex and Power in the Balkans," in Rosaldo and Lamphere, ed., *Woman, Culture and Society* (Stanford University Press, 1974).

27. Nancy Chodorow, *The Reproduction of Mothering* (Berkeley: Berkeley Unversity Press, 1978); Dorothy Dinnerstein, *The Mermaid and the Minotaur* (New York: Harper and Row, 1976).

28. Boulding, *op. cit.*

29. Much of Judith Brown's account of Iroquois women's relatively high status depends upon looking at their role in production and the control over resources they have by virtue of that role. See "Iroquois Women: An Ethnohistorical Note," in Rayna Reiter, ed., *Toward an Anthropology of Women* (New York: Monthly Review Press, 1976).

30. Mary Ryan's book, *Womanhood in America from Colonial Times to the Present* (New York: New Viewpoints, 1975) might be taken as an example of the application of the approach I am recommending. In her accounts and explanations she always makes reference to the economic situation of women and their laboring activity, both in and outside the home. She never reduces the totality of the situation at any time to this division of labor analysis, however, and always includes other elements in a particular account.

31. Heidi Hartmann, "Capitalism, Patriarchy and Job Segregation by Sex," in Eisenstein, ed., *op. cit.*, pp.206-247.

32. Barbara Ehrenreich and Dierdre English, *For Her Own Good* (Garden City, N.Y.: Doubleday Anchor Press, 1978).

33. Hartmann, *op. cit.*, p.207.

34. Heleith Saffioti, *Women in Class Society* (New York: Monthly Review Press, 1978), especially Chapter 12.

35. Hartmann, *op. cit.*, pp.209-211.

36. Ehrenreich and English, *op. cit.*, pp. 6-9; Alice Clark, *Working Life of Women in the 17th Century* (New York: Harcourt, Brace, and How, 1920); Ann Oakley, *Women's Work, op. cit.*, Chapter 2; Kathleen Case, "The Cheshire Cat: Reconstructing the Experience of Medieval Women," in Berenice A. Carroll, ed., *Liberating Women's History* (Chicago: University of Illinois Press, 1976), pp.224-249; Mary Ryan, *op. cit.*, pp.19-82.

37. Saffioti, *op. cit.*, p.53.

38. Marx, *Capital*, Vol. I (New York: International Publishers, 1967), pp.631-639.

39. Elizabeth Faulkner Baker, *Technology and Women's Work* (New York: Columbia University Press, 1964), Chapter 1.

40. *Ibid*, see also Alice Kessler-Harris, "Women, Work and the Social Order," in Carroll, ed., *op. cit.*, p.335.

41. Baker, Chapter 1; Kessler-Harris, "Stratifying by Sex: Understanding the History of Working Women," in Edwards, Reich, and Gordon, ed., *Labor Market Segmentation* (Lexington, MA: D.C. Heath and Company, 1975), pp.217-242.

42. Jane Humphries, "Women: Scapegoats and Safety Valves in the Great Depression," in *Review of Radical Political Economics*, Vol. 8, no.1, Spring 1975, pp.98-121.

43. Baker, *op. cit.* and Kessler-Harris, "Stratifying by Sex..." both detail the degree of sex segregation in the U.S. in the nineteenth century; for a comparable account for Europe, see Teresa M. McBride, "The Long Road Home: Women's Work and Industrialization," in Bridenthal and Koonz, ed., *op. cit.*.

44. Ehrenreich and English, *op. cit.*; Ryan, Chapter 3; Ann D. Gordon and Mari Jo Buhle, "Sex and Class in Colonial and Nineteeth Century America," in Carroll, *op. cit.*

45. Kessler-Harris, "Women, Work and the Social Order," pp.333-337.

46. Ann Foreman argues that the specific type of domestic labor which is allocated to women under capitalism is a form of labor peculiar to and definitive of capitalism. Wage labor, that is to say, is not the only form of labor that capitalism creates; it also creates privatized household labor, and Foreman argues that this is an integral element of the capitalist mode of production. See *Femininity as Alienation* (London: Pluto Press, 1977).

47. Ester Boserup, *Women's Role in Economic Development* (New York: St. Martin's Press, 1970); see also E.M. Chaney and M. Schmink, "Women and Modernization: Access to Tools," in Nash and Safa, ed., *Sex and Class in Latin America* (New York: Praeger, 1976).

48. See Ryan, *op. cit.*, pp.251-304.

49. *Working Papers in Socialist Feminism*, pamphlet available from the New American Movement.

SOCIALISM, FEMINISM AND GAY/LESBIAN LIBERATION

Christine Riddiough

Christine Riddiough is co-chair of the Socialist Feminist Commission of the New American Movement. She has been the editor of Blazing Star, a lesbian feminist newspaper in Chicago and has been actively involved in the women's, gay and lesbian movements for ten years. She works as an environmental health researcher at the University of Illinois.

For the last decade the idea that has moved more people to action than any other is the idea of feminism, women's rights, women's liberation. Whether in working for the ERA, demanding one's husband do his share of the dishes, taking legal action to get equal pay, or in thousands of other ways, large and small, women and some men have built a massive political movement. As the movement has developed so too have ideas about the goals and strategies of the movement. If you asked activists in the women's movement what feminism is, you'd probably get as many different ideas as there are kinds of activities. Yet there are underlying threads connecting many of these ideas. One of the major trends in feminist thought over recent years has been socialist feminism. Within this tendency much energy has gone into trying to link marxist ideas with feminist ideas in a way that will provide a unified vision of society.

Heidi Hartmann's essay is one of those attempting to make that link. She discusses the need for more emphasis on the *feminist* aspect of socialist feminism. And as a part of the basis for her argument she gives a definition of feminism that many would agree with:

> The feminist question is directed at the causes of sexual inequality between women and men, of male dominance over women. . . . [F]or feminists the object is the liberation of women. . . . [T]he object of feminist analysis [is] the relations between women and men. (Hartmann, pp. 1, 8.)

In the essay's discussion of the implications of this definition, its criticism of other approaches to feminism, its analysis of patriarchy, "The Unhappy Marriage" contributes some valuable insights into the nature of feminism and its relationship to marxism. But there are weaknesses in the essay and it is these weaknesses that need to be looked at.

A MORE PROGRESSIVE UNION OR A DIVORCE: A CRITIQUE OF HARTMANN: WHAT IS FEMINISM?

In the early seventies *Time* magazine ran an article on the women's movement. *Time*'s opinion was that Millet's lesbianism discredited her as a spokesperson for the movement and cast doubt on the validity of the movement as a whole. In response other activists criticized the article and wore lavender arm bands to show solidarity with Millett.

That episode reflects one of the major tensions within the women's movement both in recent times and in earlier feminist movements. One of the most effective ways to discourage many women from being involved in feminism has been to link feminism with lesbianism and to "charge" that women in the movement are all lesbians. The response to this has ranged from that described above to Betty Friedan's early antigay attitude that lesbians were a "lavender herring" for the movement.

The issue is more than charges and countercharges; for in reality a very high proportion of women in the women's movement are lesbians, who are involved not only in lesbian issues, but all areas of work, including those that might seem to be far removed from the interests of lesbians.

What has this to do with our definition of feminism? First of all, as the presence of lesbians in the movement has become more open, our understanding of feminism has included the liberation of lesbians. The concurrent rise of the gay liberation movement has also revealed the connection between gay rights (in a broad sense) and feminism. So the practice of the women's movement, the participation of lesbians in it has shaped our sense of what feminism is.

Secondly, feminists have been forced to investigate gay issues and to take a stand on them, resulting in a number of theoretical developments about the role of lesbianism in feminism. These developments have ranged from liberal support for gay rights to theories of lesbian nation.

Unfortunately the school of feminist thought which, at least in theory, has not dealt adequately with gay/lesbian issues is socialist feminism. This is true not only of Hartmann's essay but of the writings of many others: Eli Zaretsky, Maria Dalla Costa, Juliet Mitchell, Zillah Eisenstein. While there have been some attempts to integrate socialist feminism and lesbianism (for example, in the paper "Lesbianism and Socialist Feminism" written by the Chicago Women's Liberation Union) much of the more public debate has neglected this issue. Perhaps because of socialism's historical emphasis on economic issues, sexuality and related issues have not been dealt with—socialist feminism has continued this tendency to some extent. While lesbianism should not be the central focus of socialist feminism, to neglect it is to lose sight of some important aspects of socialist feminism. We have to place our concerns with sexuality and gay issues within the context of our definition of feminism.

To paraphrase Hartmann's essay, then, the object of feminist analysis is the relationship between human beings, between women and men *and* between women and women, men and men. The goal of feminism is the liberation of women, and included in that is sexual self-determination for all people, and the liberation of gay men and lesbians. It is not enough to say that this is implicit in other definitions of feminism because too often what is implicit is ignored.

Thus Hartmann's essay makes a critical error in not dealing explicitly with this issue of feminism. Nonetheless it offers some useful insights in its critique of past socialist approaches to feminism and the "woman question." As Hartmann points out, marxists (such as Engels, Zaretsky, and Dalla Costa) have failed to look at the oppression of women (and the oppression of gays). Rather, they have focused on the relationship of the family to capitalism. While this is important they have not linked it to the specific oppression of women. These socialists have made contributions to our understanding of the family and capitalism, but the question remains: Where do we go from here? "The Unhappy Marriage" attempts to make the next theoretical steps in its discussion of patriarchy and capitalism.

PATRIARCHY AND THE ROOTS OF WOMEN'S OPPRESSION

The core of Hartmann's argument is in her discussion of patriarchy. From this she develops her thesis on feminism. Hartmann defines patriarchy as "a set of social relations between men which have a material base and which, though hierarchical, establish or create interdependence and solidarity among men that enables them to dominate women" (Hartmann, p. 14.) She goes on to say that the "crucial elements of the patriarchy as we *currently* experience them are: heterosexual marriage (and consequent homophobia), female childrearing and housework, women's economic dependence on men (enforced by arrangements in the labor market), the state, and numerous institutions based on social relations among men—clubs, sports, unions, professions, universities, churches, corporations, and armies."(Hartmann, p. 19). Hartmann states that in order to understand patriarchial capitalism we need to analyze all of these institutions.

However, Hartmann's argument fails at two points—points that are critical to *her* goal of developing a union between marxism and feminism. Hartmann suggests that marxism is sex-blind—it fails to look at why women are oppressed, why women are subordinate to men. Yet Hartmann's own definition of patriarchy fails in the same way. Patriarchy is defined as a set of relations among men leading to male dominance of women, but that does not explain *why* it is men who are dominant.

Hartmann states, ''There seems to be no *necessary* connection between changes in one aspect of production (patriarchy/capitalism) and changes in the other''(Hartmann, p. 17). She goes on to suggest that the same may be true of racial hierarchies and says that we should perhaps define our society as ''patriarchal capitalist white supremacist''(Hartmann, p. 18). This leaves us at the starting gate—we are unable under this schema to look at society as a whole. ''The Unhappy Marriage'' fails to unite marxism and feminism, and Hartmann's efforts to move toward a more progressive union ultimately end in divorce.

This failure stems in part from an inability to reckon with the historical nature of marxist analysis. This leads Hartmann to suggest that there is some sort of ''pure'' capital outside of history. From this she sees social forms and values as coincidentally in line with the dominant values of capital. For example, Hartmann says, ''If we examine the characteristics of men as radical feminists describe them—competitive, rationalistic, dominating—they are much like our description of the dominant values of capitalist society''(Hartmann, p. 28).

We have found three critical errors in Hartmann's analysis: her too narrow view of feminism, her failure to explain women's subordination to men, and her inability to unite marxism and feminism into an analysis of society as a whole. Can we make further progress in these efforts? In the succeeding pages we shall discuss some ideas that may be helpful in doing so.

SOME BASIC PREMISES:
FEMINISM AND THE ORIGIN OF WOMEN'S OPPRESSION

An expanded definition of feminism must be aimed at the

liberation of women and gay people and at sexual self-determination for all people. This means that we have to reevaluate human sexuality and all human relationships. Some of our most basic common sense notions will go out the window. To do this we have to understand where these notions come from—how our relationships and our expectations of relationships are shaped by society and its history.

We need to look once again at the origins of women's oppression. This oppression comes from two sources: the apparent lesser strength of women and the reproductive role of women. While the former may, in fact, be socially determined, the latter, women's reproductive role, is different from men's reproductive role. It is out of that difference that differences in social roles for women and men grew, leading to the dominance of women by men. While we can't describe specifically the situation of early humans, the scenario most often put forward is that the earliest societies were hunting societies. Because of pregnancy, women were less likely to participate in the hunt. So men were the hunters and women developed the agriculture. While the development of agriculture was a critical advance for the human race, reproductive differences between men and women were critical to the development of social as well as physical differences. Men, as bearers of the old hunting culture, became dominant. In this way we can begin to understand the origins of male dominance and women's oppression as well as the beginnings of a division of labor between people.

Another aspect of reproductive differences was the development of monogamous marriage and patrilineal inheritance. While it is clear who a child's mother is, it is not necessarily clear who the father is. Through monogamous marriage and the implicit control of (women's) sexuality, it was more nearly possible to identify paternity. While this is a very schematic view of the historic development of women's oppression, it does suggest in a rather striking way the source of sex roles and sexual repression. Engel's analysis of this is summarized in the following statement:

> In an old unpublished manuscript, the work of Marx and myself in 1846, I find the following: "The first division of labor is between man and woman for child breeding." And today I can add: The first class antagonism in history coincides with the development of the antagonism between men and women in monogamous marriage, and the first class oppression with that of the female sex by the male.[1]

Does this mean that women are fated to be subordinate to men? Clearly not—in their historical development societies have built on this reproductive difference (often in diverse ways) a structure that has led to the oppression of women in the family and in the productive arena. It has further led to the oppression of gays, youth, older people and others. There is no need for this oppressive structure to remain, even given the existence of reproductive differences. Beyond that, we now live in a society that is technologically and socially capable of controlling reproduction. This gives us the potential for negating those differences between men and women.

PRODUCTION, THE STATE AND CIVIL SOCIETY

Marxists generally analyze society from a very different direction. Although Engels identified the division between men and women as the original division of labor (see the quote above), he and other marxists used this understanding as a basis for an analysis of labor, economics, production and class, and their structure as the motivating force in the make-up of society. (It is also a starting point for consideration of the oppression of women, but has not been dealt with in this manner by marxists.) Thus from Marx and Engels' view of the division between men and women one can go either into an analysis of economics or an analysis of sex. For marxists the ''mode of production'' is the basis on which society is built. Our society is a capitalist one—one in which a small group of people, the ruling class, owns the resources of society and controls the labor, while most of the rest of the people, the working class, sells its labor power to the ruling class.

In order to remain in power the ruling class must have some way of keeping control and this has traditionally been carried out by the state. Through the state and such arms of the state as the police and armed forces, the ruling class is able to maintain its dominance over the working class. This is not the only way for the ruling class to rule. A less frequently used concept is that of civil society, an idea devoloped by Antonio Gramsci in his *Prison Notebooks* and which we find useful here for our own analysis. In this view of society, the ruling class rules by a combination of coercion through the state and consent (or hegemony) through civil society. In an advanced capitalist society such as the U.S., civil society plays an increasingly important role.

This hegemony of the ruling class is developed through the institutions of civil society such as the churches and the schools. Boggs, in his book, *Gramsci's Marxism*, defines hegemony this way:

> By hegemony Gramsci meant the permeation throughout civil society—including a whole range of structures and activities like trade unions, schools, the churches, and the family—of an entire system of values, attitudes, beliefs, morality, etc. that is in one way or another supportive of the established order and the class interests that dominate it.[2]

Through ideological hegemony the ruling class gets consent of society as a whole; its ideas and values become the ruling ideas and values and are viewed as common sense. Because of this pervasive "common sense," working people will often view socialism negatively and even though economic conditions may be ripe for change, the consciousness of workers will be so shaped by the ruling class that revolutionary struggle will fail. As Boggs says, "In short, hegemony worked in many ways to induce the oppressed to accept or 'consent' to their own exploitation and daily misery."[3]

Gramsci saw the relationships between the mode of production, the state and civil society as complex, changing, and reciprocal. He felt that cultural, political, and ideological forces could shape the nature and outcome of political struggle especially if they could interfere with ruling class hegemony.

Included in the concept of civil society, then, is what Mina Davis Caulfield describes as "cultures of resistance." The role of such a culture is to resist the imposition of an alien culture and to affirm the validity of the colonized people and their resistance to domination. A culture of resistance is, in fact, an attempt to resist the ideological hegemony of the ruling class. Caulfield states:

> Imperialism assaults the total culture. . . . Imperial intrusion deeply affects social structures, economic relations, and cultural traditions. . . . In response, many colonized peoples have developed resistance strategies centering around new forms of cultural affirmation directly or subtly opposed to the massive imperial affirmation of Western European cultural superiority. . . . New cultural and institutional forms are shaped, drawing in part on the older pre-imperial culture and partly created anew in adaptation and in opposition to foreign impositions. . . . This conscious affirmation of cultural difference in the face of wholesale denigration on the part of the

powerful aliens plays an important and largely unanalyzed role in the building of both nationalist and socialist liberation movements. Marxist political analysis must take account of the cultures of resistance in Africa, Asia, and Latin America and within the United States.[4]

Carl Boggs, reviewing the book *Blues and the Poetic Spirit* by Paul Garon, talks about subversive cultures, an idea similar but not identical to the idea of cultures of resistance. Garon, Boggs says, sees blues as ''the 'music of the devil' that haunts the bourgeoisie because it challenges the very premises of established culture.''[5] Garon sees:

> ...in the emergence of an urban black subculture a force that was subversive of bourgeois hegemony. It is the secularization of Afro-American culture, the celebration of everything that is repressed and denied by capitalist morality: desire, imagination, the erotic impulses, community, equality.[6]

CIVIL SOCIETY AND FEMINISM

Civil society includes institutions outside the state and economic system—churches, schools, and families. And there are gray areas where these sectors overlap; for example, trade unions are part of civil society and the state. Through these institutions the ruling class gains hegemony—that is, a world view that includes a system of values, beliefs and so on that is accepted by all people in that society.

How does this apply to feminism (including gay/lesbian liberation)? In *Gramsci's Marxism* Boggs discusses family and sexuality as they relate to civil society:

> Though Gramsci nowhere formulates a theory of the family and sexuality, he does produce some insights into the nexus puritanism-capitalism-family that were paralleled within Marxism only by the pioneering work of Wilhelm Reich. Gramsci argued that the stablization of sexual relations within the monogamous family, with the full support of religious dogma behind it, was central to creating a work force that is efficient and obedient. In this sense the family constitutes the basic social unit of civil society, and puritanism is its underlying ideological justification. As capitalism expands and increases its reliance upon technology and bureaucratic structures, ''these new methods demand rigorous discipline of the sexual instincts...and with it a strengthening of the 'family'

in a wide sense and of the regulation and stability of sexual relations.'' Thus the repressed sexuality that is the outgrowth of the nuclear family operates to restrict psychically the worker both within and outside the workplace: ''It seems clear that the new industrialism wants monogamy: it wants the man as worker not to squander his nervous energies in the disorderly and stimulating pursuit of occasional sexual satisfaction. The employee who goes to work after a night of 'excess' is no good for his work.'' It would not be surprising, therefore, to find that the most progressive approaches to sex and morality tend to come from those groups furthest removed from the production process; nor would it be surprising, Gramsci suggests, to discover, that women's struggle against patriarchal oppression inevitably activates new patterns of thought and behavior that help to undermine bourgeois hegemony in the workplace itself.[7]

The basic unit of civil society, then, is the family and its underlying ideological basis is puritanism. We can use Gramsci's civil society concept to connect feminism and socialism through an analysis of the role of the family and its relationship to capitalism, the oppression of women, and the oppression of gay people.

The family, like society as a whole, contains contradictions. In earlier systems it was an important part of the production process, but with the rise of capitalism, the focus was on individual workers. The family unit adapted to this situation and in a capitalist economy serves the ruling class in other ways. Rather than act as part of the production process, the family acts as a part of civil society. The family is the site of child bearing and rearing and it is the chief consumer unit of society. In these roles it is responsible for the reproduction of workers (as Engels suggests in *The Origins of the Family, Private Property and the State*), including particularly the reproduction of ideology. The family teaches us our first lessons in ruling class ideology and it also lends legitimacy to other institutions of civil society. It is through our families that we first learn religion, that we are taught to be good citizens, from which we are sent out to school.

Not only are there lessons taught us in the family, but the family itself recreates the ideology of the ruling class. It is itself authoritarian and hierarchical. So thorough is the hegemony of the ruling class within the family, that we are taught that the family is the embodiment of the natural order of things. It is based in particular on a relationship between men and women which represses sexuality, especially women's sexuality. We are taught that there is a natural bond between sexuality and reproduction. Within the family this is further linked to childrearing and sex roles and sex stereotypes. These are then extended to the other spheres of life, such as work. Anything that contradicts these concepts of sexuality and sex roles is considered to be not only abnormal and contrary to common sense, but unnatural.

The family has also developed an important role within working class life, as both Zaretsky and Fernbach have pointed out. The family is the one place to which people turn for emotional and social support—support which is not available at work or in other parts of our lives. It is also a place where working people can develop an identity and a respect for themselves as human beings. So the family has support from the working class and from the ruling class, because it serves the needs of both. This makes it a very stable institution.

Women's oppression has its origins in the different reproductive roles of men and women which led, as Engels said, to the first division of labor: men's work was outside the family to a greater or lesser extent and women's work was to sustain the family. As the role of the family in society has changed so too has the nature of the oppression of women.

The family is the basic unit of civil society, but not the only unit of civil society. It is, as part of civil society, connected to the productive processes. Thus the oppression of women is not restricted to the family situation. Rather, women's oppression pervades society as a whole —in the workplace, the political arena and so on. Further, whereas women are oppressed as part of the family, other groups of people are oppressed because of their exclusion from the family. One of these groups is gay people. Gay/lesbian oppression occurs in three main ways. The first of these is in coming out, that is, acknowledging to oneself one's gayness. This experience of coming out usually is undergone in isolation and with little or no support from the people around us. We discover that not only are we apart from society, but we are also apart from our families and the values they hold dearest.

Having come out, gay men and lesbians then have to face the choice of letting other people know about their gayness; this involves a choice between oppressions of two different sorts, and by and large it is no choice at all. Having grown up in straight families and straight society, we are well aware of the stigma attached to being gay. If we do come out publicly we are faced with open hostility, discrimination, and sometimes physical violence. Thus most people stay in the closet to all but a few friends. This threat of overt discrimination and abuse is the second form that gay oppression takes, while the closet is the third. The closet is the fundamental fact of most gay people's lives—it is a way for gay people to protect ourselves but it also means hiding a significant aspect of our lives, often from our closest friends.

These forms of gay / lesbian oppression take different concrete shape for different gay people. Gay men are more likely to be subjected to harassment and abuse, while lesbians are more likely to be ignored.

Through the family we are taught, among other things, ideas about sexuality and sex roles—as Gramsci says, there is a "rigorous discipline of the sexual instincts" in the family in order to benefit capitalism. But the puritan ideology, the sexual utilitarianism of the hegemonic ideology of the bourgeoisie is challenged by the existence of gay people. Thus it is important that gay men and lesbians be kept invisible. Even our existence challenges many of the "common sense" ideas of sex roles and sexuality. This is particularly true of lesbianism—part of the ruling class ideology is that women are basically sexless, non-sexual beings. But the existence of lesbianism totally contradicts this notion. This shapes some of the ways in which gay men and lesbians are treated differently. For example, gay men are generally looked on (with disgust) as promiscuous hedonists, while lesbians, when they are thought of at all, are thought of in terms of: "what can two women do together anyway?"

So by keeping gay people, especially lesbians invisible, in the closet, the ruling class is able to maintain its ideology of (and through) the family, sexuality, and women. Overt forms of discrimination and harassment are used to keep gay people in line. Even more fundamentally, the inculcation of homophobia by people within the family maintains that homophobia as part of ruling class ideology. This is true even for gay people. Thus, coming out means challenging ruling class ideology in oneself. To some extent gay people continue to internalize homophobia even after they come out, and this acts as an internal brake to keep us in line. This psychological closeting of gay people also serves to maintain other aspects of bourgeois hegemony as well, including sexism, authoritarianism, and so on.

Finally, our analysis of civil society helps us to understand some of the differences in the way women are oppressed. As Holly Graff points out, women are oppressed under capitalism through civil society as well as in production, but the form that oppression takes will depend on other factors, principally race and class. Because the ideology promoted through civil society is not simply an ideology of male dominance over women, but in particular is the ideology of the white male ruling class, the oppression of women will vary depending on their relationship to that ruling class.

For example, because women's primary social role is supposed to be in the family, the work women do outside the home is denigrated and viewed as not as valuable as male labor. So women are often volunteer workers or are paid very low wages. Middle class women may see this as a cultural devaluing of their work, and while it will have an economic impact on them (through, for example, not getting promotions into higher level academic or managerial positions), often of equal importance will be the social devaluation of the work itself. On the other hand working class women, who are more likely to be supporting others on lower wages, will probably not have many opportunities for "advancement" and will feel this devaluation in more clearly economic terms. This will be emphasized because of the more general devaluation of working class work, so that working class women's work will seem comparatively of more equal value with men's.

Similarly, while most white women are oppressed by not being able to attain the ruling class standard of beauty, black women are oppressed by being outside those standards altogether. [8]

By using Gramsci's ideas of civil society and ideological hegemony and by linking that with our understanding of the origins of women's oppression, we can begin to see how socialism and feminism can be connected. In fact, an examination of the concepts of civil society and Hartmann's patriarchy suggest that those two concepts are in fact one and the same. The term patriarchy has the advantage of showing the importance of sexism, the family, and women's oppression. As Hartmann points out, this often gets lost in marxist analysis.

However, Gramsci's civil society shows the link between the family, the oppression of women and gays, and capitalism much more clearly. While the analysis of capitalism and patriarchy in

"The Unhappy Marriage" does not lead to any real unification of socialism and feminism, our analysis of civil society and the family does. There is much more that can and should be done, especially in the areas linking imperialism and racism with capitalism in this outline. Nonetheless, we can from this begin to raise some questions about strategy and practice for socialist feminists.

STRATEGIC AND PRACTICAL IMPLICATIONS
LOOKING AT THE CURRENT CONDITIONS

Since the rise of the women's and gay movements in the last ten to fifteen years (though there were earlier waves of both in the nineteenth and early twentieth centuries) some real gains have been made in the area of equal rights and other reform. The 1973 Supreme Court abortion decision, enactment of gay rights laws in many cities, and affirmative action programs are just a few of the concrete changes that have been made.

But in the last few years there has been a highly visible right-wing attack on all of these gains, resulting in a legislative reversal of the Supreme Court decision, public referenda on gay rights, the anti-ERA efforts, and judicial cases challenging affirmative action. This attack by the right wing is a change from their previous strategy of attacking economic issues ("right to work" laws), although parts of the right wing's work in this arena still goes on but without the same emphasis.

How can we understand these events? As has been more definitively discussed in a number of places, the women's movement arose out of the situation of the fifties and sixties—economic boom, the civil rights and antiwar movements, and "sexual liberation." The women primarily involved in its beginnings were "middle class" women, frequently white college students or college educated women. Thus many of the women's movement's original demands were rooted in that experience and didn't relate to the needs of Third World women or working class women. As the women's movement has grown, its demands have gained broader support and that support has in turn broadened its demands.

At the same time, the gay movement has followed a similar path. Though with some initial hesitation, the women's movement has been fairly supportive of gay/lesbian issues, while the gay movement has increasingly developed support for women's issues.

This support has occurred in organizations through sexual coequality in structure, and through support for issues like the ERA. The gay and women's movements are closely linked, as Hannah Frisch has pointed out:

> Gay liberation is one part of the broader feminist movement. . . . I think that this is true despite the fact that men active in the gay movement do not all see themselves as feminists and that they sometimes behave in a sexist manner toward lesbian women. No gay person can set out to fight his or her own oppression as a homosexual without thereby fighting sexism.[9]

As the women's movement has grown and the gay movement has become more visible, they have challenged many of the ideas of family, home, sexuality, women's place—ideas that help to support the established ruling class hegemony. The reaction of the right is an attempt to stave off those ideas and to maintain traditional ideas. Because the family has provided some support for the needs of the working class and because the ideas of the ruling class are so deeply engrained in our culture, this reaction has met with fairly wide support, especially in its opposition to gay rights.

WORKING FOR SOCIALIST FEMINISM IN THE U.S.

What follows are some ideas suggested by the foregoing analysis. They are based primarily on applying that analysis to the gay/lesbian community, where I have been working for the last several years. However, some suggestions will be made in other areas. In doing this we must be guided by several key ideas. First of all, in the U.S. the hegemony of the ruling class is so strong that a vitally important form of political struggle is to challenge that hegemony. Neither marxist formulations which suggest that struggle must be carried out at the point of production, nor radical feminist plans to build women's communities or a lesbian nation address this. This is not to negate the value of such efforts, but to say that by themselves they will not bring about a revolution.

However, in stressing the importance of counterhegemonic struggles we must be careful not to limit ourselves to work in arenas strictly defined as civil society. Such struggles can and do take place in the political and production spheres and often will be different aspects of struggles aimed at that sphere.

Further, when we speak about feminist work we have to see it in broad terms; too often the women's movement has confined itself (or been confined) to "women's issues." Because of the connection between women's oppression and civil society, it is clear that feminism must be more broadly defined. Feminism includes gay liberation, and the status of youth and older people. It is also connected with community issues, and so on.

In working for gay/lesbian liberation, for example, several strategic courses suggest themselves. First of all, as has been noted, being in the closet is the basis for gay oppression because of the need for the ruling class to keep gay people hidden. There are harsh penalties for gay people who do not stay in the closet. Thus a basic first step for the gay movement is to seek protection for the rights of those who do come out or are forced out in any given situation. The emphasis on legislative and judicial action which the gay movement has undertaken is thus well placed.

Such work, however, could have other effects as well. Work for gay rights could be a way of involving more gay people in broader grassroots political work. Another positive aspect would be opportunities to educate and involve nongay people with gay issues. Socialists could aim toward pushing the gay movement more in this direction.

Beyond gay rights, socialists involved with the gay movement are also concerned that we work for gay/lesbian liberation as a part of a socialist revolution. In doing this we can gain some insight into possible work by looking at gay/lesbian culture and the ways in which traditional family roles and sex roles are broken down. By emphasizing the importance of alliances and the connections of gay liberation and women's liberation, we can continue to move the gay effort out of its single issue orientation.

We can also look at the gay/lesbian culture as a culture of resistance. Many aspects of gay/lesbian culture—the bars, women's music, camp—are a part of a culture of resistance that has helped gay people survive and fight back against the stereotypes taught by ruling class hegemony. By building on these aspects we can move people from a culture of resistance to political action. We can also use that culture to challenge further ruling class hegemony among gays.

For instance, bars could be more than just social meeting places, but community centers and political foci for the gay and non-gay community. The Stonewall riot of 1969 resulted from a police raid on a gay bar. That action was spontaneous, but in other cases involvement by socialists and activists could open the community to more planned political responses. On a more on-going basis the bars can be a forum for ideas through music, newpapers, theater, and so on.

Gay/lesbian culture can also be looked on as a subversive force that can challenge the hegemonic nature of the idea of the family. It can, however, be done in a way that people do not feel is in opposition to the family per se; a simple "smash the family" slogan is seen as a threat not so much to the ruling class as to people in the working class who often rely on family ties to maintain security and stability in their lives. In order for the subversive nature of gay culture to be used effectively, we have to be able to present alternative ways of looking at human relationships.

As mentioned before, gay issues need to be tied with other issues in order for us to move to a total liberation perspective. Too often a narrow perspective has resulted in "narrow" demands that have alienated others. For instance, organizing for abortion has been an important demand within the women's movement. Yet it has not always drawn the support of diverse groups because for many women abortion is not the key aspect of reproductive rights; for many Third World women sterilization abuse and "population control" are more important issues; for lesbians sexual freedom and the right to parent are critical; for working women (especially those in industry) the right to a safe workplace is a more important question. So focusing on the abortion issue has sometimes tended to exclude or alienate many women. At the same time our under-standing of the origins of women's oppression suggest that repro-ductive rights work is critical to the liberation of women. Such work should be done but in a way that can unite people. In doing this work, we have to be careful not to be too mechanical about relating reproductive rights to women's liberation. After all, we are not only dealing with a specific material base for women's oppression but with the ideology that has been built to support that base—an ideology that asserts that "women's place is in the home," "women should be barefoot and pregnant," and so on. Our fight must not only be for the protection of specific rights, but must also put forward a different consciousness about women. The New American Movement Bill of Reproductive Rights describes an agenda for reproductive rights that includes abortion, sterilization abuse, the right to parent (including specific support for lesbian mothers), the right to a safe workplace, and several other demands.

It begins to tie together the whole range of reproductive rights issues and in doing so it forms the basis for uniting many groups of women.

These few examples give some idea of the way in which our ideas of socialist feminism can be tied to specific types of work. This work can have several goals: concrete reforms on which we can buld further work, challenging the ideological hegemony of the ruling class, uniting people around specific programs.

Finally, our work must provide a vision of the society that we are working for. This is not the same as challenging the hegemony of the working class. As Boggs says (in *Gramsci's Marxism*):

> . . . Gramsci realized that the erosion of ideological hegemony created only the possibility for advancing toward socialism; demystifying the old consciousness did not inevitably bring with it new forms of revolutionary consciousness.''[10]

Part of the responsibility of socialist feminists, among them gay and lesbian socialists, is to develop that revolutionary consciousness. And that consciousness, that socialist vision, must not simply create alternatives in a patchwork manner, but must construct a *total* alternative. Socialist feminists must work together to create a vision of society that can mobilize people and in the process begin to build a transformed society now.

FOOTNOTES

1. Engels, Frederich, *The Origins of the Family, Private Property and the State* (New York: International Publishers, 1972), pp.65-66.
2. Boggs, Carl, *Gramsci's Marxism* (London: Pluto Press, 1976), p.39.
3. Boggs, *ibid.*, p.40.
4. Caulfield, Mina Davis, "Imperialism, the Family and Cultures of Resistance," in *Socialist Revolution 20*, 1974, pp.68-69.
5. Boggs, Carl, "The Blues Tradition," in *Socialist Review 38*, 1978, p.117.
6. Boggs, *ibid.*, p.119.
7. Boggs, Carl, *Gramsci's Marxism*, *op. cit.*, pp.44-45.
8. Young, Iris, "Letter to Holly Graff," in *Women Organizing, 2* (Chicago: New American Movement, 1978).
9. Frisch, Hannah, "Gay Liberation Will Change the Culture," in *Women Organizing, 4* (Chicago: New American Movement, 1979.)
10. Boggs, Carl, *Gramsci's Marxism*, *op. cit.*, p.41.

REFERENCES

Boggs, Carl. *Gramsci's Marxism*, Pluto Press, London, 1976.

Boggs, Carl. "The Blues Tradition," in *Socialist Review*, no. 38, 1978.

Caulfield, Mina Davis. "Imperialism, the Family and Cultures of Resistance," in *Socialist Revolution*, no. 20, 1974.

Chicago Women's Liberation Union, "Lesbianism and Socialist Feminism," Chicago, 1972.

Dalla Costa, Maria. "Women and the Subversion of the Community," in Dalla Costa and James *The Power of Women and the Subversion of the Community*, Falling Wall Press, Bristol, 1973.

Eisenstein, Zillah, ed. *Capitalist Patriarchy and the Case for Socialist Feminism*, Monthly Review Press, New York, 1979.

Engels, Frederich. *The Origins of the Family, Private Property and the State*, International Publishers, New York, 1972.

Fernbach, David. "Toward a Marxist Perspective on Gay Liberation," in *Socialist Revolution*, no. 28, 1976.

Frisch, Hannah. "Gay Liberation Will Change the Culture," in *Women Organizing*, no. 4, New American Movement, Chicago, 1979.

Graff, Holly. "The Oppression of Women," in *Women Organizing*, no. 1, New American Movement, Chicago, 1978.

Gramsci, Antonio. *Selections from the Prison Notebooks*, ed. & translated by Q. Hoare and G.N. Smith, International Publishers, New York, 1971.

Healey, Richard and H. Graff, Presentations at the New American Movement Gramsci School, Detroit 1978.

Mitchell, Juliet. *Women's Estate*, Vintage Books, New York, 1973.

Riddiough, Christine. "Culture and Politics," in *Women Organizing*, no.4, New American Movement, Chicago, 1979.

Young, Iris. "Letter to Holly Graff," in *Women Organizing,"* no. 2, New American Movement, Chicago, 1978.

Zaretsky, Eli. "Capitalism, the Family and Personal Life," in *Socialist Revolution*, no.13-14-15, 1973.

THE INCOMPATIBLE MENAGE À TROIS: MARXISM, FEMINISM, AND RACISM

Gloria Joseph

Gloria Joseph is a Black revolutionary spirited feminist of West Indian parents, and views the world from a Black perspective with a socialist base. She is currently professor at Hampshire College in Amherst, Massachusetts in the School of Social Science. She has traveled in China, Cuba, India, and Africa compiling photographic essays and slide shows along the way. Her most recent publication is a book dealing with Conflicts in Feminist Perspectives: Black and White.

Hartmann's essay speaks of an "unhappy marriage between marxism and feminism" but makes no mention in the title, and does not acknowledge in the essay, the incestuous child of patriarchy and capitalism. That child, now a full grown adult, is named racism. Thus, a more appropriate title of an article that attempts to create a theory that transcends marxism and feminism would be "The Incompatible Menage à Trois: Marxism, Feminism, and Racism." The women that Hartmann is speaking about, a specific but unlabelled and apparently middle class group of feminists, can believe that they are ready to embark upon a path to a more progressive union. To pay the price of this belief is to deny the reality of being Black in America. The dimension of racism is so critical to the lives of Black folks that it must be addressed specifically, regardless of the purposes or basis of the relations that exist among diverse social groupings. Unfortunately, our society has done such an excellent job of institutionalizing racism that the internecine result has been the creation of two separate societies: one white, one Black. As a consequence, when situations occur that call for coalition, solidarity, or alliance, racism serves as a wedge which prevents groups from the strategic, systematic, and protracted cooperation which is needed for the attainment of common goals. So while Hartmann's essay represents an attempt to transcend the limitations and shortcomings of both marxist analysis and feminist analysis, I lament the absence of an analysis of the Black woman and her role as member of the wedding.*

In my response I shall focus on racism as a dimension that must be directly confronted before beginning to theorize about a compatible marriage between marxism and feminism. The reason for my original lamentation stems from the fact that I expect progressive minded writers to give adequate and appropriate recognition and credence to Blacks. When writers commit acts of omission by ignoring or neglecting Black women, I resolve once again to try to get the public to understand that Blacks must be

I wish to extend my acknowledgments to Helen and Scott Laurence of St. Croix, Virgin Islands for their rigorous critiquing throughout the development of my paper and to Jerry Surette of Cortland, N.Y. for his nimble, linguistic inputs.
*See author's note on page 106.

legitimized in their own right. Whatever the reason, the fact remains that the acts of omission prevent the public from being exposed to and informed of the reasons behind the sexual and racial inequalities which explain why interracial conflicts and problems persist.

Accordingly, my comments will focus on why racism must be addressed specifically and consistently as an integral part of any theory of feminism and marxism. In her introduction, Hartmann is well justified in taking issue with marxist analysis as sex-blind and with feminist analysis as blind to history and insufficiently materialistic. I would extend the criticism as follows: the categories of marxism are sex-blind *and* race-blind. Feminist analysis is blind to history and insufficiently materialistic. Both marxist and feminist analysis thus do a gross injustice to Black women whose historical experiences of slavery have left them with a most peculiar legacy of scars. The material conditions of the lives of the masses of Black women play a critical and influential role in directing and determining their attitudes toward feminism. These attitudes are decidedly unfavorable and unsympathetic. Hartmann also says that "only specifically feminist analysis reveals the systematic character of relations between men and women." I feel she is speaking of white men and women so I would qualify her statement by adding that "only a specific Black feminist analysis would reveal the character of relations between Black men and Black women." A specifically Black feminist approach is called for because the psychological dynamics that function among Black men and Black women in the context of existing economic conditions, are qualitatively and culturally different from those of whites.

It is not surprising that the tri-partite marxist analysis of the woman question (historical, materialist, class) typically excludes consideration of the role of Black women. While Hartmann states that the woman question has never been the feminist question, it is equally true that the feminist question has never truly embraced Black women. Black exclusion from the woman question was lucidly publicized by Sojourner Truth in 1851 in her famous and eloquent speech at the Women's Rights Convention in Seneca Falls in which she repeatedly asked her audience "...and ain't I a woman?"

Assuming that the feminist question is directed at the causes of sexual inequality between women and men, and of male dominance over women, it is important to note that sexual inequality between Black men and women has very different historical and cultural beginnings than the sexual inequality between white men and women. Consequently the present inequality is of a different nature and thereby calls for different strategies for change. Black women's participation in the labor force also has a very different history than white women's. The slave experience for Blacks in the United States made an ironic contribution to male-female equality. Laboring in the fields or in the homes, men and women were equally dehumanized and brutalized. Men and women together, toiling every day in the rain or sun, from "can't see to can't see" (early morning to late at night), shared equally the trials, tribulations, and torture. Moses Granby, an exslave, wrote illuminatingly about the slave experience. His accounts testify to the fact that atrocities were heaped upon Black women with equal ferocity and frequency as they were dealt to the men. For example, Granby on treatment of mothers with infants: ". . . women who had sucking children suffered much from their breasts becoming full of milk, the infants being left at home; they therefore could not keep up with the other hands. I have seen the overseer beat them with raw hide so that the blood and milk flew mingled from their breasts." And on treatment of pregnant slave women: "She is compelled to lie down over a hole made to receive her corpulency, and is flogged with the whip, or beat with the paddle, which has holes in it; at every stroke comes a blister."[1] The point being made here is that the dehumanization process for both male and female slaves was equally *brutal*. The specific physical mannner of brutalization was, in many instances, different due to biological differences: men could be castrated (penis castration) and women could have their babies beat out of their bellies. But the "equalizer" was the brutality.

The rape of Black women and the lynching and castration of Black men are equally heinous in their nature. Today, the Black man carries scars from his slave experience as much as the Black woman carries her scars. We use no measuring stick for the oppression suffered by Blacks.

The documented history of Black women and men in the area of labor thus reveals that the peculiar institution of slavery played a curious role in bringing about equality among Black men and women as opposed to the inequality that was fostered among white women and men. Angela Davis summed it:

> ...to extract the greatest possible surplus from the labor of the slaves—the Black woman had to be released from the chains of the myth of femininity. In the words of W.E.B. DuBois, "...our women in black had freedom contemptuously thrust upon them." In order to function as slave, the black woman had to be annulled as woman; that is, as woman in her historical stance of wardship under the entire male hierarchy. The sheer force of things rendered her equal to her man.[2]

There did, however, exist for Black women, more than for Black men or white women, a place where she could exercise a modicum of autonomy and that was in the domestic life of the slave quarters. It is true that the slave woman in her quarters, like the Black woman of today in her modern project, tenement building or suburban home, worked outside the home and was also responsible for "keeping her home." During slavery this position was influenced and encouraged largely by the white male patriarchy and in part by certain African traditions. Again, ironically, this situation presented the slave woman with a chance to exercise a degree of autonomy unfettered by white male dominance.

Circumstance contributed to the autonomous position maintained by the Black woman in her "household domain." Being a homemaker in the slave quarter was a cultural experience that was imposed upon the slaves. In spite of the wretched accommodations available in the quarter, Black women were able to be expressive, creative, and in their autonomy, were better able to continue the practice of African customs and habits.

In a discussion of marxism and the woman question, to speak of women, all women categorically, is to perpetuate white supremacy—white female supremacy—because it is white women to whom the comments are addressed and to whom the comments are most appropriate. As we have seen, marxist analysis focuses on the class question and shortchanges the woman question. To discuss women categorically is to commit a similar, parallel error whereby the reality of the operation of race relations within the woman question is denied. History clearly shows how and why Black women and white women today suffer from gender inequality. Writers must recognize, however, the Black women in American society have at least as much in common with Black men as with white women. The shared oppression of Blacks serves as the great equalizer, and racial oppression wears a crown emblazoned with the words, "I am the great Equalizer!"

Hartmann's review and critique of radical feminist views and writings on patriarchy neatly encapsulates several obvious shortcomings and spotlights several instances of shortsightedness. Hartmann devotes the remainder of the section to considerations and suggestions that should be included in the development of a definition of patriarchy. Given the obvious shortcomings of the radical feminist position acknowledged by Hartmann, I feel that it would have been wiser to utilize a wholistic approach to patriarchy, using the radical feminist position as one referent source rather than trying to develop a definition by building upon a position with an inherent weakness.

Radical feminist definitions and writings on patriarchy are to be lauded for their efforts to force society to acknowledge the personal side of political ideologies and "isms," and for illuminating the concrete effects felt in the psychological and social dimensions of personal experience; and further, for showing how the debilitating effects of patriarchy shape the material conditions of individual lives.

The radical feminist emphasis on the personal as political and the use of "patriarchy" needs shoring up, and Hartmann does some of this. To refer to patriarchy as radical feminists do, as a social system characterized by male domination over women is far too general and simplified. It offers very little instructive or new information. The radical feminists do a grave injustice to the concept of the personal as political by locating it within the context of their belief that the original and basic class division is between the sexes, and that the motive force of history is the striving of men for power and domination over women. It's like placing a gem in quicksand; i.e., the value of the personal as political can be absorbed and thereby become meaningless if its surroundings are so ill-defined, insubstantial and without foundation.

Hartmann attempts to raise critical issues and questions around the radical feminist position, but she is guilty of committing an error parallel to the one she criticizes. Hartmann's definition of patriarchy as "... a set of social relations which has a material base and in which there are hierarchical relations between men and solidarity among them which enable them in turn to dominate women..." (Hartmann, p. 14), is also too general and simplified.

For example, she gives little consideration to those whose biological color has been used to categorize them in the lowest strata regardless of sex, income, or ownership.

Hartmann is aware of the stultifying effects and destructive consequences of being blind to history, yet she remains blind to the historical role of the Black experience in the U.S. and the effects it has had on both Black and white attitudes.

In my comments, I shall emphasize those factors that must be considered in the definition of patriarchy if it is to be relevant to society today, and in particular, to the lives and souls of Black people.

THE BOTTOM LINE IS BLACKNESS

The radical feminists are credited with the documentation of the slogan, "the personal is political." In reading their arguments —their justifiable and astute arguments—my response was again a lamentation. For decades Blacks have been crying the same tune. They have cried out in Black English, in scholarly documents, in rebellions, in popular songs, in TV documentaries, and in marches and sit-ins. Black discontent, Blacks argued, "is not the neurotic lament of the maladjusted, but a response to a social structure in which *Blacks* are systematically dominated, exploited and oppressed." "*The personal is political" is not, as Eli Zaretsky would have it, a plea for subjectivity, for feeling better; it is a demand to recognize white male power and Black subordination as a social and political reality* (Hartmann, p. 13, paraphrased).

Blacks have been exhorting this lament for decades to little or no avail. It has been given little credibility or legitimacy. Blacks have been given advice and programs, characterized by the "bootstrap" philosophy, and tokenism. However, when feminists made the claim that the personal is political, and depicted their subordinate position in the social order, it became a significant part of the women's movement and the rallying point for crucial strategic moves designed to bring about changes in the power structure. When feminists recognize that the personal is political for women, while ignoring its similar application for Blacks, they assume a self-centered and self-righteous position. More importantly, applying the personal is political to Blacks would mean the inclusion of males as well as females, and this is extremely problematic for radical feminists. Nonetheless, it is a fact that must be dealt with if

Black women are to be involved in the feminist movement. In addition, the word "white" would have to be inserted in front of "males" throughout the discussion of patriarchy for the use of the phrase to be acceptable to the majority of Blacks.

Radical feminists use patriarchy to refer to a social system characterized by male domination over women. And who can argue that in western society such is not the case? But Third World people have a documented history that contradicts the "since the beginning of humankind male supremacy" doctrine. Eleanor Leacock speaks to this point:

> The fact is glossed over that in much of the pre-colonial world, women related to each other and to men in public and autono- mous ways as they carried out the social and economic responsibilities. Female sodalities of various kinds figured importantly in many third world social structures before principles of male dominance within families were taught by missionaries, defined by legal statutes, and institutionalized through the economic relations of colonialism.

> Ethnohistorical and ethnographic data are also documenting the public functions of women's organizations and their line- age roles in Africa. The distinction generally made between a male "public" sphere and a female "domestic" sphere distorts the very nature of the "preindustrial, precapitalist, and precolonial world," where "power, authority, and influ- ence within the 'domestic sphere' was *de facto* power, author- ity and influence at certain levels within the 'public sphere.'" In West African societies, the "public sphere" was not concep- tualized as masculine. The impressive political demonstra- tions of Ibo women some half century ago have been well documented.[3]

When Third World women today struggle against their own oppression, they also struggle against oppression in general. They are more concerned with strategies for change than with theories about the origin of the basic division of dominance and submis- sion. This is not to say that they are not concerned or familiar with their past. The material conditions of their present lives coupled with a heightened political awareness supplies a constant motiva- tional energy for change. If they were to diligently pursue the origin of male-female relationships, chances are that the stereo- typical views of female dependency as a universal norm would be seriously challenged. Thus, "as data about women around the world accumulate, passing statements about them as subordinate housewives and mothers, commonplace in anthropological writing, are being replaced by analyses of their decision-making roles in different types of society.''[4]

What I found most objectionable in Hartmann's definition of patriarchy was her categorical lumping together of *all* men in U.S. society into one group—Black, white, Chicano, Native American, Puerto Rican—reinforcing the purely biological distinction. She does say that patriarchical hierarchy places men of different classes, races, or ethnic groups in different places within the hierarchy. But Hartmann leaves it at that. She goes on to say that men are united in their shared dominance over women; they are dependent on, each other to maintain that dominance; that all men are bought off by being able to control at least some women; and they are dependent on one another to maintain their control over women. Historically, Black men were definitely not afforded supremacy over any females. To quote from Angela Davis' article on the Black woman:

> Excepting the woman's role as caretaker of the household, male supremist structures could not become deeply embedded in the internal workings of the slave system. Though the ruling class was male and rabidly chauvinistic, the slave system could not confer upon the Black man the appearance of a privileged position vis-a-vis the Black woman. The man-slave could not be the unquestioned superior within the "family" or community, for there was no such thing as the "family provided" among slaves. The attainment of slavery's intrinsic goals was contingent upon the fullest and most brutal utilization of the productive capacities of every man, woman and child. They all had to "provide" for the master. The Black woman was totally integrated into the productive force.[5]

During slavery the Black male was disallowed a superior position in relation to the Black female and there is really no question about Black men having control over white women. During this period Black women were the victims of the most vicious, atrocious, defiling and dehumanizing rapist behavior committed on American soil. Black men on the other hand were projected as rapists shortly after the Civil War to provide the racist white mentalities with a justification for lynching. Ida B. Wells did a magnificent job (in her article "Lynching and Rape: an Exchange of Views") of documenting crimes and proving with devastating accuracy that the "ir-rationale" for the savage practice of lynching was rarely the charge brought against the intended victim.[6] Incidentally, no white man has in the history of the U.S. ever been executed for raping a Black woman. At present, there is basically very little change in the interracial power relationships among the sexes. White men continue to dominate, exploit, and oppress all women in social, economic, sexual, and political areas. Black men have "learned" to dominate, exploit, and oppress Black women in an ersatz manner which is nonetheless genuinely degrading and oppressive to the Black woman.

It may sound rhetorical to make the blanket statement that white men dominate all women, and that Black men have "learned" to dominate Black women. But the exceptions to these cases that make the rule carry very little weight as change agents in the general order of male dominance. The societal structures dictate this dominance to a large extent. However, Black men in actuality never had and still have no power over white women; it is more accurate to say that all white women have ultimate power over Black men—penis power included. This statement requires elaboration and qualification: I would raise the question—in what area(s) do Black men have power over white women? Black men have no real economic power. Blacks own 1.2% of business equity; 1.2% of farm equity; and 0.1% of stock equity in the U.S.A.;U.S. business receipts in 1977 amounted to $2 trillion. Minority business accounted for 1.5% of this total. Political power is tied to economic power so Black male political clout suffers the same anemia as Black economic power. On the interpersonal level, a vagrant, thieving white woman can be vindicated, even lionized by crying "rape" or "assault" if the accused is Black. When Black males are in personal relationships with white women, it is very possible that the male dominates her and uses her money and body. In the final analysis, however, the white woman has the ultimate power because the judicial system is racist, the executive system is racist, and the legislative system is racist. If she wants "out" the system is on her side, and that's what I mean by ultimate power. Even the Black pimp with white women in his stable is ultimately controlled by the white males of the organized crime power elite. It will be argued that Black males have penis power over women. While the Black male may dominate, abuse, and oppress the white woman, when the deal goes down, she holds the trump card. The majority of those unions are temporary and the power that the Black male assumes is more ego power than any-thing else (although Black male misogyny reinforces male supre-macy in general). Capitalism and patriarchy simply do not offer to share with Black males the seat of power in their regal solidarity.

Towards the end of the section on patriarchy Hartmann states that it might be most accurate, for example, to refer to our society not simply as "capitalistic" but as "patriarchal capitalistic white supremist." But instead of using this as the main building block of her discussion, she glosses over the racial dimension and lumps it in a category with class, nationality, marital status, age, and sexual orientation.

Hartmann's concluding definition of patriarchy mentions a solidarity among men which enables them in turn to dominate women. I venture to say that there is more solidarity between white males and females than between white males and Black males. A nationwide questionnaire asking Black and white males their attitudes on interracial dating, marriage, neighborhoods and schools, showed that white preference for Black interracial dating, etc., remains a preference on the part of whites alone. The slight increase in interracial marriage in the past few years notwithstand-ing, the fact remains that whites bond together more on the basis of their whiteness than on their biological sex. The recent busing incident in Boston, as a case in point, showed white adults pitted against Black children; not white men against Black children or white men against all females—it was Black vs. White. And Black females will readily inform you that in a crunch, particularly in public places, it is the Black man far more readily than the white woman who will come to the defense and aid of a Black woman. Some lesbian radical feminists are proving to be an exception. They alone as a group of women will more readily offer aid or come to the defense of a Black woman. With this exception, then, Black women have to depend on their Black men for support, aid, and interest when facing a crisis or daily difficulties.

But it is also true that Black males have a much greater solidar-ity among themselves than they do with Black women. In defining patriarchy, Black males must be separated out from white males. In discussing solidarity among all males the problems of racism have to be articulated and approaches and strategies for solving them generated.[7]

Hartmann argues that "patriarchy as a system of relations among men and between men and women exists in capitalism and that in capitalist societies a healthy and strong partnership exists between patriarchy and capital" (Hartmann, p. 19). I agree that this partnership is healthy in terms of its success in perpetuating and strengthening the existing inequities and exploitation that goes on in our society. It is healthy and strong in maintaining racism, sexism, and classism. Hartmann continues her argument by explaining the partnership on the basis of the capitalist mode of production and the abuse of women's labor. Within the framework of this partnership both Black males and females are grossly exploited along with white women. But Black females are on the very bottom rung of the occupational status ladder. What Hartmann and other white feminists fail to realize is that while white men have set up the situation such that women and Blacks are exploited and in competition with one another over a few token jobs and privileges (like union admission and keys to the executive bathrooms), it has been white women themselves who have actually carried out the "divide and conquer" strategy. Whether white women have held the major seats of power in the United States or not, the fact remains that, with white males they have participated in and benefited from a social system based on the subjugation of people of color.

> The location of white women in America as the *benefactors* of racism has enabled them to ignore their whiteness. The location of Black women in American society as the *objects* of racism, has precluded the possibility that they might have their womanness as their sole identity. White women must realize that as womanness circumscribes their whiteness, (they are not white males), so their whiteness circumscribes their womanness. White feminists must come to terms with the circumscribing nature of their whiteness. [8]

The role of white males in the partnership of patriarchy and capital has to be discussed in relationship to the laborers, consumers, the exploited who are the providers for the beneficiaries of patriarchy and capital. These providers are predominantly women, both Black and white, and Black males. It is encumbent upon white feminists to: (1) recognize their implication in the partnership, as benefactors and tools; (2) address the unique problems of Black women in the labor force; (3) distinguish between the role of white men and Black men in the partnership of capital and patriarchy. In this context, Blacks are placed in an extremely powerless and precarious position, and one which is vulnerable to white male domination—since money talks.

THE BLACK DIFFERENTIAL

Hartmann raises many strategic questions surrounding the move towards a more progressive union betwen marxism and feminism. The exclusion of the race question is a serious omission and the inclusion of it further complicates an already problematic affair. But such is the nature of dealing with serious and complex theoretical problems. I raise the following point on the racial issue: if one can claim that marxism is incomplete without a consideration of feminism, it is certainly true that neither is complete without a consideration of racial relations. Of course one could argue that every relationship is unique and race relations have no patent on uniqueness; that no general theories are adequate, and from this point of view, most theories are too general. However, there is ample evidence to indicate that relations between races have a long and important history which is not reducible to relations between the sexes or classes. An analysis of racism thus should be undertaken prior to, or at least in conjunction with, the discussion of marxist feminist relations, thus facilitating a better understanding of how to integrate race into a theory of marxism-feminism.

The marxist might argue that both sexism and racism are due to an established set of classes with a proletariat engaged in producing surplus capital for the dominant classes. As the extensive brutality of women by men does not appear to be reducible to the economic factors involved, so the virulent suppression of one race by another does not appear reducible to purely economic considerations. This appears reasonable. But more than appearance of validity is required. Both empirical evidence and deeper theoretical analysis is needed. Hartmann states that sexual differences are more basic than those based on "capital," and I agree with her. But I will claim that racial differences and antagonisms are *no longer* basically due to economic exploitation.

Marxist theory did not and could not account for a role that advanced technology would play with its resulting effects on modes of production, social relations, and new social classes (e.g., nouveau riche, superstars, mafia, drug lords, etc.). Certain dimensions of marxist theory that applied to the marxist world view in the mid-1800s are no longer applicable in the 1970s. In a parallel fashion, economic considerations are no longer the basis for racial discrimination and exploitation. Racial prejudices have become so ingrained in white U.S. society that a typical racist anti-Black mentality has developed, with emotion and ignorance ruling over intellect. Education, professional jobs, and housing are three areas where empirical evidence proves that economics is no longer the prime motivator for Black exclusion and exploitation. The very fact that we had to have affirmative action plans in educational arenas speaks for itself in indicating the depth of racial biases. School systems "prefer" to lose government funding rather than comply with desegregration laws. Professional football teams would rather go with a losing white quarterback than with a winning Black one. The fact that winning teams make money cannot compete with the powerful aversion against having a Black "director" of the team. Black school teachers and administrators are the first to be dismissed when a cut-back in staffing is required. This occurs particularly in the south where the schools are predominantly Black. In many cases white teachers and administrators who remain receive higher pay than those dismissed. Realtors falsely claim that property devalues when Blacks move into a predominantly white neighborhood. Realtors systematically keep Blacks out of certain areas regardless of the Black family's income.

The claim is made, for example in banks and offices, that too many Blacks in official or administrative positions will drive away white customers and clients, and therefore for economic reasons too many Blacks cannot be hired. Where this phenomenon occurs (whites avoiding places with "too many" Blacks) the white citizens have been carefully conditioned and programmed.

Hartmann concludes her essay by saying that the struggle to establish socialism must be a struggle in which groups with different interests form an alliance; and that women should not trust men to "liberate" them "after the revolution," in part because there is no reason to think that they would know how, and in part because there is no necessity for them to do so; in fact, their immediate self-interest lies in the continued oppression of women. Black women have to be considered as one of those groups with special interests. Just as women cannot trust men to "liberate" them, Black women cannot trust white women to "liberate" them during or "after the revolution," in part because there is little reason to think that they would know how; and in part because white women's immediate self-interest lies in continued racial oppression. To date feminists have not concretely demonstrated the potential or capacity to become involved in fighting racism on an equal footing with sexism. Adrienne Rich's recent article on feminism and racism is an exemplary one on this topic.[9] She reiterates much that has been voiced by Black female writers, but the acclaim given to her article shows again that it takes whiteness to give even Blackness credibility. White feminists have to learn to deal adequately with the fact that by virtue of their whiteness they are oppressors as well as oppressed persons. "It is a mystical belief in 'womanhood' that suggests that 'woman' is the most natural and the most basic of all human groupings and can therefore transcend the race divisions of our society."[10] This is no more likely than the belief that marxist ideology can transcend sexism.

A strong viable feminist movement must give full consideration to both Black and white women. As such there is a real and obvious need for research dealing with Black feminist theory and analysis. Acknowledgement should be given to those few Black women active in these tasks. Several of these women are: Barbara and Beverly Smith of the Combahee River Collective who have made valuable contributions to Black feminist literature; Audre Lorde whose poetry is often well grounded in a Black feminist analysis; and Carroll Oliver whose pioneering work in the development of a revolutionary Black feminist theory is admirable.[11]

Black feminists have a crucial role to play in the present movement. They must include themselves from their own organized base. "The historiography about the women's movement has been distorted to depict Black women as indifferent or hostile to the feminist movement. Rosalyn Terborg-Penn asserts that Black women were concerned about the same issues that white women campaigned against—slavery, liquor, and sex discrimination—but for the most part they were discouraged by white women from participating fully in the women's movement. Prejudice and discrimination were elements that affected the daily lives of most Blacks during the 19th and 20th centuries."[12]

In order for the current movement to avoid the mistakes of the past, it is encumbent upon Black and white feminists to discover the vulnerabilities of U.S. capitalism and imperialism both of which embody male supremacy and white supremacy. Common strategies must be decided upon and clarified and then the two groups must utilize their various tactics in moving towards their common goals. The fight against white supremacy and male domination over women is directly linked to the worldwide struggles for national liberation. Protracted struggle must take place on an international level. As Black and white feminists combine forces in the struggle against male supremacy and white supremacy, they must be willing to communicate and follow a format consisting of dialogue (with the purpose of mutual education), practice, more dialogue, and more practice—moving slowly but inexorably towards advanced levels of understanding and respect for one another's differences. The similarities among women are easier to understand and should be used as building blocks towards understanding and respect for racial and class differences. The possibility of an alliance between Black and white women can only be realized if white women understand the nature of their oppression within the context of the oppression of Blacks. At that point we will be able to speak of "The Happy Divorce of Patriarchy, Capitalism, and Racism," and the impending marriage of Black revolutionary socialism and socialist feminism.

Author's note: Throughout my response I have referred to Black women rather than Third World women or other specific minorities. This is due to the respect that I hold for their different historical and cultural backgrounds. I am fully cognizant of the fact that in most cases what is applicable to Black women would also be applicable to other minority women in the U.S. However, I do not think that I could speak for all minority women when there are such significant differences among us.

FOOTNOTES

1. Granby, Moses, *Narrative of the Life of Moses Granby: Late a Slave in the United States of America* (Boston, 1844), p. 18.

2. Davis, Angela, "Reflections on the Black Woman's Role in the Community of Slaves," *The Black Scholar*, Volume 3, no. 4 (December 1971).

3. Leacock, Eleanor, "The Study of Women: Ideological Issues," unpublished, 1978.

4. Eleanor Leacock in Reiter, Rayna, ed., *Toward an Anthropology of Women* (New York: Monthly Review Press, 1975); Schlegel, *Sexual Stratification: A Cross-Cultural View* (New York: Columbia University Press).

5. Davis, Angela, *op. cit.*, p. 7.

6. Wells, Ida B., "Lynching and Rape: an Exchange of Views," San Jose State University, occasional papers series no. 25, 1977.

7. The strategies for solving problems generated by racism would involve massive propaganda campaigns, enforcement of civil rights laws already on the books, and greater economic equality. A la Cuba, institutional racism can be practically eliminated.

8. Armstrong, Pat, SUNY conference paper, 1972.

9. Rich, Adrienne, "Disloyal to Civilization: Feminism, Racism and Gynephobia," *Chrysalis* #7, 1979.

10. Armstrong, Pat, "Racism and Feminism: Division among the Oppressed," unpublished paper, 1972.

11. I consider Michele Wallace's *Black Macho and the Myth of the Black Super Woman* more dysfunctional than enlightening. Her publication, fraught with confusion and distortions, presents an ahistorical child's eye view of the Black movement. For the white media to laud this book so highly and refer to it as a major turning point in the study of male-female relations among Black people, is suspect, and an insult to the intellect of Black people.

12. Harley, Sharon, and Rosalyn Terborg-Penn, *The Afro-American Woman: Struggles and Images* (Port Washington, New York: Kennikat Press, 1970), p. xx.

THE UNHAPPY MARRIAGE OF MARXISM AND FEMINISM: CAN IT BE SAVED

Carol Ehrlich

Carol Ehrlich is co-editor of Reinventing Anarchy: What are Anarchists Thinking? an anthology of contemporary anarchist writings, and author of "Socialism, Anarchism, and Feminism." She is also part of four Baltimore-based political collectives: The Great Atlantic Radio Conspiracy, which has been producing radical audio-tapes since 1972; Social Anarchism: Journal of Practice and Theory; Research Group One, radical social science research group and publisher; and the Baltimore School, an alternative learning network.

109

One of the most vexing problems for marxist feminists has been to develop a feminist analysis within a context (marxism) that makes it difficult to have one. Patriarchy, the institutionalized domination of women by men, has historically been invisible to traditional marxists. At most, patriarchy is seen as a disfiguring but localized excrescence on the skin of capitalism, to be cured by the strong medicine of state socialism.

However, increasing numbers of marxist feminists are attempting to make visible the scope and persistence of patriarchy. It exists in hunting and gathering, horticultural, and agricultural systems as well as in capitalism; it exists in so-called egalitarian societies as well as those that are marked by sharp stratification. In capitalist countries, it exists both within and across class boundaries, and it interacts in very complicated ways with other forms of inequality such as those based on race, age, and sexual preference. And—most perplexing of all for marxists—it persists in socialist countries.

Even though patriarchy may vary widely in form and in degree from one society to the next, it seems to be present everywhere. Thus, it cannot be reduced to anything so simple as the institution of private property, and (given its persistence under state socialism) its more or less automatic disappearance cannot be counted on to happen in the communist future. Feminists who have examined the situation of women in socialist states, and who are well aware of the real gains that have been made in achieving economic and social equality, are still asking the same questions, to which there do not seem to be satisfactory marxist answers. For example: Why are there so few women in decision making positions in socialist countries? Who does the housework? Why are lesbianism and male homosexuality suppressed? Are children in socialist countries socialized according to sex role stereotypes? Are women equally represented in all occupations? Are their incomes equal to men's? How secure is the woman's freedom of choice in the areas of sexuality and reproduction? Does she have the right to bear children when and if she wants to? Or not to bear them if she doesn't want to? Is safe, effective birth control available? Abortion on request? Who decides these matters—the woman, or the mostly male leadership for reasons that have little (if anything) to do with the preferences of the women who are affected? In sum, if patriarchy still exists in socialist countries, *why*?

Theorists who try to provide marxist answers to these questions are faced with two possibilities: either marxist analyses of "the woman question" are wrong, or they are incomplete. If they are wrong—that is, if there is a fundamental defect in marxist theory that makes it incapable of explaining patriarchy—then another theory is needed. If all marxist analyses of patriarchy have been incomplete, then something needs to be added in order to make them capable of explaining the situation of women. Hartmann and other marxist feminists are attempting to build a comprehensive theory that will account for the workings of both patriarchy and capitalism, and will do so by extending marxism, not by discarding it.

Hartmann believes it possible to build a union of marxism and feminism in which both are equal partners, even though "recent attempts to integrate marxism and feminism . . . subsume the feminist struggle into the 'larger' struggle against capital" (Hartmann, p. 2). Hartmann asks, why has marxism insisted on dominating feminism in this unhappy marriage? Hartmann's answer is that although "marxist analysis provides essential insight into the laws of historical development, and those of capital in particular, the categories of marxism are sex-blind" (Hartmann, p. 2). That is, although it understands capitalism, it does not understand that the interaction of patriarchy and capitalism makes the position of women different from that of men.

Further, Hartmann points out that even those marxist theorists who have broadened the analysis of the work that women do (in particular, to focus on the crucial importance of housework and reproduction of wage workers) have still looked at women in relation to capitalism, and not women in relation to men. By doing this they have partially remedied marxism's lack of understanding of the situation of women, but their analyses are still too narrow. They have left out the elements of patriarchy: the fact that women are oppressed *because they are women*, and the fact that men (not just capitalists) benefit from the institutionalized subordination of women.

In sum, Hartmann's basic criticism of marxism is that it has looked only at the oppression of women by capital, and has overlooked the subordination of women by men. But she does not propose substituting feminist analysis for marxism—for she criticizes feminism as essentially ahistorical and for focusing on the psychological aspects of women's situation at the expense of the material. Instead, she sees both marxism and feminism as incomplete theories that must work together to provide a definitive analysis of the situation of women in contemporary capitalist society.

CAN "WHAT IS TO BE DONE" BE DONE?

From my own perspective (I am an anarchist feminist with strong roots in radical feminism), Hartmann's attempt to reestablish the marriage of marxism and feminism on an equal basis is directed primarily at marxists, not at feminists. In particular, it is written for female marxists whose political origins are not in radical feminism, and who well understand the cooptative nature of "bourgeois" feminism. Hartmann is attempting to counter the pressure from marxist males who out of a combination of blindness and self-interest urge their female comrades to "abandon all this silly stuff and become 'serious' revolutionaries" (Hartmann, p. 32); males who want women to shut up and accept a traditional marxist analysis of the woman question which would fail to build a socialism that women as well as men would want. Hartmann's essay, then, is for those who do not want to abandon marxism, but who want to find a way to make it apply to both sexes, not just one.

Why do I say that Hartmann is not writing primarily for radical feminists? The marriage metaphor (which troubled me for reasons I initially had difficulty defining) provides us with a major clue. If one were to act as a sort of political marriage counselor, one would find there could be several *different* marriages of marxism and feminism. In perhaps the most common form, the feminist awakes one morning to find herself allegedly married after a ceremony she does not even remember having attended. (Indeed, she suspects no marriage ever took place; for she certainly did not agree to it.) In another version, the marriage is fully agreed to by both partners; but both marxism and feminism enter it with such differing expectations and political assumptions that they soon discover they are fundamentally and irrevocably incompatible. In both cases, the marriage counselor would almost certainly decide that the marriage could not be saved and would recommend a quick trip to the divorce court (with, hopefully, an amicable settlement in which the two parties would remain on speaking terms).

These are the two versions most likely to be heard from radical feminists; but there are at least two more. In the third, marxism does not even know there is a serious problem—thus, would see no need for counseling. Indeed, marxism thinks feminism should be happy to be married to such a powerful partner who provides so well for her.

The fourth model is put forth by Hartmann. She assumes the marriage did take place, that it was a voluntary agreement by both partners, that serious problems did arise, but that their origin is in marxism's unthinking domination of feminism. (She does not account for feminism's allowing this domination.) Thus, if marxism can be persuaded that an egalitarian marriage is in (his? its?) best interests, the marriage can be saved. And it *should* be saved: they need each other. Romantic love? That's a bit much to ask—and anyway, everyone knows that compatibility and sharing of interests are much more important bases of a happy marriage.

If her assumptions are correct, then it is possible to build a marxist feminist theory and practice that does not treat patriarchy as a less severe problem than capitalism, and that can account for it in all its manifestations. I do not think that it is possible, for reasons that I will explore in the rest of this essay.

ANARCHISM AND FEMINISM

I agree with Hartmann that feminist analysis by itself cannot adequately account for the systematic subordination of women. That is because we are not simply women: each woman is also of a certain class, race, nationality, age, and sexual orientation. And these factors combine to produce a particular set of characteristics that largely determine her life circumstances in the time, place, and culture in which she lives. Obviously, then, although women's lives are in some crucial ways different from men's, they are also, in other crucial ways, different from each other's.

If feminism by itself cannot adequately explain these complexities, and marxism cannot adequately account for patriarchy, is there any revolutionary perspective that can? I think there is—and it is one that Hartmann does not mention: anarchist feminism.

Anarchist feminism has synthesized social anarchism (that is, a *socialist* rather than an individualist anarchism) and radical feminism in a way that has broadened and deepened both. This is possi-

ble because radical feminism and social anarchism are compatible
—more so than are feminism and marxism.[1] In fact, as Peggy
Kornegger pointed out, "feminists have been unconscious anarchists in both theory and practice for years."[2]

What is social anarchism? Although it is socialist, it is not
marxist. Like marxists, social anarchists are opposed to capitalism;
they wish to remove wealth and resources from the hands of a few
to be shared equally by all.

But there are crucial theoretical differences which lead to
significant differences in practice. These have to do with the best
ways of reaching the ultimate goal of a classless society populated
by free individuals. For anarchists, means and ends must be
consistent: freedom cannot be achieved through the paradox of
limiting it in the present. People learn the habits of freedom
and equality by attempting to practice them in the present, however imperfectly. The primary means of doing this is through
building alternative forms of organization alongside the institutions of the larger society.

For social anarchists, then, the revolution is a process, not a
point in time; and how one lives one's daily life is very important.
People don't learn that they can live without leadership elites by
accepting socialist ones; they do not end power relationships by
creating new ones.

Social anarchists and radical feminists share the belief that
power relationships (that is, relationships in which one has the
ability to compel another's obedience or control another's actions)
are inherently coercive, competitive, and inegalitarian, and that
institutionalized forms of inequality are rooted in power relationships. The limitation of radical feminism is that feminists often do
not focus on power in all its manifestations; instead, they may be
concerned primarily (or exclusively) with ways in which men as a
group wield power over women as a group. The limitation of social
anarchism—like marxism, another male-dominated body of
revolutionary theory and practice—is that it has so often neglected
to notice that patriarchy is one form of power relationship. But
unlike marxism, there is nothing about social anarchism's basic
categories that is sex-blind; indeed, the defects have been in practice, not in theory. That is why it was potentially more compatible
with feminism than was marxism.

In contrast with marxists, social anarchists and radical feminists do not work to "seize" power, but to end it, to erode it, to build new forms of organization in which power relationships cannot exist, because there is no organizational form in which they can survive.

Thus, anarchists stress ending centralized, hierarchical forms of organization right now: they cannot be the means for bringing about an ultimate end to a classless, stateless society. Although state socialism undoubtedly improves the material conditions of life for large numbers of people, it cannot lead to genuine equality and freedom for all, because the very existence of the state guarantees the continued subordination of those it governs. And anarchists do not believe that the socialist state will wither away—there are no signs of withering yet in any socialist society. It is *people* who will have to decide to get rid of the state; it will not come about because of changes in the mode of production, or because everyone has become part of the same class.

Social anarchists are far less dependent on "history" than marxists, and much more reliant upon the action of people *in the present* to create a society without power relationships on any level —material or psychological. In fact, anarchists view the material and the psychological as *interconnected* in such a complex fashion that they cannot be separated.[3] Where and how would one begin to untangle them? Material conditions help to create particular personality configurations which help to recreate particular material conditions which. . . .

For an anarchist, the implications are that one attempts to interrupt this cycle at both points: the material and the psychological. Either one alone is insufficient.

What are the limitations of the radical feminist view of patriarchal power? How is it different from an anarchist view? As I said before, its focus on patriarchy as the basic form of oppression means that it does not adequately account for the other forms of oppression women may face, and for the fact that women's lives may differ from one another's.

Further, many radical feminists have a narrower view of power relationships than anarchists do. Feminists have extended political practice enormously through their efforts to end power relationships in their own organizations: they have done this by building small groups rather than mass organizations, by systematically rotating tasks, by sharing skills and knowledge among themselves, by instituting consciousness raising groups—in short, by trying to eradicate all the structural factors that create and maintain leaders and followers.

But these practices (which are anarchistic, whether or not feminists know it) are not always endorsed when feminists look *outside* their own organizations. Although many feminists would probably attempt to change the larger society in a manner consistent with anarchist principles, others would not. There is a tendency in radical feminist thought which holds that women, although subordinate to men, have through their very state of powerlessness learned the socially necessary traits that men didn't want—gentleness, nurturance, sensitivity, and so on. And that women should organize to take control of society and govern it according to these traits.

This analysis does not see the state itself as oppressive— instead, it is the *patriarchal* state which is the problem, because it was developed and controlled by men. If women were to take over the institutions of government, they would use them to bring about a peaceful, egalitarian society.[4] This view is summed up in the motto of the newspaper, *The Matriarchist*: "We Who Nurture Will Govern." It assumes that institutions are neutral, that it is people who make them work badly (in this case, men) or well (and in this hypothetical case, women). No anarchist would make such an assumption. In order that power relationships not exist, the *conditions* for them must not exist.

In a sense, I am agreeing with Hartmann that radical feminism has overemphasized psychology at the expense of the material basis of patriarchy. But anarchist feminism does not locate power only in the psychological realm; it places it in both the material and the psychological. Anarchist feminism insists that power originates in, and is transmitted through, organizational forms which build an unequal access to economic, political, and social resources— further, that power relationships are supported by an ideology which refuses to consider any other alternative to them. And finally, anarchist feminism works to end all forms of inequality, beginning (but not ending) with patriarchy. This is what it means to say that anarchist feminism has synthesized social anarchism and radical feminism.

LESS TALK, MORE ACTION?

Political people who are engaged in the thousands of small

battles which go into daily living (and the not so small ones as well) arc often inclined to think that arguments over the sources of patriarchy and capitalism are abstract theoretical discussions which are a waste of time, make timid intellectuals feel good about their contribution to the coming revolution (which they won't know is happening anyway, because they will be too busy thinking about it), and interfere with the important task of changing the world.

Although theories of revolution that do not lead to revolutionary practice are useless, attempts to define the sources of oppression are essential if we are to find means of eradicating them. What conditions allowed patriarchy to arise, and what conditions have perpetuated it in some form, to some degree, in every society known to us? Hartmann is asking these questions and attempting to answer them; and so am I. In order to do this, I will now look at Hartmann's criticism of a radical feminist approach to patriarchy; next, I will evaluate her own attempt to provide a different definition and analysis. In doing this, I will show that Hartmann's analysis, although it extends marxism about as far as it can be stretched in this direction, can still only account for some elements of patriarchy, not all. Throughout, I will argue that anarchist feminism gives a better accounting of patriarchy; and finally, I will talk about what an anarchist feminist analysis leads us to do.

DEFINITIONS OF PATRIARCHY

If patriarchy exists everywhere, it is difficult to construct a definition that will distinguish among its variations. Hartmann criticizes radical feminist Kate Millett for providing a definition that is so broad it cannot account for the differences across societies:

> our society . . . is a patriarchy. The fact is evident at once if one recalls that the military, industry, technology, universities, science, political offices, finances—in short, every avenue of power within the society, including the coercive force of the police, is entirely in male hands.[5]

In order to distinguish capitalist patriarchy from other forms, and in order to use marxist theory to achieve feminist objectives, Hartmann offers the following definition of patriarchy. It is:

> a set of social relations which has a material base and in which there are hierarchical relations between men and solidarity among them which enable them in turn to dominate women. The material base of patriarchy is men's control over women's

labor power. That control is maintained by excluding women from access to necessary economically productive resources and by restricting women's sexuality. Men exercise their control in receiving personal service work from women, in not having to do housework or rear children, in having access to women's bodies for sex, and in feeling powerful and being powerful. The crucial elements of patriarchy as we *currently* experience them are: heterosexual marriage (and consequent homophobia), female childrearing and housework, women's economic dependence on men (enforced by arrangements in the labor market), the state, and numerous institutions based on social relations among men—clubs, sports, unions, professions, universities, churches, corporations, and armies. (Hartmann, pp. 18-19.)

Paradoxically, Hartmann's definition both includes and excludes too much. The problem results from the marxist assumption that there is a material base upon which everything rests. If radical feminist analysis is often too insensitive to changing historical conditions, too universalistic, "insufficiently materialist," as Hartmann phrases it (and I agree), marxist feminism tends to reduce the complex bundle of material and ideological factors which comprise patriarchy to the material.

For Hartmann, "the material base of patriarchy is men's control over women's labor power"; every aspect of male domination of women allegedly rests on that. Yet, I think that to say that all of the aspects of patriarchy can be crammed onto this material base puts more weight on it than it can support. Further, it does not capture the complex interlocking of the material and the psychological. This is what I mean by saying that her definition is at once too inclusive and too exclusive.

When I try to look at homophobia, monogamous heterosexual marriage, and the masculine feeling of superiority and power (all briefly mentioned by Hartmann as part of patriarchy) *only* in relation to their function in maintaining male control over female labor power, I feel as if I have suddenly been afflicted with tunnel vision. Am I seeing all there is to see? Or do I need to have my eyes checked immediately?

It is not that the connection of patriarchy with the material conditions cited by Hartmann isn't there—it is. But the analysis is incomplete; it does not go far enough.

For example: how does Hartmann account for monogamous heterosexual marriage? She says it is "one relatively recent and efficient form that serves to allow men to control both'' female sexuality and access to economically productive resources (Hartmann, p. 15). It is efficient, apparently, because men get *two* material conditions covered for the price of one institution.

However, is this a sufficient explanation, either for the existence of this particular form of the family or for the position of women within it? And is that position the same in the monogamous nuclear family across all societies? In our society, monogamous heterosexual marriage is certainly intended to restrict women's sexuality and to make it extremely difficult for women to earn a decent income. Those men (and women) who most strenuously defend traditional sex roles are likely to insist that a woman's real job is in the home, where she is (hopefully) supported by a hard-working, responsible male in return for providing him with housework, child care, and sex on demand. To back up their arguments these supporters of the family are likely to cite a view of female nature that supports occupational segregation (as Hartmann says, women are expected to clean the toilets, both inside and outside the home) and the basic rightness of lower pay for women who do work outside the home (she doesn't, or shouldn't, *need* the money), and so on.

Perhaps the monogamous heterosexual marriage will disappear in a nonpatriarchal society. (We can only guess at the answer, since there are no examples at which to look.) But I think that the problems are not so much monogamy or heterosexuality, or even marriage, as much as the ways in which they serve men in a patriarchal order. As long as people could freely choose how and with whom they wished to live, I see no reason why the monogamous heterosexual marriage (with marriage being the private choice of two people rather than an official act sanctioned by the state) couldn't be an egalitarian situation for heterosexual women and men, provided no other institutions support patriarchy.

To move from the hypothetical to the actual: if this form of the family serves both to control women's sexuality and keep her economically dependent on a man, why has it flourished in China since 1949? Why has the Chinese Communist Party encouraged it as part of their program of equalizing the sexes? And can we argue with the fact that women in China are closer to equality with men than they were before 1949?

As Judith Stacey points out in ''When Patriarchy Kowtows: The Significance of the Chinese Family Revolution,''[6] the monogamous heterosexual family has somewhat different functions than it does in the United States. Economic functions have been removed from the family and transferred to the larger society; and the state has assumed educational, recreational, and health care functions as well. In addition, the areas of sexual expression and reproduction seem determined by state policy to a degree that is barely imaginable here. The age at which one can marry, number of children, methods of birth control, premarital chastity and marital fidelity, the absolute impermissibility of homosexuality— all are matters of public policy.

Within the context of Chinese state socialism, it seems to be the state, not the family, that allows men to control women's labor power. And the state is able to do this because its citizens accept its authority, its legitimate right to determine how Chinese women (and men) will lead their reproductive/sexual lives, and how they will work. The fact that Chinese women have had their lives greatly improved is beyond doubt—but whether they can ever reach equality with Chinese men, under this or any other government, is questionable. In looking for the key to women's equality—in China, in the United States, in any contemporary society, we should search for *anarchist* answers to feminist questions.

THE COMPONENTS OF PATRIARCHY

An anarchist feminist analysis of patriarchy shows that it is composed of eight factors. I begin with those which are integral to Hartmann's analysis, and continue through those which she mentions in passing, or does not discuss at all.

(1) To reiterate Hartmann, patriarchy involves men's control of women's labor power through

(2) Preventing women's access to necessary economically productive resources, thus making them economically dependent upon a male-controlled system, and/or upon a particular man; and

(3) Controlling women's sexuality. For Hartmann this primarily means putting female sexuality in the service of men's (and particularly male capitalists') need for a replenished labor force. When an expanded labor force is needed, women's sexuality will be directed toward reproduction; when it is not needed, then women's sexuality will be directed toward attracting and servicing men.

This is correct, as far as it goes, but it does not explain *why* it is that men have decided these are the sole sexual alternatives for women; *why* it is that so many women have accepted these limitations; or *how* it is that men have been able to enforce these means of channeling women's sexuality.

Neither does it explain why it is that the sexuality of poor women is controlled in especially punitive and often contradictory ways—by limiting the availability of sex education, birth control, and abortion; through sterilization abuse; by threatening to cut women with "illegitimate" children from public assistance; by making AFDC payments inadequate *and* by failing to provide educational resources, job training, or day care facilities that would enable women to get off public assistance; by forcing many poor women to prostitution in order to survive; and by treating prostitutes (but not the men who buy their bodies) as contemptible.

(4) Male control of resources and decision making. As Kate Millett said, men are in control of all institutions. The fact that this statement is overly broad, as Hartmann pointed out, does not mean that it is untrue. And the fact that it is true makes it difficult to reduce the effects of patriarchy to control of women's labor power.

(5) Homophobia, the fear and hatred of homosexuality. Hartmann says that it stems from the belief that it threatens monogamous heterosexual marriage. But there is more to it than that. In our society, the most negative stereotype of male homosexuals is that they act like women: by descending from their superior position and copying the behaviors of the inferior sex, they have done the unforgiveable. They have given up patriarchal power.

Lesbianism too is a threat to more than just marriage. As the Radicalesbians pointed out, it is a threat to every area of male domination of women:

> Lesbian is the word, the label, the condition that holds women in line. When a woman hears this word tossed her way, she knows she is stepping out of line. She knows that she has crossed the terrible boundary of her sex role....Lesbian is a label invented by the Man to throw at any woman who dares to be his equal, who dares to challenge his prerogatives (including that of all women as part of the exchange medium among men), who dares to assert the primacy of her own needs.... For in this sexist society, for a woman to be independent means she *can't be* a woman—she must be a dyke. That in itself should tell us where women are at. It says as clearly as can be said: Woman and person are contradictory terms.[7]

Antilesbian attitudes are also a means of dividing women from each other—not only literally (since the cultural ideal is for each adult male to appropriate to himself one adult female and live with her and their offspring in an isolated nuclear unit) but psychologically and politically as well:

> As long as the label "dyke" can be used to frighten a woman into a less militant stand, keep her separate from her sisters, keep her from giving primacy to anything other than men and family—then to that extent she is controlled by the male culture.[8]

She will continue to seek male approval, identify with male-defined values, and hate herself and other women. And she will not understand why she holds these attitudes, or that there are any alternatives.

(6) Differential socialization by gender, which in most known societies is associated with sexual inequality. Views of male and female natures may vary across cultures, but in every culture known to us they are associated with females and males doing specific tasks based upon these alleged differences. In some cultures the sex-based division of labor is far less rigid than it is in others;[9] and in some cultures female roles may be highly valued if they place women in control of institutions which are central to the society, or if there is balance between male and female-controlled institutions.[10]

As Hartmann points out in an earlier article, there is widespread disagreement among anthropologists about the origins of patriarchy, its development, its universality, and the means by which we can assess its form and its extent.[11]

What, then, do we know? In reading the literature, in trying to make intelligent sense of the ethnographic and political controversies, it often seems to come down to a defense of *my* anthropologist vs. *your* anthropologist. But in general I think it is safe to say that the female is likely to be primarily if not exclusively responsible for child care, she is likely to be seen as the sexual/domestic servicer of men, and she is likely to be less highly valued for these activities than the male is for his.

Which came first, the division of labor or differential gender socialization? It's like asking the old question about the chicken and the egg; to seize upon either one commits you to a reductionist view of a process that now is equally dependent upon the existence of both.

For example: Hartmann summarizes Gayle Rubin's analysis in "The Traffic in Women: Notes on the 'Political Economy' of Sex" as follows: the division of labor leads to separate genders which leads to economic interdependence between men and women which leads to strict heterosexuality which leads to "sexual subcultures in which men and women experience life differently." (Hartmann, p. 16.) [12]

Instead of drawing these causal linkages from material conditions, I suggest we look at it this way: To the extent that socialization (based upon a differential view of male and female nature), and the division of labor are both aspects of patriarchy, of male power over women, they are a blend of the material and the ideological. To change either, we have to change both.

(7) The ideology of patriarchy, the belief that men are superior to women, includes the belief that men have the right to control the life circumstances of women. In order to assert a "right" to control others, one has to think of them as below oneself on the scale of humanity and (at least metaphorically, if not actually) as one's property. The psychological consequences of accepting a view of oneself as inferior include a feeling of self-deprecation, lack of worth, passivity, and isolation.

But the consequences are more than psychological: they affect the material conditions of one's life as well, by destroying the will to rebel, or never allowing the possibility of rebellion to arise in the first place. This point has been made by a number of feminist theorists, and is particularly well stated by Kay Boals in her article, "The Politics of Cultural Liberation." [13] Boals describes the stages of consciousness necessary for culturally oppressed groups such as colonized people, blacks in the United States, homosexuals in straight society, and women in a patriarchal system, to overcome the dominant group. Dominance is "not merely technological or economic or military, it is also emotional, cultural, and psychological, producing in the dominated a pervasive sense of inferiority and insecurity." [14] Thus, liberation involves revolt against *all* these factors, which are not in aggregate reducible to the material, or to the psychological, but which are both.

For women who are treated materially and ideologically as the property of men, it is not sufficient to gain access to economically productive resources (though it is, of course, necessary); nor is it enough to gain control over one's sexuality (though that too is necessary). Women need also to gain the *consciousness* that they are oppressed *as women*, that they are not inferior, and that patriarchy need not be inevitable. For women living in the nuclear family, isolated in pair relationships with men, living in a patriarchal culture which defines man as the measure, it can be difficult to see any option beyond living out a stereotyped femininity; and even for women who do not live in such a situation, it can be difficult to see patriarchal ideology for what it is, and to reject it. In either case, if the awareness is not there it is very hard to build a sense of solidarity with other women.

Although I am speaking primarily of conditions in our society, the principles are broader than that. The anthropologist Michelle Z. Rosaldo says in "Women, Culture, and Society: a Theoretical Overview" that if one compares cultures one finds that "women's status will be lowest in those societies where there is a firm differentiation between domestic and public spheres of activity and where women are isolated from one another and placed under a single man's authority, in the home."[15]

It is these conditions which isolate women from each other that led radical feminists to state that "the personal is political," and to analyze women's lives under patriarchy in terms of this phrase. "The personal is political" does not mean, as some people have misunderstood it, that women should go out and "do their own thing," while callously ignoring other oppressions such as class and race. Unlike some marxists, Hartmann does not make that judgment. However she does say: "'The personal is political' means for radical feminists that the original and basic class division is between the sexes, and that the motive force of history is the striving of men for power and domination over women, the dialectic of sex" (Hartmann, p. 13). As I understand it, the concept has more to do with effects than with causes. It is meant to give us a framework in which we can place the conditions that isolate and separate women, the ways in which women's lives are different from the lives of even the most sympathetic men, and the fact that the things that happen to women are neither "private" nor "personal," but are the result of being female. If the analysis has often oversimplified (sometimes even overlooked) the factors of race, class, nationality, age, marital status, and sexual orientation, it has highlighted the shared conditions of being female which cut across the other factors. It has put them in a political context, and has made it much more possible for women to work together against patriarchy in a context of self-respect, not self-deprecation.

Clitoridectomy destroys a woman's orgasmic capacity; infibulation controls her reproductive freedom. On one level, this brutal practice can be explained by Hartmann's analysis of the control of woman's sexuality in the service of patriarchy's need to control her labor power. But there is more involved: the infliction of such pain, the often severe physical problems that follow, the destruction of a human's right to sexual enjoyment and her right to control her own sexuality, the use of women (in some cultures) to do this to other women—this is sheer physical and psychological domination. It makes one wonder why women fail to resist, to refuse this assault upon their bodies, and to refuse any part in helping to cripple other women. These practices represent power relationships in their most extreme, most pathological form. They, and all other forms of ritualized, culturally condoned violence of one sex, class, or race against another, are maintained by hierarchy and authority. They will disappear only when we create forms of organization which do not permit power relationships to survive.

In the United States, clitoridectomies have not been done since the nineteenth century. Today, hysterectomy is the major form of violence against the female's reproductive anatomy. Of course, there are instances when hysterectomies are medically advisable; but there is currently a virtual epidemic of unnecessary hysterectomies. Between 1970 and 1975 there was a 25 percent jump in the number performed; the 725,000 hysterectomies performed in 1975 made it the most common major operation in the U.S.[21] Close to 50 percent are probably avoidable or medically unnecessary.[22]

Another form of violence against women is destruction of their reproductive capacity through involuntary sterilization. (This may or may not involve hysterectomy.) Although sterilization is one form of birth control which is sometimes freely chosen by the woman (or man) in question, it, too, raises questions outside the realm of the strictly medical: Why did Public Health Service hospitals sterilize over 3000 Native American women without telling many of them that the operation was irreversible, or without getting their fully informed consent? How many poor women have been involuntaily sterilized for "socio-economic" reasons—the justification used in the widely reported case of Native American

Norma Jean Serena? How many physicians believe, as did 97 percent of those surveyed in one 1972 study, that it is right to sterilize women on public assistance who have had children outside of marriage?[23] How many women of all classes and races are seen as "hysterical"? How many menopausal women are viewed as neurotic, as ready to be relieved óf a "useless, bleeding, symptom-producing, potentially cancer-bearing organ"?[24]

The answers to these questions burst the bounds of the notion of "control of woman's labor power." Beyond it is the ideology of patriarchal power—an ideology that maintains it is appropriate, it is right, it is even *in their best interests* that these things be done to women.

It is also a form of violence to make a woman with an unwanted pregnancy bear the child—out of pressure from her family, religious pressure, pressure from government policy-makers to increase the labor force, or the economic pressure of being unable to afford a safe, legal abortion. And these constraints are intensified by the internalized pressure that makes a woman think that childbearing is her major purpose in life. Although these conditions primarily describe women's situation in capitalist countries, in no industrialized country in the world—capitalist or socialist—is every woman unconditionally free to decide to have children or not to have them.

If the connection to violence seems unclear, this should make it clearer: Federally-funded Medicaid abortions decreased by 99 percent in the last 11 months of 1978 because so many restrictions were placed on them.[25] And the government's own studies "indicated that if all Medicaid funding in the U.S. were eliminated, we could expect 250 or 300 women to die each year and as many as 25,000 to suffer serious medical complications from self-induced or illegal abortions.[26] Poor women don't only die from their attempts to terminate pregnancy: The interaction of race, class and sexual oppression can be seen in the fact that childbirth mortality rates were 3.5 times higher for black women than for white in the United States in 1974. That, too, is violence.

(8) Finally, patriarchal power is expressed, maintained, and enforced through forms of violence directed specifically against women. The threat of violence need not always be carried out, if its potential is understood. Although obviously many men never commit violence against women, and men themselves are potential

victims of many forms of violence, certain aspects of it need to be understood in the context of patriarchy. Violence against women seems to be present in every form of political economy, in every form of social structure.

Often, violence is sexual in form—that is, it is an assault on a woman's sexual autonomy, or on her right to control her own reproductive capacity. Sexual violence serves patriarchy in two ways: it helps control woman's labor power through restricting her sexuality, as Hartmann suggests, *and* it helps to keep male supremacy and male solidarity unchallenged. This involves more than the control of woman's labor power: it is the control of *her*, because she is female; its associated effects are to limit where she can go and what she can do; to heighten her fear and passivity—in short, to reinforce the unequal power relationship of women to men.

Although some ethnographic evidence suggests that violence against women does not exist in all cultures,[16] it is very difficult to evaluate the accuracy of such data. Anthropologist Paula Webster notes that ethnographers are blind to the existence of sexual force against women in "societies enshrined as separate but equal, egalitarian if not matriarchal,"[17] particularly if rape is a ritual of solidarity for males, or a culturally-approved rite of passage. Data are "scattered, fragmentary, and biased"; often rape is not even mentioned in ethnographic reports, and when it is, it is generally presented from the perspective of the male, or is implicitly justified as some sort of depersonalized "norm."[18] The female is sometimes presumed to enjoy it; and this view is most easily maintained by the anthropologist's failing to ask *her* how she likes being raped.

Rape has little to do with men's sexual urges, but a great deal to do with the assertion of male power. In societies Webster studied, rape takes place for a wide range of "offenses" against the male order, or even for no offenses at all:

> women have been raped for refusing to work, for committing adultery, for flaunting male authority, for leaving the village without an escort, for learning men's secrets, for going out at night. They have been raped by groups of men or by individual men, in warfare, seduction, ritual initiation.[19]

The existing evidence indicates that rape is present in societies regardless of the mode of production; it exists in "preclass" (and presumably "egalitarian") societies as well as in societies with extreme class inequality.

Webster reports this, and more: from her account, her work has encountered a good deal of hostility and resistance from marxist feminists. However one accounts for the existence of rape across such a range of cultures, it becomes difficult, if not impossible, to place it in a marxist perspective.

Violence against women takes many forms other than rape. And even if we do not discuss past practices such as the persecution of witches, or foot-binding in China, even if we confine the discussion to forms of violence that exist right now, the list is overwhelming.

The deliberate mutilation of women's reproductive/sexual organs is a form of violence. In many countries in Africa and the Middle East, as well as in Indonesia and Australia, ritual mutilation of the female genitalia is a common practice. Females are subjected to clitoridectomy (cutting away the clitoris and labia minora) or infibulation (the clitoris is removed and the sides of the vulva are sewn shut, to be cut or ripped open only by the husband).[20]

Although poor and minority women are most vulnerable to violence in the form of forceful control of their reproductive lives, no woman is exempt. The so-called right to life supporters are out to deny abortion rights to *all* women, through any means possible: through harassment of women who have abortions and the doctors who do them; through fire-bombing clinics; through pushing for a "human life" amendment to the Constitution.

It is violent to deny abortion rights and fail to provide safe, unconditionally effective contraceptives. Consider the following:

—The oral contraceptive, initially tested on the populations of Puerto Rico, Haiti, and the Appalachians, has since been linked to blood clots, heart attacks, tumors of the liver and gall bladder, and other conditions.

—The Dalkon Shield IUD caused 17 known deaths and 247 septic abortions over a 5 year period in the United States.

—Diethylstilbestrol (DES), first used to prevent miscarriages, then later as a "morning after" pill to prevent pregnancy, has finally been banned from cattle feed because it is a carcinogen; it is still available for selected use on human females.

—Estrogen replacement therapy (ERT) for menopausal women has been linked with a staggering increase in the rate of endometrial cancer.

Other forms of force specifically directed against women are sexual harassment, abuse of female children, and battering. Often, these and all the other forms of violence fall most heavily on those women least able to live with some measure of economic or psychological independence. But they are restricted to no sub-group of women. They are sometimes isolated acts by individual men against individual women; sometimes they are the outcomes of laws and institutionalized policies which constrain categories of women, and they may be carried out by women as well as by men. Some acts or policies are generated by a man's contempt or hatred for women—or even (as, for example, support for abortion restrictions or for the sterilization of women on public assistance) by women who despise other women. Probably they are most often done simply and unreflectingly as part of *the way things are*. This is what is meant by patriarchy. It intersects capitalism in specific ways, yet it is both separate and more. And patriarchy itself is but one form of institutionalized inequality which is both cause and consequence of power relationships—relationships of dominance and subordination.

CONCLUSION

What does Hartmann's analysis lead to in practice? It is not clear. In part I think that although Hartmann and other marxist feminists are reacting to the limitations of a sex-blind theory, they are still bound by some of those limitations. Although marxism's powerful explanation of the workings of capital is undeniable, even there it excludes much of the reality of women's lives. To the extent that marxist feminists are confined within its assumptions, then, they will inevitably have difficulty designing programs of action that will overcome those aspects of patriarchy that are not specifically linked to capitalism. And marxist theory will not permit them to dig deeper to the sources of both patriarchy and capitalism.

What, then, should feminists do? Hartmann says that the radical wing of the women's movement, which she defines as including women who are "antisystem, anticapitalist, anti-imperialist, socialist, communist, marxist, whatever" (Hartmann, p. 30), does seem to have lost some ground to bourgeois feminism. In the mass media, in many women's studies courses and texts, in the membership and goals of various women's groups and commissions, in calls for a Women's Party, feminism seems more and more to have taken on a bland, safe, nonrevolutionary outlook. We cannot let this continue.

Women need to know (and are increasingly prevented from finding out) that feminism is *not* about dressing for success, or becoming a corporate executive, or gaining elective office; it is *not* being able to share a two-career marriage and take skiing vacations and spend huge amounts of time with your husband and two lovely children because you have a domestic worker who makes all this possible for you, but who hasn't the time or money to do it for herself; it is *not* opening a Woman's Bank, or spending a weekend in an expensive workshop that guarantees to teach you how to become assertive (but not aggressive); it is most emphatically *not* about becoming a police detective or CIA agent or marine corps general.

But if these distorted images of feminism have more reality for any of the women we want to reach than ours do, it is partly our own fault. We have not worked as hard as we should have at providing clear and meaningful alternative analyses which relate to people's lives, and at providing active, accessible groups in which to work.

In my years of university teaching I have found that women students come into my classes thinking that feminism is about at least some of the things bourgeois feminists say it is. They may want some of those things for themselves, or they may not; but few arrive with any sort of radical analysis. And why should they? They have never been exposed to it. But I also invariably find that many are extremely receptive to, and excited by, the principles of radical and anarchist feminism. And their responsiveness crosses lines of class and race, of age and marital status.

There are, then, alternatives. As Hartmann believes: *either* there is the trap of bourgeois feminism, *or* there is a marxist analysis which, unfortunately, completely dominates feminism on the left. In addition to these two, radical feminism is still alive: We can find it in the pages of feminist periodicals such as *Off Our Backs, Heresies,* and *Chrysalis*; in women's centers and self-help clinics and consciousness raising groups; in the groups working against rape and battering; in the attempts to restructure organizations, work and personal relationships; in some of the attempts to build what is called women's culture.

And anarchist feminism is a small, but growing, movement.

It has some very definite ideas about putting its blend of radical feminism and social anarchist ideas into practice. Anarchist feminists emphasize breaking down the state and all other forms of centralized, hierarchical, and coercive organization. They do this by working to build new forms of organization such as what is incorrectly called the "leaderless" small group. (To be successful, such a group must be well-organized and have a high level of commitment, energy, and knowledgeable participation from all its members.) In addition, they work to connect the personal and the political in all phases of theory and practice; to develop cooperation and mutual aid; to try to coordinate groups horizontally rather than vertically; to share equally all important resources—economics, politics, knowledge, and skills; to resocialize adults and socialize children in the values of equality, freedom, and personal autonomy; to end gender socialization; to end the idea and the fact of property relationships (whether of persons or things); to keep means consistent with ends; and to build an anarchist culture.

Many of these points are consistent with socialism. But the critical difference lies in the emphasis on power. If power relationships are the key to class and sex inequality alike, and to all the other forms of inequality as well, then a marxist analysis can take us only so far and no farther. And the marriage of marxism and feminism might as well begin divorce proceedings. Of course, one would hope that they might remain friends.

FOOTNOTES

1. For discussions of the connections between social anarchism and radical feminism see especially Kornegger, Peggy. "Anarchism: The Feminist Connection," *The Second Wave*, 4:1 (Spring, 1975), pp. 26-37; Leighton, Marian. "Anarcho-Feminism and Louise Michel," *Black Rose*, 1 (April, 1974), pp. 8-37; and two of my earlier articles—"Socialism, Anarchism, and Feminism," in *Reinventing Anarchy: What Are Anarchists Thinking These Days?*, H.J. Ehrlich, Carol Ehrlich, David DeLeon, and Glenda Morris, ed. London: Routledge and Kegan Paul, 1979), pp.259-277; and "Anarchist Feminism and Power," unpublished ms., 1979.
2. Kornegger, *op. cit.* p. 31.
3. For two detailed comparisons of marxist and social anarchist theories of revolutionary change, see Wieck, David Thoreau. "The Negativity of Anarchism," in *Reinventing Anarchy, op. cit.* pp. 138-155; and Benello,

C. George, "Anarchism and Marxism: A Confrontation of Traditions," in *Reinventing Anarchy, op. cit.*, pp. 156-171.

4. For example, Shanklin, Elizabeth, co-editor of *The Matriarchist*, urges the formation of a "Woman's Party" to achieve matriarchal goals through the electoral process. (*The Matriarchist*, 2:1, Spring, 1979, pp. 1, 12.)

5. Millett, Kate, *Sexual Politics* (New York: Avon Books, 1971), p. 25 (cited in Hartmann, p. 18).

6. In Eisenstein, Zillah R. ed., *Capitalist Patriarchy and the Case for Socialist Feminism* (New York and London: Monthly Review Press, 1979), pp. 299-348.

7. "The Woman-Identified Woman," in Anne Koedt, Ellen Levine, and Anita Rapone, eds., *Radical Feminism* (New York: Quadrangle, 1973), pp. 241-242.

8. Ibid., p. 243.

9. For examples of two cultures in which sex roles are relatively fluid and gender status is relatively egalitarian, see Patricia Draper, "!Kung Women: Foraging and Sedentary Contexts," in Reiter, Rayna R., ed., *Toward an Anthropology of Women* (New York and London: Monthly Review Press, 1975), pp. 77-109; and the description of the Tlingit Indians of Alaska in Constance Sutton, Susan Makiesky, Daisy Dwyer, and Laura Klein, "Women, Knowledge, and Power," in Rohrlich-Leavitt, Ruby, ed., *Women Cross-Culturally: Change and Challenge* (The Hague: Mouton, 1975), pp. 581-600.

10. See Schlegel, Alice, ed., *Sexual Stratification: A Cross-Cultural View* (New York: Columbia University Press, 1977).

11. "Capitalism, Patriarchy, and Job Segregation by Sex," *Signs: Journal of Women in Culture and Society*, 1:3, pt. 2 (Spring, 1976), pp. 137-169, esp. pp. 140-147.

12. The Rubin article appears in Reiter, *op.cit.*, pp. 157-210.

13. In Jaquette, Jane S., ed., *Women in Politics* (New York: Wiley, 1974), pp. 322-342.

14. Boals, *op. cit.*, p. 322.

15. "Women, Culture, and Society: A Theoretical Overview," in Michelle Z. Rosaldo and Louise Lamphere, eds., *Women, Culture, and Society* (Stanford, CA: Stanford University Press, 1974), p. 36.

16. See for example Draper's materials on the !Kung in Reiter, esp. p. 91; and Mead's work on the Arapesh, cited in Rosaldo, "Women, Culture, and Society," p. 18.

17. "Rape Research: One Woman's Drama," *Quest: A Feminist Quarterly*, IV:3 (Summer, 1978), p. 81; see also Webster's "The Politics of Rape in Primitive Society," paper presented at the 75th Annual Meetings of the American Anthropological Association, Washington, D.C., 1976.

18. Ibid., p. 80.

19. Ibid., p. 81.

20. For a description of the practice in Guinea, see Diana E. H. Russell

19. *Ibid.,* p. 81.
20. For a description of the practice in Guinea, see Diana E. H. Russell and Nicole Van de Ven, eds., *Crimes Against Women: Preceedings of the International Tribunal,* (Millbrae, CA: Les Femmes, 1976), pp. 150-151.
21. Reported in *The Washington Post,* 10 May, 1977.
22. Boston Women's Health Book Collective, *Our Bodies, Ourselves* (New York: Simon and Schuster, 1976), p. 148.
23. Ad Hoc Women's Studies Committee Against Sterilization Abuse, *Workbook on Sterilization Abuse.* Bronxville, NY: Women's Studies Program, Sarah Lawrence College, 1978. See esp. pp. 20-22.
24. Quotation from Connecticut gynecologist Ralph C. Wright, cited in *Our Bodies, Ourselves,* p. 148.
25. *The Washington Post,* 8 March 1979.
26. Gallagher, Janet. "Abortion Rights: Critical Issue for Women's Freedom," *WIN Magazine,* 8 March 1979, p. 11.

WHAT IS THE REAL MATERIAL BASE OF PATRIARCHY AND CAPITAL?

Sandra Harding

Sandra Harding teaches philosophy of social science and feminist theory at the University of Delaware. She has edited several collections of papers and published articles on topics in those areas. Dis-Covering Reality: Feminist Perspectives on Epistemology, Metaphysics, Methodology and the Philosophy of Science, edited with Merrill Hintikka, will be published in 1981. She is active in a checkered collection of local and national feminist organizations.

135

CAN THE "UNHAPPY MARRIAGE OF MARXISM AND FEMINISM"
BE SAVED?

The "marriage" of marxism and feminism has indeed been
like the marriage of husband and wife depicted in English common
law: as Heidi Hartmann's essay has put it, "marxism and feminism
are one, and that one is marxism"(Hartmann, p. 2)[1]. But can this
marriage be saved? Is a more progressive union possible in theory or
in political practice? From the perspective of the historical,
materialist, feminist explanatory framework which can be
constructed from some recent attempts to develop an historical,
materialist, feminist theory of the nature of "the species"
produced under our division of labor by gender,[2] one of the old
partners to the unhappy marriage seems hopelessly ill-suited to a
more progressive union. As usual, the major problem is the
husband (marxism) and thus with the terms of any future union.
The ahistorical and nonmaterial character of some feminist
descriptions and explanations of social life can be corrected in the
newly emerging explanatory framework. But the shallow and sexist
character of many elements of the marxist conceptual framework
raise real questions as to whether either marxist theory or marxist
political practice can maintain its identity as marxist in any more
progressive union with feminist theory and practice. As feminists
have long understood, we need to create "new men" before any
truly liberated union is even conceivable.

Hartmann's essay is especially interesting since it leads us to
the brink of this assessment of the viability of a "more progressive
union." However, like a number of others who have tried to reconcile feminism and marxism, I think she fails to draw the conclusions
which her illuminating criticisms of the unhappy marriage very
naturally suggest.[3] Hartmann's analysis of the various ways in
which "the woman question" has never posed "the feminist
question" is valuable indeed. Furthermore, her essay begins to
move us toward a better understanding of the real causes of our
social life when it shows us how present day capital and patriarchy
form a partnership in which each partner has resources which make
it very flexible in adapting to the shifting material base of the
other. Capital mediates patriarchy, and patriarchy mediates

capital. This perception leads to the argument that feminism must be allowed to—and *must*—be a stronger partner in the more progressive union which is required to defeat the partnership of capital and patriarchy. The criticism of theory leads to a criticism of the marxist strategic claim that the best revolutionary practice, given limited resources, is for all oppressed peoples to unite in the struggle against capital. This claim could be true only if patriarchy were entirely caused by class oppression. As Hartmann shows, struggle aimed only at capital will fail since not only is patriarchy an independent cause of gender oppression, but also the underlying supports for capital in patriarchal relations of oppression will be overlooked.

However, it is here that Hartmann fails to draw the "natural" conclusions. Consequently, her argument ultimately settles for what, from a feminist perspective, remains merely a utopian partnership of marxism and feminism because it does not show us the real material base of patriarchy and capital. Thus in my opinion Hartmann's account, too, ultimately mystifies social relations in a way clearly beneficial to both patriarchy and capital. In the first section of this essay I shall sketch out Hartmann's "utopian solution," and also the "radical solution" to which her analysis in fact leads us. The radical solution requires us to ask a different set of theoretical and strategic questions than marxists have even been willing to consider. In the second section my argument is that Hartmann tries to correct only for what is a mere sin of omission—the "sex-blindness" of the marxist categories. In fact, the marxist categories are also guilty of a sin of commission: they are fundamentally *sexist as well as sex-blind*. To support this claim, I show in the third section how Hartmann's revision of the "material base" of capital and patriarchy merely broadens the domain of that traditional concept but does not make the required revisions in the category itself. "Material base" has been restricted to economic relations in marxist theory. Hartmann in trying to reconcile feminism and marxist theory has extended the traditional concept to show how the *economic* aspects of the division of labor by gender in the family maintain both patriarchy and capital. I think Hartmann is right about this, but I think we also need to understand the "material base" in a different and less reductionistic way. The necessary revision of the concept itself can be constructed from the recent writings of Nancy Chodorow and Jane

Flax.[4] This revision in the concept of the material base of capital and patriarchy emerges from an explanation of the historical and material conditions under which psychological interests in domination relations in general are reproduced. It provides an historical, materialist, nondeterministic explanation of the "production and reproduction of the species"—that is, of such distinctive historical persons as men, women, capitalists, workers, heterosexists and homosexuals, racists and their victims. In the fourth and last section, I demonstrate some virtues of this radical solution to the unhappy marriage. For one thing, the radical solution shows the "curious coincidence" of stereotypically masculine and stereotypically entrepreneurial traits neither to be curious nor a coincidence. For another, it provides a long-needed psychological underpinning to marxist social theory but avoids the problems of ahistorical, nonmaterialist, and deterministic psychological theories in a way freudian theory cannot. Third, it raises a new and important set of research questions. Finally, the radical solution leads us to the importance of creating and participating in new kinds of political practices.

Hartmann is ambivalent both about what the more progressive theoretical union between marxism and feminism should be, and also about who, in actual political practice, could be the partners in such a theoretically "liberated marriage."

On the one hand, she shows that patriarchy and capital are interlocked in an equally and mutually supportive economic and ideological system—in a symbiotic relationship. Consequently she seems to propose that feminism and marxism *as theories* must similarly interlock in an equally mutually supportive opposition. From this perspective, it seems irrelevant *who* the real, live feminists and marxists are. From this perspective, it is conceivable that they could all be men. (Hartmann would not support this, of course; but on the basis of the dominant perspective in her essay, there are no theoretical grounds to object to such a practice.) The new more progressive union can be constructed by individuals of *either* gender: the "empty places" of the new union may be filled by individuals irrespective of their gender.

On the other hand, in some places Hartmann's arguments lead to a different and more startling conclusion. Her arguments imply that patriarchy and capital, as economic and ideological institutions, are not themselves the disease but only the symptoms of a far deeper and more general illness. The underlying illness involves gender-based personality differences created by the material conditions of infant care. These conditions create patterns of dominating social relations which are more general than class oppression and gender oppression, as well as adult men's psychological investments in not giving up their controlling positions in *either* patriarchy or capitalism (not to mention their dominating roles in race relations and the selective institutionalization of heterosexism). Whatever else it may be, the "more progressive union" of marxism and feminism must be a union against male controlled institutions. The radical conclusions lead us to some pertinent theoretical and strategic questions about this historically obvious but usually ignored fact. The first is, why is it that *all* institutions in society, including socialist organizations, are controlled by men? Second, should a marxist expect an adequate answer to the first question to be produced by men? Third, should a marxist think it possible to *convince* men, who are the dominating group, to relinquish voluntarily their control of social life? Fourth, what then can be the revolutionary role of men at this moment in history?

Consider the first question about the male control of institutional life. To answer this we must solve the problem of the unhappy marriage of marxist and feminist *theory*. Marxist *theory* has not provided a way to explain adequately the causes of male dominance. Hartmann's account shows the need for a radical solution to this problem. Hartmann argues that the marxist categories will not *permit* an adequate description of the historical, material regularities of social life or an explanation of their underlying determinants—that is, the marxist scheme will not permit an adequate account of *either* class oppression or gender oppression. Hence, she argues that new categories of analysis must be constructed which are adequate to this job. The new categories, this new explanatory scheme, will allow us to capture the symbiotic relations between patriarchy and capital and the roots of this symbiosis in a deeper historical and materialist pattern of dominating social relations. Hence on the radical approach there will be no independently recognizable marxism—nor, of course, will there be a feminism which is ahistorical or nonmaterial.[5] But there *will* be an account of why it is that *men* control and thus have material interests in maintaining both patriarchy and capital; the new explanatory scheme must have theoretical room for such an explanation. Thus, with this radical conclusion, such a feminist perspective would have the potential to produce a more general theory which will include much of the substance of the older marxist theory and of utopian feminism, but which has far greater explanatory power.[6]

Consider the second question. Who could be the authors of this new, revolutionary theory? Hartmann shows that as a general rule and at least in the short run, all men (including men on the left) have a variety of interests in refusing to recognize their role in the patriarchal relations contributing to gender oppression and class oppression.

> As a general rule, men's position in patriarchy and capitalism prevents them from recognizing both human needs for nurturance, sharing, and growth, and the potential for meeting those needs in a non-hierarchical, non-patriarchical society. But even if we raise their consciousness, men might assess the potential gains against the potential losses and choose the status quo. Men have more to lose than their chains. (Hartmann, p. 33.)

> It is not clear—from our sketch, from history, or from male socialists— that the "socialism" being struggled for is the same for both men and women. For a "humane socialism" would require not only consensus on what the new society should look like and what a healthy person should look like, but more concretely, it would require that men relinquish their privilege. (Hartmann, p. 32.)

We should not expect men, who have more to lose than their chains, to produce the needed theory.

With respect to the third question, what's required for men to "relinquish their privilege" is not a mere statement by men that they intend to give up masculine perogatives, but a new set of political practices which will produce both nonpatriarchical institutions and the "new men" capable of developing the required feminist perspective based on *their* daily experience. Without nonpatriarchical institutions, men whose masculine privilege has truly been relinquished will not exist, since masculine privilege is not freely chosen by individual males. It is conferred on all males, regardless of their wishes, by the practices of patriarchal, capitalist, racist, and selectively heterosexist institutions. We are discovering that those practices weave more deeply into the social fabric of our daily lives than we can yet even fully grasp.

Thus Hartmann's arguments lead *us* to conclude that present day men should not be expected to produce the theory which can defeat patriarchy / capitalism, and that mere statements of feminist intent on their part, or efforts to convince them on women's part, will not change this assessment. There is not a useful analogy with marxist theory here since it is far easier individually to relinquish class privilege than it is individually to relinquish gender privilege. (Women historically have "changed class" through marriage, to cite just one way class privilege can be individually relinquished.)[7] Gender privilege will be deniable by individual men only when it has been relinquished by the entire gender. But then we will not live in a patriarchy or a class society, and feminism will at last (and only then) be truly identical with humanism. Thus Hartmann's arguments lead *us* to the conclusion that it is women, armed with the newly emerging historical, materialist, autonomous feminism, who now stand at the revolutionary place in history.

We have now arrived at the fourth and very painful question—one from which marxist feminists have carefully averted their attention. In traditional marxist debates, there was no agonizing over how to obtain an analoguously "more progressive union" of the proletariat and the bourgeoisie. There was thought to be little reason to spend much energy considering the question of the revolutionary role of capitalists. No sympathy was to be extended to factory owners; no helpful reeducation programs for the bourgeoisie were high on the list of revolutionary projects to which the proletariat should devote its energy. But feminists must figure out what is to be the revolutionary role of men—at least of the men they work with politically and those with whom they share family bonds and relations of intimacy. (From this perspective, feminist separatism becomes an understandable, though necessarily temporary, political strategy.) What is the solution to "the man question"? The resistance of men on the left to an historical, materialist, feminist analysis is largely a measure of the collective failure of men and women to address this question theoretically or to resolve it in practice. In the final paragraphs I shall suggest some necessary requirements for solving the man question.

ARE THE MARXIST CATEGORIES OF ANALYSIS ONLY "SEX-BLIND"?

Hartmann is led away from the radical solution because she corrects only for the sex-blindness of the marxist explanatory scheme. She argues that the woman question has never been the feminist question because of the fact that marxists have consistently failed to analyze adequately the nature and consequences of the division of labor *within* the family. Hartmann asks one important question about this labor: who benefits from women's labor within the family? Not just capital, she points out. Men *as men* also benefit from this labor in a variety of ways. This should not surprise us, she argues, since we can see that through their positions in capital as well as in patriarchy all men as men (as well as a few as capitalists) control the conditions of women's labor within the family. She argues that the failure of marxists to understand this dynamic is illuminated once we see that the categories of marxist analysis are sex-blind while, in contrast, history has obviously not been sex-blind. An adequate understanding both of history and of appropriate political strategies requires a solution to this problem:

> . . . "class," "reserve army of labor," "wage-laborer," do not explain why particular people fill particular places. They give no clues about why women are subordinate to *men* inside and outside the family and why it is not the other way around. *Marxist categories, like capital itself, are sex-blind.* The categories of marxism cannot tell us who will fill the "empty spaces." Marxist analysis of the woman question has suffered from this basic problem.(Hartmann, pp. 10-11.)

Hartmann's important question about the nature and consequences of the division of labor within the family leads her to extend the traditional marxian notion of material base to include men's *economic* and ideological control of women's labor within the family. She takes as her touchstone here the famous passage from Engels to which feminists have returned again and again in the attempt to construct the "more progressive union" with marxism.

> According to the materialist conception, the determining factor in history is, in the final instance, the production and reproduction of immediate life. This, again, is of a twofold character: on the one side, the production of the means of existence, of food, clothing, and shelter and the tools

necessary for that production; on the other side, the production of human beings themselves, the propagation of the species. The social organization under which the people of a particular historical epoch and a particular country live is determined by both kinds of production, by the stage of development of labor on the one hand and of the family on the other.[8]

This passage has consistently led marxist feminists to corrections of the marxist explanatory scheme which remain ultimately inadequate. On the one hand there are the social relations of "the production of the means of existence, of food, clothing, and shelter and the tools necessary for that production." Until recently, it was assumed that the categories needed for this analysis were those which marxist theory has produced—economic categories such as class, reserve army of labor and wage laborer. (Note that these categories have been constructed to describe and explain just those aspects of social life where men dominate, and through which they define culture—what constitutes distinctly *human* interaction with nature.) But what are the appropriate categories for understanding the social relations of "the production of human beings themselves, the propagation of the species"? Engels himself, in spite of his implied call for an analysis of the independent causes of the social relations producing persons, went on to explain these relations as largely a consequence of the control of the labor of production and reproduction of "the means of existence." Subsequent attempts to resolve the woman question followed this lead, as Hartmann demonstrates. But though Hartmann shows how marxist theory—the marxist explanatory scheme—does not have the categories adequate for understanding the causes of these relations, in fact she extends, unrevised, the traditional economic notion of material base so that now it covers both the economic relations within the family and the economic relations between the family and the workplace. She provides a causal analysis of the consequences for the social relations of the workplace of the economic division of labor within the family.

But family life is structured by a lot more materially based social relations than merely economic ones. The restriction of material causes to economic ones is an unjustifiably reductionist restriction, as the next section of the essay will show. Hence even after Hartmann's analysis we still do not have categories permitting us to describe and explain the social relations of the area in which, in capitalist society, women as a gender are contained—often in reality, always in ideology. More importantly, economic relations can not capture most of the social relations in which infants and children participate: it is through more materially-based social relations than merely economic ones that biological animals are turned into social persons—that the species is produced and reproduced. Hence the complete material base of the social relations *producing within the family different kinds of persons* escapes Hartmann's revision of the marxist explanatory scheme. It is true that the marxist explanatory scheme is sex-blind in its failure to give the economic aspects of the division of labor within the family the causal relation to capital which in fact they have. But it is also sexist in that economic categories such as class and material base (understood in the traditional way as economic base) are not even the appropriate categories with which to understand crucial aspects of the social relations of family life.[9] Since, as Hartmann argues, the social relations of family life maintain not only patriarchy but also capital, a courageous (or foolhardy) writer should claim that in this sense *the marxist categories are not only sexist but also classist.* They are constructed in such a way as to capture only *part* of the material base (here understood in my way) of class oppression.[10]

WHAT IS THE MATERIAL BASE OF PATRIARCHY AND CAPITAL?

To see how this misunderstanding of the extent of the correction required in the marxist categories affects Hartmann's account, consider the alternative notion of the material base of patriarchy and capital.

Where earlier marxists had argued that the economic relations of wage labor alone support both capital and patriarchy, Hartmann again and again argues that the economic relations of family life also support both patriarchy and capital. As she puts it, the material base of patriarchy and capital also lies in men's control of women's labor in the family. But to assume that economic relations exhaust the list of causal social relations is an old error in the dominant strain of marxian theory. The material base is not in fact limited to economic relations. Marxist thought has often tended toward a narrow and reductionist materialism which is in fact inherited from the dualistic metaphysics/epistemology which at least some marxists explicitly reject. This dualistic tendency has led marxists to divide social relations into two mutually exclusive categories: economic relations, and all other social relations, which are usually thought of as psychological relations. The reductionist tendency sees the latter as including social relations structured by an entire realm of individual and collective mental life, from individuals' ideas and attitudes to culture-wide beliefs such as ideologies, and as entirely caused by the former. This is of course a caricature of the worst reductionist excesses of marxist theory, and no respectable marxist would profess such an obviously inadequate conceptual scheme today—at least not out loud. Nevertheless, echoes of this reductionist view constantly surface in marxist analyses, and Hartmann's essay is no exception in this respect. (It will become evident later in this essay that the dualism itself has its source in the historical, material, social relations which maintain capitalism and patriarchy, and is itself a patriarchal division.)[11]

What other social relations besides economic relations might constitute the material base of patriarchy and capital? Hartmann asks the question: "Who benefits from the division of labor by gender?" But there is another question we must ask about the social relations of family life. In the case of the family, what is produced is, simply, the species, since it is in the family that human biological animals become social persons. Currently this species is one in which classism, sexism, racism, and heterosexism are endemic. We know how in the workplace the real social relations of the production process help to determine the nature of the products produced. So the new question is: what is the nature of these *products* (i.e., adult social persons) which the social relations of the division of labor by gender in the family play a significant role in producing.

First we must note an obvious but important *dis*similarity between the "means of existence" produced through the division of labor in the workplace and "the species itself" produced initially through the division of labor in the family. Material goods such as food, clothing, and shelter are not human—they have no conscious or unconscious perspective on the process responsible for their production—no understanding of it, no experience of their own production. In contrast, the products of the division of labor by gender in the family are human beings who experience the process of becoming social persons. They have an understanding, however imperfect, of what their production process is and of what kind of final product they are supposed to become. In fact, their experience of their own production helps to shape the kinds of persons they will become.

Why has there been so little attention paid to the differences which the material conditions of the division of labor in the family make in the nature of the social beings who emerge from families into the public world? One reason is that this dissimilarity between things and people has been overlooked and downplayed. But a second reason is that infantile experience—the infant's perspective on the division of labor by gender—has been repressed both in individual memory and in our accounts of social life. This repression in individual adults and in the stories we tell about ourselves which we call history and social science leads us to rationalize and explain away many social events and processes which actually lack real explanation.[12] Finally, there appears to have been so little historical and cross-cultural variation in certain crucial aspects of the division of labor by gender that it, and the whole sex gender system it generates, appear natural.[13] These crucial aspects are that it is women who care for infants—and thus always a woman from whom we separate and individuate ourselves, and that women are universally devalued. These two phenomena appear to be what nature provides rather than what culture constructs, and they have been treated as natural by virtually all prior social theories, including marxist theory. Thus these apparently virtually universal aspects of the division of labor by gender do not even appear to be an important subject for social inquiry.

It is not a new marxist project to look to the production process to understand the nature of the human products produced. Max Horkheimer and others in the Frankfurt School had considered the role of the family in producing the kind of personality which is comfortable in authoritarian social institutions.[14] But they were concerned mainly with boys' social relations with their fathers. There was little concern in their writings with the social relations of infants of either sex to their major caretakers—their mothers.[15] I am going to skip over the differences between the analyses of Nancy Chodorow and Jane Flax,[16] in order to focus on the more adequate and explanatorily powerful notion of material base which we can construct from these writings. Drawing on the object relations analysis of post-freudian psychoanalytic theory, these theorists distinguish (as, in a mutilated form, Freud did) the biological birth of the infant and the psychological birth of the social person. Biological birth is an event of short duration which is relatively uninfluenced by social variables. But the psychological birth of a person is a process which takes about three years and which is greatly influenced by the social environment in which it occurs. Infants become persons during this period. Their natures—their personalities—are not fixed or determined during this process, but the kinds of persons infants become are greatly influenced by the particular social relations the infant experiences as it is transformed, and transforms itself, from a biological infant into a social person.

A NECESSARY DIGRESSION

At this point we must jump ahead and examine two objections to the kind of ahistorical and determinist psychological account one might still suspect this is going to be. Objections are always raised by marxists, first of all, to claims that individuals' social natures are fixed or determined at any age or in any way, and secondly to claims that it is psychological states which are the most fundamental causes of social relations. Neither claim will be made by me. The theory to be sketched out is neither an ahistorical or deterministic one, nor is it psychological in the traditional, dualistic sense. But I have found it hard for people to hear what the theory does propose until these objections are explicitly addressed. Hence the need for this digression to answer claims I will not make.

Consider first the objection to the ahistorical and deterministic character of any psychological theory. The theory to be outlined claims only what would appear to be an obvious social fact: that we are psychologically *influenced* by our interaction with our social and physical environments. It substitutes the notion of historical limits for ahistorical determinants. Limits have a width in that we can move around in them—there are alternatives available within them. Determinants do not have a width. And a width of historical limits can be extended or narrowed by changing social environments. In order to strengthen our understanding of the difference between ahistorical determinants and historical limits it will be helpful to consider how we are not even physically determined, though there are many ways at any historical time that each of us is physically limited, and though there obviously are species-wide limits to the ways in which we can change our physical bodies.

First of all, we are born with certain limitations on how our physical bodies can and will be changed, for there are normal physical developmental processes. (What's *labelled* "normal" and "physical" and what is normal and physical are important matters for discussion, but each species does have certain such normal physical developmental processes, such as the emergence of reproductive ability and aging processes.) But there are also many ways in which interactions with our environment change our bodies: the kind of diet we have, the kind of work we do, and the kind of air we breathe obviously change our bodies. These changes are usually individually unplanned though they are influenced by our forms of social organization. And then there are the planned changes we make in our bodies—shaving hair, developing muscles, going on a diet, transplanting limbs and organs, changing sex. But all these changes are made within physical limits. Some of these limits are historically specific—*now* the air is polluted in cities; *now* heart transplants are possible for a few. Some of the limits are biological —that is, species-wide—for perhaps creatures of our design could never grow wings to support us in flight across the Atlantic; perhaps we could never adapt to life on the moon without an artificial physical environment; perhaps much of the damage done by syphyllis or arthritis is physically irreversible. Thus we are biologically limited but not determined or fixed by either historical conditions as individuals or by the laws of nature as a species. We can make individual and collective changes in our social lives which extend or narrow our physical limits. We don't know and never will know exactly what our historical and species-wide limits are, but we do know that they are there.

Similarly, the theory to be outlined asserts that there are certain psychological limits established in individuals by the time a biological human has been transformed into a social person around the age of three. Some of these are developmental, some historical, some species-wide.[17] Examples of developmental limits are the facts that we can't recreate our adolescent personalities, nor can we have the sense of our sexual potential at eight which we have at eighteen. Historical psychological limits include those created by being socialized into our culture's sex roles, or into feudal relations. Species-wide psychological limits might include needing an integrated sense of oneself, or needing to feel one belongs to some social grouping of other people. But many psychological changes are made in persons after they are three years old; and many more are possible than we actually do make since the width of limits gives us space within which to change psychologically. Some psychological changes are developmental, such as changes associated with the physical changes of puberty, or with noting that one is probably closer to the end than to the beginning of one's life. Some are individually unintended changes resulting from the social relations within which we interact with others and with nature: dealing with marriage, or motherhood, or sudden poverty, or new positions of responsibility. And there are the planned changes we make in our psychological lives: the decisions to learn not to crumple under criticism, or to eliminate some stereotypically classist, racist, or sexist personality trait we discover in ourselves. Of course the changes we plan will not occur unless we enter into appropriate new interactions with social others—interactions having clear historical and material conditions. We don't know and never will know exactly what our historical and species-wide psychological limits are, but we can see that they are there.

Thus the theory to be outlined is neither ahistorical nor deterministic. Instead it suggests a relationship between the historically specific and the species-wide material conditions of the social relations of infancy, on the one hand, and the kinds of psychological interests produced under these conditions, on the other hand. These psychological interests—these personalities —are changeable, but within limits. And our interest will be in exploring the kinds of intentional changes adults can make *within* these limits (testing the width of the limits) and in how those limits which are historically produced can themselves be stretched for us and for future infants.

Second, consider in a preliminary way the objection to psychological determinism. The theory to be sketched out claims not that psychological states are the fundamental cause of social conditions, but that certain real, material, historically specific aspects of the division of labor by gender cause the production of social persons with psychological investment in reproducing patriarchy and capital. But this historical, material base of the production of social persons is simply not limited to, or even primarily, an economic base, though economic relations clearly mediate it. It is instead the actual physical division of labor by gender itself, and the consequent physical/social relations of the infant to its environment which constitute the material base. The nature and consequences of these aspects of the division of labor by gender will become clearer if we return to explore the concept of material base which can be constructed from the writings of Chodorow and Flax. To summarize the point of this digression, the theory to be considered is not ahistorical, deterministic, or idealistically psychological.

BACK TO THE REAL MATERIAL BASE

Marxists have primarily looked at the ways in which adult individuals' interactions with particular social structures (e.g. the structure of office life in twentieth century United States) have produced and reproduced social persons with interests which they think will be satisfied within such structures. And they have looked at how the politically powerful ones among those very same kinds of social individuals have produced and reproduced the social structures which they think will be comfortable for them. (Actually they have looked at classes of persons. But classes contain individuals.) History shapes humans at the same time that the more powerful humans are shaping history. Chodorow and Flax look at how this process works earlier in the production of persons. They look at how the social structures of infant care produce *gendered social* individuals from the raw material of biological animals. Gender and personhood are inseparable, for there are no persons who are not distinctively gendered by the process of becoming persons. However, gender differences are intimately related to differences in our ways of relating to others, to ourselves, and to nature. Thus the gender contours left on boys and girls by having to become persons through interactions with particular, historical forms of infant care show up in all of the social structures humans design. Since it is largely men who have designed and still control all of our social institutions, an understanding of the production and reproduction of gender becomes crucial for understanding significant contours of social structures which might initially seem far removed from the sex/gender system. Dinnerstein lists some of the other kinds of systems of relationships inseparable from the sex/gender system:

> The gathering impulse to break loose from our existing gender arrangements . . . is part of the central thrust of our species' life toward more viable forms. It is of the same order as, and inseparable from, our long effort to identify and surmount the forces that make us each other's murderers, tyrants, prey: the

effort toward what in a male-dominated world is still called
brotherhood.... Another member of this constellation is the
project of making friends with our bodies, and healing the
life-sapping split which in our case alone divides the basic
activity impulse that we share with other beasts into work on
the one hand and play on the other. Another is the project of
achieving perspective on the role that we have carved out for
ourselves, half blindly, in nature.... Another is the project of
reconciliation between the rational and the pre-rational layers
of our sentience.... [18]

As noted earlier, there are two striking features of the social
structure of infant care, the social structure within which we all are
"psychologically born." First, it is always a woman (or women)
who is the primary caretaker for the infant under the organization
of labor from prehistory through the present. Thus, as newborn
male and female androgynes, who can not distinguish themselves
from their first caretakers, come to understand themselves to be
separate social individuals with desires and needs which are
separate from and often conflicting with those of their initial
nurturer, that first "other" from which they separate is always a
woman. The only aspect of women's work which evidently is
universal is just this: it is women who are the primary caretakers of
infants. Thus for all infants, men appear as significant inhabitants
of their universe only after infants have passed into the age of
reason—only after they have succeeded to a considerable degree in
differentiating themselves from their mothers (and I use the term
mother to stand for whatever female or females nurse the child and
perform the early child care) and only after they are no longer
totally vulnerable and helpless. Under the present organization of
labor, men initially appear to us, whether we are little boys or little
girls, only abstractly, distantly, and without particular physical or
emotional significance for us. By the time we get to know them, we
can deal relatively rationally with the fact that they have interests
and desires which conflict with ours and with the fact of their
imperfection as objects of desire. The initial, horrible discoveries
that humans are imperfect, that they have wills of their own, that
they frustrate our projects—this discovery has been made about a
woman, about the person on whom we were dependent for
survival, about the person from whom we were having difficulty
distinguishing and separating ourselves; and these discoveries were
made before we had learned to deal with life rationally.

The second striking feature of the social structure of infant care is that gender is not value-neutral. Being a woman is less highly valued than being a man. Thus the person from whom we first individuate ourselves both devalues herself and is perceived as devalued, and this shows up both in the different quality of mothering given to infant boys and infant girls and in the different *experience* which male and female infants have of becoming a person—of the production of their small part of the species. Female infants discover that they are to become women while male infants discover that they are to become men. The discovery of the sex/gender system by male and female infants, and of their future roles in it, has different consequences for males and females. The stereotypically masculine personality develops through separation from its first other—a devalued woman in interaction with whom he first experiences his own body and her body. Her body becomes the first model for the bodies of others, of persons who are perceived as unlike himself. Emerging into the beginnings of rational life and collective social life, what he has left behind is his pre-rational and nourishing interactions with a woman. The frantic maintenance of dualisms between mind and body, between culture and nature, between highly-valued self and devalued others, take their first forms in the process of becoming a male person who must individuate himself from a devalued woman. Thus infant boys' psychological birth in families with our division of labor by gender produces men who will be excessively rationalistic, who will need to dominate not only others but also their feelings, their physical bodies, and other bodies—nature—in general.[19] They will be excessively competitive and concerned primarily with their own projects. They will maintain an excessive separation or distance from the concerns of those around them, especially those unlike themselves. It produces misogyny and male-bonding as prototypes of appropriate social relations with others perceived to be respectively unlike and like themselves. And, as Jane Flax argues, our division of labor by gender itself produces the repression of infantile experience in both boys and girls and consequently a great deal of covert adult acting out of unresolved infantile projects.

Our division of labor by gender produces in girls, in contrast, a more ambivalent relationship to the mother from whom they individuate themselves as social persons, and hence a more ambivalent relationship to the poles of the dualisms. Adult women, who have maintained strong emotional attachments to women—their first love throughout childhood—in general are excessively nurturant and altruistic (even to supporting authoritarian personality traits in men); they are excessively focused on emotional life and excessively unable to separate themselves or achieve objective distance from the concerns around them. Their involvement in heterosexual relations, though economically of the greatest significance, is of less emotional significance than these relations are for men. For men, infantile sexual and emotional experiences were with a person of the same kind as their adult partner. Chodorow and Flax are concerned more with the reproduction of females' roles in the sex/gender system, since they are interested in how mothering itself is reproduced under the present division of labor by gender. But since we are focussing on the natures of the humans who design and control patriarchy and capital, it is the reproduction of the stereotypically masculine personality, developed through the experience of separating from a devalued woman, which interests us more. In both cases, the infant becomes the invisible perpetrator of much of human history.

From this perspective, the underlying social dynamic of racism takes on a clearer form. As a social institution, designed and controlled by men, as all social institutions have been, the vast panorama of the history of race relations becomes one more male drama in which the more powerful group of men works out its infantile project of dominating the other. Race relations are fundamentally social relations between men, where women find themselves supporting characters or, occasionally, thrust forward to leading roles in a script they have not written and can not direct.[20]

And from this perspective, female homosexuality—lesbianism—becomes not a personal preference, or even merely a sexual choice, but an increasingly predictable opportunity for women to experience themselves as social persons who are not other, who are not systematically devalued in their social relations in a world they did not design. Male homosexuality, in contrast, has two very different dynamics. For some men, it offers the possibility of the ultimate male community—the complete separation from everything perceived as feminine. For others, it offers the possibility of participating in the repressed and lost part of male personality, that part associated with the feminine.

Of course stereotypical masculine and feminine personality traits are reinforced and rewarded in many ways after the age of three. And there are real economic interests on the part of both capitalists and men in maintaining gender polarization. But for those of us who want to change history, to win the struggle against both patriarchy and capital, this autonomous feminist theory directs our attention to additional fronts on which the battle must be waged. We must both become ourselves and create other persons who are new people. To do that we must understand, and change, the historical, material conditions under which persons are produced in the capitalist form of patriarchy.[21]

To recapitulate the argument of this section, Hartmann argued that it is economic aspects of the division of labor by gender which provide part of the material base of both patriarchy and capital. I am arguing that we can construct a less utopian concept of the material base of patriarchy and capital from the historical and materialist gender-based personality theories of Chodorow and Flax. This alternative concept not only resolves some of the problems which were puzzling about the old concept, but also allows us to construct a more powerful theory of how social life is produced and reproduced. In a nutshell, the historical and material conditions of the production and reproduction of the species play a crucial causal role in setting limits for what the material conditions for the production and reproduction of the means of existence will be. It is the division of labor by gender as experienced by infants—the products of that labor—which emerges in adults to make men *want* to dominate others, to make men conceptualize nature and others in ways which make such domination appear appropriate and natural, and to make men and women unaware of and thus unable to understand these aspects of their own natures. The particular social forms in which the psychological interests in dominating others will be expressed will vary historically in the sorts of ways in which Hartmann shows patriarchy mediating capital and capital mediating patriarchy. Should we be surprised if the fingerprints of masculine personalities are to be found on the social institutions men design? Should we be surprised that patriarchy and capital are structured in the way they are or that they are so closely intertwined?

Let me again stress that it is indeed historical and material conditions to which the gender-based personality theories direct our attention. Though virtually universal to date, this division of labor by gender is nevertheless historically specific.[22] It is not now either natural or necessary, for men can share the primary care-taking of infants and women can share the designing of our social relations inside and outside the family. It could be women *and* men from whom the infant individuates itself; it could be men *and* women who initially appear to us as rational creatures. And it is a set of material conditions that are the issues: the actual division of labor by gender and the physical/social relations of the infant to its environment. The new concept of the material base of social life allows us to understand not only the historical and material conditions producing psychological interests in patriarchy and capital, but also those responsible for interests in various other kinds of dominating relationships: the interests in producing and maintaining the various dualisms where mind or intellect must dominate feelings, emotions, the body, physical nature and other social persons.

SOME ADDITIONAL VIRTUES OF THE RADICAL SOLUTION

Hartmann notes the curious phenomenon of the "coincidence" of stereotypically masculine personality traits and of the desired personality traits of the capitalist entrepreneur. Why is it, she asks, that "the characteristics of men as radical feminists describe them" and the dominant values of capitalist society coincide? (Hartmann, p. 28.) She offers two explanations of this phenomenon.

> In the first instance, men, as wage-laborers, are absorbed in capitalist social relations at work, driven into the competition these relations prescribe, and absorb the corresponding values.... Secondly, even when men and women do not actually behave in the way sexual norms prescribe, men *claim for themselves* those characteristics which are valued in the dominant ideology. (Hartmann, p. 28.)

It is true that both of these phenomena happen: much of social life is overdetermined, and desired personality characteristics are reinforced in many ways. But if gender-based personality differences originate in our prerational infantile experience (in the unconscious), and if these personality differences which reproduce and maintain sexism are the same as those which reproduce and maintain classism, then it is infantile experience of the division of labor by gender which is producing "the characteristics of men as radical feminists describe them" and the dominant values of capitalist society. This is no coincidence: it is two effects of a single cause. Capitalism and patriarchy are not really partners in a union. They are siblings[23] sharing the genes of psychological interests in maintaining the domination of others. This is not "curious" once we note that it is men who control both institutions. Thus the radical solution resolves the puzzle of the curious coincidence of stereotypically masculine personality traits and the desired personality traits in capitalist society.

Another virtue of the radical solution is that it avoids the justly deserved criticisms which marxists and feminists have raised to the most significant earlier attempt to locate the causes of social life in infantile experience—namely freudian theory.[24] Consider how five fatal problems for freudian theory are not problems for this historical, materialist psychological theory. First, critics object to the freudian claim that certain historically specific characteristics of middle class women and children in nineteenth century Vienna *are* in fact characteristics of all women and children in all societies at all times. In contrast, the theory we are considering explicitly examines how psychological development varies according to the historical, material, social relations of the division of labor by gender—relations which are themselves mediated by economic social relations. There is no reason to assume psychological theories cannot be historically and materially based, whatever the intentions of their creators and whatever the bad examples we have had before us.

Second, critics object to the freudian claim that men, women, and children should be like the expressed ideal in Freud's Vienna. In contrast, our theory supports this criticism and argues that just this sort of unjustifiable normative claim is, in fact, part of the arsenal used to maintain sexism and classism.[25]

Third, critics argue that the focus on psychological life supports a typical strategy of the oppressors, mystifying the real economic sources of human misery and, hence, disarming the forces for revolutionary change. We have already dealt with the narrow, reductionist, and patriarchical tendency to understand causal social relations as only economic relations.

Fourth, critics charge that freudian theory locates social ills in the private domain of the family instead of in the public domain of the economy, and that this, too, is a typical strategy of the oppressors enabling them to avoid dealing with the real sources of human misery. Liberal democratic theory does indeed use the mother as a scapegoat for social ills in many ways, and freudian theory has been useful to it in such projects. Nevertheless, since it is in the family (whatever its form) that individuals get psychologically conscripted into gender systems, class systems, racism, and heterosexism, it is a theory of such conscription which we need to understand the next generation's psychological investment in classism and sexism. Furthermore, the division of labor by gender is itself understood to be supported in part by ongoing relations of class, race, heterosex, and gender oppression in economic and public life more generally. Thus the family is not in this theory an isolated cause of social ills but, instead, the intergenerational conduit for interests in reproducing them. The family is the location of the processes whereby it is insured that this generation's interests in class, gender, race, and obligatory heterosexuality will be inherited by the next generation. The assumption that there is a clear division between public issues and private issues, or that causal influences are all from the former domain to the latter, is an assumption that reductionist and sexist marxism has uncritically inherited from liberal thought.

Fifth, it has been correctly charged that freudian theory has a built in class and ethnocentric bias in its focus on nuclear families. Generally only the middle class—and not even all the middle class —is reared in such families. Upper class children have little contact with such a family and are often nursed by people they are very clearly not supposed to become: southerners are reared by black mammies; upper class children elsewhere are reared by lower class nurses. Poor children are often reared in fatherless families and in family groupings containing many other people besides parents and siblings. (And what about the role of the siblings?) And, in other societies, family is defined in many different ways. But in contrast, the trouble making division of labor which the infant experiences should be understood as involving not a nuclear family, but socially devalued women doing the infant childcare where men control public life. The caretakers need not be biological mothers. There need not be only one such woman (the kibbutz nurseries and the nurseries of China, Cuba, and the Soviet Union are still staffed entirely by women).[26] And the early identification between mother and child need not be as strong as in stereotypical nuclear families in order to create the sufficient conditions for the production and reproduction of dominance interests. The important thing to keep in mind is that there have never been children raised anywhere, as far as we know, where even one of the two crucial division of labor features is entirely lacking. Women are devalued everywhere in some way or other, and women perform the primary infant caretaking everywhere and consequently are the gender to interact physically and emotionally with the psychologically birthing social person. We can get a lot of variation in family style—all the variation in human history, in fact—and still have these two factors constant.

A third virtue of this radical solution is that it sets for us a number of fruitful new research questions. One set of these questions asks what, in historical fact, are the variations in the division of labor by gender as experienced by infants? What difference in adult personalities does such variation make? For instance, what differences are correlated with being nurtured by several women instead of just one? What differences are correlated with cases where men have significant emotional and physical interaction with the infant? What personality differences are correlated with being nurtured by women of a different class from the infant's? A second set of questions focuses on the differences in personality formation correlated with variation in other social relations into which the person enters after the age of three. What other social relations—economic or other—offset or support early personality formations? What social institutions offer resistance to gender categories? For instance, how do homosexual communities and communities where men share early infant care decrease the connections between gender and personhood in the adults and children living in these communities? A third set of questions not entirely separate from the first two, focuses on variations in the expression of gender-based personalities. What are the favored expressions of patriarchy, of class society, of other mind/body dualities in a society, and how are these related to variations in the division of labor by gender as experienced by infants and as countered or supported by other mediating social relations?

Finally, the radical solution directs our attention to the importance of discovering new political practices. Our division of labor by gender must be ended if the domination relations structuring capital and patriarchy are to be eliminated. And we must learn how to do this wisely—a difficult task. What is clear is that the new practices must offer resistance to the coincidence of gender and personhood if we are to transform ourselves individually and collectively. An autonomous women's movement, resistance to the public institutional practices supporting gender categories (often through support of race, class, and heterosex forms of gender), alternative forms of infant care, lesbian communities—these are in fact emerging as they must. The role of men in history will depend on the extent to which individual men are willing to initiate and participate in gender-resisting *practices*. Men may have more to lose than their chains, but they can also gain the opportunity to participate as equals—as humans—in shaping a more liberating human history.

CONCLUSION

Hartmann states that women have an important role to play in the struggle against patriarchy and capital and that this role has been both misunderstood and minimized by the various varieties of marxist feminists. However, I have argued that Hartmann herself tends to underestimate the significance of women's role in revolutionary struggle. She seems to settle for what remains, ultimately, merely utopian categories within which to understand the partnership between capital and patriarchy which the more progressive union of socialism and feminism is to counter. Once the roots of this partnership are correctly understood as a pact between genetic siblings, we can see that women can not expect men to liberate anyone from class oppression either as long as stereotypically masculine and feminine personalities are produced and reproduced as they evidently are under the present division of labor by gender. Thus women must take the lead not only in the struggle against patriarchy, but also in the struggle against the underlying interests men have in controlling both patriarchy and capital and in perpetuating dominating relations through various kinds of oppressive relations with others. We are at the moment in history when women must seize the lead in creating a theory and practice which are truly scientific in that they are more comprehensively historical and materialist. Women are now the revolutionary group in history.

FOOTNOTES

1. Earlier versions and later parts of this paper have been presented at the joint meeting of the Radical Caucus of the American Philosophical Association and the Society for Women in Philosophy, Washington, D.C., December 1978, at the symposium on Feminism and the Philosophy of Science, Houston, January 1979, and at the Research on Women Seminar at the University of Delaware, April 1979. I have been working for over two years on joint projects on the topic of this paper and on related topics with Nancy Hartsock and Jane Flax. I owe them an incalculable debt for helping me to understand both the need for an autonomous feminist theory and how we might begin to construct it. I have indicated specific points I owe to them throughout the essay, but my debt to them is much greater than these specific points. Some of Flax's recent work is listed in the following note. Two of Hartsock's published essays are "Fundamental Feminism: Process and Perspective," in *Quest: A Feminist Quarterly* II (Fall, 1975), and "Feminist Theory and the Development of Revolutionary Strategy," in Zillah Eisenstein, ed., *Capitalist Patriarchy and the Case for Socialist Feminism* (New York: Monthly Review Press, 1978). Both have larger works in progress. For helpful comments I also thank Alison Jaggar, Leslie Friedman Goldstein, Kathryn Parsons, and Margaret Phelan.

2. Nancy Chodorow, *The Reproduction of Mothering* (Berkeley: University of California Press, 1978); Jane Flax, "The Conflict Between Nurturance and Autonomy in Mother-Daughter Relationships and Within Feminism," *Feminist Studies* 4:2 (1978); "Political Philosophy and the Patriarchal Unconscious: a Psychoanalystic Perspective on Epistemology and Metaphysics," forthcoming in *Dis-Covering Reality*, ed. Sandra Harding and Merrill Hintikka (Dordrecht: Reidel, 1981). These two authors have most clearly developed the feminist implications of the post-freudian object relations psychoanalytic theory of Margaret Mahler, D.W. Winnicott and Harry Guntrip. See Margaret S. Mahler, Fred Pine, and Anni Bergman, *The Psychological Birth of the Human Infant* (New York: Basic Books, 1975); D.W. Winnicott, *The Maturational Processes and the Facilitating Environment* (New York: International Universities Press, 1965); Harry Guntrip, *Personality Structure and Human Interaction* (New York: International Universities Press, 1961). Gayle Rubin's essay, "The Traffic in Women: Notes on the 'Political Economy' of Sex," in Rayna Rapp Reiter, ed., *Toward an Anthropology of Women* (New York: Monthly Review Press, 1975), was available in manuscript for several years before publication and alerted feminist marxists to the possibilities of rethinking what Freud was really describing, unbeknownst to him. Dorothy Dinnerstein's *The Mermaid and the Minotaur: Sexual Arrangements and Human Malaise* (New York: Harper & Row, 1976) does not directly draw on object relations theory, but

arrives at a number of conclusions similar to those of Flax, Chodorow, and Rubin.

3. One such illuminating but ultimately unsatisfactory attempt is Batya Weinbaum's *The Curious Courtship of Women's Liberation and Socialism* (Boston: South End Press, 1978), about which more will be said later.

4. See note 2.

5. Examples of ahistorical, nonmaterialist feminist theories can be found in Shulamith Firestone's *The Dialectic of Sex* (New York: William Morrow and Company, 1979), and in Mary Daly's *Gyn/Ecology: The Metaethics of Radical Feminism* (Boston: Beacon Press, 1978).

6. "Foremothers" of the theory can be found in Simone de Beauvoir's *The Second Sex* (Paris, 1949), and Juliet Mitchell's *Women's Estate* (New York: Random House, 1971).

7. Or alternatively, class alone is not a category within which women's social labor can be adequately understood. Nor, from this perspective, is class alone then a category within which men's social labor can be adequately analyzed.

8. Frederick Engels, "Preface to the First Edition," *The Origin of the Family, Private Property and the State,* edited with an introduction by Eleanor Burke Leacock (New York: International Publishers, 1972), pp. 71-72.

9. Nancy Hartsock pointed out to me that the categories are sex-aware—i.e., sexist. In the different respects indicated above I think they are both sex-blind and sexist, though I am not happy with this terminology. The point I am making is that not only have the economic categories not been applied appropriately to women's labor within the family, but that also economic categories are not the appropriate ones to capture all of the material base of social life. Perhaps it would be better to say that the categories are sexist in two different ways, but I shall retain Hartmann's terms for criticism of their application.

10. Batya Weibaum, like Heidi Hartmann, provides an illuminating and powerful account of the "sex-blindness" (and, in Weinbaum, age-blindness) of the marxist explanatory scheme. She too is peripherally aware that biological animals become distinctive social persons through interaction with others in the historical, material, social conditions of infancy. For instance, she notes that we might reflect "how the formative years of childhood determine the basis for adulthood. Sex role analysis might further refine the analogy: to understand men and women, we must examine the comparative experience of boys and girls." (p. 138.) But she, too, ultimately thinks economic categories adequate for understanding social life if only we more carefully analyze the division of labor by gender and age within the "household" (an economic category) and in the workplace. She shows us who the players really are, but only in the drama of economic relations. And she cannot show us how, *before*

men and women enter economic relations, they are prepared for their parts in the drama. (The book is independently valuable for its picture of how and why feminist struggles have been at certain times welcomed but later hidden and denigrated by socialist movements.)

11. Jane Flax and Nancy Hartsock have both pointed this out.

12. Flax, *op. cit.*

13. I say "appears to be" because what we know about social life historically and cross-culturally has largely been provided by men, and men have real material interests in understanding these phenomena as universal and natural. Feminist scholarship must re-examine and probably rewrite all of our descriptions of social life. The beginnings of this project are evident, for example, in the Reiter volume, *op. cit.*, in *Women, Culture, and Society*, Michelle Zimbalist Rosaldo and Louise Lamphere, ed. (Stanford: Univeristy Press, 1974); in Berenice A. Carroll, ed. *Liberating Women's History* (Urbana: University of Illinois Press, 1976).

14. See Max Horkheimer, "Authority and the Family," in *Critical Theory* (New York: Herder & Herder, 1972), and Frankfurt Institute of Social Research, "The Family," in *Aspects of Sociology* (Boston: Beacon Press, 1972).

15. One place where this sort of criticism of the Frankfurt School can be found is in Chodorow, *op. cit.*, pp. 36-40, and 187-190.

16. Cf. note 2.

17. "Species-wide" since persons, whatever their individual psychological peculiarities, are psychologically distinguishable as a species from termites, apes, and dogs.

18. Dinnerstein, *op. cit.*

19. Cf. William Leiss, *The Domination of Nature* (Boston: Beacon Press, 1972), for an illuminating discussion of the history of this concept from the bible through the industrial revolution and later which stops short, however, at just the point where a theory of gender-based personality differences would pull together his attempts to discover the *psycholgoical* roots of this idea.

20. For what black women have to deal with, and for their perceptions of the problem, see *The Black Scholar* issues of February 1972, March 1978, March/April 1979, and May/June 1979.

21. The phrase is Hartsock's.

22. Eleanor Leacock, in "Women's Status in Egalitarian Society: Implications for Social Evolution," *Current Anthropology* 19:2 (1978), tried to defend Engels by arguing, among other things, that there is nothing inherently oppressive about the division of labor by gender. It is only the *economic* use to which the division has been put in class societies which is oppressive. This kind of claim is plausible only if one succeeds in ignoring the infant's perspective on the division of labor by gender. As the "Comments" following the essay point out, Leacock does not even

succeed in convincing us that there are or were entirely egalitarian societies.

23. Hartsock's phrase.

24. Conversations with Kathryn Parsons lead me to see the importance of explicitly addressing these criticisms.

25. Rubin, *op. cit.*, makes this clear.

26. An illuminating exploration of the consequences of the failure of Czechoslovakian socialists to confront this problem can be found in Hilda Scott's *Does Socialism Liberate Women?* (Boston: Beacon Press, 1974).

CAPITALISM IS AN ADVANCED STAGE OF PATRIARCHY: BUT MARXISM IS NOT FEMINISM

Azizah Al-Hibri

*Azizah Al-Hibri was born
and educated in Lebanon.
She has degrees from the
University of Beirut and the
University of Pennsylvania.
She is currently teaching
philosophy at Texas A&M
while continuing research on
Islam and feminism, and the
origins of civilization and
technology. She is author of
Deontic Logic and co-editor
of Technology and Human
Affairs. She has also written
numerous articles and papers
on feminism as well as
other areas in philosophy.*

INTRODUCTION*

"The Unhappy Marriage of Marxism and Feminism" attempts to expose the interrelations between patriarchy and capitalism but fails in one important respect. It accepts uncritically, and from the outset, the widely-held belief that patriarchy and capitalism, though interrelated, are *conceptually* (or ideologically) independent.

As a result we find Hartmann talking about the partnership between patriarchy and capital; and her task becomes one of revealing the extent of this partnership in our society (Hartmann, p. 19). Unfortunately, such a view of patriarchy and capitalism does not reach the heart of the matter. It also can and does lead to serious consequences. For example, it is as a result of this view that Hartmann can see no *"necessary"* connection between the *changes* in one aspect of production (say, economic), and changes in the other (production of people in a patriarchy), although she sees them as "closely intertwined" (Hartmann, p. 17). This leaves the door wide open for arguments of the following kind: while difficult, it is not altogether impossible for women to be liberated in a capitalist society *qua women*, though not qua workers. For after all, according to Hartmann, it is the superimposition of the patriarchal gender hierarchy on the capitalist hierarchy which instructs the capitalist as "to who fills the empty places" in his hierarchy (Hartmann, p. 24). This superimposition is, according to her essay, the result of the "adaptation" of capital to "the pre-existing forms that perservere in new environments'" i.e., to patriarchy (Hartmann, p. 24). Thus one can argue that if we can finally destroy this lingering form of oppression, i.e., patriarchy, we may end up with a sex-egalitarian capitalist society, or who knows.... maybe a matriarchal one!

---

*I would like to thank Hala Maksoud and Cynthia Gillette for the many valuable discussions I had with them concerning their criticisms of an earlier version of this essay. I would also like to thank the editor of this volume, Lydia Sargent, and Harriette Andreadis for their helpful comments.

In my essay I shall aim at the root of the relationship between patriarchy and capitalism and show that conceptually, *capitalism is an advanced stage of patriarchy*. Given that framework, the assessment of marxism and its relation to feminism, patriarchy, and capitalism emerges with surprising clarity. This I hope would be the basis of a more useful political strategy as well as more realistic expectations. In the latter part of this essay I shall present a case study of the praxis of Lebanese and Palestinian marxist organizations, which documents my claims about the relation between feminism and marxism.

PRELIMINARY THESES

An impressive amount of evidence is available in support of this claim: capitalism is an advanced stage of patriarchy. Only part of it will be selected in this article. The selected data tends to be academic in character. However, similar results to those established here could be arrived at on the basis of common sense and observation.

In developing the argument in support of the above claims, three different theses will be introduced, discussed and used at various stages in the argument. In asserting each thesis as true of the male, it is not being simultaneously denied of the female. That issue is not raised explicitly in this essay. However, it is argued that there is an important difference between the male's experience of his being in the world, and the female's. The argument developed in this essay establishes implicitly that, if true of females, these theses are not true of them either in the same way or to the same degree by virtue of the *specificity* of the female's experience of her being in the world.

Second, it will be noticed that the argument is based mainly on data obtained from western culture. This is a result of the assumption that the readership of this article will be more familiar with such data. But what is being presented here is not an account of the western female-male relationship; rather it is an account, cast in western mold, which provides a structural or symbolic framework for understanding the female-male dialectic of opposites.

Third, the question as to how the present stage of this dialectic can be transcended, is left open. But the framework presented in the essay does not at all foreclose such a possibility. On the contrary, it contains the very elements necessary for such transcendence.

THESIS I: THE MALE DESIRES IMMORTALITY

Aristotle puts it this way, "But we must not follow those who advise us, being men, to think of human things, and, being mortal, of mortal things, but must, so far as we can, make ourselves *immortal*..."[1] (Italics al-Hibri).

Hannah Arendt argues that, "imbedded in a cosmos where everything was immortal, mortality became the hallmark of human existence."[2] She later concludes that, "by their capacity for the immortal deed, by their ability to leave non-perishable traces behind, men, their individual mortality notwithstanding, attain an immortality of their own and prove themselves to be of a 'divine' nature."[3]

Arendt defines immortality as "endurance in time, deathless life on earth...."[4] Put in this way it becomes clearer that men generally desire immortality. Only recently did modern thinkers finally face the psychologically complex issues of death and fear of dying. The promise of an afterlife can also be seen as a way of allaying the anxieties of people about their mortality. This explains to some extent the increased religiosity of people as they approach death. During the Salt II talks, the seriously ill leader of the U.S.S.R., Brezhnev, was heard to say, "*God* will not forgive us if we fail."[5] (Italics al-Hibri)

THESIS II: THE MALE CONSIDERS REPRODUCTION A PATH TO IMMORTALITY

There is an Arabic saying that "he who reproduces does not die." The importance of having children for the male is quite well known. But what we need to keep in mind is that the desire for offspring is directly connected to the desire for *immortality*. Fathers try to live their lives all over again through their sons. In the *Symposium*, Socrates introduces Diotima of Mantineia, a wise and revered woman with whom he had a most interesting dialogue about immortality and love. In that dialogue Diotima argues that "to the mortal creature, generation is a sort of eternity and immortality."[6] For,

the mortal nature is seeking as far as possible to be ever-lasting and immortal: and this is only to be attained in generation, because generation always leaves behind a new existence in the place of the old.[7]

When Socrates shows astonishment at her words, she elaborates adding at one point, "Marvel not then at the love which all men have of their offspring; for that universal love and interest is for the sake of immortality."[8] Later, Socrates concludes his account of Diotima's views saying that he was persuaded of their truth, "and being persuaded of them, I try to persuade others."[9]

One might also remember that the desire for having a son to carry the family's name is one of patriarchy's ways of giving immortality to the great....great grandfather whose name was immortalized through the generations of his male descendants. A woman, of course, rarely immortalizes her own male (or even female) ancestors in our patriarchy. More often, she only gets the chance to participate in immortalizing the male ancestors of her husband. For instance, my family can trace its family tree back several centuries. but all the names on that tree are male. It was a shocking experience to me when I realized that I cannot trace my matrilineage back for more than two generations. Women have been characteristically less obsessed with immortality than men.

THESIS III: THE MALE CONSIDERS PRODUCTION A PATH TO IMMORTALITY

Production can be of words, as in poetry; or of deeds, as in society; or more generally of tools, as in technology. But the key requirement is to produce that which reflects a person's individual talent (or essence), and consequently objectify it in the outer world, giving the producer permanence. This mode of immortalization is seen as superior to that obtained through reproduction. (Perhaps because it can last longer than one's immediate offspring and is not dependent on the wish or ability of others to participate. Hence it needs no mother and is not dependent on the wish or ability of the offspring to procreate). Even Diotima concurs. According to Socrates she wonders, "Who, when he thinks of Homer and Hesiod and other great poets, would not rather have their children than ordinary human ones?"[10] And Arendt too,

> The task and potential greatness of mortals lie in their ability to *produce* things—works and deeds and words,—which would deserve to be and , at least to a degree, are at home in

everlastingness, so that through them mortals could find their place in a cosmos where everything is immortal except themselves.[11](Italics al-Hibri)

Since we are concerned here with the relation of patriarchy to capitalism, let us concentrate at this point on economic production. In discussing labor, Marx makes the following statement:

In my *production* I would have objectified my *individuality*, its *specific character*, and therefore enjoyed not only an individual *manifestation of my life* during the activity, but also when looking at the object I would have the individual pleasure of knowing my personality to be objective, *visible to the senses* and hence a power *beyond all doubt*.[12]

In the *Economic and Philosophic Manuscripts* Marx says,

The object of labor is, therefore, the *objectification of man's species-life*: for he *duplicates himself* not only, as in consciousness, intellectually, but also actively, in reality, and therefore he sees himself in *a world that he has created*.[13] (Double Italics al-Hibri)

For these reasons Marx sees alienated labor as most serious, for it is "activity as suffering, strength as weakness, *begetting as emasculating*."[14] (Italics al-Hibri)

What strikes us in these passages is the recurrence of terminology more befitting the description of reproduction than production. The product is basically seen as the objectification, not only in consciousness, but in the real world of the specific character of the individual; it is duplication, it is creation, and its alienation is *emasculating*. Diotima is quite straightforward about it—for her, the product is also a child, but not a mortal one.

A FEMINIST THEORY ON THE ORIGINS AND DEVELOPMENT OF PATRIARCHY AND (MALE) TECHNOLOGY

Going back to early man, it seems obvious that there were a number of things that the early male had to contend with. But perhaps the most interesting experience for him would have been the female. For, the female was the being in nature most similar to him, and yet quite different. This fact supplied at once two components in their relationship; those of identity and difference. The component of identity between male and female contributed to the centrality of this relationship in the lives of humans. The difference complicated that central relationship.

THE GROUNDS FOR REGARDING THE FEMALE AS AN OTHER

The most obvious difference between the male and the female is the genital difference and related phenomena. One such phenomenon is that females can bleed suddenly and heavily without dying, (perhaps this is the earliest reason for associating women with magic, since few men would have survived such bleeding then.) Another is that the bleeding can stop just as suddenly as it starts. Furthermore, once in a while a woman's body can change in shape and then produce a miniature human being. That human being, is subsequently nourished off the female body and grows to start another full life. Meanwhile, nothing happens to the male body. It does not change, it does not reproduce, it has no nourishment for children even after they are brought into the world by females. In terms of life changes, the male body may have seemed barren and boring. The anthropologist Leo Frobenius quotes an Abyssinian woman commenting on the complexity and richness of the female's body relative to that of a male: "His life and body are always the same. . . .He knows nothing."[15]

Such differences between male and female provide adequate foundations for the male to develop the notion of the female as an Other. Nevertheless, the female Other is not a diffused Other, that is, anything different from Self. Rather, it is a most focused, specific, and special Other, by virtue of the fact that it is another consciousness with a basic underlying similarity. It is thus a complimentary Other; and for this reason it occupies a central position in man's concern with Otherness.

It is reasonable to assume that during early times human knowledge of biological functions was so primitive that the male could have hardly known his role in reproduction. Since intercourse and childbirth (or even visible pregnancy) are separated by such a significant time lag, the development of the notion of causality here could not have been either immediate or simple. Bronislaw Malinowski in *The Sexual Life of Savages* lends credence to the conclusion. Commenting on the beliefs of the Trobrianders concerning conception, he says,

> The primeval woman is always imagined to bear children without the intervention of a husband or of any other male partner; but not without the vagina being opened by some means. In some of the traditions this is mentioned explicitly.

Thus on the island of Vakuta there is a myth which descibes how an ancestress of one of the sub-clans exposed her body to falling rain, and thus mechanically lost her virginity.[16]

This dialogue with a male native of the Trobriand Islands is recounted by Molinowski,

"What, then, is the cause of pregnancy?" he answered: "Blood on the head makes child. The seminal fluid does not make the child. Spirits bring at night time the infant, put on women's heads—it makes blood. Then, after two or three months, when the blood [that is, menstrous blood] does not come out, they know: 'Oh, I am pregnant!'"[17]

Thus, at the dawn of history the male had ample reason to experience the female Other as a substantial ego threat. For, in contradistinction to the male, the female exhibited a greater permanence. Not only did she constantly recover from her bouts with bleeding, but more significantly, she constantly reproduced herself—she had the key to immortality and he did not. The male, then, had cause to experience himself as inferior and more mortal. For this revealed him, by contrast, as excluded and cut off from the cycle of ever-regenerating life. * The male's negative experience of his being in the world might also have been reinforced by the additional fact that the male has always been dependent in his early childhood on the female for his very existence.

It is understandable that under such a state of affairs substantial amounts of alienation and frustration are generated in the male; culminating in feelings of inadequacy, jealousy, or hostility towards the female. Philosophical questions of the sort raised by Plato and Aristotle, may well have found their primitive roots in this situation. The questions facing a male dissatisfied with his being in the world would be of the following sort: "What is my significance?," "What am I good for?," "What is my role in life? my destiny?," "What kind of a being am I?" These same questions were raised again by females thousands of years later, after their alienation and frustration came into being and intensified in an oppressive male culture.

THE MALE'S RESPONSE TO HIS HUMAN CONDITION:
THE EMERGENCE OF PATRIARCHY
AND (MALE) TECHNOLOGY

As a free human being whose essence is defined by his choices and not only by the given, the male had, since early times, the option of setting out to meet this challenge. At least two courses of action were available to him. First, to appropriate the gift of the female and her offspring. This action would integrate him into the cycle of life if only indirectly. Later discoveries concerning the role of the male in conception may have further reinforced this mode of immortalization for him, and prompted the shift of male dominance from the brother and father of the female to her mate or husband. For, the appropriation of offspring would have been given for the first time a biological, or objective justification. The male could then see himself for the first time as appropriating what was already his; his immortalization becoming more direct than ever. Furthermore, this could partly explain why the male has gone to great lengths in minimizing the obvious and substantial contributions of the female to reproduction. He has often described the female as a mere container, an incubator; while he held that his sperm supplied the life principle. If this analysis is correct, then it was not private property, not natural law that made the male appropriate reproduction from the female. Rather, it was his unabashed desire and struggle for immortality in a world that seemed determined to deny it to him.

A second course of action available to the male was that of making himself useful (and later indispensible perhaps). This approach unlike the first was not necessarily based on the notion of domination but could easily be integrated with it. Historically, the most salient male application of this approach may be found in the area of technology, an area which captured specifically the male imagination. Tools that the male produced were useful in simplifying and securing certain processes in life. Thus they were ideal as compensation for a perceived inadequacy. It also gave the male for the first time some feeling of power. As Freud and others were quick to observe ''with every tool man is perfecting his own organs.''[18] The male was no longer helpless; he was no longer stuck with his human condition. Through technology he discovered that he could improve his condition utilizing artificial means of his own creation. Therefore, this technological endeavor was particularly suited to the feelings of inadequacy or hostility in the male. It supplied both the possibility of liberation from his perceived inferiority to the female, and also the possibility of a better more effective foundation for her domination (first approach). But most importantly, in production, the male finally gave concrete expression to his urge for having offspring, i.e. for immortality.

The product as Diotima., Marx, and others reveal, became the child. Production became an imitation of reproduction. The male's minimizing the importance of reproduction in favor of production could be interpreted as the male's way of emphasizing his own significance and of forcing himself deeper into the cycle of life.

Thus, one may conclude that both male technology and patriarchy are based on the male's feeling of inadequacy and mortality vis-a-vis the female, and his desire to transcend his human condition by forcing himself into the cycle of life from which he *perceived* himself to be cut off through no fault of his own.

THE GROUNDS FOR REGARDING NATURE AS AN OTHER

There is another dimension associated with the male's feeling of being cut off from the cycle of life. The male has often observed that the female is somehow at one with the rhythms of the universe, of nature. Her bodily rhythm is attuned to it, and nature like the female reproduces and nourishes its "children." Nature thus became "Mother Nature" and the connection between the female and nature became exaggerated and magical to the human eye. The belief in the affinity of the female to nature was accepted (though to different degrees and in different ways) by both males and females with interesting results. During the very early stages of technology:

> . . . Agriculture was invented by people living within a magical worldview and *by virtue of* that world view. Most likely it was. . . an invention of women, who perceived in the fecundity of seed and soil an image of their own sexuality. From that initial poetic insight the technics of cultivation burgeoned into a splendid variety of sexual-spiritual symbols. The new agrarian cultures saw the earth as a mothering womb, the seed and rain as sperm, the crops as a bearing of offspring.[19]

But it is perhaps this view of nature as female that finally led to the male's attempt at extending his domination to nature itself. The category of female Other was enlarged to engulf nature as well. For it too had the gift of immortality, of reproduction, and mothering. On Nature too the male was dependent, and against it his feelings of inadequacy were confirmed. Thus while initially nature like woman was dreaded and respected, it later became, like the female, the target of male domination and hostility through male technology. Tools, which were initially produced for constructive purposes, became agents of subordination and destruction for both woman and nature. Man had tasted power and immortality through domination and production. He had defied woman and nature; and domination through production seemed to have paid off.

THE FEMALE RESPONSE AND HER GRADUAL EXCLUSION FROM POWER

It is reasonable to believe that the female did not keep up with this technological twist of events for two reasons. First, her experience of the world was substantially different from that of the male. She was planted deeply into the cycle of life and the womb of nature. Thus she had no reason to feel cut off, frustrated, or shortchanged. Her anxiety about mortality, if there, was not exaggerated by those feelings. So she had good reason to relate to the world in a more relaxed fashion. For example, she had no reason to be driven to produce, although she did produce. (Note that later she was driven by patriarchy to reproduce in order to retain her social position, etc. and that came to be interpreted as an expression of the "mother instinct"!) Nor did her production need to be (initially at least) tainted by hostility and frustration. It was instead oriented primarily towards improving the quality of life (agriculture, for example) and not towards enhancing her powers of domination. With the male's concentration on the latter orientation, a male power-base was gradually formed with no effective parallel female opposition. Secondly, the male who understood the extent of power conferred upon him by technology, understandably denied woman access to his technology. Thus while patriarchy served male efforts in denying the female access to technology, technology was used by the male to reinforce patriarchy. We may also note that technology provided an answer to the male's original philosophical questions. For he had found a function that characterized his contribution (or function) in life. While women reproduced, men produced (and that, the male said, was more important). This was a balance of division of labor that the male could live with. It would hardly have been acceptable for him if women reproduced and also produced, while men only produced. Hence to preserve the fragile male ego it became desirable, among other things, to exclude women from production (housework notwithstanding).

THE ROLE OF RELIGION

It is important at this point to note that man's attempt to gain immortality through production did not go totally unquestioned in the course of history. As Arendt points out,

> The fall of the Roman Empire plainly demonstrated that no work of mortal hands can be immortal, and it was ac-companied by the rise of the Christian gospel of an everlasting individual life to its position as the exclusive religion of Western mankind.[20]

Various historical events served to reveal the inadequacy of the male's attempt for gaining immortality through pro-duction. Together, they made two facts quite clear: (1) as Arendt observed, the products fabricated by males, themselves disintegrated in time; and (2) even when these products temporarily escaped the onslaught of time, they ended up immortalizing either themselves or someone other than the producers. More often than not, the individual identity and life story of the producers was lost.

Religion provided a timely solution to this crisis. If man behaved in accordance with certain laws and upheld certain values, he could gain, not immortality but better yet, an ever-lasting life in heaven. But again such a solution would not do if women were equally capable of gaining everlasting life. For then again, women would have the possibility for both immor-tality and everlasting life; while men would have the possibil-ity of the latter only. This problem was solved along similar lines as those used in the realm of production. God was de-clared male, and man was declared created in his likeness. Eve became the symbol of temptation and sin; and woman was consequently judged a less likely candidate for salvation and everlasting life in heaven than man. Mary Daly summar-izes these and related developments as follows:

> The infamous passages of the Old Testaments are well known. I need not allude to the misogynism of the church Fathers—for example, Tertullian, who informed women in general: "You are the devil's gateway," or Augustine, who opined that women are not made to the image of God. I can omit reference to Thomas Aquinas and his

numerous commentators and disciples who defined women as misbegotten males. I can overlook Martin
Luther's remark that God created Adam lord over all living creatures but Eve spoiled it all. I can pass over the
fact that John Knox composed a "First Blast of the Trum-
pet against the Monstrous Regiment of Women." All of
this, after all, is past history.[21]

One result of the substitution of the goal of everlasting
life for that of immortality is that technological activity, during this period, slackened considerably and became a
secondary concern. St. Augustine, for example, argued that
the ideal state of affairs was one where the person attended
chiefly to the development of his comtemplative knowledge
(of eternal things) while at the same time directing his reason
to the good use of material things "without which this life
cannot go on."[22] Clearly then, during St. Augustine's days,
society had become sufficiently dependent on technology and
its artifacts as to be unable to do away with them without
substantially threatening the quality of life; but they no
longer occupied a central position in society.

One problem with religion's promise of everlasting life
was that it could not be substantiated. The promise had to be
accepted on faith. Slowly, man started exhibiting restless-
ness about entrusting such a major concern to the unknown.
At the same time, accumulated scientific theories in the
West continued to present ever stronger reasons to doubt
the biblical accounts of creation and of man himself. The
Copernican   revolution,   the   Newtonian   revolution,   the
Darwinian revolution, and later psychoanalysis, all of these
inflicted deep wounds on the male ego.[23] They also shook his
faith in religion.

THE WILL TO POWER

A process of secularization began. The otherworldly restraints on technological progress and on human behavior
weakened steadily. Finally, Nietzsche proclaimed that "God
is dead."[24] With the proclaimed death of God the crisis was
deepened. For now, man found himself alone in the world.
Walter Kaufmann summarizes Nietzsche's reaction to this
new situation as follows:

...Nietzsche concluded that if we renounce supernatural religions and accept a scientific approach to man,
we lose the right to attribute to man as such a unique
supernatural dignity. Such dignity is not...a fact but a
goal that few approach. There is no meaning in life
except the meaning man gives his life, and the aims of
most men have no surpassing dignity. To raise ourselves
above the senseless flux, we must cease being merely
human, all-too-human. We must be hard against
ourselves and overcome ourselves; we must become
creators instead of remaining mere creatures.[25]

Nietzsche called the man who is hard against himself, who
overcomes his passions and transcends his limitations in order to
become creative "the *Übermensch*." The *Übermensch* is the man
who rejects the Christian slave-morality characterized by humility,
meekness, and charity, and goes beyond himself by overcoming
certain things in himself. But Nietzsche does not elaborate on what
is to be overcome. As a result, the concept of the *Übermensch* was
left wide open for interpretation in accordance with the needs of
the times. For example, Nietzsche's sister assured Hitler that he
was what her brother had in mind when he spoke of the
Übermensch.[26] Similarly, Nietzsche's concept of the Will to Power
was interpreted as a drive for domination characteristic of the
Übermensch.[27] Thus, it is indicative of the changing values of these
times that the *Übermensch* was taken to be exemplified by
someone whose desire for power was not restrained by any ethical
considerations including those of Christian morality. For, as
Dostoyevsky said, with God dead everything became permissible.

This interpretation of Nietzsche's philosophy was a modern
response to man's new situation. For, with the proclaimed death of
God, modern man in Western society found himself thrown into a
world he did not choose, and deprived of a right he thought was
his; the right given to him in Genesis, namely that of dominion
over nature. Furthermore, his hopes for either immortality or
everlasting life were dashed by his assessment of the accumulated
historical evidence. So he set out to cope with his anguish and
solitude by taking his life into his own hands. This is one
significance of the *Übermensch* myth. The other one is that in the
absence of diety, all restraints on one's power were removed. So
when modern man in Western society set out to re-establish his
dominion over earth on a new foundation, he did not shrink from

turning his undisguised power against other men whom he regarded as inferior adversaries.

OPPRESSIVE IDEOLOGIES ARE ESSENTIALLY PATRIARCHAL

As we saw earlier, the concept of the female Other was enlarged to engulf nature as well. Throughout history, various developments in male ideologies continued to enlarge this concept further. For example, with the ascent of religious ideology, the concept was enlarged again to engulf "heathens" and "sinners." But with the emergence of the modern ideology of unrestrained domination, the category of the Other was suddenly enlarged enormously, setting the stage for important historical developments. The new expanded category of the Other now contained all sorts of "others"; woman, nature, black, red, Jew, Arab, native, etc. . . . . The original patriarchal principle of domination was now finally extended to virtually all *men* as well. These extensions made possible new forms of relations among groups of people. For example, the concepts of feudalism, colonialism, capitalism and imperialism are all based on the expanded version of the patriarchal principle of domination. Each one of these concepts (which we do well to regard as abstract tools), involves the extension of man's domination to other men. In feudalism the lord dominated the peasant, in colonialism the invader dominated the natives, in capitalism the capitalist dominated the worker, and finally in imperialism (defined by Lenin as the highest stage of capitalism) the capitalist dominated the natives.[28]

These concepts, as they appeared in their historical order, seem to indicate contrary to our argument a movement towards increased freedom (not domination) of man. But at this point it is helpful to remember Hegel's famous master-slave dialectic.

According to Hegel, in the *Phenomenology*, when two individuals meet, two self-consciousnesses, each trying to reaffirm the certainty of itself as true being, come face to face.[29] The subsequent actions are devoted to eliciting recognition from the Other. To that end, a struggle follows in which each attempts to cancel the Other. Thus they embark on a struggle till death. But this approach for achieving recognition fails because a dead person cannot give recognition. So now a new kind of struggle is substituted which is hoped to be more satisfactory: the struggle to enslave the Other, i.e. to "cancel him dialectically." A consciousness is cancelled dialectically when it negates its own independence and subordinates its own desires to another. The recognized party becomes the lord at this point, the Other becomes the slave. But this again does not work! For what the lord has achieved is the recognition of a slave, not a free Other, and that is not good enough.

A third and more advanced stage in this struggle for recognition is described by Sartre in his discussion of traditional love. In this discussion, it is suggested that the lover wishes the beloved to choose freely to subordinate his/her own freedom to the freedom of the lover.[30] He points out that the lover does not want to possess an automaton, rather he wants to possess a freedom as freedom. He wants to be loved by a freedom which wills its own captivity.[31] How is that to be achieved? Sartre answers:

> I manifest by my acts infinitely varied examples of my *power over the world* (money, position, "connections," etc.)...I must capture [the Other's freedom] by making it recognize itself as *nothingness* in the face of my *plentitude of absolute being*.[32] (Italics and bracketed phrase author's.)

But this stage, though seemingly more egalitarian than the previous one, is still based on the principle of domination. For what is being sought at this stage remains the subjugation of the Other. Furthermore, if we are to take seriously the examples given above of "my power over the world (money, position, 'connections,' etc. . .)," then we may conclude that despite its apparent egalitarianism this kind of relationship favors the subjugation of the female. For the oppressed female in our society is hardly in a position to match male achievements, let alone to lure the male with her own. Nor is she in a position to reject at will males who possess such instances of power, without regretting the consequences. Surely, she is not without her traditional weapons, but these, as various feminists have pointed out, only serve to perpetuate her oppression. Thus Shulamith Firestone concludes, "It is not the process of love itself that is at fault, but its political, i.e., unequal power context: the who, why, when and where of it that makes it now such a holocaust."[33] This mode of relations can of course be generalized to cover nonlove relations even among males themselves, for example boss-employee, etc.

The three stages presented above can be viewed as covering different eras in human history: the first describes relations in the primitive stage; the second describes those of feudalism and colonialism, while the last describes those of capitalism and imperialism.

What this means is that the change from feudalism and colonialism to capitalism and imperialism, just like the abandonment of primitive societies, is not the result of increasing respect for the freedom of others. On the contrary, it is a movement dictated partially by the male's dissatisfaction with the result of the modes of domination (of the expanded female-nature-male Other). In each case technology plays a major part in determining the form of the next stage of human relations. For example, the first industrial revolution made it possible for feudalism to fade into capitalism. But this is only one more instance of technology serving patriarchy and vice versa. Underlying the entirety of this movement is the male's severe feelings of inadequacy, and hence his need for recognition and affirmation of self-worth. Since the solution to such feelings of inadequacy can never come from the outside, the male is doomed to continue experimenting with different modes of domination until the roots of the problem are finally recognized and faced. The male has to come to terms with his own being.

This means that marxism is a step beyond the third stage in achieving this recognition. For the third stage itself fails because the male realizes that the female, who has been excluded from the economic and political sphere, is not choosing freely when she chooses him. Similarly, the newer stage will fail for a simple reason. Why would any being choose to subordinate her/his freedom to any Other, if she/he is truly free? One may choose to admire, support, cooperate with another, but that is different and hardly suffices to silence the fears of inadequacy in the male.

But there is also another mover of history whose power has been limited at certain times, powerful at others. It is the subordinated Other: the slave, the worker, the woman. In Egypt, in the Middle Ages, the slaves rose and established their own kingdom, the Mamluk kingdom (''mamluk'' means literally ''possessed by another,'' i.e. slave, in Arabic). Recently, workers became a major political force in history. Women are in the process of developing such power. This means that the oppressor must seriously address himself to the desires and wishes of the oppressed, as much as he might hate it, or risk losing control (the Shah of Iran chose to ignore this rule and paid for it). Thus some of the movement in history is the result of the force exerted by the oppressed (who have their own reasons for revolting, some of which may be related to a desire to have their own base of power and domination) and not only the reflection of the dissatisfaction of the oppressor with the quality or extent of his domination.

THE PROPER PLACE OF MARXISM IN THE DIALECTICAL MOVEMENT OF HISTORY

This means that one must not overlook the positive aspect of the historical movement from capitalism to marxism. A major force behind the change lies in the worker's rejection of his oppression, a rejection which can itself cancel the oppressor altogether (assassinate, depose, or exile him). Thus marxism can be seen partly as a positive response to the exploitation of capitalism. For under capitalism the oppressive male repeats an earlier pattern of oppression against the female. But the target of this new oppression is also the worker (traditionally, this has meant the male, i.e., the worker outside the home). What happens here is that the capitalist (and in a different way, the feudal lord too), appropriates the labor and product of the worker. To put it differently, he appropriates the male's child just as he has previously appropriated the female's. For by doing so he accumulates power indirectly through the efforts of others. This is supposed to enhance his feelings of adequacy and contribute towards his desired immortality (witness the Johnson Library, the Rockefeller Foundation, IBM, etc.).

Marxism is the system through which the worker reappropriates his labor and product, thus liberating himself from the control of the capitalist. From this vantage point, marxism becomes the struggle for liberating man from the capitalist exploitation by man. That is, it is in principle, an attempt to limit or remove the male's capitalist exploitation of other males. It is an attempt to shrink the ever-enlarging category of the Other. This means that for the first time in history we are seeing an attempt to contain the continuous expansion of the principles of domination in patriarchy. As such, it is clearly a step forward in the struggle against patriarchy in that it will liberate some men, but it is hardly the whole struggle.

Marxists are aware of the conceptual affinity of the struggle of females and minorities to their struggle. Thus, they have given these struggles some attention in their analysis. This may help females gain a foothold in a male world in order to wage the next stage of struggle, but that is all. Marxism will not liberate women simply because marxists are (generally) not feminists; they are not out to question the patriarchal principle of domination itself; but only some aspects of it. This dynamic becomes clearer when we look at the practice of certain marxist organizations *vis-a-vis* women.

A HISTORICAL SKETCH: THE STATUS OF ARAB WOMEN BEFORE AND AFTER ISLAM

Prior to the birth of Prophet Mohammad (570 A.D.), and the subsequent spread of Islam, the Arabs lived in what came to be known later as the era of *Jahiliya*, meaning ignorance. In those days, Arab women were more possessed of self-determination, even with respect to issues concerning sexuality, than they are today. For example,

> The women in Jahiliya, or some of them, had the right to dismiss their husbands, and the form of dismissal was this: if they lived in a tent, they turned it around so that if the door faced East, it now faced West, and when the man saw this, he knew that he was dismissed, and he did not enter.[34]

Also, it was not uncommon for women to initiate or break off sexual unions with men; or to be married to several men either simultaneously or successively.

Physical paternity was generally considered unimportant, and society exhibited substantial matrilineal as well as matrilocal trends. Two kinds of marriage were common: the *sadica* marriage, and the *ba'al* or dominion marriage. The first exhibited a matrilineal trend, the second a patrilineal one. The two kinds of marriage existed side by side until the dawn of Islam. Fatima Mernissa in *Beyond the Veil*, comments on those two forms:

> Sadica marriage (from sadic, ''friend,'' and sadica, ''female friend'') is a union whose offspring belong to the woman's tribe. It is initiated by a mutual agreement between a woman and a man and takes place at the house of the woman, who retains the right to dismiss the husband. In ba'al marriage the offspring belong to the husband. He has the status of a father as well as that of his wife's ba'al, i.e., ''lord,'' ''owner.''[35]

In Islam, *sadica* marriages were outlawed as a form of adultery, and certain forms of ba'al dominion marriages were reinforced. Physical paternity became most important, with patrilineage replacing matrilineage. Inheritance laws were introduced that favored sons over daughters. In short, Islam provided patriarchy with a solid religious foundation.

ISLAM'S VIEW OF WOMEN

The attitudes of women toward Islam during its early days were varied. Some women were very enthusiastic towards the new religion and actively participated in it. Some even asked the prophet in marriage (although at least one of them, Leila Bint Al Khatim, changed her mind when it became clear to her that she could not tolerate the role of a wife in a polygamous household). On the other hand, other women were quite hostile towards the prophet, and even celebrated his death by dyeing their hands with henna, and playing the tambourine.[36]

Perhaps part of the explanation for this wide disparity of female attitudes towards Islam lies in the fact that Islam, while providing a firm foundation for patriarchy in the Arab society, outlawed patriarchy's most vicious forms, and retained some positive views of women. For example, female infanticide was practiced in certain tribes, but the practice stopped after Islam. Such a practice, together with the presence of *sadica* as well as dominion marriages in *Jahiliya*, indicates that society was living under transitional conditions of ideological and social tension. The role of Islam was to resolve this tension by working out a patriarchal compromise which retained for women some of their earlier status, but legitimized the male's right of dominion. Thus, insofar as it was a compromise, Islam, unlike Christianity for example, did not assert the inherent inferiority of women.[37] Also, it portrayed them, not as passive, but rather as active and powerful agents. But insofar as Islam was a patriarchal compromise, it regarded women as dangerous beings, precisely because they were seen as active and powerful. (Muslim women are especially feared because of their potential sexual power over men.) As Mernissi puts it,

> In Western culture, sexual inequality is based on belief in women's biological inferiority . . . in Islam there is no such belief in female inferiority. On the contrary, the whole system is based on the assumption that the woman is a powerful and dangerous being. All sexual institutions (polygamy, repudiation, sexual segregation, etc.) can be perceived as a strategy for *containing her power.*[38] (Italics author's)

This underlies the basic differences in the struggle for liberation between Western and Arab women. Arab women, who are predominantly Muslim, are generally very conscious of their ample potential for equality with men; and hence of the basis of their oppression as explicitly political, social and religious, but not biological.

For example, when I was a child I spent a lot of time reading books and asking questions. My grandfather, who was the absolute patriarch of my extended family until he passed away (and perhaps later as well), was observing me closely. He was a well-known religious leader who adhered very closely to the tenets of Islam. One day he seated me near him in the living room, as he did with important guests, and told me that he had been following my interests, and that he believed strongly that my intellectual abilities were quite promising. He mentioned that he was an old man, and that I was quite young. Nevertheless, he added, he was going to tell me two things that I should keep in mind until I got older. He said, "you will not understand them now because you are too young; but remember them, and when you grow up you will understand them." Then he gave me two brief lectures on a mystical interpretation of religion, and on the problem of colonialism and imperialism in the Arab World. I was extremely pleased with his words and so was my father. But neither of us found it unusual that my grandfather held such a conversation with a granddaughter instead of a grandson. For Islam does not hold that women are inherently inferior or that they have inferior capabilities. On the contrary, women can be as capable as men, and that is why certain modes of restraining became necessary in Muslim patriarchy. Thus, it was this same grandfather who, a few years later, insisted that all his granddaughters, including myself, cover their hair and flesh in public.

But it was not until my college years in the American University of Beirut, and later in the United States, that I came to see my capabilities questioned *because* I was a woman. Coming from my background I found such questioning not only puzzling but quite disconcerting. It just did not make any sense. Furthermore, in the Western context of my education, the traditional Muslim modes for restraining women did not make any sense either. Thus, I developed a feminist consciousness before I even heard of the movement; my own history necessitated it.

THE NEGATIVE IMPACT OF WESTERNIZATION

The Arab male, on the other hand, experienced the Western

cultural impact quite differently from the female. While the females saw in Western culture some glimpses of what a traditionally unrestrained life would be like, the male saw in it a reaffirmation of the truth of male dominance in society. Hence, although the Arab male rejected being dominated by a Western power, he was ultimately open to integrating the Western version of male dominance into his traditional set of beliefs. As a result, the modern Arab is infected with the Western view that women are inherently inferior, while he retains at the same time much of the traditional restraints on her power. This fact may often be disguised by the Arab male's need to project publicly a modern image of himself, a need quite common in developing countries. But in actual practice, and especially in his private life, the Arab male continues to exhibit freely this new blend of female oppression.

Thus, although modernization regained for the Arab woman some of her long lost rights, it did so for a very high price. It eroded further her status in society by pronouncing her as inherently inferior, while maintaining most of the vestiges of the traditional modes of oppression. After centuries of lack of self-determination, modernization came to compound that problem and deny Muslim women any possibility of self-respect. This partly explains the impatience of some Muslim women with modernity, and their call for adherence to the religious order (witness events in the Muslim, but not Arab, country of Iran).

THE MARXIST ORGANIZATIONS

It is within this historical context that the activities of Lebanese and Palestinian marxist organizations in Lebanon, can best be understood and evaluated. These organizations continue to exhibit an attitude of oppressive modernity *vis-a-vis* the female. For sure, the liberation of the female was on the agenda, but what kind of liberation? An angry female Palestinian poet, May Sayegh, comments,

> The PLO Charter talks of the equality of men and women and the elevation [tarqia] of women's role in the revolution. Elevation! Even the word (tarqia) is wrong and suggests that they're going to teach her to play the piano or do watercolors or something equally ''elevating''! In fact neither equality nor elevation have been brought about and there is no single organized program to implement.[39] (bracketed word added)

The marxist notions of primary and secondary contradictions have often been used to silence such complaints within these organizations. It is argued that the primary contradiction is that between the Lebanese and Palestinian people on the one hand, and the forces of imperialism, including its local agents, on the other.

It is then argued that the female-male contradiction within the organizations specifically, and the society as a whole, is a secondary contradiction which should not be exploded until the primary contradiction is resolved. Thus to raise feminist criticisms and demands within these organizations is often seen as divisive, bourgeois, and irresponsible. Meanwhile, women are expected to endure and sacrifice silently. A similar situation arose during the Algerian war of liberation, and the Palestinian women are well aware of the fact that as soon as the Algerian war ended, the women were back in the homes. Thus, Palestinian women continue raising the issue of woman's liberation despite males' attempts to dissuade them.

Another argument often used to tone down women's demands for change within organizations is that the milieu in which the organizations operate is predominantly Muslim and conservative. To challenge its values would weaken popular support for the movement. For example, when the Marxist Democratic Popular Front for the Liberation of Palestine (DPFLP), ignored this milieu in Jordan several years ago, and established training camps where men and women lived in the same camps, the Jordanians in the area were appalled and the organization lost substantial amounts of support.

Indeed, the conservative milieu in which these organizations operate has caused resistance (except in cases of extreme duress) not only to such moves as housing males and females in the same training camps, but to the very participation of females in training. Um Samir, a female Palestinian, describes her own experience:

> After the battle of Karameh in March 1968, I joined Fateh and received military training. I spent the battles of 1970 at a military base, sleeping there—at that stage families didn't protest against this. But before it was different. I remember once I returned home after 10 days at a base, stinking, filthy, longing only for a bath and a change of clothes, and my father gave me the most awful scolding. "Where have you been? In America or what? What do you think you are? What do you think *we* are?" And so on and so on. He used to shout at me but other fathers beat their daughters, locked them up and even

threatened to kill them, so I was lucky. But when the fighting
was on in September all the girls used to sleep away from home
because it was too dangerous to come home every night, so
their families had to accept it.[40]

Clearly, the values of the milieu can be modified and
changed. Nevertheless, even if we were to accept the need to avoid
challenging the values of the milieu at a certain stage, there is no
reason for us to accept sexist values within the marxist organizations themselves. At most, the argument presented above can be
used to temper certain feminist demands involving the public
behavior of, and relations among, cadres. It cannot be used to
exempt their internal organizational relations from scrutiny. To
illustrate this point concretely, let us examine some of the relations
within these organizations.

In a booklet published by the General Union of Palestinian
women, Khadija Abu Ali, a Palestinian woman, questions women
from the various Palestinian organizations, marxist and otherwise,
about female-male relationships within their organizations.[41] It
turns out that in all these organizations, the male continues to
relate to the female along traditional lines, and that women in
these organizations have often suffered from damaging rumors
spread by their male comrades about their personal lives. For this
reason, the women point out, many commandos keep their wives
and sisters from joining their organizations.

I know of a case where a leading member of a marxist Palestinian organization met his future wife as she trained in that same
organization. He married her and made her quit. I met them both
one evening and questioned them about her quitting. He
answered every point I raised that evening, but he never gave her a
chance to say a word.

This problem also exists in Lebanese marxist organizations. In
one case, it took women cadre over a year to convince their comrades to publish in the party's weekly publication an article about
the rights of the female. In another case, a marxist husband continued advancing within the ranks of the party, while his wife got
stuck with the housework.

''Abir,'' a Palestinian woman, sums up the situation this way:

Men are my comrades but deep down they don't believe I'm
really their equal. Socially we haven't caught up with our political development—we're all walking on an advanced political
leg and dragging a backward social leg behind, impeded and

crippled. I'm 36 and I haven't yet met a man who has really shaken off the conventions about women. I feel that an Arab woman has to marry if she wants to live in society. We can't live freely on our own; even my brother, who's a revolutionary wouldn't and couldn't accept my being involved with a man, so in this social situation you are forced to marry if you want to relax and be happy. One can't live with someone in secret and if you do it openly everybody else changes in their relations toward you. And the leaders are hypocritical about it all. At public meetings they talk about liberating women but they really believe, and some of them say it openly, that a woman does her revolutionary duty by ironing her husband's shirts, cooking his dinner and providing a cosy and restful ambiance for the warrior.[42]

An additional barrier to the liberation of Lebanese and Palestinian women is indeed the present warlike situation. This situation is a barrier, not because it militates that women defer their struggle, but for a much more fundamental reason.

Faced with the daily possibility of his death, the male's desire for immortality becomes highly exaggerated. As a result, the male attempts to immortalize himself not only through words and deeds, but also through procreation. This general fact holds true in the Lebanese-Palestinian arena. Witness for example the high birthrate in the Palestinian camps. As May Sayegh put it, "there is no birth control program in the camps because women want to replace the heavy Palestinian losses."[43] In other words, reproduction has been elevated to the status of a national duty of women. But contrary to May Sayegh's claim, it does not seem at all clear that it is the women who want all these children. Fahimeh, another Palestinian woman, says,

> We once tried to do something about birth control—got films from the U.N. family planning office and a woman doctor to give explanations. Some of the women agreed that they were worn out—"God damn all these children"—but most were frightened that the pill would harm them or that *their husbands would change toward them*.[44] (Italics al-Hibri)

The conclusion here is that the marxist organizations in Lebanon are merely paying lip service to the feminist cause. Although they have contributed to breaking the old modes of oppression in the home for many women, they seem to have done so only in cases coinciding with organizational interests. In other cases, the so-called primary contradiction, or else the husband (as the case may be), takes precedence.

The failure of the Lebanese and Palestinian marxist organizations to adopt the goals of the feminist revolution is not at all accidental. For one, there does not exist yet within these organizations an adequate foundation of feminist theory that would necessitate such an adoption and inform the practices of the cadres. Furthermore, these organizations are predominantly male in membership and leadership (females have been repeatedly discouraged by the practices within these organizations; however, some are still trying). As males they have a vested and ancient interest in the preservation of some form of patriarchy.

I do not see a feminist revolution sweeping these organizations in the near future. For conditions under which males feel that their own survival is at stake tend to stiffen their attitudes in favor of patriarchy. Alternately, the conditions under which feminism blossoms are those of peace and security. Perhaps this is a basic reason for women's aversion to war.

CONCLUSION

Strategically, then, the struggle against capitalism, racism, imperialism and any other product of man's attempt at domination of the Other must be based on an understanding of their basic patriarchal nature, and must therefore be regarded as part and parcel of the feminist struggle. This understanding provides a firm and clear basis for supporting socialist, nationalist and other liberation movements around the world despite their frequent antifeminist practices. For they are merely patriarchy devouring itself, weakening itself. Placed within the proper feminist strategy, these movements could usher in the beginning of the gradual defeat of the male principle of dominance.

Furthermore, this understanding supplies the basis for healing the rift that has appeared repeatedly in the feminist movement between Western women and women of the so-called Third World.[45] During the meetings of the 1980 *Non Governmental Organizations Forum* which met in Copenhagen in conjunction with the World Conference of the U.N. Decade for Women, many women from Western countries repeatedly criticized women of the Third World for shortchanging ''true feminists'' by insisting on bringing up the political problems infecting the Third World today, for example, occupation, war, torture, the role of multinational corporations, and so on. This led "The Third World Caucus of the 1980 NGO Forum" to "call for a women's conference representing only our nations whose struggles, hopes and problems differ substantially from those of the West."[46] The fact of the matter is that despite the uneven development of the feminist struggle around the world, the political problems of the Third World are essentially patriarchal and must therefore be actively embraced as part of the international feminist struggle. Such a stance would immediately diffuse Third World suspicions of the feminist movement as the passtime of bored white females, or worse yet as an imperialist attempt at dividing the ranks of the oppressed in the Third World itself. This can only serve in advancing the cause of feminism there, and strengthening international feminist unity.

Finally, the theory outlined in this article provides a solid basis for formulating strategic as well as tactical feminist policies for dissipating male control. Like our oppression, the feminist liberation of humanity will also happen gradually and will entail our neutralizations of the male's tools of oppression, and of the male's deep-seated hostility towards the female. This turns out to be a crucial but most dangerous process in which one of the highest risks we could run is that of succumbing to the male logic of power struggle. However, a total renunciation of power tactics is also quite unrealistic. This makes the task of feminist liberation a highly complicated as well as a highly sophisticated task.

FOOTNOTES

1. Aristotle, *Nicomachean Ethics*, 1177b 31; in *The Works of Aristotle*, trans. and ed. by W.D. Ross (London: Oxford University Press, 1944), Vol. 9.
2. Hannah Arendt, *The Human Condition* (Chicago: The University of Chicago Press, 1969), p. 18.
3. *Ibid.*, p. 19.
4. *Ibid.*, p. 18.
5. *Time*, 25 June 1979, p. 15.
6. Plato, *Dialogues*, trans. B. Jowett, ed. J.D. Kaplan (New York: Pocket Books, 1951), p. 212.
7. *Ibid.*, p. 213.

8. *Ibid.*, p. 213.

9. *Ibid.*, p. 219.

10. *Ibid.*, p. 215.

11. Arendt, p. 19.

12. Karl Marx and Frederick Engels, *Collected Works* (New York: International Publishers, 1975), Vol. 3, p. 227.

13. *Ibid.*, p. 277.

14. *Ibid.*, p. 275.

15. Adrienne Rich, *Of Woman Born* (New York: W.W. Norton, 1976), p. 126.

16. Bronislaw Malinowski, *The Sexual Life of Savages* (New York: Harcourt, Brace & World, 1929), p. 182.

17. *Ibid*, p. 188.

18. Sigmund Freud, *Civilization and Its Discontents*, trans. and ed. by James Strachey (New York: W.W. Norton, 1961), p. 37.

19. Theodore Roszak, *Where the Wasteland Ends* (New York: Doubleday & Co., 1972), pp. 373-4.

20. Arendt, p. 21.

21. Mary Daly, *Beyond God the Father* (Boston: Beacon Press, 1973), p. 3.

22. Frederick Copleston, S. J., *History of Philosophy* (New York: Image Books, 1962), Vol. 2, part 1, p. 73.

23. See similar remarks made by Sigmund Freud, *Collected Papers*, ed. J. Riviere and J. Strachey (New York: The International Psycho-Analytical Press, 1924-50), Vol. 4, pp. 351-55.

24. Friedrich Nietzsche, *Thus Spake Zarathustra* (New York: Macmillan, 1914), p. 6.

25. Walter Kaufmann, "Nietzsche, Friedrich," *Encyclopedia of Philosophy*, p. 512.

26. Friedrich Nietzsche, *Beyond Good and Evil*, trans. Walter Kaufmann (New York: Vintage Books, 1966), p. 198.

27. For more on this see *Nietzsche as Philosopher*, by Arthur Danto (New York: Macmillan Co., 1965), esp. pp. 214-232.

28. V.I. Lenin, *Essential Works*, ed. Henry Christman (New York: Bantam Books, 1966), pp. 177-270.

29. G.W.F. Hegel, *The Phenomenology of Mind*, trans. J.B. Baillie (New York: Harper's Torchbooks, 1967), pp. 229-35.

30. J.P. Sartre, *Being and Nothingness*, trans. Hazel E. Barnes (New York: The Citadel Press, 1968), pp. 342-3.

31. *Ibid.*, p. 343.

32. *Ibid.*, p. 348.

33. Shulamith Firestone, *The Dialectic of Sex* (New York: Bantam Books, 1971), pp. 132-3.

34. Fatima Mernissi, *Beyond the Veil* (New York: John Wiley and Sons,

1975), p. 35.

35. *Ibid.*, p. 34.

36. *Ibid.*, p. 32.

37. For more on this see my introduction to Part II on th history of technology in *Technology and Human Affairs*, which I co-edited (St. Louis: C.V. Mosby, forthcoming).

38. Mernissi, p. xvi.

39. Soraya Antonius, "Fighting on Two Fronts: Conversations with Palestinian Women," *Journal of Palestine Studies,* Vol. 8, no. 3, Spring 1978, p. 30.

40. *Ibid.*, p. 38.

41. Kadija Abu Ali, *Muqaddamat Hawl Waqi' al Mar'ah Wa Tajribatha Fith-Thourat-el-Falastiniah*. Published by the General Union of Palestinian Women, 1977. (The study was conducted for the period 1967-1971.)

42. Antonius, pp. 39-40.

43. *Ibid.*, p. 31.

44. *Ibid.*, p. 43.

45. The Third World Caucus of the 1980 NGO Forum stated that, "We reject totally the designation 'Third World' or 'Developing Countries,' as expressing a Western point of view regarding the achievements of our people." The full text of the statement was published in the daily *Forum* paper, *Forum 80*, Copenhagen, 25 July 1980, p. 5.

46. *Ibid.*, p. 5.

MARXISM AND FEMINISM: UNHAPPY MARRIAGE, TRIAL SEPARATION OR SOMETHING ELSE?

Lise Vogel

Lise Vogel has been active in the women's liberation movement and in the left for more than fifteen years. She has just completed a manuscript, Beyond Domestic Labor: Women's Oppression and the Reproduction of Labor Power, from which her contribution to this volume has been adapted. She currently lives in New York City, and teaches in the department of sociology at Nassau Community College.

In 1975 the first version of "The Unhappy Marriage of Marxism and Feminism" began to circulate within the socialist-feminist wing of the North American women's movement. Both the essay's title and its argument found an enthusiastic welcome, setting the terms of a discussion that continues today. The authors at that time, Heidi Hartmann and Amy Bridges, had grasped the current mood of the socialist feminist movement and put it into words. In the wake of the events and activism of the late sixties and early seventies, socialist feminists were growing increasingly skeptical that socialist theory and practice could be transformed to accord with their vision of women's liberation. Along with Hartmann and Bridges, many had come to the conclusion that "the 'marriage' of marxism and feminism has been like the marriage of husband and wife depicted in English common law: marxism and feminism are one, and that one is marxism." And they agreed, furthermore, with the paper's strategic imperative that "either we need a healthier marriage or we need a divorce" (Hartmann, p. 2).

The imagery used by Hartmann and Bridges in the earlier essay has since been elaborated. Later versions of the paper added a hopeful subtitle: "Towards a More Progressive Union." Others have informally embellished the sexual metaphor of a marriage between marxism and feminism. In place of an unhappy marriage they offer a string of humorous, if faintly bitter, alternatives: Illicit tryst? Teenage infatuation? May-December romance? Puppy love? Blind passion? Platonic relationship? Barren alliance? Marriage of convenience? Shotgun wedding? and so on. As the title of this essay indicates, one might describe the relationship not so much as an unhappy marriage as, in some sense, a trial separation. That is, to the extent that marxism and feminism are distinct entities, whose union may result in conflict as well as mutual support and healthy offspring, the socialist feminist movement has generally maintained them in a state of trial separation. At bottom, however, the image of a marriage between autonomous persons, each with his or her own identity, is inadequate theoretically to the task of representing the relationship between marxism and feminism. Here, I would agree with Rosalind Petchesky's suggestion that the goal is, rather, to "dissolve the hyphen" between marxism and feminism, and with Joan Kelly's projection of a "doubled vision" that will enable us to achieve a unified social outlook.[1]

The following pages trace the development of socialist feminist theoretical work over the past fifteen years in order to assess its contributions, to point to certain persistent weakness, and to evaluate socialist feminist usage of marxist theory. My discussion of the socialist feminist literature constitutes an implicit critique of Hartmann's analysis of its insufficiency. Hartmann's pessimism rests on a conviction that marxism must inevitably remain sex-blind, and that therefore it cannot produce an adequate understanding of women's situation. Hartmann suggests, furthermore, that socialist feminists have generally subordinated their feminism to their marxism, and consequently have been unable to move beyond marxism's presumed limitations. In opposition to Hartmann's reasoning, I would maintain that the problem is neither with the narrowness of marxist theory nor with socialist feminists' lack of political independence. Rather, socialist feminists have worked with a conception of marxism that is itself inadequate and largely economistic. At the same time, they have remained relatively unaware of recent developments in marxist theory, and of its potential application to the question of women's oppression. This state of isolation is, however, coming to a close, and socialist feminists are once again affirming their commitment to marxism as the theoretical foundation for socialist practice in the area of women's liberation.

In our critique of the socialist feminist literature, Hartmann and I agree on many points. In my view, however, the problem at issue is not the quality of some marriage between marxism and feminism, but the state of marxism itself. As Hartmann observes, "many marxists are satisfied with the traditional marxist analysis of the woman question. They see class as the correct framework with which to understand women's position. Women should be understood as part of the working class; the working class's struggle against capitalism should take precedence over any conflict between men and women. Sex conflict must not be allowed to interfere with class solidarity (Hartmann, p. 31). Like Hartmann, I strongly reject such assumptions as to the adequacy of marxist work on the so-called woman question, for they deny the specificity of women's oppression and subordinate it to an economistic view of the development of history. Unlike Hartmann, I hold that the problem of women's oppression, like all social phenomena, can be addressed within the terms of marxist theory. We do not need some new synthesis between marxism or socialism, and feminism. Rather, it is marxist theory itself that must be developed, and socialist practice that must be transformed.

MITCHELL AND THE STRUCTURES OF WOMEN'S OPPRESSION

Initial efforts to develop a socialist feminist theoretical perspective focused on the family unit and the labor of housework in contemporary capitalist societies. The opening argument, an article on "Women: The Longest Revolution," by Juliet Mitchell, actually appeared well before the development of the socialist feminist movement proper. First printed in 1966 in *New Left Review*, a British marxist journal, Mitchell's piece began to circulate widely in the United States two years later. It rapidly became a major theoretical influence on the emerging socialist feminist trend within the women's liberation movement. The 1971 publication of Mitchell's book, *Woman's Estate,* based on the earlier article, reinforced its impact.

Mitchell begins "Women: The Longest Revolution" with what was, at the time, the first intelligent critique of the classical marxist literature on the question of women. As an alternative, she presents a theoretical framework that places women within four structures: production, reproduction, socialization, and sexuality. Each structure, she claims, develops separately and requires its own analysis; together, they form the "complex unity" of woman's position. Mitchell then surveys the current state of the structures. Production, reproduction, and socialization show little dynamism, she says, and indeed have not for years. The structure of sexuality, by contrast, is currently undergoing severe strain, and constitutes the weak link—the structure most vulnerable to immediate attack.

While one structure may be the weak link, Mitchell notes that socialist strategy will have to confront all four structures in the long run. Furthermore, "economic demands are still primary" in the last instance. In this context, Mitchell makes a number of sensitive strategic observations about socialist practice on the so-called woman question. In place of abstract programs, she concludes, the socialist movement requires a practical set of demands which will address the four structures of woman's position.[2]

Questions about Mitchell's analysis of women's situation arise in several areas. First, the discussion of the empirical state of the separate structures is extremely weak, a failure that has, or should have, consequences in the realm of strategy. To maintain that "production, reproduction, and socialization are all more or less stationary in the West today in that they have not changed for three or more decades" grossly misrepresents not only postwar history but the evolution of twentieth century capitalism. Moreover, as Mitchell herself sometimes recognizes, the contradictions produced by rapid movement in all four of her structures form the very context for the emergence of the women's liberation movement.

A second problem in Mitchell's analysis is her treatment of the family. While she mentions the family at every point, Mitchell denies the category "family" any explicit theoretical presence. Its place is taken by the triptych of structures that make up the woman's world: reproduction, socialization, and sexuality. At the same time, the actual content of these structures has an arbitrary quality, and Mitchell fails to establish clear lines of demarcation among them. Women are seen as imprisoned in their "confinement to a monolithic condensation of functions in a unity—the family," but that unity has itself no articulated analytical existence. Similarly, production functions as an aspect of experience essentially external to women, even in the domestic sphere. Here, Mitchell once again misreads history. Furthermore, she persistently devalues women's work, and accords it no clear theoretical status.

Finally, Mitchell's manner of establishing a structural framework to analyze the question of women requires critical examination. The four structures that make up the "complex unity" of woman's position operate at a level of abstraction that renders social analysis almost impossible. They provide a universal grid on which women—and, implicitly, the family—can be located irrespective of mode of production or class position. Rather than central determinants, societal variation and class struggle appear, if at all, only as afterthoughts. Furthermore, the manner in which the four structures combine to produce a complex unity remains largely unspecified, as well as abstract and ahistorical. As a result, Mitchell's theoretical approach resembles the functionalism of bourgeois social science, which posits quite similar models of complex interaction among variables. Oddly enough, the content of her four structures also derives from functionalist hypotheses, specifically, those of G.P. Murdock. Despite her staunchly marxist intentions, then, Mitchell's theoretical perspective proves inadequate to sustain her analysis.[3]

Even with its problems, easier to recognize at a distance of more than ten years, Mitchell's 1966 article played an extremely positive role within the developing socialist feminist movement. Its differentiation of the content of women's lives into constituent categories helped women's liberationists to articulate their experience and begin to act on it. Its perceptive overview of the classical marxist literature on women provided a base from which to confront both dogmatic versions of marxism and the growing influence of radical feminism. Its insistence, within a marxist framework, on the critical importance of social phenomena not easily characterized as economic anticipated the socialist feminist critique of economic determinism. And the political intelligence of its specific strategic comments set a standard which remains a model. Theoretically, Mitchell's central contribution was to legitimate a perspective that recognizes the ultimate primacy of the economic level, yet allows for the fact that other aspects of women's situation not only have importance but may play key roles at certain junctures.

BENSTON, MORTON, AND DALLA COSTA: A MATERIALIST FOUNDATION

By 1969, the North American women's liberation movement had reached a high point of activity, its militance complemented by a flourishing literature, published and unpublished. In this atmosphere, two Canadians, Margaret Benston and Peggy Morton, circulated and then published important essays. Each piece offered an analysis in marxist terms of the nature of women's unpaid work within the family household and discussed its relationship to existing social contradictions and the possibilities for change.[4]

Benston starts from the problem of specifying the root of women's secondary status in capitalist society. She maintains that this root is "economic" or "material," and can be located in women's unpaid domestic labor. Women undertake a great deal of economic activity—they cook meals, sew buttons on garments, do laundry, care for children, and so forth—but the products and services which result from this work are consumed directly and never reach the marketplace. That is, these products and services have use-value but no exchange-value. For Benston, then, women stand in a definite relationship to the means of production, distinct from that of men. Women constitute the "group of people which is responsible for the production of simple use-values in those articles associated with the home and family." Hence, the family is an economic unit whose primary function is not consumption, as was generally held at the time by feminists, but production. "The family should be seen primarily as a production unit for housework and child-rearing." Moreover, because women's unpaid domestic labor is technologically primitive and outside the money economy, Benston argues that each family household represents an essentially preindustrial and precapitalist entity. While noting that women also participate in wage labor, she regards such production as transient and not central to women's definition as a group. It is women's responsibility for domestic work which provides the material basis for their oppression and enables the capitalist economy to treat them as a massive reserve army of labor. Equal access to jobs outside the home will remain a woefully insufficient precondition for women's liberation if domestic labor continues private and technologically backward. Benston's strategic suggestions therefore center on the need to provide a more important precondition by converting work now done in the home into public production—the socialization of housework and childcare. In this way, she revives a traditional socialist theme, not as dogma but as forceful argument made in the context of a developing discussion within the contemporary women's movement.

Peggy Morton's article, published a year after Benston's, deepened as well as sharpened the analysis of the family as an economic unit in capitalist society. For Morton, Benston's discussion of unpaid household labor as the material basis for women's oppression leaves open a number of questions: Do women form a class? Should women be organized only through their work in the household? How and why has the nature of the family as an economic institution in capitalist society changed? Morton proposes a more precise definition of the family: It is the economic unit whose function is the maintenance and reproduction of labor power—meaning the labor power of the working class. In this way, she ties the argument more closely to the workings of the capitalist mode of production, and focuses on the contradictions experienced by working class women within the family, in the labor force, and between the two roles. In particular, she suggests that as members of the reserve army of labor, women are central, not peripheral, to the economy, for they make possible the functioning of those manufacturing, service, and state sectors where low wages are a priority. While the strategic outlook in the several versions of Morton's paper bears only a loose relationship to its analysis, and fluctuates from workers' control to revolutionary cadre-building, her discussion of the contradictory tendencies in women's situation introduces a dynamic element that had been missing from Benston's approach.

Both Benston's and Morton's articles have a certain simplicity that even at the time invited critique. In the bright glare of hindsight, their grasp of marxist theory and their ability to develop an argument appear painfully limited. Benston's facile dismissal of women's participation in wage labor requires correction, as Morton and others quickly pointed out. Moreover, her delineation of women's domestic labor as a remnant from precapitalist modes of production, which has somehow survived into the capitalist present, cannot be sustained theoretically.[5] Morton's position, while analytically more precise, glosses over the question of the special oppression of all women as a group, and threatens to convert the issue of women's oppression into a purely working class concern. None of these problems should obscure, however, the theoretical advances made by Benston and Morton. Taken together, their two articles established the material character of women's unpaid domestic labor in the family household as an object of theoretical interest. Each offered an analysis of the way this labor functioned as the material basis for the host of contradictions in women's experience in capitalist society. Morton, in addition, formulated the issues in terms of a concept of the reproduction of labor power, and emphasized the specific nature of contradictions within the working class. These theoretical insights had a lasting impact on subsequent socialist feminist work, and remain an important contribution. Moreover, they definitively shifted the framework in which discussion of women's oppression had to be located. Where Mitchell had analyzed women's situation in terms of roles, functions, and structures, Benston and Morton focused on the issue of women's unpaid labor in the household and its relationship to the reproduction of labor power. In this sense, they rooted the question of women in the theoretical terrain of materialism.

Mariarosa Dalla Costa, writing from Italy less than two years later, took the argument several steps further.[6] Agreeing that women constitute a distinct group whose oppression is based on the material character of unpaid household labor, she maintains that on a world level, all women are housewives. Whether or not a woman works outside the home, "it is precisely what is particular to domestic work, not only measured as number of hours and nature of work, but as quality of life and quality of relationships which it generates, that determines a woman's place wherever she is and to whichever class she belongs." At the same time, Dalla Costa concentrates her attention on the working class housewife, whom she sees as indispensable to capitalist production.

As housewives, working class women find themselves excluded from socialized production, isolated in routines of domestic labor which have the technological character of precapitalist labor processes. Dalla Costa disputes the notion that these housewives are mere suppliers of use-values in the home, and therefore supposedly external to the workings of capitalism and to the class struggle. Polemicizing against both traditional left views and the literature of the women's movement, she argues that housework only appears to be a personal service outside the arena of capitalist production. In reality, it produces not just use-values for direct consumption in the family, but the commodity labor power. Moreover, housework produces surplus-value, and housewives are therefore "productive workers" in the strict marxist sense. Appropriation of this surplus value is organized by the capitalist's payment of a wage to the working class husband, who thereby becomes the instrument of woman's exploitation. The survival of the working class depends on the working class family, "but *at the woman's expense against the class itself.* The woman is the slave of a wage slave, and her slavery ensures the slavery of her man. . . . And that is why the struggle of the woman of the working class against the family is crucial." Because working class housewives are productive laborers who are peculiarly excluded from socialized production, demystification of domestic work as a "masked form of productive labor" becomes a major strategic task.

The polemical energy and political range of Dalla Costa's article had a substantial impact on the women's movement on both sides of the Atlantic. Unlike Benston, Morton, and other North American activists, Dalla Costa seemed to have a sophisticated grasp of marxist theory and politics. Her arguments and strategic proposals struck a responsive chord in a movement already committed to viewing women's oppression mainly in terms of their family situation. Few noticed that Dalla Costa, like Morton, talked only of the working class, and never specified the relationship between the oppression of working class housewives and that of *all* women. What was most important was that Dalla Costa, even more than Benston and Morton, seemed to have situated the question of women's oppression within an analysis of the role of their unpaid domestic labor in the reproduction of capitalist social relations. Moreover, since her article functioned as the theoretical foundation for a small but aggressive movement to demand wages for housework, which flourished briefly in the early 1970s, it acquired an overtly political role denied to most women's liberation theoretical efforts.[7]

THE DOMESTIC LABOR DEBATE

Dalla Costa's vigorous insistence that ''housework as work is *productive* in the Marxian sense, that is, is producing surplus value'' intensified a controversy already simmering within the socialist feminist movement. The debate revolved around the theoretical status of women's unpaid domestic labor and its product. Published contributions took the form of rather intricate and dry elaborations of marxist theory, usually printed in British or North American left journals. With some justification, many in the women's movement soon regarded this ''domestic labor debate'' as an obscure exercise in marxist pedantry. Yet critical issues were at stake, even if they usually went unrecognized. In the first place, the discussion deepened Benston's insight that housework is a material activity which results in a product, and offered several distinct interpretations of the theoretical character of that activity and product. Second, serious political issues haunted the debate. Each theoretical position corresponded, more or less closely, to definite political and strategic views of the relationship of women's oppression to class exploitation and to the evolution of revolutionary struggle. Unfortunately, protagonists in the debate rarely stated these implications clearly, with the result that the domestic labor debate remained, for most activists, irrelevant.

Finally, and perhaps most significant, the debate's reliance on categories drawn from *Capital* suggested a confidence that the material basis for women's oppression could be analyzed within the framework of Marx's economic writings. Those socialist feminists who rejected the terms in which the domestic labor debate proceeded, or who saw it as an interesting but peripheral footnote to the development of a theory of women's situation, challenged this confidence. Implicitly or explicitly, they therefore took on the task of proposing an alternative framework utilizing new and better theoretical categories. As Hartmann later put it, "If we think marxism alone inadequate, and radical feminism itself insufficient, then we need to develop new categories" (Hartmann, p. 29).

The substance of the domestic labor debate involved three related questions, not always adequately distinguished: What does unpaid domestic labor in the household produce? Is domestic labor productive, unproductive, or something else? What is the wage and what does it pay for? In general, the problem of how the commodity labor-power gets "produced" in capitalist society lay at the heart of the debate. Differences arose around the precise meaning and application of marxist categories in carrying out an analysis of this problem.

Ten years after the domestic debate began, certain questions appear to be settled. As it turns out, it is relatively easy to demonstrate theoretically that domestic labor in capitalist societies does not take the social form of value-producing labor.[8] Benston's original insight that domestic labor produces use-values for direct consumption had been essentially correct. In the scientific sense, then, domestic labor cannot be either productive or unproductive, and women are not exploited. At the same time, domestic labor is indispensible for the reproduction of capitalist social relations. Just what domestic labor is, rather than what it is not, remained a problem only superficially addressed by participants in the domestic labor debate. Some suggested it constitutes a separate mode of production, outside the capitalist mode of production but subordinate to it. Others implied domestic labor is simply a special form of work within the capitalist mode of production. Most left the question unanswered. The problem of specifying the character of domestic labor, and issues concerning the wage and women's wage work, now represent the central concerns of most theorists working with traditional marxist categories. As for politics and strategy, few today would fall into the economic determinist error of using their analyses of the material foundation for women's oppression to draw easy conclusions about the role of women in revolutionary struggle.

Benston, Morton, Dalla Costa, and the participants in the domestic labor debate set an important agenda for the study of women's position as housewives and the role of domestic labor in the reproduction of social relations. Their work proceeded, however, within certain limits, not always clearly circumscribed. In the first place, they focused mainly on the capitalist mode of production. Second, they concentrated almost exclusively on domestic labor and women's oppression in the working class. Third, they generally restricted their analysis to the economic level. Fourth, they tended to identify domestic labor with housework and childcare, leaving the status of child-bearing undefined. These various limitations might have been defended on theoretical grounds, but they rarely were. In any case, socialist feminists began to study a number of other questions which required consideration. For example, the domestic labor debate shed little light on the problem of whether housework is analytically the same in different classes within capitalist society, and even less on the theoretical status of domestic labor in noncapitalist societies. Socialist feminists also turned their attention to the child-bearing and child-rearing components of domestic labor, and investigated the problem of why domestic labor falls generally to women. Since women's oppression is not specific to capitalist societies, furthermore, many wondered how to reconcile its particular contemporary character with the fact that women have been subordinated for thousands of years. Similarly, they asked whether women are liberated in socialist countries, and if not, what obstacles hold them back. Finally, the relationship between the material processes of domestic labor and the range of phenomena which make up women's oppression, especially those of an ideological and psychological nature, became a key issue. In general, these questions spoke more directly to the experience and political tasks of activists in the women's movement, and they quickly advanced to the center of socialist feminist theorizing.

PATRIARCHY AND THE MODE OF REPRODUCTION

While Juliet Mitchell had advised that "we should ask the feminist questions, but try to come up with some Marxist answers," by the early 1970s, many socialist feminists disagreed.[9]

They argued that the quest for marxist answers to their questions led down a blind alley, where the feminist struggle becomes submerged in the socialist struggle against capitalism. To move forward, then, socialist feminism had to construct new theoretical categories.

At first, socialist feminists turned to the radical feminism of the late sixties for concepts that could account for the depth and pervasiveness of women's oppression in all societies. Radical feminists typically considered the struggle between the sexes to be universal, and indeed, the essential dynamic underlying all social development. At the same time, some radical feminist writings seemed to be extensions or deepenings of the insights offered by Marx and Engels. Shulamith Firestone's *The Dialectic of Sex*, for instance, claimed to go beyond the merely economic level addressed by Marx and Engels, in order to uncover the much larger problem of sex oppression. "The class analysis is a beautiful piece of work," Firestone wrote, "but limited." In proposing a dialectic of sex, she hoped ''to take the class analysis one step further to its roots in the biological division of the sexes. We have not thrown out the insights of the socialists; on the contrary, radical feminism can enlarge their analysis, granting it an even deeper basis in objective conditions and thereby explaining many of its insolubles." Similarly, Kate Millett's *Sexual Politics* acknowledged Engels as a major theorist of what she called the sexual revolution. Her presentation of Engels' work transformed it almost beyond recognition, however, into a contribution to her understanding of patriarchy. Marxist theory nevertheless "failed to supply a sufficient ideological base for a sexual revolution, and was remarkably naive as to the historical and psychological strength of patriarchy." In broad strokes, Millett depicted Nazi Germany, the Soviet Union, and freudian psychology as comparable instances of reactionary patriarchal policy and ideology, arguing that patriarchy will survive so long as psychic structures remain untouched by social programs. For Millett, the sexual revolution requires not only an understanding of sexual politics but the development of a comprehensive theory of patriarchy.[10]

Firestone's and Millett's books, both published in 1970, had a tremendous impact on the emerging socialist feminist trend within the women's movement. Their focus on sexuality, psychological phenomena, and on the stubborn persistence of social practices oppressive to women struck a responsive chord. The concept of patriarchy entered socialist feminist discourse virtually without objection. Those few critiques framed within a more orthodox marxist perspective, such as Juliet Mitchell's, went unheard. Although acknowledging the limitations of radical feminism, many socialist feminists, particularly in the United States, simply assumed that "the synthesis of radical feminism and marxist analysis is a necessary first step in formulating a cohesive socialist feminist political theory, one that does not merely add together these two theories of power but sees them as interrelated through the sexual division of labor."[11] No longer was the problem one of using marxist categories to build a theoretical framework for the analysis of women's oppression. Like the radical feminists, these socialist feminists took marxism more or less as a given, and did not seek to elaborate or deepen it. The trial separation of marxism and feminism had begun in earnest.

In their effort to accomplish the socialist feminist synthesis, socialist feminists explored two related themes: patriarchy, and the mode of reproduction. The concept of patriarchy, taken over from radical feminism, required appropriate transformation. Millett had used the term to indicate a universal system of political, economic, ideological, and, above all, psychological structures through which men subordinate women. Socialist feminists had to develop a definition of patriarchy capable of linkage with the theory of class struggle, which posits each mode of production as a specific system of structures through which one class exploits and subordinates another. In general, socialist feminists agreed with Hartmann's formulation that "marxist categories, like capital itself, are sex-blind," while "categories of patriarchy as used by radical feminists are blind to history" (Hartmann, p. 2). Obviously, they concluded, the next step would be to "integrate the insights of radical feminism and marxism" by means of a transformed concept of patriarchy, thereby capturing the social phenomena that somehow escape marxist categories. Some suggested that the theory of patriarchy could explain why certain individuals, men as well as women, are in particular subordinate or dominant places within the social structure of a given society. Others believed that issues of interpersonal dominance and subordination could best be addressed by a theory of patriarchy. Although socialist feminists often focused on the psychological aspects of these hierarchical relations, they argued that patriarchy is not just an ideological superstructure. "Patriarchal authority," wrote Sheila Rowbotham, " is based on male control over the woman's productive capacity, and over her person." That is, patriarchy has a material foundation in men's ability to control women's labor, access to resources, and sexuality. Through these formulations, socialist feminist theory began to extend what was actually a traditional marxist understanding of patriarchy as a form of household labor organization and property control, in order to encompass the sex division of labor. The origin of sex divisions of labor, and the relationship between patriarchal structures and the workings of a given mode of production continue to be key problems for socialist feminist theorists.[12] The precise nature of the autonomy which socialist feminists claim for patriarchy also remains to be specified. In this connection, some socialist feminists have begun to focus on a new concept, the mode of reproduction— comparable to, but relatively autonomous from, the mode of mode of production which characterizes a given society.

As with the concept of patriarchy, there is little agreement on the substance of the mode of reproduction. Some simply identify the mode of reproduction with what appears to be the obvious functions of the family. Despite the empiricism of this approach, it clarifies the conceptual tasks which socialist feminists confront. In Renate Bridenthal's words, "the relationship between production and reproduction is a dialectic within a larger historical dialectic. That is, changes in the mode of production give rise to changes in the mode of reproduction," and this dialectic must be analyzed. Similarly, some participants in the domestic labor debate have postulated the existence of a "housework mode of production" alongside the capitalist mode of production, but subordinate to it. The socialist feminist concept of a mode of reproduction converges, moreover, with recent suggestions by marxist anthropologists that the contemporary family, as well as some primitive domestic community, acts as a perpetual source of human labor power. An analogous concept of the mode of reproduction is often implicit in the work of socialist feminists who study the relationship between imperialism and the family in dependent third world countries.[13]

The concept of a mode of reproduction seems to offer a way to incorporate the notion of patriarchy into a more rigorous marxist framework. Indeed, a quite similar concept of an autonomous, family-based mode of production—"simple commodity production''—has a long history within marxist studies of social development.[14] Largely in ignorance of this history, socialist feminists have partially recreated it. At the same time, the effort to delineate the mode of reproduction as an explanation of women's oppression, and of the relationship between family and society, has brought socialist feminist theory closer to current developments in marxism. And it has made it more difficult to view marxism as a rigid body of dogma brutally overwhelming the vital force of feminism in an unhappy marriage.

TOWARDS A UNITARY THEORY OF WOMEN'S OPPRESSION

In reviewing the theoretical work produced in the context of the socialist feminist movement, certain major themes and leading ideas stand out. Taken together, they indicate the important contribution made by socialist feminism to the development of theory on the question of women. Simultaneously, they suggest some of its limitations.

Socialist feminist theory starts from a correct insistence that behind the serious social, psychological, and ideological phenomena of women's oppression lies a material root. It points out that marxism has never adequately analyzed the nature and location of that root. And it hypothesizes that the family constitutes a major if not the major terrain which nourishes it. With this position, socialist feminism implicitly rejects two fallacious, as well as contradictory, currents in the legacy of socialist theory and practice on the woman question. First, the socialist feminist emphasis on the material root of oppression counters an idealist tendency within the left, which trivializes the woman question as a mere matter of lack of rights and ideological chauvinism. Second, socialist feminists' special concern with psychological and ideological issues, especially those arising within the family, stands opposed to the crudities of economic determinist views of women's oppression. These perspectives—implicitly summed up in the slogan "the personal is political"—establish guidelines for the socialist feminist consideration of women's oppression and women's liberation. Through them, socialist feminism returns, wittingly or not, to the best of Marx and Engels on the woman question. At the same time, it promises to take that work beyond its still very rudimentary form.

Socialist feminists recognize the inadequacies as well as the contributions of Engels' discussion of the family and property relations in the *Origins of the Family, Private Property and the State*. Like Engels, they locate the oppression of women within the dynamic of social development, but they seek to establish a more dialectical phenomenon as its basis than Engels was able to identify. Such a phenomenon must satisfy several implicit criteria. It must be a material process which is specific to a particular mode of production. Its identification should nevertheless suggest why women are oppressed in all class societies—or, for some socialist feminists, in all known societies. Most important, it must offer a better understanding of women's oppression in subordinate as well as ruling classes than does Engels' critique of property. Socialist feminist analyses share the view that child-bearing, child-raising, and housework fit these criteria, although they offer a wide variety of theoretical interpretations of the relationship between these activities and women's oppression.

Some socialist feminists try to situate domestic labor within broader concepts covering the processes of maintenance and reproduction of labor power. They suggest that these processes have a material character, and that they take place, furthermore, *within*—not outside of— social production. For elaboration of this position, which shifts the immediate focus away from women's oppression per se, and on to wider social phenomena, they turn to Marx's economic writings, and especially to *Capital*. At the same time, they resist, as best they can, the contradictory pulls of economic determinism and idealism inherited from the socialist tradition.

The relationship between the capitalist wage and the household it supports represents yet another major theme. Socialist feminists point out that marxism has never been clear on the question of who the wage covers. The concept of the historical subsistence level of wages refers, at times, to individuals, and at other times, to the worker "and his family." Sensitivity to this ambiguity has inspired a series of attempts to reformulate and answer questions concerning divisions of labor according to sex in both the family and wage labor. While some such efforts stress concepts of authority and patriarchy, others focus on questions involving the determination of wage levels, competition in the labor market, and the structure of the industrial reserve army. Whatever the approach, the identification of the problem in itself constitutes a significant theoretical step forward.

Socialist feminist theory also emphasizes that women in capitalist society have a double relation to wage labor, as both paid and unpaid workers. It generally regards women's activity as consumers and unpaid domestic laborers as the dominant factor shaping every woman's consciousness, whether or not she participates in wage labor. From this position flows an important strategic conclusion. Socialist feminists maintain, against some opinions on the left, that women can be successfully organized and they point to the long history of militant activity by women in the labor movement, in communities, and in social revolution. They observe, however, that mobilization demands a special sensitivity to women's experience as women, and they quite properly assert the legitimacy and importance of organizations comprised of women only. Socialist feminist theory takes on the political task of developing a framework to guide such organizing efforts.

Finally, socialist feminist theory links its theoretical outlook to a passage from Engels' Preface to the *Origin*:[15]

> According to the materialistic conception, the determining factor in history is, in the final instance, the production and reproduction of immediate life. This, again, is of a twofold character: on the one side, the production of the means of existence, of food, clothing and shelter and the tools necessary for that production; on the other side, the production of human beings themselves, the propagation of the species. The social organization under which the people of a particular historical epoch and a particular country live is determined by both kinds of production: by the stage of development of labor on the one hand and of the family on the other.

The citation of these sentences, repeated in article after article, accomplishes a number of purposes. It affirms the socialist feminist commitment to the marxist tradition. It suggests that Marx and Engels had more to say about the question of women than the later socialist movement was able to hear. It seems to situate the problem of women's oppression in the context of a theory of general social reproduction. It emphasizes the material essence of the social processes for which women hold major responsibility. And it implies that the production of human beings constitutes a process which has not only an autonomous character, but a theoretical weight equal to that of the production of the means of existence. In short, Engels' remarks appear to offer authoritative backing for the socialist feminist focus on the family, sex divisions of labor, and unpaid domestic work, for its strategic commitment to the autonomous organization of women, and for its theoretical dualism. Yet, the passage actually reflects Engels at his theoretical weakest.[16] Socialist feminist insights into the role of women in social reproduction need a more solid basis.

Despite the strengths, richness, and real contributions of socialist feminist theoretical work, its development has been constrained by loyalty to an already established strategic perspective, as well as by its practioners' insufficient grasp of marxist theory. With their roots in a practical commitment to women's liberation and to the development of the women's movement, participants in the socialist feminist movement have only recently begun to explore their relationship to trends and controversies within the left. At the theoretical level, the exploration has taken the form of a new wave of publications seeking to delineate the substance of socialist feminism more clearly. Many have begun, furthermore, to situate women's oppression within, rather than alongside, a marxist theory of social reproduction.[17] In other words, the trial separation of marxism and feminism is gradually coming to an end—not in a marriage, happy or unhappy, nor in a divorce, but in the transcendence of contradictions that have festered between them for more than a century.

FOOTNOTES

1. Rosalind Petchesky, "Dissolving the Hyphen: Report on Marxist-Feminist Groups 1-5," in Zillah Eisenstein, ed., *Capitalist Patriarchy and the Case for Socialist Feminism* (New York: Monthly Review, 1979). Joan Kelly, "The Doubled Vision of Feminist Theory," *Feminist Studies*, 5, No. 1 (Spring 1979), 216-227. Norma Chinchilla argues that marxism and feminism are not comparable in "Ideologies of Feminism: Liberal, Radical, Marxist," Social Sciences Research Reports, No. 61 (February 1980), School of Social Sciences, University of California, Irvine.
2. Juliet Mitchell, "Women: The Longest Revolution," *New Left Review*, No. 40 (November-December 1966), pp. 11-37; *Woman's Estate* (Baltimore: Penguin, 1971).

3. Murdock argued that the universal nuclear family incorporates the "four functions fundamental to human social life—the sexual, the economic, the reproductive, and the educational [i.e., that pertaining to socialization]." George P. Murdock, *Social Structure* (New York: Macmillan, 1949), p. 10. For critiques of Mitchell along similar lines, see also Chris Middleton, "Sexual Inequality and Stratification Theory," in Frank Parkin, ed, *The Social Analysis of Class Structure*, (London: Tavistock, 1974), pp. 179-203, and Joan Landes, "Women, Labor and Family Life: A Theoretical Perspective," *Science and Society*, 41, No. 4 (Winter 1977-78), pp. 386-409. On the family in functionalist theory, see: D.H.J. Morgan, *Social Theory and the Family* (London: Routledge, 1975); Veronica Beechey, "Women and Production: A Critical Analysis of Some Sociological Theories of Women's Work," in Annette Kuhn and Annemarie Wolpe, eds., *Feminism and Materialism* (Boston: Routledge, 1978), pp. 155-197; as well as Lise Vogel, "The Contested Domain: A Note on the Family in the Transition to Capitalism," *Marxist Perspectives*, 1, No. 1 (Spring 1978), 50-73, and "Women, Work and Family: Some Theoretical Issues," paper presented at the 1980 meetings of the Society for the Study of Social Problems, New York, New York. Louis Althusser sketches the larger context for this critique in his *Essays in Self-Criticism* (London: NLB, 1976).

4. Margaret Benston's article circulated under the title "What Defines Women?" and appeared as "The Political Economy of Women's Liberation" in *Monthly Review*, 21, No. 4 (September 1969), 13-27. Peggy Morton's original essay, "A Woman's Work is Never Done, or: The Production, Maintenance and Reproduction of Labor Power," was abridged in *Leviathan* in May 1970 and revised for publication in Edith Altbach, ed., *From Feminism to Liberation* (Cambridge, Mass: Schenkman, 1971), pp. 211-227.

5. For early critiques of Benston, see Morton, "A Woman's Work;" and Mickey and John Rowntree, "Notes on the Political Economy of Women's Liberation," *Monthly Review*, 21, No. 7 (December 1969), 26-32; Roberta Salper, "The Development of the American Women's Liberation Movement, 1967-1971," in Salper, ed., *Female Liberation*, pp. 169-184; Lise Vogel, "The Earthly Family," *Radical America*, 7, Nos. 4-5 (Fall 1973), pp. 9-50.

6. Mariarosa Dalla Costa's article, "Women and the Subversion of the Community," was first published in Italian in 1972 and appeared simultaneously in English in *Radical America*, 6, No. 1 (January-February 1972), pp. 67-102. A corrected translation is found in *The Power of Women and the Subversion of the Community* (Bristol: Falling Wall Press, 1973), pp. 19-54.

7. For a fine analysis of the campaign for wages for housework, see Ellen

Malos, "Housework and the Politics of Women's Liberation," *Socialist Review*, No. 37 (January-February 1978), pp. 41-71.

8. For useful recent critiques of the domestic labor debate, see: Maxine Molyneux, "Beyond the Domestic Labour Debate," *New Left Review*, No. 116 (July-August 1979), pp. 3-27; Maureen Mackintosh, "Domestic Labour and the Household," in Sandra Burman, ed. *Fit Work for Women* (London: Croom Helm, 1979), pp. 153-172; Paul Smith, "Domestic Labour and Marx's Theory of Value," in *Feminism and Materialism*, ed. Kuhn and Wolpe, pp. 198-219; and Terry Fee, "Domestic Labor: An Analysis of Housework and Its Relation to the Production Process," *Review of Radical Political Economics*, 8, No. 1 (Spring 1976), pp. 1-8. Early notes of sanity were struck by Ira Gerstein, "Domestic Work and Capitalism," *Radical America*, 7, Nos. 4-5 (Fall 1973), pp. 101-128, and by Jean Gardiner, Susan Himmelweit, and Maureen Mackintosh, "Women's Domestic Labour," *Bulletin of the Conference of Socialist Economists*, No. 11 (June 1975). Unfortunately, few could hear them at the time.

9. Mitchell, *Woman's Estate*, p. 99.

10. Shulamith Firestone, *The Dialectic of Sex* (New York: Morrow, 1970), pp. 4, 11; Kate Millett, *Sexual Politics* (New York: Doubleday, 1970), p. 169.

11. Citation: Zillah Eisenstein, ed., *Capitalist Patriarchy*, p. 6. For Mitchell's critique of radical feminism, see *Woman's Estate*, pp. 82-96; also, Charnie Guettel, *Marxism and Feminism* (Toronto: The Women's Press, 1974), and more recently, Roisin McDonough and Rachel Harrison, "Patriarchy and Relations of Production," in *Feminism and Materialism*, ed. Kuhn and Wolpe, pp. 11-41.

12. Sheila Rowbotham, *Woman's Consciousness, Man's World* (Baltimore: Penguin, 1973), p. 117. Other early influential socialist feminist discussions of patriarchy include Hartmann and Bridges, "Unhappy Marriage;" Gayle Rubin, "The Traffic in Women: Notes on the 'Political Economy' of Sex," in Rayna R. Reiter, ed., *Toward an Anthropology of Women* (New York: Monthly Review, 1975), pp. 157-210; and Joan Kelly-Gadol, "The Social Relation of the Sexes: Methodological Implications of Women's History," *Signs*, 1, No. 4 (Summer 1976), pp. 809-823. More recently, see: McDonough and Harrison, "Patriarchy;" Hartmann, "Unhappy Marriage;" and especially Veronica Beechey, "On Patriarchy," *Feminist Review*, No. 3 (1979), pp. 66-82.

13. Renate Bridenthal, "The Dialectics of Production and Reproduction in History," *Radical America*, 10, No. 2 (March-April 1976), 5. For other explicit conceptualizations of the mode of reproduction, see: John Harrison, "The Political Economy of Housework," *Bulletin of the Conference of Socialist Economists*, No. 7 (Winter 1973); Isabel Larguia,

"The Economic Basis of the Status of Women," in *Women Cross-Culturally: Change and Challenge*, ed. Ruby Rohrlich-Leavitt (The Hague: Mouton, 1975), pp. 281-295; Bridget O'Laughlin, "Marxist Approaches in Anthropology," *Annual Review of Anthropology*, 4 (1975), pp. 365-366; Jean Gardiner, "The Political Economy of Domestic Labour in Capitalist Society," in *Dependence and Exploitation in Work and Marriage*, ed. Diana Leonard Barker and Sheila Allen (New York: Longman, 1976), pp. 109-120. In the context of the study of imperialism, a notion of the mode of reproduction is implicit in: Mina Davis Caulfield, "Imperialism, the Family, and Cultures of Resistance," *Socialist Revolution*, No. 20 (October 1974), pp. 67-85; Carmen Diana Deere, "Rural Women's Subsistence Production in the Capitalist Periphery," *Review of Radical Political Economics*, 8, No. 1 (Spring 1976), pp. 9-17; Heleieth Saffioti, "Women, Mode of Production, and Social Formations," *Latin American Perspectives*, 4, Nos. 1-2 (Winter-Spring 1977), pp. 27-37. Anthropologist Claude Meillassoux has put forth the concept of the domestic community, notably in *Femmes, greniers et capitaux* (Paris: Maspero, 1975). Important reviews of Meillassoux, which discuss the concept of reproduction, include: Maureen Mackintosh, "Reproduction and Patriarchy," *Capital and Class*, No. 2 (Summer 1977), pp. 119-127; Bridget O'Laughlin, "Production and Reproduction," *Critique of Anthropology*, No. 8 (Spring 1977), pp. 3-32; and Rayna Rapp, "Review of Claude Meillassoux...," *Dialectical Anthropology*, 2, No. 4 (November 1977), pp. 317-323.

14. The recent revival of interest in "simple commodity production" and the "natural economy" has sparked a lively discussion. Some examples: Barbara Bradby, "The Destruction of Natural Economy," *Economy and Society*, 4, No. 2 (May 1975), pp. 127-161; Scott Cook, "Value, Price and Simple Commodity Production," *Journal of Peasant Studies*, 3, No. 4 (July 1976), pp. 395-427; Judith Ennew, et al., " 'Peasantry' as an Economic Category," *ibid.*, 4, No. 4 (July 1977), pp. 295-322; Mark Harrison, "The Peasant Mode of Production in the Work of A.V. Chayanov, *ibid.*, 4, No. 4 (July 1977), pp. 323-336, and "Chayanov and the Marxists," *ibid.*, 7, No. 1 (October 1979), pp. 86-100; Harriet Friedmann, "Simple Commodity Production and Wage Labour in the American Plains," *ibid.*, 6, No. 1 (October 1978), pp. 71-100; Kevin Kelly, "The Independent Mode of Production," *Review of Radical Political Economics*, 11, No. 1 (Spring 1979), pp. 38-48. For the Soviet debate, see Susan Solomon, *The Soviet Agrarian Debate: A Controversy in Social Science, 1923-1929* (Boulder: University of Colorado, 1977).

15. Frederick Engels, *The Origin of the Family, Private Property and the State* (New York: International, 1972), pp. 71-72.

16. Beverly Brown, "Natural and Social Division of Labour: Engels and the Domestic Labour Debate," *m/f*, No. 1 (1978), pp. 25-47. Lise Vogel, *Beyond Domestic Labor: Women's Oppression and the Reproduction of Labor Power* (forthcoming), Chapter 5.

17. See, for example, the special "Women's Issue" of *Critique of Anthropology*, Nos. 9-10 (1977), or the collection *Capitalist Patriarchy* edited by Eisenstein. Important recent articles include: Veronica Beechey, "Some Notes on Female Wage Labour in Capitalist Production," *Capital and Class*, No. 3 (Autumn 1977), pp. 45-66, and "On Patriarchy;" Janet Bujra, "Female Solidarity and the Sexual Division of Labour," in *Women United, Women Divided*, ed. Patricia Caplan and Janet Bujra (London: Tavistock, 1978), pp. 13-45; Norma Chinchilla, "Ideologies of Feminism: Liberal, Radical, Marxist;" Felicity Edholm, Olivia Harris, and Kate Young, "Conceptualizing Women," *Critique of Anthropology*, Nos. 9-10 (1977), pp. 101-130; Jane Humphries, "Class Struggle and the Persistence of the Working-Class Family," *Cambridge Journal of Economics*, 1 (1977), pp. 241-258; Joan Kelly, "The Doubled Vision of Feminist Theory;" Maureen Mackintosh, "Domestic Labour and the Household;" Mary McIntosh, "The Welfare State and the Needs of the Dependent Family," in *Fit Work for Women*, pp. 153-172; Molyneux, "Beyond the Domestic Labour Debate;" O'Laughlin, "Production and Reproduction;" Paddy Quick, "The Class Nature of Women's Oppression," *Review of Radical Political Economics*, 9, No. 3 (Fall 1977), pp. 42-53.

CULTURAL MARXISM: NONSYNCHRONY AND FEMINIST PRACTICE

Emily Hicks

Emily Hicks is currently a member of the socialist feminist network in Los Angeles. She is on the curriculum committee of the Socialist Community School and will be teaching a course on psychoanalysis and feminism in the spring. She plans to continue to support the feminist analysis of the media through Women Against Violence Against Women and the Women's Building.

The fundamental problem with marrying marxism and feminism, or divorcing them for that matter, is that they both, separately and together, lead to a narrow formulation of their respective oppressions and a narrow understanding of the dynamics of society. In either case, union or divorce, we are left with an unsolved or subsumed woman question or what appears to some women to be a solved woman question but no solution to racism or classism. Marxism as Hartmann defines it will not explain the woman question; feminism as feminists describe it, including Hartmann, has not satisfactorily generated an analysis which encompasses class, race, and sex. Putting them together will not solve the problem of analyzing and understanding the many ways in which the three interact.

In my opinion, the problem of marrying marxism and feminism cannot be solved. It is time to reformulate the problem.

The main problem for the left today is that it has been unable to develop and articulate a theory and practice that is attractive to various oppressed groups in the United States. Nor has it offered a viable alternative to capitalism which will take into account the fact that *not everyone is identical* in terms of her consciousness, needs, material and psychological conditions, and desire for change. For instance, a group that the left might have expected to oppose capitalism, young working women, has turned to the right. While these women have been hearing the arguments for abortion and the right to choose abortions, they have not seen women in the movement personally dealing with the emotional and physical pain of abortion. But they have heard and been exposed to the emotional arguments and actions of the prolife movement. The prolife groups have, in fact, dealt with the emotional needs of these women. Another group, young industrial workers, have not rushed to join the left. And while gays, feminists, and blacks have become increasingly vocal, visible, and powerful in their criticism of the United States, a great many of them have continued to find enough material and psychological fulfillment from the current system. (Of course, this does not hold true for the unemployed.) Among the more fortunate, some have new homes, new cars, higher pay, and less degrading jobs allowing others more oppressed to continue to hope for these "goals." So while these oppressed groups may oppose or criticize the United States government and the economic system, they do not at the same time see the left and its analysis and programs as the solution. Instead, they perceive: (1) the inability of the left to meet their needs; and (2) the inability of the left to change the political system anyway. Both these perceptions of the left have tended to collapse into one: "Nothing will change anyway so I may as well learn to get along with my small piece of the pie."

Hartmann's proposed progressive union will not solve these problems. There can be no shotgun wedding of marxism and feminism as Hartmann defines them. Not even a living together.

Instead, the task for socialist feminists is to develop a cultural marxism that can adequately explain the intricate interactions of the oppressions of race, class, and sex; a cultural marxism that helps give a clearer articulation of our various voices: feminist, black, chicano, Native American, Asian, male, female, gay, lesbian, heterosexual; a cultural marxism which understands human needs—family, ritual, religion, sex, fun, insanity, pain, fear and so on.

A marxism that uses the concept of *nonsynchrony* can help develop this understanding. By nonsynchrony I mean the concept that individuals (or groups), in their relation to their economic and political system, do not share similar consciousness of that system or similar needs within it at the same point in time. Thus, while the white working class women mentioned earlier may be strongly anticapitalist, they are not necessarily going to be proleft or prosocialist because their needs may be for broader equality within the status quo. Similarly, during the 1930s in Germany, large numbers of people aligned with the Nazi Party and its programs because under certain conditions due to a certain perception of the present, huge numbers of people wanted fascism.[1] But a cultural marxist concept of nonsynchrony rejects the idea that the people of Germany were ignorant or misled. Rather, it realizes that fascism was able to meet people's cultural and sexual needs in the broadest sense. I do not mean to imply that sexual satisfaction was direct.[2] Of course, fascism did not provide orgasms for everyone; but it did take root in the sexual make-up, including the guilt feelings and anxieties, of its followers.[3] This sexual make-up matures in a cultural context which varied among classes and cultures. The attitudes towards the mother, the family, and the authority of the father were a part of this cultural context. Fascism flourished in systems of patriarchy. Attitudes in rural families were different from those of urban families, and differences could be found among various rural groups.[4]

A cultural marxist concept of synchrony would help leftists analyze and understand that although conformity can be cowardly, it may also be motivated by more than cowardice: by a hope, a desire, to fulfill a need. For instance, the anglo middle class women's movement includes some women who go along with certain political stands and positions, such as support for the Equal Rights Amendment, not only because they are caught up in the fashionable enthusiasm of its supporters, but because they have a need to share in a vision which goes beyond the given situation of women. There are anglo middle class women who are not feminists, who are afraid of a new way of life. Their rejection of feminism is in keeping with their rejection of new values, of change. Then, there are anglo middle class women who stay in bad marriages, low paying jobs, wondering if they could go back to school, but do nothing about their situation because they feel weak and afraid. These three subgroups of anglo middle class women share an experience of the world which is similar; it is urban, or at least suburban; and it is modern or in touch with the present. Even the anglo middle class woman who is not sympathetic to feminism may find herself being promoted at her job due to her company's attempt to follow affirmative action guidelines.

What about women who do not share this experience of the present? A middle-aged Hispanic woman who works in the garment industry in Los Angeles will not be promoted due to affirmative action guidelines. She works in an industry which is still mostly nonunionized. She may speak Spanish most of the time and be further separated from mainstream North American life by the language barrier. She may have a nonurban background and be uncomfortable with the dangers and difficulties of city life. Her way of life may be much older than that of the women described above. In spite of her contact with television, the newspapers and modern life, she maintains her "old" ways. For example, unlike the groups above, she might go to a *curandera* or spiritual reader rather than the therapists or self-discovery groups which attract the women described above. A nonsynchronic analysis would help leftists include disparate groups of women with disparate concerns.

The new right, which is living in the same technologically developed world as the first group of women, and is in touch with the present, nevertheless opposes the thrust of the modern world. It has made coherent links among affirmative action, gay rights, the ERA, busing, and abortion, and is against all of them. However, it is against these in a timely, informed, up-to-date way, using the mass media to its benefit by appearances on talk shows telling millions of television viewers that they are quite happy to stay in the family role.

The three examples we have considered, sub-groups of anglo middle class women, the Hispanic middle aged garment worker in Los Angeles, and men and women in the new right movement, constitute examples of three attitudes toward the present: the contemporaneous, the noncontemporaneous, and the ultra-contemporaneous. The latter two groups are not synchronous with the present. The problem for the left and for feminists is to formulate a decentralized notion of the present which can gain the sympathy of all women, not just those with contemporaneous attitudes towards the present. A cultural marxism that uses the concept of nonsynchrony can probe the cultural context in which class, race, and sex interact.

Hartmann calls marxism a methodology: "we believe marxist methodology *can* be used to formulate feminist strategy." She then points out that in the marxist feminist approaches she has discussed, "marxism dominates their feminism" (Hartmann, p. 10). The problem in Hartmann's analysis is not the perception that marxism dominates, but the view that it is a methodology which can be put to various purposes as one might use any tool. Rather, the method of marxism is one with its philosophical and political assumptions. To do better it is not simply a question of using the marxist method more efficiently but of changing its assumptions and thereby its content.

A marxist theory of nonsynchrony could serve this need. It would not be sex-blind, and although it could not predict who would fill the "empty places," it could have something to say about the processes which shape that channeling. Marxism would no longer be a neutral tool employed by feminists but instead a theoretical framework wholly compatible with feminist needs.

The marxism I envision is not only a "theory of the development of class society, of the accumulation process in capitalist societies, of the reproduction of class dominance, and of the development of contradictions and class struggle" (Hartmann, p. 10). In the *Early Manuscripts*, Marx discusses alienation, the relationship of humans to nature, the notion of needs, which together provide the basis for understanding why some groups continue to be subordinate to others. He suggests a way to look at the continued subordination of women to men. Marx does not provide an answer to the question of the origin of the oppression of women, nor has anyone else. Even so, by studying how needs change, we can begin to consider how the nonsynchronous may surface and where possibilities for women overcoming subordination to men may arise.

Juliet Mitchell also divides theory from method when she writes: "it is not 'our relationship' to socialism that should *ever* be the question—it is the use of scientific socialism [what we call marxist method] as a method of analyzing the specific nature of our oppression and hence our revolutionary role."[5] This notion of scientific socialism and marxist orthodoxy since Engels dismisses those texts which could allow for an understanding of the emergence of the nonsynchronous.

The structuralist assumptions of Mitchell's *Woman's Estate* result in static categories which do not allow for an understanding of how various spheres of production, reproduction, sexuality and childrearing relate to each other and how they differ according to class, race, and sex. These categories may give insight into the life of the white middle strata woman, but they are certainly not universal.

THE RELATIONSHIP BETWEEN CLASS, RACE, AND SEX

The relationships between class, race, and sex are what invalidate the universality of Mitchell's categories. Production, reproduction, sexuality, and childrearing differ among classes, racial groups, heterosexuals, and homosexuals. "The Unhappy Marriage" quotes Engels' claim that economic production and the production of people in the sex/gender sphere together determine the social organization under which people of a particular historical epoch and a particular country live. Hartmann hopes that racial hierarchies may be understood in this context.

Hartmann understands racism in terms of "color-race systems." However, although she illustrates one system with the case of South Africa, she does not develop the relation between color race systems and economic systems. Sylvia Wynter has explored the way in which the norm of whiteness has inscribed itself into the very structures of economic systems. She writes in "Sambos and Minstrels": "it was that normative culture of blanchitude that inscribed the globe, binding the structures of production under the hegemony of its imaginary social significations."[6] She notes that the "relatively milder" treatment of blacks in Latin America is due to its relative underdevelopment, and that as capitalist development has taken place, racism has increased. Further research could study underdevelopment in terms of nonsynchrony.

According to Wynter, whites in the United States had to solve a contradiction historically, that of being a settler and the bearer of the egalitarian creed of "democracy." The solution was paternalism: "by representing the identity of Sambo as childlike, by instituting the process of infantilization, the slave master constituted himself as *Paternal Father*."[7] That is, the slave master not only treated Sambo as a child literally and physically, as well as maintained the ideology that Sambo was a child, but actually entered Sambo's imaginary representation of him or herself so that Sambo actively participated in his or her own infantilization. However, there were slaves who refused to allow the slave master to articulate their identities. Wynter calls them the Nats, alluding to Nat Turner. Wynter describes this other face of Sambo: "Indeed, it was Sambo who made possible the mirrors of aristocracy in which Southern planters preened and their wives coquetted and were courted. But it was a rococo aristocracy and the guilt could suddenly crack if Sambo turned the Janus face of Nat."[8]

Wynter argues that the notion of the subject as fixed and unchanging is itself based on repression: "the strategies of capitalism as a mode of domination depends on the modes of social repression which assigns standardized prescribed ego identities to their assigned places, for the functioning of the social machine."[9] Hartmann refers to this process as the filling of empty places: "Capitalist development creates the places for a hierarchy of workers, but traditional marxist categories cannot tell us who will fill which places" (Hartmann, p. 18). Once the identity of the subject has been articulated, there can be no escape from the assigned place unless the subject refuses to accept the given designation and to articulate his or her own identity.

Wynter's analysis is based on the argument that the Sambo/Nat stereotype is not merely a second aspect of the mode of production and reproduction of people. Rather, it is an integral part of production itself: the plantation model is the source and origin of using the workplace as the site of the ideological domination of the worker. That is, in the social configuration of the workplace, the separation of ideology and production is not valid. That workers who spoke different languages were put next to each other in the beginning of industrialization in the United States was as important a part of the organization of the work process as the procedures of production. Since the workers did not understand each other, they could not organize themselves to challenge their bosses. A variation continues today in an industry such as canning in Canada, where Chinese-speaking women eat and take breaks separately from English-speaking women, a separation enforced by the herding of women into separate rooms by supervisors. Such separation prevents political organization and is a crucial part of getting fish eggs out of fish and into cans profitably. That women are subject to sexual harassment in offices is as important a part of the production process as is the division of labor among receptionists, file clerks, and typists. For undocumented workers in the garment industry today in Los Angeles, a high level of sexual harassment is maintained by the immigration authorities. Complaints are easily met by turning women over the the *migra*, the immigration authorities. As women in higher education know, female undergraduates provide a pool of sexual servants for male graduate students, and female graduate students provide similar services with typing and research skills as well for male faculty members. While an undocumented worker succumbs out of fear of deportation, women participate in maintaining the system of sexual favors in universities by believing that sexual intercourse with their male dissertation advisor will help them in some way. Of course, at best, their department chair will drop them and at worst, he will marry them and prevent their ''careers'' with the production of his children.

Although Hartmann understands that it is insufficient to label ''color-race systems'' as merely ideological, her solution, that they are a second aspect of the mode of production, is no solution at all. Wynter's theory is much richer because it argues that the Sambo/Nat stereotype is part of production. That is, Hartmannn still diminishes the importance of race. Wynter does not subsume race under class but allows both full status as primary by analyzing the interaction and inseparability of the two.

Hartmann holds that although capital is not all-powerful, it is tremendously flexible: "Capital accumulation encounters pre-existing social forms, and both destroys them and adapts to them...The ideology with which race and sex are understood today, for example, is strongly shaped by the reinforcement of racial and sexual divisions in the accumulation process" (Hartmann, p. 24). The flexibility of capital is the most insidious in the realm of culture. Here, we may find forms of resistance, but also of cooptation. While Wynter's analysis stems from a cultural politics, she is aware of the degree to which capitalism is able to deal with both Sambo and Nat, and to take from black culture what it needs:

> Amidst the stagnation of all other areas of cultural activity, the bourgeois world found a source of cultural life on which to feed, if the barest minimum of an affective and emotional life were to be sustained in the wilderness of technological rationalization. Thus, the minstrel shows, like the rest of black culture—its spirituals, its blues, its jazz—were incorporated in a form that kept its relative inclusion intact. Black culture, black music in particular, became an original source of raw material to be exploited as the entertainment industry burgeoned. Once again, blacks function as the plantation's subproletariat hidden in the raw material.[10]

The task of cultural marxism is to find the contradictory forms inside of mass culture, the entertainment industry, the barely visible spasms of capital's flexing its muscles. It is here that nonsynchronous elements may survive.

THE FLEXIBILITY OF CAPITAL

I have discussed the importance of the notion of nonsynchrony in understanding human needs. Nonsynchrony can also elucidate capital's ability to displace its crises. Marx argued that there was a tendency towards a falling rate of profit in capitalist society because value could only be produced by living or human labor, and as desire for profit continued to develop technology, the ratio of dead or machine labor to living labor would decrease. He grew increasingly attentive to capital's ability to displace its contradictions in the economic sphere from the core in the industrial sector in advanced capitalist countries, to the periphery, both the geographic periphery and the peripheral sectors such as the service sector. This displacement can be understood in terms of nonsynchrony: capitalism's crises are not experienced in all sectors in the same way. The effect of capital's flexibility is presently being felt most acutely by women and blacks. We noted that some blacks, women, and gays have gained economic power in recent years, and that they have begun to look to capitalism to fulfill their needs. In fact, capitalism has strengthened itself by bringing some blacks and women into the state sector and has thereby infused it with new living labor. The displacement of the crisis to the margins and then the integration of the margins into the core meant that in the period of expansion of the sixties, many women and blacks were brought into the core. However, women were absorbed into the state sector, not the industrial sector. Now as the second recession of the seventies continues into the eighties, women and blacks are the first to be laid off. Although blacks and women are permanently discriminated against, they are not permanently excluded. The chart below illustrates the relations between the flexibility of capital and class, race, and sex.

		Expansion of State Sector		Recession in State Sector	
		Included	Excluded	Included	Excluded
Suffer discrimination		black and white women chicanos all workers over 55	65% black youths		black and white women black youths
Do not suffer discrimination		white men	experienced white men		white youths all workers over 55

THE FLEXIBILITY OF CAPITAL AND ITS EFFECTS

THE FLEXIBILITY OF CAPITAL AND ITS EFFECTS

By discrimination, I mean lower pay and exclusion from certain jobs. Discrimination can take the forms of sexism, racism, and ageism. In a period of expansion, black and white women are included in the economic system but still suffer discrimination. They are brought into the state sector as secretaries and at various levels of civil service jobs. One reason they are chosen to fill these jobs is that white and black men have already been used in the industrial sector, so that there is a vacancy which needs to be filled by a previously unexploited workforce. Sixty-five percent of black youths have suffered discrimination and unemployment in recent years. The lowest on the list of employability, they are marked as excluded in both periods of expansion and recession. White men suffer neither discrimination nor exclusion from employment in periods of expansion. Workers over fifty-five years old of both sexes suffer discrimination of ageism but may still find themselves employed as long as the economy expands. Employment for gays and lesbians is difficult in all periods.

When a recession occurs, the last hired, all those who suffer discrimination but were included during the period of expansion, are the first laid off. No group which suffers discrimination can find employment in a tight job market. Black and white women find themselves continuing to suffer discrimination and also unemployed. Only those white men with experience can be assured jobs. Now, even white teenagers find it difficult to find work.

Recently, the expansion of the state and service sectors has arisen out of three conditions: (1) the general economic expansion which depends on the intervention of the state into the economic sphere; (2) legitimation; (3) investment. That is, as the entire economy expands, the bureaucracy must also expand. Those who have been unemployed are now given jobs in the state sector or are paid by the state. The guarantee of jobs or income even at substandard levels reproduces the ideology of welfare capitalism: it maintains the belief that capitalism provides for all citizens. Finally, capital needs to disaccumulate as well as to accumulate. Disaccumulation is the investment of capital into services and government, in which no product is produced. The state sector is the site of both accumulation and disaccumulation. To a certain extent, the state sector may be said to disaccumulate capital because workers in this sector are nonproductive. That is investment here is wasteful in relation to the historical level of material culture and the current level of technological competence. However, wasteful production and investment in services bring a rate of profit equal to or higher than that of the productive sectors. State expenditures for the building of hospitals, schools, and weapons accumulate capital.

Capital faces two powerful foes in its attempt to avoid the tendency toward a falling rate of profit: (1) the limits imposed upon investment in underdeveloped nations by revolutionary movements; (2) the drain on the expansion of the economy from disaccumulation. It attempts to fight these problems by creating more consumers and articulating new needs for commodities. Disaccumulation itself is transferred from one sector to another, in a sort of floating crap game. A socialist feminist perspective must see itself in terms of both of these. If women are drawn from the periphery, the private sphere of the home, into the state sector, they are helping capital to disaccumulate. A nonsynchronous response to this situation can begin with an analysis of women and cutbacks in the state sector. Women bear the brunt of cutbacks not only because of blatant sexism but because the crises of capital have been displaced to the state sector. When capital is required for productive investment the state sector becomes a barrier to new accumulation. The confrontation between factory owners and workers in the industrial sector has been displaced to the state sector: now governors tell teachers, firefighters, and the police that they will not receive increases.

With unionization, state sector wages have begun to approach those of the private sector. The purpose of investing in the state sector is then undermined: capital faces difficulties in disaccumulating. This is an argument for unionizing women no matter how sexist unions are.

The expansion of the public sector has been accompanied by the production of myths about the character of the state: it is held to be a neutral complex of services where persons help clients. State workers conceive of themselves as librarians, helping eager readers to the books just for them. Since women, as I have already discussed, participate in nurturing activities anyway, they are pretrained for public sector jobs. Against these helping hands, the ideological forces of productivity are at work. The public sector reproduces the same division of labor and hierarchy as the private sector. Women union organizers who have worked in both sectors claim that differences are insignificant except insofar as it is easier to get access to workers in the public sector.

Recently, there has been resistance in unexpected places: in June 1979, there was a general strike of municipal workers in Toledo; in 1978-79, one out of every six teachers in the United States went out on strike and state workers threatened a strike which forced the legislature to override Governor Brown's veto of a substantial wage increase in California. I call this resistance unexpected because it is local and it is in industries which are peripheral to the centralized logic of capital. The strikes of municipal workers and teachers are symptomatic of the displacement of the crises of capital.

This resistance is following a different strategy than that of the left. It is decentered. While the left continues to fight fire with fire, the strategy emerging in the state sector is to fight fire with water; that is, the left continues to organize itself in centralized parties and organizations while in the state sector, there is an impulse towards self-management. While in Europe there has been support for autogestion by the left, the response in the United States to urban women fighting for crosswalks and steetlights has been to belittle their struggles. The strikes of teachers are considered less important than the strikes of miners. The importance of collective bargaining rights in California for teachers won in 1979 has been underestimated; even union contracts help to limit the movement of capital When neighborhood women fight to maintain the quality of everyday life in their neighborhoods, they organize themselves in a way which breaks down the division of labor: a student with a car helps a mother by taking her child to the hospital; a mother shares childcare and shopping with the other mothers. The harassment of teenagers is protested by concerned parents and other members of the community. Block parties are held and holidays are celebrated by neighborhoods rather than within individual families.

SEXUAL DIVISION OF LABOR

Hartmann recalls that the left has always been ambivalent about the woman's movement as it may be "dangerous to the cause of socialist revolution" (Hartmann, p. 31). She adds that feminism may be threatening to left men and that many left organizations benefit from the labor of women. These fears are connected: a consolidation and centralization of forces has historically occurred in periods of economic crises. Those goals such as breaking down the division of mental and manual labor and sharing tasks are subsumed under the higher needs of scarcity and survival. In many revolutions, economic crises have occurred and a centralized response has been employed, the question arises whether or not there is an internal connection between centralization and the situation of women; does centralization foster hierarchy?

It is well known that the woman's movement arose in part out of (1) a critique of male domination; (2) a call for the democratizing of the household; (3) a critical view of the private sphere and its separation from the public sphere; and (4) the demand that a division of labor which fosters hierarchy be abolished.

Male dominance was felt by large numbers of women at home, at the workplace and in political activities. Consciousness raising groups played a valuable role in providing a space in which instances of sexism could be articulated and enumerated. Out of collective strength, many women fought within their families, at their jobs, and with their male political comrades. The result for some women included leaving their children, coming out as lesbians, going back to school, leaving school, getting fired, getting abortions, organizing day car centers. organizing feminist health care collectives, dressing differently, thinking differently. Many women have felt a power from the struggles of other women, even in the face of the present economic crisis, which continues to sustain them. Women have entered fields formerly closed to them; some have fought sexism professor by professor, book by book, in order to get into/through law school, medical school, and university positions.

The sharing of household tasks and the movement "Wages for Housework" were two methods which addressed the problem for many women of the double shift. The home front became a battleground. Women discovered it was often more difficult to explain how to do a household task than to do it; that even helpful husbands, boyfriends, and sons were still helping rather than taking full responsibility.

With the development of capitalism, women have been marginalized to the private sphere, a situation which has engendered an inequality, which persists even after they enter the public sphere. Attempts to break down the division between these spheres has been somewhat successful in getting women out of privatized existences and into the public sphere. Feminists have called for a male consciousness raising. While the logic of capital will continue to drive women into the public sphere, or back into the private sphere when economically necessary, it does not appear that it will ever drive men into the private sphere permanently. This realization led many women to recognize that only a radical restructuring of society can hope to achieve the freeing of women from the private sphere and the hegemony of the public sphere.

Some women recognized that the sexual division of labor in conjunction with the division of labor was the root of hierarchy. As long as men held jobs in which they were paid more and had more power than women, sexism would remain. Many women have been critical of the socialist movement for not taking up these questions. The division of labor in capitalism and the centralization of many socialist organizations resemble one another in that both relegate women to the menial, the underrecognized, the underpaid. The distinction between mental and manual labor is maintained.

These relations repeat themselves in left political organizations: daycare is considered less important, and is left out of more and more conferences, as Hartmann mentions. Although socialist feminists agree that the concerns of women must come now, not after the revolution, the structure of left organizations makes this unlikely. To what extent does the division of labor between the intellectuals who determine labor policy, men for the most part, and the organization people, the recruiters, and those responsible for the newsletters, mailings, cultural activities and running socialist schools, women for the most part, still exist in left organizations? How many women speak at national conventions in plenary sessions?

Frederick Taylor's, "principles of scientific management," help in understanding the division of labor. Taylor's tests provided managers with methods with which to get the most production out of a worker. Although his tests may seem far from the present problems of women, one of his principles, the selection of the work, is timely. Taylor claimed that there was a range of human attributes including tact, energy, grit, honesty, brains, education, special or technical knowledge, judgement or common sense, manual strength and dexterity and good health. Three traits characterized a common laborer, four or five a foreman, and eight or nine, possibly, a plant superintendent. Unfortunately, being a woman could mean remaining a laborer even with all ten, which Taylor forgot to add. But if we were to rewrite this list for a political organization, it might look like this: tact, energy, the sense to know when to dispense with honesty, political experience, special or technical knowledge, such as the ability to speak before large audiences, political judgement which can only come from experience, manual strength and dexterity, and good health. Many women in left organizations are thought to have energy and manual dexterity. When asked to type, they do so energetically. Fewer are thought to have the same level of political education as the more advanced men. Younger women rarely feel they've the experience to develop political judgement. Even when they do, it is considered less valuable than a man's. Many women suffer from health problems which are caused by the present socio-economic system: various birth control complications, infections, abortion problems, cysts, breast cancer, hysterectomies. Few women are able to address a large groups of leftist men. The result is that for the sake of efficiency, even groups committed to developing equality do not break down the sexual division of labor which seems to arise naturally. One woman is just so good at recruiting, another with money, and the men just happen to know about labor and energy, and to have more experience arguing for resolutions at conventions.

While corporate managers discredit unions, all groups on the left discredit grievances of women within their organizations. Favoritism by older, more experienced members encourages being a nondisruptive woman comrade and discourages criticism. Male and female leaders play favorites and act in arbitrary ways regarding younger women, especially disgruntled ones. Women who must do mailings, typing, handle money, have the meetings at their homes, and clean up afterwards while also working at jobs and doing an inordinate amount of political work, or "taking on too much," are sometimes forced to work even faster before rallies, forums, demonstrations, conferences, and conventions, and yet do not get more recognition. The specialization and subdivision of jobs such as calling members on the phone, getting rooms and halls for events, folding and stapling mailings, making leaflets and posters, break down skill and the knowledge of the whole work process. How often is the discussion bulletin in a political organization filled with position papers written by men and short reports by women. Who types, collates, mails and distributes these? How many left male professors do not know how to refill a stapler, so that they staple until it runs out and a woman is called upon to refill it?

CULTURAL MARXIST PRAXIS

We must engage in nonsynchronous praxis at three levels: (1) an alliance with working class women; (2) cultural criticism which seeks to find contradictory forms inside of mass cultural images of women as well as to encourage the development of feminist art; (3) a decentralized response to crisis. The first of these is presently being attempted. There are coalitions which manage to reconcile the needs of Black and Puerto Rican women with those of white women by addressing forced sterilization as well as abortion. Judy Chicago's "Dinner Party" and the work of many artists in Los Angeles represent the attempt to do collective art work. Although Women Against Violence Against Women has been successful in criticizing the presentation of women by the media and presenting alternative images of strong women who are not victims but survivors, some feminist artists have not yet gone beyond condemnation of sexist images. The challenge is to find contradictions inside of what we already know is sexist. The most difficult problem is the formulation and development of a decentered response to crisis. As Hartmann writes, we are made to feel our work is a waste of time compared to unemployment and inflation. But our work should include an analysis of unemployment and inflation, not to legitimize our work, but because a nonsynchronous response must go beyond "women's concerns" as we have too narrowly defined them.

The displacement of the crises of capitalism occurs not only within economic relations, but in the realm of politics and culture as well. When a woman fireperson insists upon nursing her child at the fire station while on duty, her act carries connotations whose threat exceeds that of offending public taste. It is the convergence of the issues of childcare, the felt need of a woman to be with her child, the entrance of politics into a public servant job, the age old notion that nursing is the original explanation for the division of labor. If a woman can get down a fire pole as fast as a man, even immediately after nursing her baby, the theory that women were historically more vulnerable because of nursing and therefore stayed close to home is severely undermined. The act of a fireperson nursing her baby while on duty at the station is an example of nonsynchronous praxis. It could not have been predicted as a logical extension of the women's movement, given present antibaby, proaportion attitudes, nor would it have been suggested by the left as a tactic. It occurred at the margins, in the state sector, and the act was committed by a woman who neither considers herself a leftist not a feminist. Her felt need to be with her child is nonsychronous with the norm of the feminist. Her desire to work as a fireperson is nonsynchronous with the norm of the woman in capitalist society.

A cultural marxism can fight the tendency of both marxist and feminist movements to be self-centered. By developing a decentered response to the crises of capitalism in the cultural realm and by encouraging nonsynchronous practice, it can bring together various groups which would otherwise be divided due to differences of class, race, and sex. A cultural marxism can appreciate and support nonsynchronous praxis by recognizing nonsynchronous human needs and addressing these needs. It can develop a discourse which is not centered around one norm, but is flexible and open to the utopian, and the generation of opposition from the least likely places. A cultural marxism can allow for an array of possibilities of perceiving the present and of a variety of utopian moments, a multilayered response to a multilayered reality.

FOOTNOTES

1. Wilhelm Reich, *The Mass Psychology of Fascism*, trans. Vincent R. Carfagno (New York: Farrar, Straus & Giroux, 1970).
2. Ernst Bloch, "Nonsynchronism and the Obligation to Its Dialectics," trans. Anson Rabinbach, in *New German Critique*, no. 11, Spring 1977, p. 26: "The desire of the white color worker not to be proletarian intensifies to orgiastic pleasure in subordination, in magic civil service under a duke."
3. Reich, p. 59.
4. Nicos Poulantzas, *Fascism and Dictatorship, The Third International and the Problem of Fascism*, trans. Judith White, trans. eds. Jennifer and Timothy O'Hagan (London: NLB-Verso, 1979).
5. Juliet Mitchell, *Woman's Estate* (New York: Random-Vintage, 1971), p. 92. Quoted by Hartmann, p. 13.
6. Sylvia Wynter, "Sambos and Minstrels," *Social Text*, Vol. 1, no. 1, Winter 1979, p. 150.
7. Wynter, p. 151.
8. Wynter, p. 151.
9. Wynter, p. 152. From Gilles Deleuze and Felix Guattari, *Anti-Oedipus, Capitalism and Schizophrenia*, trans. Robert Hurley, Mark Seem, and Helen R. Lane (New York: Viking, 1977).
10. Wynter, p. 149.
11. This figure was widely reported in newspapers in 1979.

MOTHERS, FATHERS AND CHILDREN: FROM PRIVATE TO PUBLIC PATRIARCHY

Carol Brown

Carol Brown has her PhD from Columbia and a tenured position at the University of Lowell in Massachusetts. She was a marxist before she was a feminist and has grappled with the contraditions ever since. Her sisters in the Marxist Feminist Conference have contributed the most to an intellectual and emotional synthesis of the issue. She is engaged in a collective study of divorced mothers.

Heidi Hartmann's essay, "The Unhappy Marriage," has shown the economic basis of patriarchy and its relations to capitalism. Her analysis of the interrelations among classes of men shows how their conflicts and accommodations have enabled men as a sex to control the labor power and lives of women to the benefit of men. In particular, she has shown how capitalism interacts with patriarchy to remold women's position both in the labor force and in the family. We can take this further by developing an analysis of the difference between public and private patriarchy.

The question of responsibility for children is an important one for the feminist movement. The fight against men's rights to women's family labor has been long, and partially successful, yet as women gain more apparent freedom from restrictive family laws, their situation in the family and in society does not improve. Women's position as the bearers and rearers of children appears an unchanging and insurmountable obstacle to equality. But it is not unchanging and therefore not insurmountable. It is hoped that this analysis of child custody in the United States will further our understanding of the political and economic forces at work.

The labor force and the family are specific elements in what we can call public patriarchy and private patriarchy.[1] The private patriarchy includes the individual relations between men and women found in the traditional family, in which the individual husband has control over the individual wife, her daily reproductive labor and the product of her labor, the children. But patriarchy is not just a *family system*. It is a *social system* which includes and defines the family relation. It is in the social system that we find the public aspects of patriarchy: the control of society—of the economy, polity, religion, etc.—by men collectively, who use that control to uphold the rights and privileges of the collective male sex as well as individual men. The husband's family-centered control over his wife's daily labor is upheld by the publicly-centered monopolization of jobs, law, property, knowledge, etc., by men.

The intersection of public and private patriarchy comes in family law.

CHILD CUSTODY AND FEMALE HEADED FAMILIES

Hartmann has shown how capitalism accommodated to partriarchy by providing men with both control of the economic system and a monopoly of family-waged jobs that push women into personal dependence on and personal service to their husbands. The servitude of women is the payoff to men of all classes for acceptance of the status quo.

But in a certain number of cases men do not seem to want this privilege. In many cases they desert their families, walking away from their ostensible rights. In case of divorce, they let their wives have custody of the children, usually without even asking for custody from the court. The female-headed family resulting from divorce and desertion has become a prominent feature of U.S. family life. Ten percent of all families with children are female-headed. Ninety percent of all single-parent families are female-headed. Many of these divorced mothers eventually remarry, but there is no guarantee of that.[2]

That mothers keep the children when a marriage dissolves seems so natural today that it comes as a surprise to discover that the phenomenon is recent. One hundred and fifty years ago it was considered equally natural for fathers to keep the children, and their desire to do so was backed by the power of the state. In the early nineteenth century divorce was virtually illegal. Runaway wives were tracked down and returned to their husbands by the police, like runaway slaves. Men had "paramount" and "natural" rights to custody of their children; mothers were entitled to reverence but no rights.

Today divorce is completely legal; the no-fault reforms being adopted in most states do not even require that there be a reason. Men are running away from their families and are being tracked down by Health, Education and Welfare Departments and local courts. Mothers *de jure* have equal rights to custody and *de facto* have primary rights. Although some men are asking for custody, most men do not ask for or want it, and judges tend to award custody to mothers regardless of desire. AFDC supports husbandless mothers. New programs for displaced homemakers seek to make it easier for divorced and deserted mothers to take over the father's traditional role of economic support.

If the male-headed family is the bulwark of patriarchy, why do so many men leave their marriages and give custody of the children to their wives? Why does the patriarchal state take away from men a paramount right they have held since their earliest codification of English common law?

The answer, I think, comes from the interaction of capitalism and patriarchy. Building on Hartmann, we can analyze that as monopoly capitalism developed there was a shift from private patriarchy centered on the family to public patriarchy centered on industry and government. Children are no longer valued as they were in earlier times for their unskilled labor but rather are valued today for their future skilled labor. For this reason, children themselves and the labor required to rear them have changed from a valuable family asset that men wished to control to a costly family burden that men wish to avoid. Simultaneously, public patriarchy takes over more directly the labor of women in child bearing and child rearing through state policies, public support and professional caretaking. Male-headed families are no longer needed to maintain patriarchy. Neither the patriarchal system as a whole nor individual men suffer from permitting the widespread formation of female-headed families. As a result, divorce and mother-custody become the law of the land. Women gained not so much a private right as a public obligation.

MEN, WOMEN AND CHILDREN

How do capitalism and patriarchy intersect where children are concerned? Hartman has shown that the division of labor in our society is simultaneously capitalist and patriarchal. Under capitalism, production for profit is the central focus of the economy, but, as Marx said, the reproduction of labor is equally important.[3] Reproduction includes maintaining and nurturing the current population as well as developing the new generation. The reproduction of labor itself demands much labor, which must be organized to the benefit of production. Profits are made from production. The reproduction of labor, although necessary, is a cost that capitalism seeks to decrease. The patriarchal division of labor determines in large part which people fill which positions. Men on the whole are found in production and profit-making; women in reproduction of the labor force. Reproduction serves the needs of production; women serve the needs of men.

We tend to think of production as part of the public world (out of the home) and reproduction as part of the private world (in the home). This is not quite true. Public and private have always been intertwined, in a historically changing relation as capitalism and patriarchy have developed.

Under fuedalism the family was the center of production as well as reproduction. The husband virtually owned his wife, and children were valued as the family's labor force. The home was not as private as it is today, but was more obviously part of the economy.[4]

Under competitive capitalism the factory, not the home, became the locus of production. Men were pulled out of the home into factories, stores and offices; women were pushed out of the public arena and into the home. (See Hartmann, p. 22). The effect of the interaction of capitalism and patriarchy was that production became men's work under the control of the capitalist ruling class, and reproduction became women's work under the control of their husbands.

As family enterprise declined, children became less valuable to the family and more valuable to society, that is to say, to the capitalist class as future skilled workers. Thus we find the nineteenth century controversies over compulsory public education and child labor laws.

A woman's reproductive labor, including the work of rearing children, continued to be valued by her husband for his current maintenance and for the children who were presumed to support their parents in the parents' old age. Benefit also went to the capitalist class which obtained at the cost of one wage earner the production of the wage earner himself, the reproductive labor of his wife in maintaining him and his children, and the future labor of the children.

The change from competitive capitalism to monopoly capitalism involved another transformation in the relation of men, women and children. The rise of monopoly capital came in 1880-1920; the period of consolidation in the 1960s.[5] Under monopoly capitalism, reproduction began to move outside the home. Today reproduction is part of a coordinated network of social organizations and policies under the hierarchical control of the ruling class. Although the traditional patriarchal family continues to exist, and women's labor continues to be bound in part to their husbands and their homes, husbands *per se* no longer control *en masse* the kind of reproductive labor that is performed and the circumstances under which it is performed. Hospitals, schools, restaurants, stores, mental health agencies, offices and so forth are the places in which reproduction is carried out and in which women work for pay.

Even housewives are increasingly subject to direct outside control of their consumption labor, their child rearing and their homemaking.[6] In 1970 a prominent family sociologist, Marvin Sussnam, analysed the future role of the family to be the coordination of bureaucratic policies, and the role of the family sociologist to be teaching the family (which in practice means teaching the housewife) how to carry out the coordination.[7] Thus both in paid and in unpaid work, women are increasingly subject to the demands of public patriarchy.

The increase of public patriarchy carries with it a change in the social class structure of control. All husbands had patriarchal powers over their wives. All men do not have power over social institutions. Public patriarchy increases the power of higher level men over all women and decreases the power of lower level men over any women. Even the higher level men have lost personal legal control over any given woman, although they retain economic control.

THE PROCESS OF CHANGE

Before monopoly capitalism, the main role of the public patriarchy was to uphold the rights of individual men through family laws and economic exclusions that ensured women's dependence. Today the ruling class that controls the public patriarchy takes upon itself control over the reproduction of labor power, pulls women out of the home into the labor force, and, by legislation or judicial decision, abolishes the rights of individual men over women. But men's rights over individual women are supposedly one factor keeping men of all classes loyal to the system. Patriarchies are systems of cooperation among classes of men as well as systems of conflict over economics. Why did the male sex—ruling class, middle class, working class—permit, perhaps even struggle to bring about, the decline in its own power over individual women? The answer is that people cling to that which is valuable but abandon that which is valueless. The private family has lost much of its value to patriarchy, both public and private.

Profit is one reason. The needs of capital to develop new markets led to mass production of consumer goods that replaced home production and home labor. The profit to be gained from employing cheap labor led employers to hire women as workers.[8]

In addition, monopoly capitalism needs highly skilled, stable, and predictable labor power.[9] Thus the development of human capital needs to be as well controlled as the machines and organizations. Individual families may be unwilling or unable to fulfill these needs for high levels of services.[10] The kind of social environment and services required to produce workers capable of and willing to move vast units of capital successfully, efficiently, and safely can only be developed by vast public policies controlled by the establishment and implemented by reproduction units as large as the production units.[11]

The public patriarchy of monopoly capital does not benefit from individual men's continuing control. The locus of control over women's reproductive labor has changed from the family to the political economy. Husbands are no longer needed to maintain the patriarchy or to maintain the continued reproductive labor of women. Husbands may even be a hindrance. Basic to capitalism is the idea of free labor, labor not bound to any one employer. As women's work became detachable from the family we saw the breakdown of the husband's right to control his wife's property, wage, domicile, sexual activity, child production, even name.[12]

Within the sphere of private patriarchy, the value of women's domestic labor declined. A wife's home labor is still important and desirable, but it is less necessary for a man's survival and comfort. A wife's personal labor can now be replaced by commercial products, such as self-cleaning ovens. The labor of women is available outside the home. Waitresses serve food and clean tables; nurses tend sick bodies; therapists provide shoulders to cry on. Third, women are publicly available, giving service with a smile on their jobs or sex with a smile after hours. Thus men do not have the incentive to find and cleave unto just one woman until death do them part. Finally, a woman's potential public participation gives her bargaining chips in the marriage which enable her to refuse some of her husband's demands, thereby decreasing even further the benefits the husband can obtain from the relationship and increasing her own chances for independence from him.[13]

I am not arguing that the private family is dead or dying. As Hartmann has shown, the public patriarchy continues to uphold and encourage male domination within the family. I do argue, however, for the increased importance of public patriarchy and for the decreasing importance of private patriarchy in structuring the reproductive labor of society. Although women are still primarily engaged in reproduction and a large number are still laboring at home supported by their husbands' incomes, the female sex unquestionably has a different relation to the labor force, to money, and to the formal organizations of society than it did in the nineteenth century. The relationship of husband's income and wife's labor is increasingly mediated by the formal institutions of public patriarchy.

CHILDREN AND FAMILY LAW

In order to illustrate the change, I will concentrate on an examination of the changes in family law concerning custody of children. I will show historically that custody changed from father right to mother obligation as the economic role of children in the family changed from a benefit to a cost.

Child labor on farms and in factories and family businesses continued well into industrialization. In 1820, "43 percent of all textile workers in Massachusetts, 47 percent in Connecticut and 55 percent in Rhode Island were children."[14] Children continued to form a significant component of the labor force in a variety of industries through the Civil War.[15] A marked decline of children in manufacturing took place in 1880-1890, although "as late as 1901, one urban family in five had working children."[16] These children's wages were important to their parents. Today, "families in which the father has a low-paying job do not receive nearly as much income, proportionately, from the employment of sons and daughters as such families did in the past. Nor does the employment of the wife make up for the income which formerly might have been earned by several sons and daughters."[17]

Child labor legislation and compulsory school laws, both controversial policies resisted by elements of both capitalism and the working class, contributed to the decline.[18] Morrison and Commager note that between 1870 and 1890 "the percentage of children between five and seventeen who were in school increased from 57 to 78, while the average daily attendance increased five-fold."[19] Thus we see the transition of children in the economy from workers with a pay package to resource-consuming trainees for a future system.

Today economists do not talk about the value of children at

all, but about their cost. Some refer to children as units of consumption, pleasurable but costly.[20] The history of birth control shows a strong demand by married couples for limitation of child bearing since at least the 1880s.[21]The high cost of children is invariably cited as a reason.

The economic value of mothering is low as a result. To an individual husband, there is no economic value in supporting his wife's child rearing labor. Indeed, the time she spends with the children may interfere with the time and energy she spends with him, and he may be required to contribute labor to the children himself. To the public patriarchy, the value of the mother's labor is slight. The skilled work of education and indoctrination is done by paid labor of teachers and others, more carefully controllable than a mother is. Her economic contribution is in the one-to-one work of feeding and clothing, nurturance and emotional health, tasks which are necessary and desirable but far too labor-intensive to pay for while maintaining a profitable economy.

The children still have value as potential labor; therefore the establishment takes a great interest in seeing them raised well. There is as a result a quiet battle going on between the private family and the public system, part of the class struggle. The family would like the public to take over the costs in the form of better schools, more day care centers, better child health services. The public system wants the family to continue bearing the costs, and cuts back or ceases increasing the public services.

The support of children remains a haphazard affair. The public patriarchy tries to push the burden onto men, who have an economic incentive to push it onto women, who cannot bear the cost because of the patriarchal wage structure. Raising women's wages to the family-supporting level would destroy much of the economic basis of patriarchy. Instead, men are permitted to divorce and desert their families. The public welfare system is forced to provide a minimum subsistence to a mother raising the new generation of cheap labor.[22] The welfare system tries to track down the fathers and make them pay the welfare costs if possible; simultaneously it tries to get the mother off welfare into a job where she can support the children herself.[23]

No one is happy with the outcome from any political perspective. In the meantime the birth rate continues to decline to such a low level that the establishment is worried about replacing the population.

DIVORCE LAWS

We recognize that the legal system has a class bias, since intrafamily litigation is a middle and upperclass phenomenon. Desertion has always been a poor man's (sic) divorce. Nevertheless, the law affects everyone, and both reflects and creates social limits.

The changes in divorce and in child custody are inseparable in reality. However, in order to perceive the trends more clearly, it is necessary to describe them separately.

Under English common law divorce, which gives both spouses the right to remarry, was forbidden, although legal separation was possible. Only 317 divorces were granted by act of Parliament before 1857.[24]

Although few divorces were recognized in the early U.S. republic, the rate of marital breakup appears to have been higher than in England. Divorce was permitted on various grounds such as adultery or desertion.[25]

Liberalization by adding grounds was widespread in the 1830s and 40s. A major leap toward open divorce came in the 1840s in the New England states, which industrialized early and used many women and children workers. In the 1840s every state in New England added an "omnibus clause" permitting divorce for any sufficient reason. Connecticut's 1849 statute permitted divorce for "any such misconduct...as permanently destroys the happiness of the petitioners and defeats the purpose of the marriage relation,"[26] which is about as close to the present "no-fault" divorce as a law can get. For years Connecticut served as a divorce mill for New Yorkers whose own state laws were restrictive. Omnibus clauses were also found in Pennsylvania, Indiana, Louisiana, and Arizona. For awhile Indiana and Utah were known as divorce mills.[27]

Liberalized divorce was a feminist issue. As early as the women's rights conventions of 1852 and 1854 pleas were made for greater divorce freedom and for permitting women to retain after divorce their property and their children.[28] Said Kraditor writing about a later period, "Few feminists would disagree with Carrie Chapman Catt's statement that states with liberal divorce laws were to women what Canada had been to fugitive slaves."[29]

There were several reasons for a more liberal divorce system in America. One was that in general American courts prided themselves on being more liberal toward personal freedom among "decent" citizens than the English. Second, the employment of women made divorce possible, since an alternative to a husband's income was available. But neither employment nor wages were great enough to cause a stampede. A third reason was that Western migration and fluid social structure left many women abandoned by their husbands. Divorce enabled them to find new husbands.

In the meantime abandoned wives presented a legal problem. Under common law a married woman could not earn and keep her own wages, make contracts, own property, or be sued for debts. Yet all these had to be done if the woman and her creditors were to survive. If the desertion was permanent, liberalized divorce was the answer. Another alternative, one bishop termed the "usual practice," is to give an abandoned wife the right to act as a *feme sole*, a single woman, thus enabling her to take responsibility for her financial affairs.[30]

The liberal era of divorce in the East ended in the 1880s, a victim of the Victorian reaction against the breakdown of the home caused by capitalism. Omnibus provisions were repealed and divorce reform leagues founded to restrict the rights of divorce.[31] By this time, however, liberalized divorce had moved west, with the mountain and Pacific states liberalizing in the 1870s. The actual rate of divorce kept rising regardless of restricted grounds, going nationally from 28 per 100,000 population in 1870 to 53 in 1890 and 84 in 1906.[32]

A Uniform Marriage and Divorce Bill which would have given the federal government the right to regulate marriage, divorce, legitimacy, and child custody was introduced in Congress between 1894 and 1925 by conservatives. (Said co-sponsor George W. Norris, "Every time a home is broken up, the onward march of civilization is halted.")[33] Although the attempt failed, we can see in it the growing self-consciousness of public patriarchy.

Investigations repeatedly showed the cities to have higher divorce rates than rural areas. The 1880s are a decade in which the breakdown of the family produced many official investigations, reports and campaigns (e.g., Carroll Wright.)[34] "Poor man's divorce" had also become a social issue by the 1880s, as charity workers and others viewed with alarm the rising rates of desertion by urban working class husbands.[35]

In the twentieth century, divorce continued to rise irregularly.

E.A. Ross, a prominent sociologist, in 1909 blamed economic changes for the increase:

> Now that the machine has captured most of the domestic processes and the middle-class home is sustained by the earnings of the husband, the wife, from a helpmate, has become a luxury. If, now, there is a rift in the lute, the husband becomes aware of carrying a burden, and resents things that are overlooked when the wife is a true yoke-mate.... The old economic framework of the family has largely fallen away, leaving more of the strain to come on the personal tie. Husband and wife are held together by love, conscience and convention, but very little by the profitable co-partnership which once contributed so much to the stability of the home.[36]

He continued by saying that intelligent wives resent their enforced idleness, and this contributes to the woman's unhappiness.

By the 1970s the divorce rate was generally considered to be sky-rocketing, this time popularly blamed on women's rising labor force participation rate and the women's movement. The reform of this decade was "no-fault" divorce, in which the parties simply had to assert that the marriage had broken down. By 1976 Foster and Freed report that all but three states have added "marital breakdown" as a ground for divorce.[37] Again we have to point out that although the women's movement advocated easier divorce, "no-fault" was not voted into existence by feminists. It was voted in largely in recognition that restricted grounds do not restrict divorce, and that there is no social benefit in restricting divorce.

CHILD CUSTODY

The history of child custody does not show the dramatic transitions of divorce history, but rather a slow diminution of father-right and a slow expansion of mother-custody. Until recently the only public group concerned with child custody was the women's movement, whose promother policies did not vary. A dramatic shift has taken place in the last few years, and this will be dealt with in turn.

Roscoe Pound, an oft-cited judicial scholar, outlined the traditional rights of parents to include the chastity of the female child, the social pleasures of a child (companionship, love, respect), and the services of a child, "the latter a form of property like any other." The economic value of children is clear from his explication:

> The remaining claim, the claim to the services of the child, is an interest of substance, and as a purely *economic claim* does not differ from the interest in other *economically advantageous* relations. As between parent and child immediately the parent may claim obedience and respect as matters related to his personality, and as interests of substance, *service for the profit of the household,* and in case the parent is indigent, support from a child of age, capacity and sufficient means.[38](Italics, Brown.)

The profit to be made from this property included personal labor on the parents' behalf, labor in the family enterprise, and money earned elsewhere to which the parent was entitled. In return, the parent was obligated to provide physical and economic maintenance, education, and discipline. These rights and obligations were issues in the nineteenth century.

FATHER RIGHT

Under the English common law the father had the sole "natural" and "paramount" right to a child's custody, care, control, and services. Blackstone was approvingly quoted by U.S. jurists as saying that a mother as such is entitled to respect but no rights. Cases are cited in England of suckling infants torn from their mothers' breasts with the approval of the court.[39] If the father gave custody to the mother or to another party such custody was only temporary—he retained the *right* to custody at all times.

The U.S. courts modified common law in several ways. Whereas English courts had often considered themselves helpless in the fact of the father's paramount right, U.S. courts gave to themselves the power to make the decision on the grounds, always present but rarely used in England, of *parens patrie*, loosely meaning that the courts have the right to make parental decisions in the child's best interests.

One of the earliest law books, widely used as guidance for cases, is Kent's *Commentaries* of 1827, centered on New York law but used throughout the nation. Kent perceived the father's right to be reciprocal with obligation:

> And in consequence of the obligation of the father to provide for the maintenance, and in some qualified degree, for the education of his infant children, he is entitled to the custody of their persons, and to the value of their labor and services.[40]

He later points out that "the courts will even control the right of the father to the possession and education of his children, when the nature of the case appears to warrant it."[41]

However, this modification of father-right, although it would become important in the future, was of small practical importance through the middle of the nineteenth century. A well-known 1860 case in New Hampshire gives a good example of continuing judicial thinking on the subject:

> Prima facie, however, the right of custody is in the father; and when the application is resisted upon the ground that he is unfit for the trust, by reason of grossly immoral conduct, harsh usage of his child, or other cause, a proper regard to the sanctity of the parental relation will require that the objections be sustained by clear and satisfactory proofs.... And while we are bound also to regard the permanent interests and welfare of the child, it is to be presumed that its interests and welfare will be best promoted by continuing that guardianship which the law has provided, until it is made plainly to appear that the father is no longer worthy of the trust.... The breaking of the ties which bind the father and the child can never be justified without the most solid and substantial reasons. Upon the father the child must mainly depend for support, education and advancement in life, and as security for this he has the obligation of law as well as the promptings of that parental affection which rarely fail to bring into the services of the child, the best energies and the most thoughtful care of the father.[42] (Girl awarded to father.)

Thus we see that the best interests of the child are assumed to be served by father-custody.

A second early modification of English common law was to admit *some* legal interest on the part of the mother. Kent's rule was that "the father has first title to guardianship by nature, and the mother the second."[43] That the mother is admitted to have a right at all can be traced to the same cause as the *feme sole* rulings: if a father abandoned his children, *someone* had to take responsibility for them. The mother's legal interest was not very great. Says Williams,

> Under the early common law, the father was entitled to custody of the children as against the mother, and the cases were few and exceptional in which their custody would be given to her, although she lived apart from her husband on account of his misconduct.[44]

There is no one date at which the custom changed; rather there was a slow progression, nudged along by a growing women's movement. Married women's property acts, such as New York's in 1840, could be interpreted as giving women a share of the property rights in their children.[45] Equal rights legislation often specified it. The Kansas Act of 1859 said:

> The legislature shall provide for the protection of the rights of women, in acquiring and possessing property, real, personal and mixed, separate and apart from the husband; and shall also provide for their equal rights in the possession of their children.[46]

BEST INTERESTS

"Best interests of the child" usually became the language of the early statutes when these replaced common law.[47] Although there is historical continuity, the use of such a concept is a larger reform than might appear. Best interests does not in law give the father his traditional paramount right.[48] The effect was to increase the chance of the mother gaining custody. However, best interests legally bypasses the mother's rights as well. Said a New York judge in 1847, "the real question is not, what are the rights of the father or mother to the custody of the child, but what are the rights of the child."[49] Thus during the period that mothers were gaining more rights vis-a-vis their husbands, both mothers and fathers were losing family-centered rights to the state. If the mother did get custody, it was not necessarily because she had more right than the father, but because she could better fulfill the obligation to the child that the state wanted fulfilled. In practice, judges continued to cite common law when giving custody to the father, and to cite best interests when giving custody to the mother.

TENDER YEARS

In deciding what was for the best interests of the child, the rule of thumb that children of tender years belong with their mothers slowly gained ascendency, being written into the New Jersey statutes in 1860, and the Michigan statutes in 1879.[50] Precedent setting cases giving mothers custody of children of tender years are cited from various states in the 1840s, 50s, and 60s, although father-right continued to dominate.

By 1887 Hochheimer (and he is echoed by Field in 1888) asserts the general acceptance of the tender years doctrine:[51]

In awarding the custody of children upon a decree of divorce or separation, the courts look primarily to the fitness of the parties and their adaptability to the task of caring for the children, taking into consideration the age, sex, state of health, and other circumstances in the lives of the children. . . . The general inclination and tendency of the courts are in the direction of giving the younger children, and female children of all ages, to the mother.[52]

By Hochheimer's 1889 edition he refers to the tendency as a "well-settled practice":

In fact, it is now well recognized, that in certain cases, other things being equal, the mother is in a superior position in regard to a claim to the custody of the children. Cases, therefore, of contests between parents as to the custody of the children are not generally deemed to present questions of much difficulty or delicacy.[53]

Just how young a child had to be in order to be of tender years was an issue. The New Jersey legislature said age seven, the Michigan legislature said twelve, but in 1905 a New York judge gave a child from his mother to his father at age five, saying rhetorically that if he was not then old enough to leave his mother, when would he be.[54] This case illustrates that the tender years doctrine did not guarantee the mother custody once her children grew older and needed less tender care.

Despite the controversies, it is clear that the 1880s and subsequent decades saw the consolidation of the idea that mothers are likely to gain custody because the children need them.

CHILD SUPPORT

Fathers who totally abandoned their families obviously did not support them. There was, however, a question of whether a divorced father legally *had to* support his children. Kent in 1827 had stated that in a separation the husband was entitled to his wife's property but the wife was entitled to maintenance for herself and the children. By the 1880s, when divorce was the issue and equal rights a framework, obligations were not clear. The argument on both sides is best summed up by the findings of a 1918 Oregon case, State v. Langford:

One line of authorities proceeds upon the theory that the duty of the father to support the child and the obligation of the latter to serve the former present reciprocal rights and duties, and that therefore to award the custody of the child to the mother is to deprive the father of the child's services, and hence the loss of the right to the services of the child operates as a release from the duty to support; but a majority of the well-considered precendents denounce and condemn this cold and illogical doctrine, which not only ignores the rights and welfare of the child, but also enables an unfaithful husband and unnatural father to compel his wife to divorce him, on account of grievous wrongs done by him, with the assurance given to him in advance that when she does divorce him she will not have lost the maternal instinct, but will cling to the child, and thus enable him further to wrong her by cowardly casting his burden upon her; for the great weight of judicial authority is to the effect that a father is not released from his obligation to support his child by reason of the fact that the mother has secured a divorce and has been awarded custody of the child by a decree which makes no provision for the child's maintenance.[55]

The support of husbandless mothers had become a public issue as early as the 1880s.[56] When working class husbands deserted their families, they left their families destitute. The issue of who was going to pay for the children was part of the larger controversy about mothers' aid which continues today in AFDC.[57] With fathers refusing and mothers unable, the government was increasingly called upon to provide the money.[58] Today the majority of female-headed families are supported by welfare for some length of time.[59] The public policy of courts forcing the cost back onto the divorced father whenever possible solidified around the turn of the century. Specified an 1890 court, "The obligation to support is not grounded on the duty of the child to serve, but rather on the inability of the child to care for itself. It is not only a duty to the child, but to the public."[60] That men did not pay the court-ordered support was as obvious then as now.[61]

During the time of transition, children's labor still held some value. Kent specified that the father was entitled to the child's custody "and to the value of their labor and services." He did not deal with divorce. By the later nineteenth century the issue was controversial:

When the converse question as to the right to services is presented, it is held that because the father has the legal duty to support, he is entitled to the services of the child even though it is in the mother's custody.... Some cases did decide that if the mother in fact supports, she has the right to services though the duty of support is legally chargeable to the father[62]

The mother's right to the child's earnings was specified by Oregon in 1880 and Pennsylvania in 1896. By the time of Vernier's compilation of state laws, most dating from 1900 to 1920, twenty-two states considered the mother equal to the father and therefore as entitled to the child's earnings as he was, and twenty specified that services go with custody regardless of who provides child support.[63]

All of this presumes that the child has some earnings worth fighting for. Yet by the 1930s child labor was virtually abolished, and the right that women had won was meaningless. *Women fought for rights and gained obligations.*

MOTHER PREROGATIVE

By the 1920s the arrangement now standard was settled. Mothers gained custody in divorce; fathers were ordered to pay child support but often did not, and the economic relation between parent and child was to the benefit of the child. The courts, and behind them the state, had the right to determine the child's treatment and the parents' obligations.

A mother's equal right to custody after divorce was specifically written into the divorce statutes in many states between 1900 and 1930.[64] The assumption that the mother's custody was in the best interests of the child began to jell into a certainty.

James Schouler in 1921 speaks of mothers the way earlier commentators spoke of fathers:

The love of the mother for her child, regardless of conditions and environments, has been proven by the history of the ages, and while her devotion can be counted upon most unfailingly, it is sad to say that sometimes the tie between father and child is a different matter, and requires the strong arm of the law to regulate it with some degree of humanity and tenderness for the child's good.[65]

More states modified their statutes to specify best interests in the 1930s and 40s, when depression desertions and postwar divorces brought the issue to public attention. The child's best interests were presumed by courts to require the mother's custody.

Thus we see a complete turnaround from early common law. By 1961 Nelson could say:

> It is universally recognized that the mother is the natural custodian of the young. In legal contests for the custody of minor children, the law favors the mother. If she is a fit and proper person to have the custody of the children, other things being equal, the mother should be given their custody, in order that the children may not only receive her attention, care, supervision and kindly advice, but also may have the advantage and benefit of a mother's love and devotion for which there is no substitute. A mother's care and influence is regarded as particularly important for children of tender age and girls of even more mature years. It is generally conceded that these children will be reared, trained and cared for best by their mother. Accordingly the courts will ordinarily award the custody of children of tender age, especially girls, to their mother, unless it is clearly shown that she is not a fit and proper person to have the custody of her child.[66]

Courts accepted a broad definition of fit and proper. Robert Metry cites a Kentucky case in which "Even where the mother had shot and killed her ex-spouse's second wife, she was given custody of a ten-year old daughter. She was found to be a good parent, her other act notwithstanding."[67]

The feelings for the mother's custody were at times harshly antifather, as this exchange at the 1975 American Bar Association convention showed:

> Mr. S__ stressed that what many fathers now want is not just extended visitation but true parental rights: i.e., an equal voice in decisions affecting the child's future. She was immediately attacked by numerous male members of the panel and audience, who unequivocally declared that any father who says he wants extended visitation or continued parental rights is a liar. . . . It was again roundly asserted that paternal love is a myth and any father who says he loves the child enough to want more than weekend visits are (sic) given in bad faith.[68]

FATHER RIGHT?

By the late 1960s it appeared that women had won the right to their children similar to the feudal father-right. But this was not true. The courts had been assuming that mother-custody would best serve society's interest in good child rearing. Said a Missouri court in 1955, "With all his technological and social advances, man has found no substitute for the care and affection of a mother."[69] Once this assumption was attacked, women turned out to have few rights at all.

In the 1970s Justice for Divorced Fathers and other men's organizations publicly campaigned for father-custody on the grounds of sex discrimination against men and the best interests of the child. Colorado, Florida, Indiana, Oregon, Wisconsin, and others have passed laws specifying, in the words of the Oregon statute, "no preference in custody should be given the mother over the father for the sole reason that she is the mother." Old shibboleths about female-headed families causing juvenile delinquency, school failure and male homosexuality have been brought back as ammunition.[70]

The women's liberation movement and mothers working have been used as arguments that women are not better suited for parenthood than men. The campaign has seen some success:

> Possibly to the chagrin of feminists, mothers are no longer the automatically preferred parents in custody disputes. Increasingly states are abandoning the "tender years presumption" in statutory and case law, and fathers are being awarded custody of their young children when it is clear that it is the best interests of the children.[71]

The doctrine of tender years has been rejected by statute or court decision in twenty-six states.[72]

This trend may have the effect of restoring the father's paramount right. If the father wants the children for the social pleasures of this new unit of consumption, he is increasingly able to get them. If he does not want them, and most do not, then he need not have them.[73] The freedom is his. There are even a few cases of fathers of illegitimate children gaining custody over the objection of the mother.[74] Traditionally, illegitimacy guaranteed the mother sole and paramount right. It appears that in addition to losing a presumption they have had for a hundred years, mothers may be losing rights they have held for centuries.

IMPLICATIONS FOR STRATEGY

We have seen that as children changed from a valuable family asset to a costly family burden, divorce became easier and legal custody of children shifted from father-right to mother-obligation.

The reasons can be traced to the changed role of children under monopoly capitalism and the concommitant change from private, family-based patriarchy to public, industry-based patriarchy. Public patriarchy benefits individual men in enabling them to shift the financial and labor burden of their children onto the mothers, while retaining access to women's services through the formal organizations, both governmental and industrial, of capitalist patriarchy. This explanation also accounts for the increase in illegitimacy, caused by men not marrying the women who bear their babies. Women have fought for and gained some benefit from this change, the major benefit being greater rights to their children and greater freedom from individual men. But the freedom has by no means brought equality, and will not as long as, under capitalist patriarchy, reproduction serves production and women serve men.

The female-headed family is still a minority of families, and will probably remain so. The patriarchy upholds male domination of the family, and there are benefits to men in their position as private patriarchs. These include the social pleasures of the children, the services of the wife, and the prestige and social status of head-of-family. But these benefits do not always obtain, especially at the lower economic levels where children are costly, the pleaures of their company few, and where the lack of money and the overwork decreases the services and pleasures of the marriage. This same lack of benefits increasingly holds true at the middle income levels for the same reasons. When the benefits do fail, the changes in the patriarchal system have made it possible for men to cut their losses, obligating the women to the children and enabling men to gain the benefit of women's reproductive labor either through the marketplace or through a new girlfriend or wife. The new arrangement has increased the freedom of men to choose between burdens and benefits.

Women's changing economic roles have locked them into the reproductive aspect of society both at home and at work, doubling their burden and removing the secondary benefit of marital guarantees that private patriarchy had provided. Some of these guarantees were also oppressions, and women are better off for being able to leave. But a woman who leaves her husband, or whose husband leaves her, is not freed of patriarchy; she has simply become less subject to private patriarchy and more subject to public patriarchy.

What are we going to do about this? A realistic strategy for today has to accept the reality of both patriarchy and capitalism; it has to consider both what is possible and what is desirable. Women should not become overly pessimistic about the increasing power of the public patriarchy. Women have always been tied to reproduction and children. The shift to public patriarchy has given women more rights to their children than they previously had, and has provided some public assistance payments and job possibilities that enable women to escape the bondage to powerful husbands that was the fate of previous generations. The increasing power of public patriarchy has brought with it the increasing collective strength of women. Greater consciousness of the role of capitalism and the state, as well as greater freedom to act publicly has made it possible for women collectively to organize and win battles as workers, as citizens, and as reproducers.

It is to be hoped that eventually we can overthrow both capitalism and patriarchy; in the meantime women have to do all they can to improve the situation now. Linda Gordon has noted about the struggle for birth control that "even while unable to overthrow their rules, women could and did change the terms of their labor and limit the privileges of their masters."[75] It is with this goal in mind that I turn to the question of female-headed families and custody of children.

It is not easy to figure out even what the eventual goal would be. Children are a social pleasure to their parents as well as a burden. Some women want more than anything to be relieved of the burden; some women want more than anything to retain the social pleasure. One overall policy would not be right for all women. What women need is the freedom to choose custody, and the right to retain control once they have chosen. What is happening now is that men are getting the freedom and the public patriarchy is getting the control.

In general, our strategy should be to try to turn "mother-obligation" into "mother-right"—the right to choose motherhood or nonmotherhood. This is an aspect of the overall goal of the women's movement for reproductive freedom.

PRIVATE PATRIARCHY

Women never won the "paramount" rights to their children that men previously had. For reasons I will explain below, I do not think women should fight for paramount right. I think women should fight for "primary" right, similar to Kent's "first guardianship by nature." At present women have only the equal right to *ask* for custody from the court, but the court may deny the mother in the best interests of the child. The courts have been assuming that the mother's custody was in the best interests of the child, but the assumption is under attack, as I have shown. If a best interest argument is made on the grounds of which parent has greater economic resources, social prestige and recognition, and access to the reproductive labor of others, then men, because of their superior position in patriarchal capitalism, will be able to win in a large number of cases. Women should fight for their *right* to their children on the grounds of their motherhood—the labor and emotional nurturance that they have invested in their children. A mother who wants to retain custody of her children should be able to keep it unless an overwhelming public interest is served by her losing it. Her right to her children should come before the right of the father or any other party.

I do not argue for permanent and unassailable mother-right, for three reasons. First, there *are* the bests interests of the child to be taken into account. All biological mothers are not good mothers, and there is a public interest which all women share in wanting children to be well treated. Second, actual custody fights take place not merely between the biological mother and the father, but also between mother and foster mothers, adoptive mothers, even grandmothers. *Social* motherhood is a goal to be fought for; we should therefore not limit it. Third, a paramount right to what others see as a burden too often becomes a paramount obligation. We do not want to force women into permanent servitude; we want to free them of it.

When custody does involve patriarchy and the rights of women, the argument for mother-custody is a strong one. The argument is made by Goldstein *et al* in *Beyond the Best Interests of the Child* that custody should be awarded once and for all to one parent, and that no further challenges should be allowed.[76] Although this does seem to be tying on a burden, perhaps it is strategically the best. In a large number of actual cases women receive custody when the children are young; then, when the children become older and are more pleasure than work, and the father perhaps remarries, the woman's children may be taken from her. Permanent custody would assure her that she need not fear losing her children to the father's greater power. If we are to have the burden, let us at least have the rights that go with it.

If fathers do want to share the social pleasures of the child, they should be required to show proof of mothering. If they want custody, they should prove that they have done 50 percent or more of the child-rearing labor. If they want visitation rights or joint custody, they should be required to pay equitable child support, perhaps as great a proportion of their income toward the child as the mother is paying of hers toward the child, and the men should be required to perform their share of the labor. Within the last year, disturbing decisions have let men who were not paying their child support continue to have visitation rights, thus enabling them to have the social pleasures of their children without sharing the burden.[77]

A man's remarriage, where he has a new wife to do the labor, should not be considered as grounds for taking the children away from their own mother.

Court arguments made along these lines might also help the still-married mothers. By defining the rights and obligations of parents to children outside of marriage, a new definition within marriage may come into public consciousness.

PUBLIC PATRIARCHY

The numerically and perhaps politically more important issue is the 90 percent of single parent families in which women carry all the burden. Most often the women not only have the sole care of the children, but also the sole financial burden. There is a contradiction in strategy here: if we make demands on the public patriarchy for more support of female-headed families, we increase the scope of the public patriarchy. Thus one might argue that we should avoid such involvement. However, if we do not make such demands, women heading families will suffer an unjustified burden of labor and cost that not only oppresses them, but also forces all women into greater dependence on individual men and the private patriarchy for lack of alternatives.

Given the choice, there is no question that women must make demands on the public patriarchy. Issues include higher welfare benefits that recognize the value of the labor of child rearing; chilren's allowances that are not tied to a means test, relieving the private family of a burden that benefits society; more child care services that are paid from public tax funds; more low-cost legal assistance to women involved in divorce and custody fights, since women do not have the money that men have; more legal pressure on men to pay their child support.

The strategies I have been suggesting direct themselves to this society, assuming the continuation of public patriarchy. Over the long run, we do not want merely an improvement in our condition of subordination. We want an end to the subordination, the destruction of patriarchy both private and public, and equal power in society to decide not only family policies but all other policies.

Therefore, women have to fight both patriarchy and capitalism. Many of these suggestions do both, since the subordination of reproduction to production is basic to capitalism. Demanding more share of the surplus for the reproducers is an attack on the capitalist structure. Moreover, it is an attack on the economistic ideas of much of socialism. In ignoring the importance of reproduction, socialism runs the risk of recreating the patriarchal structure.[78] At the same time, a feminism that concentrates on "women's" issues without understanding and attacking the entire economic structure of capitalism will remain relegated to a secondary role in the total struggle. Since we are fighting not merely against capitalism but for a socialism that brings human liberation, the presence in the socialist movement of conscious feminism will help to bring about the future we desire.

FOOTNOTES

1. Carol Brown, "The Political Economy of Sexual Inequality," forthcoming.
2. Ruth Brandwein, Carol Brown and Elizabeth Fox, "Women and Children Last: the Social Situation of Divorced Mothers and Their Families," *Journal of Marriage and the Family*, Vol. 35: August 1974, pp. 498-514.
3. Karl Marx, *Capital*, Part 7, Chapter 23 (New York: International Publishers, 1906).
4. Phillippe Aries, *Centuries of Childhood: A Social History of Family Life* (New York: Knopf, 1970).
5. James O'Connor, *The Fiscal Crisis of the State* (New York: St. Martins Press, 1973); Roger Alcaly and David Mermelstein, eds., *The Fiscal Crisis of the Cities* (New York: Vintage, 1977).
6. See for example: Rosalyn Baxandall, Elizabeth Ewen, and Linda

Gordon, "The Working Class Has Two Sexes," *Monthly Review*, Vol. 28, No. 2: July-August 1976; also Batya Weinbaum and Amy Bridges, "The Other Side of the Paycheck: Monopoly Capital and the Structure of Consumption," *ibid.*; also Barbara Ehrenreich and Dierdre English, *For Her Own Good* (Garden City: Anchor-Doubleday, 1978).

7. Marvin Sussman, "Family Systems in the 1970s: Analyses, Policies and Programs," *Annals*, No. 396: 1971, pp. 40-56.

8. Valerie Kincaid Oppenheimer, *The Female Labor Force in the United States* (Berkeley: Institute for International Studies, University of California, 1970).

9. Peter B. Doeringer and Michael Piore, *Internal Labor Markets and Manpower Analysis* (Lexington: Lexington Heath, 1971).

10. Francis Fox Piven and Richard A. Cloward, *Regulating the Poor* (New York: Pantheon, 1971).

11. Manuel Castells, *The Urban Question* (Cambridge: MIT Press, 1976).

12. Leo Kanowitz, *Women and the Law: the Unfinished Revolution* (Albuquerque: University of New Mexico Press, 1969).

13. *Dair Gillespie, "Who Has the Power? The Marital Struggle," Journal of Marriage and the Family*, vol. 33: August 1971, pp. 445-458; also Robert O. Blood, Jr. and D.M. Wolfe, *Husbands and Wives: The Dynamics of Married Living* (Glencoe: Free Press, 1965); also Jesse Bernard, "No News, But New Ideas," in Paul Bohannan, ed., *Divorce and After* (Garden City: Doubleday Anchor, 1964).

14. Stanley Lebergott, *Manpower in Economic Growth* (New York: McGraw Hill 1964).

15. *Ibid.*

16. *Ibid.*

17. Robert W. Smuts, *Women and Work in America* (New York: Columbia University Press, 1959).

18. Michael Katz, *The Irony of Early School Reform* (Boston: Beacon Press, 1970).

19. Samuel E. Morrison and Henry Steele Commager, *The Growth of the American Republic* (New York: Oxford University Press, 1962).

20. For example, Gary Becker, "A Theory of Marriage: Part I, *Journal of Political Economy*, Vol. 81: July-August 1973, pp. 813-846.

21. Linda Gordon, *Woman's Body, Woman's Right* (New York: Grossman, 1976); Peter Fryer, *The Birth Controllers* (London: Secker and Warburg, 1965).

22. Siney Bernard, *Fatherless Families: Their Economic and Social Adjustment* (Waltham: Papers in Social Welfare No. 7, Brandeis University, 1964).

23. Judith Cassetty, *Child Support and Public Policy* (Lexington: Lexington Books, 1978).

24. Carl A. Weinman, "The Trial Judge Awards Custody of Children of Divorced Parents," *Law and Contemporary Problems*, Vol. 10: 1944, p. 726; also Margaret Puxon, *The Family and the Law* (Bristol: Macgibbon and Kee, 1967).

25. G.E. Howard, *A History of Matrimonial Institutions*, Chicago: University of Chicago Press, 1904; Arthur W. Calhoun, *A Social History of the American Family from Colonial Times to the Present* (Cleveland: Arthur H. Clark, 1919).

26. K.N. Llewellyn, "Behind the Law of Divorce," *Columbia Law Review*, December 1932 and January 1933.

27. *Ibid.*

28. Elizabeth C. Stanton, Susan B. Antony, and Matilda J. Gage, *History of Woman Suffrage* (New York: Fowler and Wells, 1881, *passim*).

29. Aileen Kraditor, *The Ideas of the Woman Suffrage Movement* (New York: Columbia University Press, 1965, pp. 115-16).

30. Joel P. Bishop, *Commentary on the Laws of Marriage and Divorce* (Boston: Little, Brown, 1881).

31. Gustavus Myers, "Rapid Increase in Divorce," in Julia Johnsen, ed., *Selected Articles on Marriage and Divorce* (New York: H.W. Wilson, 1925).

32. *Ibid.*

33. "Divorce and the Means of Diminishing It," (no author), in Johnsen, *op. cit.*.

34. Carroll Wright, *A Report on Marriage and Divorce in the United States* (Washington, D.C.: Commissioner of Labor, 1891).

35. Calhoun, *op. cit.*, p. 268.

36. E.A. Ross, "Significance of Increased Divorce," in Johnsen, *op. cit.*

37. Henry Foster, Jr. and Doris Freed, "Divorce in the 50 States: An Overview As of August 1, 1978," Monograph No. 6, *Family Law Reporter*, Vol. 4, No. 41: 22 August, 1978.

38. Roscoe Pound, "Individual Interests in Domestic Relations," *Michigan Law Review*, Vol. xiv, No. 3: January 1916, pp. 176-196.

39. Grace Abbott, *The Child and the State*, 2 vols. (Westport, Conn.: Greenwood Press, 1968)(originally published 1938).

40. James Kent, *Commentaries on American Law* (New York: Halsted, 1827).

41. *Ibid.*

42. State v. Richardson in Robert Bremner, ed., *Children and Youth in America: A Documentary History* (Cambridge: Harvard University Press, 1970, Vol. 1).

43. Kent, *op. cit.*

44. Delsie Williams, "The Care and Custody of Children in Mississippi," *Mississippi Law Journal*, Vol. 16, No. 3: March 1944, p. 281.

45. Mary A. Greene, "The American Mother's Right to Her Child," *The American Law Review*, Vol. 52: May-June 1918.

46. Bremner, *op. cit.*

47. Paul Sayre, "Awarding Custody of Children," *University of Chicago Law Review*, Vol. 9: June 1942, pp. 672-92.

48. Until the 1960s, eight states continued to recognize father-right. *Handbook of Women Workers 1969* (Washington, D.C.: U.S. Department of Labor, Women's Bureau, 1969).

49. Lewis Hochheimer, *The Law Relating to the Custody of Infants* (Baltimore: Harold B. Scrimger, 1887, 2nd edition).

50. *Patrick Payton*, "Factors in Determining Child Custody in Iowa," *Drake Law Review*, Vol. 20: pp. 383-395.

51. G.W. Field, *Legal Relation of Infant, Parent and Child, Guardian and Ward* (Rochester: Williamson and Higbie, 1888).

52. Hochheimer, *op. cit.*

53. Hochheimer, *op. cit.*, 1889, 3rd edition.

54. Sinclair v. Sinclair, in Bremner, *op. cit.*, p. 128.

55. State v. Langford, 1918 in Bremner, *op. cit.*, p. 126.

56. Charles Stewart, *Disintegration of the Families of Working Men* (Chicago, no publisher, 1893).

57. Blanche Cole, *Perspectives in Public Welfare: A History* (Washington, D.C.: U.S. Department of Health, Education and Welfare, 1969).

58. Emma O. Lundberg, "Aid to Mothers of Dependent Children," *The Annals*, Vol. xcviii: November 1921.

59. Robert L. Stein, "The Economic Status of Families Headed by Women," *Monthly Labor Review*, Vol. 93: December 1970.

60. Porter v. Powell 1890 in Bremner, *op. cit.*; see also Hon. L.B. Day, "The Development of the Family Court," *The Annals: Progress in the Law*, Vol. cxxxvi: March 1928.

61. Cassetty, *op. cit.*

62. "Reciprocity of Rights and Duties Between Parent and Child," (no author), *Harvard Law Review*, col. 1, No. 42: November 1928, pp. 112-114.

63. Chester G. Vernier, *American Family Laws* (California: Stanford University Press, 1932).

64. Joseph Landisman, "Custody of Children: best interests of children vs. rights of parents," *California Law Review* Vol. 33: June 1945, pp. 306-316.

65. James Schouler, *A Treatise on the Law of Marriage, Divorce, Separation and Domestic Relations* (Albany: Matthew Bender and Co., 1921, 6th edition).

66. F. Reed Poore, David Rieg and E. Ent, *Nelson on Divorce and Annulment* (Mundelein, Ill.: Callaghan and Co., 1961).

67. Robert Metry, "Tender Years: a Diminishing Doctrine," *Journal of Family Law*, Vol. 5: 1965, pp. 114-116.

68. "Report on Family Law Section Meeting at ABA Convention," (no author), *Family Law Reporter*, Vol. 1, No. 40: 26 August 1975.

69. Long v. Long, Missouri, 1955, quoted in Leo Kanowitz, *Sex Roles in Law and Society: Cases and Materials* (Albuquerque: University of New Mexico Press, 1973).

70. Alan Roth, "The Tender Years Presumption in Child Custody Disputes," *Journal of Family Law*, Vol. 15: 1976-7, pp. 423-462. See for rebuttal of such assumptions Elizabeth Herzog and C.E. Sudai, *Boys in Fatherless Families* (Washington, D.C.: U.S. Department of Health, Education and Welfare, Children's Bureau, 1971).

71. "No Special Treatment," (no author), *Family Law Reporter*, Vol. 4, No. 9: 3 January 1978.

72. Foster and Freed, *op. cit.*

73. Paul C. Glick, *The Future of the American Family*, Current Population Reports, Special Studies (Washington, D.C.: U.S. Bureau of the Census, January 1979), pp. 23-78.

74. *Family Law Reporter, passim*.

75. Gordon, *op. cit.*

76. Joseph Goldstein, Anna Freud and Albert J. Solnit, *Beyond the Best Interests of the Child* (New York: The Free Press, 1973).

77. *Family Law Reporter*, 1978. *passim*.

78. Hilda Scott, *Does Socialism Liberate Women* (Boston: Beacon Press, 1974).

THE MARRIAGE OF CAPITALIST AND PATRIARCHAL IDEO-LOGIES: MEANINGS OF MALE BONDING AND MALE RANKING IN U.S. CULTURE

Katie Stewart

Katie Stewart has been active in the women's movement in Cambridge, Massachusetts and Ann Arbor, Michigan and taught in the Women's Studies Program at the University of Michigan from 1977 to 1980. She is now living in a coal-mining community in West Virginia, researching a doctoral thesis in anthropology on the relationship between male-bonding and class consciousness.

Heidi Hartmann outlines a theory of capitalist patriarchy which recognizes historical and on-going dynamics between these two hierarchies and grounds each of them in a set of distinct social relations. As such, her essay "The Unhappy Marriage" suggests radical revisions of those marxist and feminist perspectives which have treated class and gender hierarchies in isolation from one another and either blended the two or subsumed one under the other. But while Hartmann provides many critical insights into the failures of ahistorical feminism and sex-blind "traditional" marxism, she argues that marxism's historical and dialectical materialism, when applied to patriarchy as well as capitalism, can provide the methodological basis for a new, more adequate understanding. I would like to propose, to the contrary, that additional insight will be required into the ways in which people experience hierarchy in their daily lives and interpret these experiences in culture. A truly historical theory of capitalist patriarchy must maintain a central focus on the relations of domination and subordination which define these hierarchies for the people living under them and on the processes by which we act to create, reproduce, and change them. To the extent that marxism limits its focus to objective, specifically economic structures and relegates subjective experience and meaning to a secondary, superstructural realm it does not address, and may actually obscure, essential questions concerning the relationships between acts and their meanings, structures and praxis, consciousness and culture. I argue, then, that a materialist theory of patriarchy such as the one which Hartmann has proposed is not in itself a sufficient theoretical basis for understanding the relationship between class and gender hierarchies. We need, rather, to dissolve the traditional marxist dichotomy between objective and subjective realities in order to develop a new perspective on both capitalism and patriarchy which is rooted in people's experiences of them.

In this essay I present an analytic framework for understanding the dynamics between patriarchy and capitalism as these are experienced by men in particular social and historical contexts. I suggest that cultural interpretation can provide crucial insights into these experiences since it is in culture that individuals continually express, interpret, and reinterpret them. I take culture to be a systematic, internally structured, world view which emanates from individuals' experiences of "self" in relation to others rather than a simple "reflection" of acts, behaviors, and relationships or a functional "mystification" and "legitimation" of abstracted objective structures such as "patriarchy" and "capitalism." In hierarchies, where categories of people are ranked in relation to one another and hold differential degrees of power and authority, status fundamentally influences one's identity. This status-identity, I argue, forms the central process through which experiences of hierarchy are translated into cultures of hierarchy, or, in this case, into the meanings which men attribute to class and gender. Dynamics between patriarchy and capitalism, then, can be located in men's sometimes congruent, sometimes conflictual status-identities in these two systems—the first ranking men in relation to one another and the second ranking them as a uniform gender over women. Finally, I propose that political relations of solidarity or of conflict and competition among men further structure their understandings of their own and other genders and classes.

To illustrate these points I present an analysis of colonial, Victorian, and contemporary meanings of gender and class in U.S. culture. Meanings of gender and class have permeated every level of U.S. culture throughout our history, affecting our most basic understandings of all social interactions and our interpretations of the forces which shape society. But these meanings are by no means uniform; their various forms in particular historical periods and among distinct social groups reflect men's historically specific experiences of the dynamics between their gender and male-ranked statuses.

The Puritan culture of colonial New England farm communities contained two quite distinct themes which expressed the male dominant and male-ranked status-identities of landowning adult men. The first theme, which stressed the human creation of society and competitive individual achievement, referred to men's ranked statuses as fathers and sons, landowners and servants, political officials and ordinary citizens, church leaders and followers. But a second theme—that of natural hierarchies, ascribed, God-given roles, and a harmonious brotherhood of men—predominated over the values of competitive individualism. This second, dominant theme expressed men's uniform gender identity as male dominants. In the late eighteenth and early nineteenth centuries, however, patriarchal kinship bonds were weakened by capitalist land speculation; the uniformity of male landowners and family heads was broken by growing distinctions of class, occupation and wealth and by greatly intensified competition among men. The dominant theme of Victorian culture, then, emphasized male-ranked status-identities over the status-identity of the male dominant; conflict and competitive individualism became the core meanings. The culture of the contemporary United States is still predominantly individualist. This is, however, far more true of middle class culture than it is of working class culture. Whereas middle class men derive much of their status-identity from their professional rank, working class men emphasize their natural, ascribed characteristics as male dominants. In each of these cases—Puritan, Victorian, and contemporary working class and middle class cultures—men's status identities are formed in a dynamic tension between male-ranking and male dominance. This dynamic is most clearly evident in men's sports groups, social clubs, unions, and fraternal societies. Its implications for political action and political consciousness are far reaching. By revising the strictly materialist theory of hierarchy to recognize these subjective dimensions of domination and subordination we can more fully understand men's praxis in gender hierarchies and develop strategies to combat it.

THE PURITAN DILEMMA: SOCIAL STRAINS BETWEEN THE INDIVIDUAL FAMILY HEAD AND THE BROTHERLY PATRIARCHAL COMMUNITY

I have said that Puritanism contained two conflicting views of male status-identity. The first view, with its focus on male-ranking, defined masculinity and high social status as achievements effected by individuals' effort, self-control, rationality, self-reliance, and free willful action. The individual male family head, acting in his own self-interest, was seen as the prime mover of society and the source of social progress. Some men succeeded while others failed; each man was ranked in relation to every other according to his worldly successes. The second, dominant view, however, focused on men's status as gender dominants; in it, men's status-identity depended on cooperation among all men in a community and their conformity to given, ascribed roles. The individual family head was subject to a larger moral and political authority symbolized in the image of an all-powerful God; willfulness was sin and any attempt to interfere with the natural social order created by God invited defeat. Status distinctions among men were treated as natural ascribed roles rather than reflections of individual differences of effort, intelligence, or skill. Society was seen not as a loose collection of distinct families but as an organic unity in which each family was the same as every other.

Meanings of individual achievement and human agency, then, expressed men's efforts to achieve status over other men while those of a natural ascribed order embodied men's experiences of a "natural" gender status—a status which would be disturbed or undermined by individual men's efforts to distinguish themselves from others. Conflicts between these meaning systems centered around the relative autonomy or interdependence of family heads. They voiced increasing political tensions, throughout the seventeenth and eighteenth centuries, between the individually achieved power of family heads and men's collective identities as members of a community which was organized by patriarchal kinship bonds and based on the simple authority of adult men over women and children.

THE ACHIEVING FAMILY HEAD

At the founding of New England farm communities family heads were allotted individual parcels of land. Although community members also used common pastures and general fields at first, these were soon subdivided into additional individually owned and oriented plots. The settlement pattern, which originally clustered households around a village nucleus, soon shifted to dispersed individual households.[1] With little economic specialization, independent family economies formed the basic unit of production, distribution, and consumption. The family head controlled the labor of his dependents and maintained a strict division of labor based on sex and age.[2] Sons depended on land inheritance, daughters on dowries, to marry and establish new households. Fathers often held on to the ownership of their land through most of their lives or even until death, thereby delaying sons' marriages by many years and insuring their continuing economic cooperation in working their fathers' land. Family heads used the affinal kinship ties established by their own and their daughters' marriages to form important political alliances and economic partnerships or exchange networks.[3]

The family, then, was the focus of all social relations and the center of adult male status. All individuals were required, sometimes by law, to "reside under some orderly family government": those who did not were considered dangers to society. Within the family men held their positions of power by virtue of their supposed peculiar abilities of self-control, physical strength, and rational intelligence.[5] Since women and children lacked these traits, they were required to simply obey the family head and to follow the code of conduct he imposed.[6] Women were physically and spiritually "endangered" by pregnancy and childbirth; they were urged to seek salvation through intense prayer and careful adherence to moral standards during these "trials."[7] Their subjection to natural forces bound them to infants who were seen as "depraved" creatures without reason or moral sensibility. Women were relegated exclusive responsibility to care for their children's physical needs for food, clothing, cleanliness, and warmth while men had the primary responsibility for their moral and social training. Even as well-supervised "helpmeets" women were often chastised for impeding their children's moral development by showing them too much natural, untempered affection.[8]

Thus women and children were relegated to a sub-social natural world while men's abilities linked them to a supernatural realm above society. Men's capacity to understand God's Commandments made them like him; "made in God's image" they embodied the moral structure of society. Replicating God's force through active domination, they made their passive subordinates human, created social relations, and achieved their own statuses.[9]

But far from establishing a uniform "male" status-identity, these traits merely provided the media through which individual men could compete with one another and establish a hierarchical ranking among themselves. Actual achievements were measured in degrees of control over family charges, material wealth, and positions of power in the church and town government. Each man formed an individual contract with the God of the Covenant and worked to carry out its terms through self-control and determined effort. In this view, the general calling, which made all Puritans children of God, gave only an outward appearance of piety and produced a "deceptive unity"; there were imposters in every church and in every family.[10] In short, "Since every group contained unbelievers, no group as such was capable of salvation."[11] Society was divided into "better, middling and meane sorts" according to individuals' differential achievements.[12] In this view indentured servants and wage-earning farm laborers, who together constituted approximately 20 percent of the adult male population,[13] lacked necessary resolve and were therefore subordinated, as "children," to particular land-owning family heads. Some individual family heads were weak. Lacking rational self-control they were both unable to properly control their family charges and in danger of being polluted from contact with them. Children should be taken from fathers who failed to educate them properly or who spoiled them by allowing too much natural affection to permeate the natal family and some husbands had to be constrained from allowing their wives to act inappropriately. Love and instinctual desire were the causes of Adam's original fall from grace. Marriage should be a rational covenant; men who married lower status women were thought to be the victims of an "improper love."[14]

> Man had originally an Empire and Dominion over these creatures here below. But sin hath inverted this order and brought confusion upon earth. Man is dethroned and become a servant and a slave to those things that were made to serve him, and he puts those things in his heart that God hath put under his feet.[15]

Active domination was necessary, too, to overcome the polluting influences of subordinates' natural depravities.

> . . . our children, servants, . . . are apt to profane the Sabbath: we are therefore to improve our power over them . . . and to constrain them . . . lest God impute their sins to us, who had the power to restrain them and did not; and so our families and consciences be stained with their guilt and blood.[16]

High ranking men (church elders, town fathers, large property owners) controlled not only their own family charges but those of the "weak" men as well. Ultimately, men overcame the potential dangers of instinct and the natural forces in the family by proving their ability to achieve power and status over other men. Family heads strove to increase their land holdings and their political alliances with other patriarchs. Even small differences in wealth could determine whether or not a man had a right to vote; voting requirements generally included a minimum level of taxable property ownership which excluded some of the lesser holders as well as all of the landless men.[17] The church elders and the "select men" or "town fathers," who ruled in town government were expected to be extremely rational and self-controlled—the characteristics deemed necessary for achievement.[18] Selectmen, in fact, were generally among the wealthiest members of the community. Prestige titles such as "esquire" and "gentleman" also roughly corresponded to wealth and wealth was among the criteria used to assign church seats in a rank ordering which marked the status of every man in the congregation.[19]

In this view, then, gender status, which marked natural distinctions between the sexes, was a necessary precondition for men's competitive achievement in relation to other men. But no natural status was assured; both gender and male-ranked statuses had to be achieved by individual family heads. Any "false unity" of man and woman or man and man invited individual mediocrity and social decay.

THE ESSENCE OF GOD AND THE BROTHERLY COMMUNITY

A second view—that of a brotherly community and a system of natural hierarchal roles—dominated Puritan culture throughout the seventeenth century and most of the eighteenth. It emphasized a unified group over the divisions of individual statuses and nucleated families. Communities were structured by a uniform Puritan congregation; all were children of God and, as the chosen people, all were descendents of a single father, Abraham. The village common was symbolically cogent as the center of a residential, religious, political, and economic community; household farms radiated out from it and family heads congregated there at the meeting house for religious services, town meetings, and haymarket exchanges. The houses of the founding fathers of the community surrounded the common. A community authority was vested in town fathers and church elders who apportioned land, made political decisions, regulated trade, and defined the moral rights, and responsibilities of ascribed roles. Kinship networks, far from being limited to the separate descent groups and affinal ties of individual family heads, included lateral ties between brothers and sisters and formed larger, encompassing descent groups unified under a single ancestor. Each unit of society—family, kinship, community, church, and state—was formed as a collectivity under a figure of authority and all units and authorities were bound together by the essence, or ultimate authority, of God.

God gave family heads the authority to own land and to dominate their family charges.[20] Indentured servants and wage-earning farm laborers were defined as children and subject to the same paternal authority. In the words of one family head, "My servants are in some sense my children. . . . And, as for the methods of instilling piety which I use with my children (they) may be properly and prudently used with them."[21] Family heads, town fathers, church elders, and state officials all had the same moral authority to determine what was best for their charges.[22] The rank ordering of church seats was based on age, parentage, social position, and service to the community as well as wealth.[23]

Status within this hierarchy rested, simply, on the fulfillment of an ascribed role. Hard work within one's calling assured redemption; only idleness and unnatural aspiration were worthy of scorn. The work of female "helpmeets" and children, as well as that of the family head, were recognized as real contributions to society and the fulfillment of moral responsibility.[24] Family heads and town fathers were enjoined to practice strict self-control and to orient their thoughts to collective rather than self-interested concerns.[25] They were required to work

> . . .*for the common good*, that is, for the benefit and good estate of mankind. In man's body there be sundry parts and members, and every one hath his several use and office which is performeth not for itself, but for the good of the whole body, as the office of the eye is to see, of the ear to hear, and the foot to go. Now all societies of men are bodies, a family is a body and so is every particular church a body, and the commonwealth also; and in these bodies there be several members which are men walking in several callings and offices. . . The common good of man stands in this. . . And for the attainment hereunto, providence designed the persons to bear them. . .he abuseth his calling, whosoever he be, that against the end thereof employs it for himself, seeking wholly his own and not the common good.[26]

Subject to a larger authority, fathers as well as mothers could be publicly punished for the crime of premarital pregnancy[27] and wives as well as husbands could seek divorce on grounds of impotency, infidelity, or physical abuse.[28] Family heads who failed to carry out their responsibilities were among those arrested as witches.[29]

The growing autonomy of nuclear families from their larger kinship systems and the relative freedom of family heads to control their family charges and to achieve economic and political status was the primary focus of the concern to assure individuals' subjugation to the group and the larger authority.

> Civil government. . . became an absolute necessity after the fall of man. The sin of the first Adam had so vitiated human nature that family governors could no longer be trusted to maintain the order that God had commanded. They might control their children and servants, but who was to control them? Who was to settle the quarrels into which their degenerate natures would lead them? God had given family governors no power over life and death. Clearly a superior authority was called for.[30]

Marriage banns had to be publicly announced or posted, civil magistrates presided over weddings, marital disputes could be called into court without the initiative of either spouse, and appointed deputies inspected families and attended to disorders of every kind. In heaven there would be no nuclear families at all—all would be husband, wife, parent, child and friend to all others. Children were sent out to live and work on neighboring farms (which were probably those of patrilineal relatives since these tended to hold adjacent lands) in order to counteract the "excessive affection" which permeated natal families. Spouses were urged to moderate their marital affection since it "would only end in death" while ties between members of extended familial descent groups, on the other hand, were seen as stable and everlasting. Building on the cooperation between members of extensive kinship systems, classificatory and fictive kin terms defined all respectable members of the community at large as "brothers" and "sisters."[31]

One essence linked God, man, land, community, and church together in a single moral order which originated in the family.[32] But rather than isolate his family each man was to bind his family to others; rather than act alone he was to act in concert with others. Individual happiness and salvation rested not on willful achievement but on submission to the role, or calling, to which God had assigned each person. Individual differences of intelligence, skill and so on were not recognized: it was precisely in their acceptance of a natural hierarchy—both within the family and among men outside the family—that all men were kept essentially "equal" as children of God. During the voyage to the new England John Winthrop addressed the other passengers on board the Arbella explaining that when God required that "Some must be rich, some poor, some high and eminent in power and dignity, others mean and in subjection" his purpose was to insure that

> every man might have need of another and from hence *they might be all knit more nearly together in the bond of brotherly affection*; from hence it appears plainly that no man is more honorable than another, or more wealthy etc.[33]

New residents had to petition the town fathers to be recognized as voting inhabitants and many were denied. Only land-owning family heads could vote and only those aged forty-five or older could be elected to be town fathers.[34] Town fathers formed a ruling oligarchy[35] although lesser offices and functions were distributed and rotated among men of all statuses.[36] Town fathers appointed town workers and special committees, initiated legislation, settled property and marital disputes, and levied taxes in *closed* meetings. All voting family heads participated in town meetings but in these "consensus was reached, and individual consent and group opinion were placed in the service of social conformity... men talked of politics, but ultimately they sought to establish moral community."[37] Those who could not prove that they had the saving grace necessary for church membership were excluded, and contentious or deviant individuals could be expelled from the town.[38]

Subjection to a common authority produced *equality of uniformity* among men. As the governor of the Massachusetts Bay Colony, Winthrop claimed that the good subject was one who willingly accepted the authority of the state while the sinful and *self-defeating* subject "eternally struggled to overthrow his yoke."[39] The civil liberty about which family heads were beginning to speak could only be maintained, according to Winthrop, when it was conbined with obedience and subjection to authority.

> The other kind of liberty I call civil or federal, it may also be termed moral in reference to the covenant between God and man, in the general moral laws, and in the political covenants and constitutions, amongst men ourselves. *This liberty is the proper end and object of authority, and cannot subsist without it*, and it is a liberty to that only which is good, just and honest... if you stand for your natural corrupt liberties... you

will not endure the least weight of authority...*which is set over you for your own good.*

Any act of self-interest or self-indulgence was a threat to community order. A man who acted for himself acted against others; wealth which was achieved rather than ascribed from God created the poverty and misery of others and all acts of aggression and violence were condemned regardless of the circumstances. Any man who caused another to lose face could be subject to public punishment.[42] As each family head's authority rested on the authority of all family heads, through God, he should deny his earthly family and deny himself to follow Him. Otherwise, men were threatened by an urge to achieve—a competition and uncertainty—that would destroy them all.

SUMMARY: THE PURITAN DILEMMA AND ITS TRANSFORMATIONS.

The two views of status were dynamically related in Puritan culture as a whole, forming a dilemma which focused on achievement versus ascription, competition versus brotherly affection, and the individual versus the community order. Achievement was a right of individuals and a necessity for a dynamic society but it also created destructive competition among men and threatened the very basis of their authority. A belief in men's equality of birth and their equal opportunity, coupled with a recognition of male-ranked social statuses and women's subordination to men, lead to an assertion that individual men on the one hand, and the sexes on the other, ultimately had unequal personal abilities and social worth. But this was encompassed by a dominant understanding that all people (including women) shared an equality of substance; a uniformity, by virtue of their common ancestry and their universal subjection to a larger authority: a predetermined social order superceded all individual interests and agency.

Still, why the Puritan dilemma? Why was there a continuing conflict between ascription and achievement in Puritanism despite the predominance of meanings of a natural hierarchy? And why, as I will demonstrate in the sections which follow, is the same conflict evident in the predominantly traditionalist culture of the contemporary working class and in the predominantly individualist views of the Victorians and the contemporary middle class? In each case, the themes of a natural hierarchical social order and individual freedom and achievement are interacting and in each case the conflict between these themes focuses on the individual man versus the male collectivity, the autonomous nuclear family versus the integration of all families in a larger community brotherhood.

For the Puritan family head achievement and autonomous control over his nuclear family meant his separation from his male patrilineal kin. Marriage represented an achievement: with it he established his own household, laid claim to his parcel of the patrilineal lands, formed immediate affinal alliances with his wife's kin, and eventually established his own descent line, passing *his* land on to *his* sons. Originally, the divisive effects of such achievement were held in check by the strength of the more extensive descent groups which structured on-going cooperation between fathers and sons, brothers and cousins. These large descent groups formed power blocs in the community; they placed their members in office and were allotted new lands of varying sizes depending on their relative strength in numbers and on the amount of land which each, as a group, already owned.[43] Pollution ideology focused not just on women, but on the nuclear family in general: efforts by individual men to claim autonomous ownership of their wives, children, and land would break the bond of brotherly affection and lead, ultimately, to their own self-destruction. The problem of achievement and the nuclear family, then, referred to a very general concern to maintain a solitary status-identity among the men of lineage.

The tensions in the kinship system between individual family heads and extended lineages were exacerbated by a growing land scarcity; partible inheritance no longer provided sons with sufficient lands for farming and fathers shifted to an increasingly impartible system.[44] Descent lines lost members as each succeeding generation of fathers saw more of their sons forced to leave their natural communities in order to farm land in the west or to adopt nonagricultural callings.[45] The average age of men's marriage dropped as fathers lost control over their sons.[46] And sons, who had once relied on kinship networks to achieve the family head status and upward mobility were now required to leave these networks in striving toward the same ends.[47]

In the second half of the eighteenth century, particularly the last quarter, the rapid development of capitalist markets in land and in agricultural goods and artisans' products and services further undermined patrilineal kinship as the center of community organization.[48] Agriculture and craft production became increasingly specialized and purely economic exchanges replaced kinship reciprocities. The home industries of helpmeets and daughters were organized more and more by a commission system rather than by direct production for and management by the family head. [49] As land was bought and sold with increasing frequency, land grants were no longer controlled by communities and doled out by town fathers; emigrating sons were replaced by land speculators who became "inhabitants" by virtue of their property ownership without regard for community residence or family status.[50] With land a free commodity, family heads worked to augment their holdings; some succeeded while others were dispossessed. The ranks of the landless nearly doubled as did the proportion of wealth held by the richest ten percent.[51] Wealth and class replaced traditional patriarchal status markers. Wealthy farmers and nonresident land speculators argued that property should be more strongly emphasized in the criteria used to elect selectmen. The influence and moral authority of ministers and selectmen declined as did the use of symbolic prestige titles. Town fathers no longer represented a consensual body of land owning family heads; the new political ideology deemphasized communal spirit and emphasized, instead, the importance of the town meeting as a forum for conflicting local opinions and the political participation of individuals with distinct interests.[52] Universal suffrage for all "freemen" referred to an equality among men which specifically denied traditional ascribed hierarchy; democracy defined the rights of each individual man distinct from all others and achieving his status in conflict and competition with them.

At the same time, gender ideology shifted its focus from the helpmeet, the tempting Eve and the polluting mother to a new virginal and moral mother. As ascribed male-ranking lost its political cogency, the autonomous nuclear family was elevated to a new status and granted the power to determine society writ large. This, however, was not won without real costs to a stable and unifying male status. The achieving individual was made a "blank slate" at birth,[53] sons were removed from the stabilizing family,[54] and working class "children" became adult men and women whose amorality and sin not only lead to their own self-destruction but also *diseased* other men and caused *decay* in "the family."

THE VICTORIAN IMAGE OF THE LIMITED GOOD: DILUTED MASCULINITY AND SAVAGE COMPETITION

The Victorian ideology of petty-bourgeois shop owners and farmers developed the image of the moral mother, posed a strict dichotomy between the female family sphere and the male work world, and expressed a powerful theme of distrust and uncontrolled conflict among men. Shops and offices were removed from the family residence, free laborers were increasingly employed over apprentices and indentured servants, farmers' daughters went to earn their dowries in the first textile mills[56] and so on. These men, like the Puritans, looked beyond the family for their full status-identities. But with work and family divided and the single authority of God-land-man-church-community and state broken, male dominance no longer assured a status with other men or provided the moral authority through which individuals could achieve status over other men. The rivalry and pressure of competition gave men the impetus to develop their energies and will in order to ''make themselves (in the) whirl and contact with the world.''[57] But it also undermined men's ''natural'' role to dominate their families and ultimately reduced self-controlled, rational achievement to an uncontrollable competitive instinct.

In unseating the town fathers and freeing themselves of natural constraints on achievement, men had produced confusion and exposed themselves to a constant threat that their energies would be diluted. Without a stable ''male'' status they could destroy themselves as easily as they could make themselves and they were confused and driven mad with anxiety about political and other success.

> no son is necessarily confined to the work of his father. . . all fields are open. . . all are invited to join the strife. . . they are struggling to their utmost tension. . . their minds stagger. . . they are perplexed with the variety of insurmountable obstacles; and they are exhausted with the ineffectual labor.[58]

The family inspired images of natural and unchanging forces such as water and sun but these referred to woman rather than to God and the essence of man: what had once been God's limitless ocean was now woman's domesticated stream.[59] Woman's ''merely biological'' motherhood became the force which created a moral society. The condition of her womb determined her children's physical and moral capacities, her breast milk contained a substance through which she transferred to her children the natural affection which was now necessary to their growth, and her intuitive morality made her the natural parent and sole guardian of all spiritual purity.[60]

> the influence of the woman is not circumscribed by the narrow limits of the domestic circle. She controls the destiny of every community. The character of society depends as much on the fiat of woman as the temperature of the country on the influence of the sun.[61]

Fatherhood, in contrast, was reduced to the role of providing sperm and material necessities: the father's exclusive creative force in reproduction and his moral power were sacrificed in his competition for wealth in the wilderness outside the family. Fathers were portrayed as harsh and authoritarian: their efforts to arrange their children's marriages elicited protests and resentment and they were besieged by frightening images of "marauding gangs" of youths bent on their own, and the moral order's, destruction.[62]

Men struggled to achieve gender and male-ranked statuses in two mutually-exclusive spheres. They were "utterly unable to concentrate their energies on any particular point,[63]"in the division between home and the economy each sphere was a danger to men's now *limited* energies. Men who did not transcend the moral, personal, affectionate, cooperative and spiritual relations in the family would only stagnate in the amoral, impersonal, emotionless, competitive and materialistic relations among men in the world outside. Where women worked in the home "only for pure affection, without thought of money or ambition"[64] men were *by nature* "bent on the acquisition of wealth."[65] But each man battled, alone and naked, in an economic wilderness. They looked to their private families for respite from "the alternations in commercial affairs... the sudden and unexpected reverses of fortune."[66]

> A home!... the altar of your confidence (is) there: the end of your worldly faith is there: and adorning it all, and sending your blood in passionate flow, is the ecstasy of the conviction, that *there* at least you are beloved: that there you are understood: that there your troubles will be smiled away: that there you may unburden your soul, fearless of harsh, unsympathetic ears: and that there you may be entirely and joyfully—yourself.[67]

Men had to guard against the pollution of women's menstruation, pregnancy, and birth but in order to be rational, aggressive, coura-geous, virile, materialistic and worldly they required contact with woman's exactly complementary characteristics. It was only in rela-tion to the emotional, passive, timid, asexual, spiritual, submis-sive, pious, pure and domestic woman,[68] that men's characteristics symbolized achievement. Without the balancing and stabilizing effects of gender contrasts in the family, men's activities in the work world were reduced to uncontrollable instincts.

Images of sex and economics were mixed in metaphors of "spent sperm," "mother earth," and "virgin land."

> Woman should be inexhaustible and undemanding resources. But the hope came with the guilty fear that men were depend-ent on women—indeed, hope and fear sprang from the same matrix. Men were dependent for power on that from which they wished to be independent.[69]

Men "plowed virgin land" to extract its resources and "recruited (their) exhausted energies with each fresh contact with (their) mother earth."[70] But at the same time "Women became insatia-ble consumers of male resources...and men's relationship with them a ceaseless expenditure that could drain them dry and make them unmanly, passive and dependent like women."[71] Men were urged to limit their sexual intercourse which was likened to "div-ing for pearls in the slimy bottom of the ocean...they are found only here and there and (a man) would stick and die in the mud in which they were embedded."[72]

On the one hand, then, men were saved and renewed in their relations with women while on the other they were threatened and consumed. The problem, however, lay not in female pollution per se; men were susceptible only to the extent that they lacked resolve or were ruled by their instinctual, uncontrollable desires. Repro-ductive sex was beneficial; men deposited their sperm, and their male status in a fertile female vessel.[73] Non-reproductive sex and masturbation, however, depleted the "sperm" necessary to achieve political and economic success; in "wasting" their precious sperm "men drivel away their existence on the outskirts of socie-ty...they are at once a lead weight, a sluggish, inert mass in the paths of this busy, blustering life, having neither the will not the capacity to take a part in the general matters of life."[74] Young men who masturbated would stunt their growth so that they would eventually father only runts and girls.[75] In masturbation, "All the faculties are weakened. The man becomes a coward; sighs and weeps like a hysterical women. He loses all decision and dignity of character."[76] As a thing in itself, orgasm represented only the loss of self-control; it was likened to an unpredictable paroxysm of pain. Finally, in this view, "sexual license was characteristic of slum life and, like drink, one of those traits which kept the poor poor."[77]

The privatized family was a stable natural world in which a man could be safe and sure of himself but the world beyond it had no natural order. The market, like the Puritan's God, became a self-determining force untouched by human interference.[78] But where God's order had directly ranked men and established an ultimate male authority the market only freed men from ascribed statuses and marked their individual abilities to achieve wealth. Democracy, too, defined equal rights for free men but could not unite men. Reflecting only self-interest and competition, it was frightening and arbitrary: "the licentiousness of a lawless democracy, without virtue or intelligence, is...more terrible than the oppression of despotism."[79] Moral and political reformers argued for renewed self-control, faith in providential order, a return to the land, and a reemphasis on steady work, frugality and simple and honest industry. But the image of the self-made man, exerting his will to conquer nature and to create his own destiny, prevailed. Men's status could not rest simply on contact with their mother earth and the natural influence of the moral mother. They would have to both "plow virgin lands" and protect their virgins from rape by other men.[80] The "excesses" of some men polluted all men, replacing self-control with sexual instinct and willful achievement with "animal" competition.

Without a uniform essence which could define a community of men while it also predetermined their differential social statuses, a code for conduct was no longer sufficient insurance of a stable social order. Absolute principles and rights were abstracted from social context. Individualism and biological determinism developed together in a world view that argued for individual interests in a society ruled by instincts, symbolized gender hierarchy and male ranking in body idioms of penises and wombs, explained individuals' differential accomplishments by biological characteristics of races and classes, and made individuals "blank slates" at the same time that it made them the genetic recipients of their parents' traits.

True masculinity rested on freedom and required willful effort. But men were not united in the struggle and individual failures weakened the male "race," creating a downward spiral of lost manliness. The problem lay in the value on individual achievement which defined masculinity itself; in asserting his strength each man entered, necessarily, into competition with other men.

I have argued that the images of a brotherhood of men and a natural hierarchy on the one hand, of competition and individual achievement on the other, were in a dynamic tension in Puritan and Victorian culture. I suggest that this tension expresses two conflicting but interdependent meanings of masculinity—the one ascribed and the other achieved—and that the conflict between them is derived from the co-existence of male dominant gender hierarchy and non-gender hierarchies which rank men.

In Puritanism, masculinity was derived from men's ascribed roles; all men were alike in their positions as family heads or breadwinners, and all men shared a uniform and stable status as male dominants. They formed a unity of brothers in their subordination to God's ultimate moral authority and were constained from individual achievement. Men were ranked in an *explicit* hierarchy which demanded obedience from subordinates but these roles, like male dominance itself, were predetermined in a natural social order and did not reflect individual worth. A predominantly individualist culture, such as that which emerged in nineteenth century Victorianism, presents a strikingly different view of masculinity. The values of democracy, achievement, equality, and individual rights and freedoms made each man an autonomous agent and freed him from the constraints of a given social order. The emphasis shifted from brotherhood to competition, from an equality of substance (or uniformity) to equal opportunity, from an ascribed male status to the achieved status of each individual man against all others. A "real" man had to prove himself in active competition with other men. Since structurally-determined hierarchy was specifically denied, men's ranked statuses were taken as reflections of their differential abilities. Subordinate men, in this view, were lazy and content to be poor and uneducated; they, like women, were ruled by natural forces and irrational, uncontrollable instincts.

Despite their distinct emphases on the community of men and the achieving individual, Puritan and Victorian cultures expressed the same conflict. Where the Puritans worried that men were losing their essential and uniform connection to God, Victorian men obsessed over preserving their limited life force and saw themselves as savages battling, alone and naked, in an economic wilderness. Both cultures focused their concern on the relationship between male dominance in the nuclear family and the system of male ranking in the larger society; where the Puritans argued that family order duplicated that of the whole social order, and that men would destroy themselves in vain efforts to achieve, the Victorians believed that men must overcome the natural, polluting forces of the family and natural instinct in order to "make themselves" through competition and the achievement it engendered.

INDIVIDUAL ACHIEVEMENT AND BROTHERHOOD IN CONTEMPORARY UNITED STATES CULTURE

Today, the dominant U.S. culture is individualistic. Both equality and achievement depend, however, on competition, and individual differences must be constantly asserted and reasserted. Without competition and individual differences, we are told, we would all be living on welfare and dependent on the state. Social conformity in the suburbs is seen as a blight on society, and a continuous symbolic threat of "communism" periodically erupts into an articulated political theme. For most Americans, communism means a forced and absolute *equality* which would destroy all individual incentive to achieve, and a totalitarian regime which would dismantle democratic pluralism.[81] In short, we confound substantive equality with conformity and consensus with an undesirable uniformity.

The threat to individual achievement and freedom is no idle one for American men. On the one hand, they compete as individuals for school grades, sports stardom, sexual prowess, good jobs, and so on. But on the other hand they bond as male peers and as members of sports teams, unions, fraternities, and fraternal organizations; in all of these groups self-interested motives are specifically devalued in relation to the interests of the group or to some larger abstract goals such as patriotism and humanitarianism. In all of them, too, there are strong sanctions against individuals' attempts to assert their superiority over other members of the group. Finally, the very equality of men in these groups is ensured by an elaborate hierarchy of given roles culminating in a strong and central leader whose authority may be absolute. Decisions are based on consensus, and it is a consensus which may be more or less dictated by the leader.

The symbolism of sports in the U.S. portrays a conflict between individual achievement and team cooperation. Popular spectator sports such as football, basketball, baseball, and hockey are both extremely competitive and played by teams. Individualism is expressed in elaborate ''rags to riches'' myths, in an emphasis on star players and all-star teams, and spectators' sympathy for underdog teams would could win against the odds. In winning, which is, afterall, the object of the game, one team establishes its superior ability. Formal rules and impartial referees are used to enforce an equal opportunity out of which this natural inequality, reflecting differential abilities, can emerge. The spirit of competition is ruined when games are fixed, when one team uses unfair advantage in recruiting players, and when players use artificial stimulants and pain-killers during a game. A ''good'' game is one played between well-matched teams in which competition is fierce and the outcome is unpredictable. As such, the ethic of American sports is in sharp contrast to that of traditional European village games where one team generally had more horses to ride and was also deliberately given an uphill advantage.[82]

But where American sports culture is strictly egalitarian individualistic in defining interactions between teams, it is much more traditional, or social, in the norms it establishes for relationships among members of a single team. Each player has a given position in a group formation and a given role in a team effort. The team is a force in itself; it is larger than its individual parts and has a spirit which bolsters and supercedes individual abilities. Team colors, uniforms and emblems become fetishes and spectators develop long-standing team loyalties which have little or nothing to do with a team's record of wins and losses.

According to the sports code, players are expected to develop full social characters as well as physical strength and competitive fortitude; boys are encouraged to play team sports in the belief that this will teach them patriotism, loyalty, altruism, respect for authority, discipline, self-control. . .even Christianity itself.[83] All players are subject to social control; they may be benched, socially ostracized, suspended, removed from the team, or blacklisted. And they are all subordinated, together, to the authority of the coach; he may regulate their hair and clothing styles, their diets, their bedtimes and even their sexual activities. In the words of one University of Texas football player, ''Our coaches would tell us about the necessity for self-discipline, but what that really meant was obedience... (The) threat of punishment reinforced our total dedication and tacitly demanded that we should never question our coaches' authority. Like good soldiers, our job was to follow orders, not to think about them.''[84]

In the context of a uniform identity for all team members and their subjection to a single authority in the figure of the coach, individuals are expected to subordinate their interests and achievements to those of the team. Group formations, team spirit and team cooperation are stressed. The quarterback is a star in his roles to announce team plays in the huddle and to put the team's ball in motion. The player who makes a touchdown must share his glory with the other team members who worked to keep the field open. The star athlete draws the antagonism of his teammates if he plays too ''selfishly'' or if he fails to exert his full effort *for* the team.[85] Obedience to the coach is part and parcel of team loyalty; as such, it supercedes both individual achievement and the rules of the game. The coach decides who plays and who doesn't, he humiliates individuals, or the team as a whole, for poor performance, he orchestrates the plays of the game, and he has the legitimate authority to order players to cheat by deliberately interfering with passes, shoving, tripping, elbowing, and so on. All of these are acts for which individuals can be penalized, fined, and even taken out of the game. It is only as a member of the team, within the given structure of the team, and under a coach that an individual is spurred on to compete and to achieve. The ideology of equal potential and individual ability in the game is contradicted by a traditionalistic definition of team unity. At the same time, however, team solidarity depends on competition with other teams and on winning. Competition, then, is the means through which individual men develop and assert their masculine fortitude and abilities but it must also be bolstered by in-group loyalty and the submission of individuals to the team and to the authority of the coach.

Secret fraternal societies, such as the Masons, the Elks, the Kiwanis club, the Lions, and the Knights of Templar, stress the power of the group over the individual even more strongly. All of them define themselves as a group of men in distinction from others, whether on the basis of religion, occupation, class, ethnicity, or race.All have initiation rituals, degrees of membership and an elaborate hierarchy of officers. All are headed by a central figure who often has tremendous symbolic importance in defining the membership as a unified group of brothers; the Knights of Templar, for instance, travel each year to their regional leader's birthplace for their annual meetings. In all of them, members prove their unselfish motivation by raising charity funds for physically handicapped people—usually children—and by acting in various "big brother" capacities.

The Knights of the Ku Klux Klan, although certainly distinct from these other fraternal societies by virtue of its hate and violence, has the same structure and *avowed* purposes in their most extreme form. The nature of the KKK, as outlined in the Klansman's manual, is defined by its six functions; it is patriotic, military, benevolent, ritualistic, social and fraternal. In its benevolence, "it gives itself to the task of relieving and helping the suffering and distressed, the unfortunate and oppressed (in) a program of sacrificial service for the benefit of others." Socially, it unites "in companionable relationship those who possess the essential qualities for membership. It is so designed that kinship of race, belief, spirit, character, and purpose will engender a real, vital and enduring fellowship among Klansmen." And fraternally, "Fraternal love has become the bond of union . . . every Klansman (is impelled) to seek to promote the well-being of his fellow Klansmen."[86]

The KKK was originally formed during postbellum reconstruction in reaction to the emancipation of the slaves. In the 1920's, it was reconstituted, with millions of members, in the nativist backlash against immigration. Now, in the late 1970's and early 1980's, it is being renewed once again—this time in conjunction with the antifeminist and new right movements to defend the traditional family. In each case, it has emerged as a defense of white, Protestant, all-American masculinity against a *democratic threat* to extend individual freedoms and rights to blacks, to women, to immigrants, to Jews, and to Catholics. The problem for Klansmen, however, lies not simply in the extension of rights to inferior groups, but in democracy itself and in achievement and the recognition of individual differences.

Fraternal order history records the failure of many patriotic societies that were organized on a so-called democratic basis.

Without...the military form of government which is designed to provide efficient leadership, intelligent cooperation...uniform methods, and uniform operation...even the Knights of the Ku Klux Klan would degenerate into a mere passive, inefficient social order. The military must and will be preserved for the sake of true, patriotic Americanism, because it is the only form of government that gives any guarantee of success. We must avoid the fate of the other organizations that have split on the rock of democracy.[8]

The military function dictates the hierarchy of officers from the highest—the Imperial Wizard—to the Grand Dragons, the Great Titans, the exalted Cyclops, and the subordinate officers and aids of each of these. And authority

is vested primarily in the Imperial Wizard....there shall always be *one* individual, senior in rank to all other Klansmen of whatever rank, on whom shall rest the responsibility of command...and whose decisions, decrees, edicts, mandates, rulings, and instructions shall be full of authority and unquestionably recognized and respected by each and every citizen of the Invisible Empire.[8]

No other member of the Klan can compete with, or hope to achieve, the ultimate authority of the Imperial Wizard. All positions in the Klan are treated as ascribed, naturally ordered roles whether they are those of the first, probationary order of Citizenship or of the progressively higher orders of Knighthood, American Chivalry, and the Superior Order of Knighthood and Spiritual Philosophies.

In its very appeal to "red-blooded American manhood" the Klan demands uniformity in a cooperative equality of substance. "In this crusade there are few occasions for individual plays. Success is possible only through the most unselfish playing for the team."[8] Under the single authority of the Imperial Wizard, Klansmen are united to defend womanhood, brotherhood, selflessness, and responsiblility; the primary symbols of the Klan—the cross, the flag, the robe and the mask—all express meanings of selfless uniformity and a powerful masculinity which is established through self-sacrifice. Christ's blood transformed the cross from a symbol of disgrace and shame to one of faith, hope, and love. The flag, "purchased by the blood and suffering of American heroes, represents the price paid for American liberties." The robe is used "to signify that we do not judge men by the clothes they wear and to conceal the difference in our clothing as well as our personality. There are no rich or poor, high or low, in Klancraft. As we look upon a body of Klansmen robed in white we are forcibly reminded that they are on a level." And "With the mask we hide our individuality and sink ourselves into the great sea of Klancraft."[90]

All are united in defending the sacred chastity of womanhood.

> The degradation of women is a violation of the sacredness of the human personality, a sin against the race, a crime against society, a menace to our country, and a prostitution of all that is best, and noblest, and highest in life. No race, or society, or country can rise higher than its womanhood.[91]

In this effort, the nuclear family is treated as the center and source of all moral and social order.

> The American home is fundamental to all that is best in life, in society, in church, and in the nation. It is the most sacred of human institutions...Every influence that seeks to disrupt the home must itself be destroyed. The Knights of the Ku Klux Klan would protect the home by promoting whatever would make for its stability, its betterment, its safety, and its inviolability."[92]

In their uniformity, and in their subjection to a single absolute authority, Klansmen feel no contradiction between the power of the individual father-husband over his family and the brotherhood of the Knights. Natural hierarchy and an encompassing social order assure the power of every individual by constraining both competition and achievement.

Fraternal societies represent attempts to deal with a very general conflict between two meanings of masculinity in American culture: the achieved masculinity of individual men in competition with others and the ascribed masculinity assumed in self-sacrificing male bonding. Men's peer groups, for instance, recognize marriage as an institution which divides men. In marriage and fatherhood each man achieves an adult status as an individual; he frees himself from his natal family to become the father of *his* children, the breadwinner of *his* household, and the sole sexual partner of *his* wife. But in so doing he also breaks or weakens bonds with his father, brothers, and peers. Men say they are "caught," "tamed," and "henpecked" in marriage. Brothers and peers throw ritual bachelors parties for the groom in which they reassert their solidarity as a group of men and express hostility toward the women who drive wedges between them. Peer groups are maintained, even after marriage, in country clubs, professional associations, card games, baseball and bowling teams, neighborhood bars, and hunting and fishing groups; in these, men are drawn out of their families against the protests of their wives.

The sub-cultures of the working class and the professional managerial class diverge in their distinct emphases on ascribed and achieved male status. Working class traditionalism defines a natural and uniform masculinity, stresses male bonding and devalues achievement while middle class individualism codes both family and occupational status as achievements which reflect men's differential abilities. The working class man sees his family and work positions as natural, predetermined male roles which dictate his explicit authority to dominate his wife and children and his responsibility to provide for them. His status, far from representing his freedom from tradition, extended kinship, and structural determinants, depends on these. He is expected to locate his household in his "old neighborhood" and often shares an apartment or duplex with his own or his wife's extended kin. His family is a natural unit which is like every other family and which defines proper gender and age codes for conduct over and above personal characteristics of individuals. Both husband and wife discuss their marital problems and other personal concerns with same-sex siblings and friends rather than with their spouses.[93] A man recognizes kinship ties and other personal connections as normal and legitimate means of obtaining jobs, and he attributes job promotions or lay offs to economic conditions beyond his control. He is born into a class—a fact of life which places a structurally determined ceiling on his ability to achieve high status.[94] He "works hard," seeking steady employment and job security; in working he fulfills a given obligation and sacrifices himself for his family.

The married man is burdened with staid family and work responsibilities; his male virility is trapped and domesticated. He reserves his nights out with the boys and asserts a natural, pure masculinity by "holding his liquor," exhibiting his physical strength and proficiency, and accumulating masculine objects such as powerful cars, snow mobiles, hunting guns, and mobile recreational vehicles. This manliness, like the natural role of the father-husband, expresses a uniform status which demands self-sacrifice. A real man is symbolized as a shirtless, brawny, and virile manual laborer in distinction from the pale, flabby, and effeminate white collar "paper pusher"; a man who buys into middle class status pretensions is weakened and corrupted. Upward mobility itself carries with it feelings of isolation, worthlessness, and guilt for having betrayed one's peers. Fathers not only expect their sons to fail in efforts to achieve higher status but condemn such aspiration.[95] The male code of honor demands loyalty to one's peer group and to one's traditional class-defined work role.[96] The middle class family is seen as an amoral and weak collection of self-interested individuals in which wives and children no longer respect the authority of the family head. The middle class suburb is a threatening image; it is a lonely, crime-ridden settlement of strangers who are continually divided by their efforts to achieve wealth and occupational status over others on the block.[97] The mythic working class hero characteristically disregards, or rises above, "petty" status ranking. He may be the John Wayne whose naturally superior abilities place him, without conscious effort on his part, above other men. Or he may be the John Henry who sacrifices his own life saving his weaker and more vulnerable workmates. Finally, he may be a character like the Billy of Merle Hagggard's song, "Billy Overcame His Size,"—a small and weak man who transforms the taunts of other men into praise by dying for them in Vietnam. Working class men place a high value on a "laid back" attitude which indicates that a man is not concerned with achieved status or interested in competing with others to better his own position.

Individuals in peer groups are ranked in a given order according to natural markers of masculinity such as tolerance for liquor, physical stength, sexual prowess, penis size, and ability to hunt, fight, bowl, etc.[98] A man who attempts to achieve a higher status is heckled by other members of the group.[99] Highest ranked individuals, or leaders, may have extraordinary power as the focus of the group, the initiators of group activities, and the decision makers of the group. But leaders also bear the heaviest responsibilities to the group; they must be fair minded, generous, and active in resolving conflicts between lower status individuals.[100] Strong negative sanctions are used against individuals who brag or flaunt their status; conceited individuals must be put in their place and all members of the group face a continuous threat of humiliation as the objects of pranks and derogatory sexual jokes. Self-interest is subordinated to collectivity; group opinions must express a consensus and exchanges are structured by a system of generalized reciprocity.[101]

Union ideology, too, demands unity among brothers of a local and binds locals together in an international family. Internationals are generally headed by powerful authority figures who are appointed by their predecessors rather than elected by the union membership. Conflicts over democratic versus authoritarian union structures raise the same issue stressed by the KKK—that democracy somehow weakens the power and efficiency of the group. At the same time, leaders must be selfless, responsible for the interests of all union brothers, and devoted to the union cause. The leaders of locals, in particular, should be workers from the rank and file; their only interests should be to fulfill their duties as their brothers' representatives—duties which demand self-sacrifice. On the local level "Leadership...assumes an almost sacred quality, and anyone who profanes his role by evidencing personal ambition is an object of strong disapproval." The worst that can be said of a union leader is that he is an opportunist or that he is ambitious.[102]

Middle class men, in contrast, stress individual achievement as a personal goal and a social good. A man must effect his own progress through education, will, self-control, and planning; he measures his self-worth in his achieved social statuses. Science and rationality are valued over personal loyalties, professional jobs requiring intellectual skills and advanced education are valued over natural and simple manual labor. Competition is elevated to an absolute good; it motivates individuals to reach their full potential and, as such, benefits society as a whole. Morality is maintained primarily in a set of absolute individual rights. Hierarchical positions are seen as the result of free choice and individual effort in a democratically structured society.[103]

A man's family represents a private individual achievement rather than a traditional, structurally-determined male status. To become a free adult, each man must establish an independent nuclear family housed in a private dwelling. Extended kin are not incorporated into the household unit and kinship ties are recognized only selectively according to individual preferences and shared lifestyles and interests rather than uniformly maintained according to the natural criterion of blood bonds. It is vaguely immoral, a sign of weakness, to allow one's kin to interfere with marriage choice or to use kinship influence in obtaining jobs and promotions.[104]

In contrast to the working class family ideology, the middle class father-husband's authority to dominate his wife and children is not explicit or overt. The family is seen not as a set of predetermined sex and age roles but as a democratically organized collection of individuals with unique needs and talents. Spouses should be good companions with common interests and personalities; they must be able to communicate with one another, they share a single set of friends, and they participate in recreational activities as a couple. Ideally, parents share child care responsibilities and even household tasks to some extent; when a woman takes primary responsibility for these she does so, in this view, through personal choice. Self-control is emphasized over an external social control; parents explain issues and values to their children rather than impose rules on them, win or coax them rather than use force. Each child is seen as being endowed at birth with all of the potentialities for good; parents nurture this potential by protecting their children from an environment which may thwart or corrupt it.[105]

The middle class man works "for his family" but not as a simple act of self-sacrifice; he expects to derive legitimate personal satisfaction in the achievement of professional success. He gains high status in relation to other men by achieving an harmonious and respectable family as well as by his own wealth, occupation, education, and cultural taste. His wife's and his children's personal talents and achievements also reflect on his status. ". . . the man is held ultimately responsible if . . . the family, or any of its members should fail. If his wife cannot discharge the social obligations which facilitate his business or profession, it is he who is considered to have shown poor judgement in his choice."[106] His status is not natural; it must be continually maintained and bettered. His family is an adjunct to his occupational status; free from extended kin and community ties, it can be relocated to suit his opportunities for upward mobility. At the same time, the family is the one place where this man, like the Victorian man, "may be himself, relieved of pressing responsibilities, free of competition, sure of warmth and companionship."[107] His membership in professional associations and exclusive and expensive country clubs mark only an achieved status; in these men's groups rankings are subject to sudden shifts, individual displays of superiority are only weakly tempered, exchanges are characterized by strictly balanced reciprocity, and those who do not work to maintain bonds are quickly forgotten or ostracized.[108] Even fraternal societies of the middle class—such as the Kiwanis club—constitute relatively loose bonds in which achievement criteria weaken uniform male identity and group coherence. All of these groups are used as a means of promoting individual ends; men display their successes and establish important professional and business contacts. The "college boys" in Whyte's study of a working class community established a club with this same loose structure in their efforts for individual advancement—a structure which was dramatically different from the traditional hierarchical structure of the "corner boys'" groups. Where the corner boys used consensus, focused on a single leader, and recognized hierarchical roles with corresponding obligations to the group, the college boys based decisions on majority vote, had difficulty choosing a leader (since all were equally qualified by virture of their college educations), and failed to establish any common understandings of authority, responsibility, and obligation. According to Whyte, the college boys' club was unstable, ineffective, and short lived; members did not maintain bonds with other members, or relate as a group, outside of meetings and individuals left the group to pursue individual opportunities.[109] Where traditionalist groups assert a natural and uniform masculine status, these democratic individualist groups value statuses which are achieved by individuals. A simple male status is transformed into an intricate system of relative and fluctuating ranked statuses; male unity is weakened and disrupted by "self-interested" competition.

CONCLUSIONS

Ideologies of hierarchy express people's—in this case, men's—experiences of their status-identities as dominants or subordinates (or high and low ranked individuals) in hierarchical social relations. The coexistence of male dominance in gender hierarchy and male-ranking in class hierarchies produces a dynamic tension in men's full status identities.

In the traditionalism of the Puritans and the contemporary working class, men's uniform gender status is generalized to apply to all social roles; individual differences among men are specifically denied. Men are "achievers" by virtue of their gender dominance; they see themselves as more natural than women and more knowledgeable of public affairs. But male dominance can only be maintained through loyalty to a group of male peers, a kinship network, and a class. Hierarchies are explicitly recognized, but ranked statuses reflect positions of birth or class—ascribed social roles—rather than differential personal worth. Women are explicitly labeled as subordinates and expected to show formal deference to men. But their household labor is recognized as socially valuable and they, like men, are afforded legitimate social status to the extent that they fulfill their given gender roles. Both sexes maintain ties with extended kin and same-sex peers and the two sexes are symbolically united in the context of larger, non-gender hierarchies such as class and ethnicity.

Individualism, such as that of the Victorians and the contemporary middle class, treats hierarchically-ranked positions, including that of the male dominant, as achievements — as freedoms from natural *and social* constraints. The nuclear family is idealized and isolated from extended kinship networks; it represents a man's individual achievement and embodies his occupational status. A rationalized democratic ideology of the family reproduces the egalitarian individualist ideology of male ranking in the public world. Given social roles and "natural" male dominance are deemphasized in beliefs that all members of a family should seek individual fulfillment through achievement. In the end, however, it is men who are seen as the achievers and women are left bound to nature. In denying the existence of socially-constructed hierarchy, egalitarian individualism employs a seemingly contradictory view—that of biological determinism and absolute differences in individual worth—to explain why subordinates are subordinate. It is precisely in this view that women's biological capacity to bear children and social capacity to nurture have been treated as determinants of women's status and evidence of a distinctively female personality.

The perspective on cultures of hierarchy outlined in this essay differs from both "materialist" and "idealist" perspectives; it posits that meanings of hierarchy are not a simple reflection of hierarchical relations any more than they are a direct determinant of those relations. Heidi Hartmann's thesis is directed to dispelling the notion that patriarchy is an atavistic hangover or an ideological residue which is no longer grounded in a social reality. But in her focus on a material base of patriarchy she accepts the either-or terms of the "atavistic hangover" concept rather than critique its assumed dichotomy between belief and reality to relate contemporary patriarchal culture to contemporary patriarchal social relations. Culture is reduced either to men's rational, objective interests in dominating women or to a vague and automatic function of abstracted economic structures. *A closer examination of cultures of hierarchy reveals a complex and dialectical relationship between structures and individuals' experiences and understandings of them.* And a recognition of the process of status-identity in this relationship provides an understanding of the dynamics between patriarchy and capitalism occurring on a level which is at once subjective and clearly rooted in social structures located outside the individual. Where Hartmann argues that men's material interest in exploiting women's home labor motivated them to organize for a family wage and to exclude women and children from the paid work force I would argue that such motivations are formed in a complex cultural process and structured as much by male ranking as by male dominance. It was not a simple or direct economic interest which caused middle class Victorian men to transfer parental responsibility for their suddenly unproductive children to their wives and which now motivates contemporary middle class men to claim equal parental responsibilities with women. Most importantly, it is crucial to realize that working class and middle class men, by virtue of their distinct positions in the capitalist male-ranking system, express very different meanings of and motivations for male dominance despite their shared interest in it.

Men's ideologies of hierarchy, then, cannot be treated as simple reflections of their objective and rational interests. Nor can such meanings be seen as simple functions of capitalism and patriarchy or interpreted in relation to the abstract characteristics of these systems. Hartmann argues, "If women were degraded or powerless in other societies, the reasons (rationalizations) men had for this were different. Only in a capitalist society does it make sense to look down on women as emotional or irrational" (Hartmann, p. 28). No doubt these gender stereotypes have particular fuctions in capitalist societies, but they are by no means unique to them; the beliefs that women are emotional, irrational, and closer to nature are near cultural universals, appearing in the cultures of the simplest societies as well as in those of advanced state capitalist societies. Sherry Ortner[110] relates these universal meanings to female practices of child bearing and caring for infants. Jean Baker Miller[111] and Albert Memmi[112] suggest, further, that these characteristics are those which are used to describe any group of people in a subordinate position; in our culture, women, children, and working class and ethnically subordinated men are all seen as somehow less cultural, less socialized or civilized, less intelligent, and less self-controlled than white middle class men in images such as "natural black rhythm," the physical strength and sexual virility of black and working class men, and the emotional, naturally nurturant motherhood of women. At times of social and cultural conflict with subordinates white middle class men express the full meanings of danger and threat contained in these images of the "other": the black man becomes a "rapist," the woman a "castrating bitch" feminist, children a marauding gang of juvenile delinquents, and the working class man a violent and backward "redneck." Rather than assume that values such as rationality are a function of a depersonalized, economistic and bureaucratic capitalist system, we need to explore the ways in which their meanings express experiences of the central politcal relations of dominance and subordination in a given society at a given time; they may be formed, for instance, in dominants' perceptions of themselves as active agents of social control and as people who are distinct from their subordinates by virture of their ability to free themselves of natural constraints. Hartmann argues that ". . .capital creates an ideology, which grows up along side it, of individualism, competitiveness, domination, and, in our time, consumption of a particular kind. Whatever one's theory of the genesis of ideology one must recognize these as the dominant values of capitalist societies" (Hartmann, p. 10). But I would stress, again, that even these values are not unique to capitalist societies, that they have distinct meanings for working class and middle class men (e.g., the meanings of maleness in working class men's consumption), and that they have been constructed out of historical conflicts between patriarchal and capitalist authority systems.

New efforts to understand the processes producing, reproducing, and opposing capitalist patriarchy must begin with a recognition of cultures of hierarchy as expressions of people's daily, subjective experiences in these structures rather than as functional reflections of the structures themselves or as direct expressions of objective interests in them. Hartmann makes a significant contribution to such an understanding in her depiction of the broadly social and fundamentally political bases of male dominance in structures of sexuality, marriage, parenting, paid and unpaid work, the state, and various institutionalized relations among men in clubs, sports, unions, professions, religions, and ethnic and racial groups. But she defines these, first and foremost, as functions which enable men to control women's labor, focusing on economic exploitation as the determining structure of this hierarchy. I would focus, rather, on the central political relations of gender domination and subordination; economic exploitation is certainly important in these relations but it does not in itself define them or determine their dynamics. To understand historical conditions of gender hierarchy we must look to the dynamics between three sets of political relations—of competition or solidarity among men and among women and of conflict or stasis in relations between women and men—and locate the social, but not necessarily specifically economic, bases of these relations. Capitalism, too, must be understood not simply as an economic structure which exploits workers' labor but as a social system formed in political struggles between workers and capitalists and in the conditions of competition or solidarity within each of these groups. As Hartmann points out, ''. . . nothing about capital itself determines who (that is, which individuals with which ascribed characteristics) shall occupy the higher, and who the lower rungs of the wage labor force'' (Hartmann, p. 24). But capitalism has not evolved solely under the laws of capital; as a set of political relations, it has been fundamentally influenced by the sexual, racial, and class composition of occupational rungs. The very definition of capitalism must include an analysis of the ways in which all of these rankings have structured the historical dynamics between the working class and the capitalist class. In the same way, the political dynamics of patriarchy have been influenced by capitalist work hierarchies which rank men in relation to other men and women in relation to other women. Historical relationships between capitalism and patriarchy, too, have been defined not simply by the conflicting or mutually supporting interests of capitalists and men but by the interrelated status rankings among men, among women, and between women and men.

Strategically, then, our efforts must be to effect change in a wide range of relations and institutions which structure political struggles between women and men, workers and capitalists. This task is complicated by the subjective processes of status-identity in which individuals interpret their world and the potential for changing it. Theories to understand the processes of change cannot be restricted to documenting objective conditions which would free subordinates from their dependence on dominants (e.g., unionization, equal pay for equal work); they must also address the problem of mobilizing subordinate groups whose political ideologies express their particular experiences of gender and class hierarchies.

I have argued that working class men's class solidarity is effected by their solidarity as men. It is not surprising, then, that all male or primarily male trade unions have not worked to organize female workers or to include women in their membership. In addition, the structure of trade unions and the particular meanings of collectivity among working class men are shaped by the tension between male bonding and occupational status-ranking among men. Competition and divisive status-ranking are constrained in an ideology which values uniformity and conformity to ascribed social roles in a given social order. To the extent that this ideology devalues self-interested action and achievement itself, it may promote fatalism and hierarchical undemocratic union structures. Members of local unions bond together as "brothers" in defense against the capitalist class but they do so under the authority of strong father-like leaders of internationals. In sports groups and fraternal societies, too, cooperation among men is assured only by their shared subordination to a central authority figure. And in a generalized defensive solidarity working class men glorify individual failure and value only those achievements which reflect "natural" masculine characteristics and roles (e.g., physical strength, skill in traditional male occupations, the achievement of a family wage). They do not, for the most part, challenge the basic political inequalities of the capitalist economy or seek class solidarity with women workers.

Middle class men, on the other hand, value achievement and rational self-conscious action. But in their emphasis on ranked occupational statuses this achievement orientation is also competitive and individualistic. Freedom is valued over solidarity, social responsibility is abstracted from social context and expressed as a formal morality of contract, and an absolute formal authority is vested in science, law, and professional training. Middle class men join groups in order to augment their individual statuses; membership in professional associations and elite country clubs represents a high status and an achievement in itself and is also seen as a means of acquiring important business and professional contacts.

A political ideology to promote progressive collective action must recognize the power of the individual to act in society and actively change it at the same time that it also recognizes existing social constraints. In the processes of male bonding and male-ranking these two aspects of consciousness are dichotomized and placed in opposition to one another. The focus on group cohesion and loyalty in working class male bonding limits human agency to the fulfillment of ascribed roles while the emphasis on free individual achievement in middle class men's status ranking denies the existence of social hierarchies and abstracts action from its social context. The women's movement, too, suffers from a conflict between solidarity and status-rankings among women. The radical and liberal sectors of the women's movement are each constrained by their respective emphases on a defensive gender solidarity and equal opportunity with men. The radical feminist concept of sisterhood is progressive in its value on solidarity among all women but it can also take on meanings of uniformity which deny real differences in the lives of women of different classes and races as well as individual differences among women of a single class and race. The value of consensus decision making, too, expresses a uniform and militantly egalitarian female gender identity but this can also stifle constructive conflict and enforce conformity to a single set of values and a single standard of behavior. Differences between women and men may take on an absolute and ahistorical quality and stereotypically female charac-teristics such as nurturance and the open expression of emotions may be exaggerated and idealized while achievement-orientation, rationality, "self-interest" and success may be coded as "male" and condemned. The dominant liberal sector of the movement, on the other hand, expresses individualist values of free choice, equal opportunity, and occupational achievement. Armed with the dominant culture's epithets of women as emotional and irrational, liberal feminism has scorned women whose identities and concerns are based in the more traditional female status markers of mother, wife, and homemaker. The individualism of the professional self-made woman, like the traditionalist sexism of the working class man, embraces one status system—capitalist or patriarchal— as an alternative to and defense against the other. The liberal individualist ideology of free choice and individual effort denies the existence of structural constraints on women's lives and exacerbates status-ranked divisions between middle class and working class women, white and minority women, and heterosexual women and lesbians.

Socialist feminist analysis must begin with a recognition of both social and cultural dynamics between capitalist and patriarchal hierarchies. By identifying the processes by which women and workers invest their identities in various existing statuses (e.g., the self-sacrificing mother, the strong man, the economic achiever) and build their political ideologies from these status-identities we can develop a more systematic understanding of why subordinates support some progressive changes while resisting or opposing others. We can also identify critical problems in need of change (e.g., women's nearly exclusive parenting of young children, enforced dichotomies between work and family roles, status distinctions between manual and mental labor) and identify links between the structural determinants of capitalist patriarchy and people's subjective experiences and interpretations of it. It is only by recognizing and acting to change our experiences and meanings of hierarchy that we can build effective women's and workers' movements and begin to construct new, nonhierarchical economic and sex-gender systems.

FOOTNOTES

1. John Demos, *A Little Commonwealth: Family Life in Plymouth Colony* (New York: Oxford University Press, 1970); Philip Greven, *Four Generations: Population, Land and Family in Colonial Andover, Massachusetts* (Ithaca: Cornell University Press, 1970); Greven, "Family Structure in Seventeenth-Century Andover, Massachusetts," *The Family in Social-Historical Perspective*, edited by Michael Gordon (New York: St. Martin's Press, 1978); Samuel Morison, *The Oxford History of the American People*, Vol. 1 (New York: Mentor Books, 1972).
2. Edith Abbott, *Women in Industry* (New York: Appleton and Company, 1910); Demos, *A Little Commonwealth*; Edmund Morgan, *The Puritan Family* (New York: Harper and Row, 1966).

3. Greven, *Four Generations*; Greven, "Family Structure in Seventeenth-Century Andover, Massachusetts."

4. Abbott, *op. cit.*

5. Ruth Bloch, "American Feminine Ideals in Transitions: The Rise of the Moral Mother," *Feminist Studies*, Vol. 4, no. 2, 1978, pp. 101-126; Ann Gordan and Mari Jo Buhle, "Sex and Class in Colonial and Nineteenth-Century America," *Liberating Women's History*, eidted by Berenice Carroll (Urbana: University of Illinois Press, 1976); Aileen Kraditer, *Up from the Pedestal* (New York: New York Times Books, 1968); Cotton Mather, *A Family Well-Ordered* (Boston: n.p., 1699); Morgan, *The Puritan Family*.

6. Bloch, "American Feminine Ideals in Transition"; Mather, *A Family Well-Ordered*; Morgan, *The Puritan Family*.

7. Bloch, *op. cit.*

8. Bloch, *Ibid.*; Morgan, *op. cit.*; Robert Wells, "Family History and Demographic Transition," *The Family in Social Historical Perspective.*

9. Hector St. John De Crevecoeur, "On Eighteenth-Century Womanhood," *Women and Womanhood in America*, edited by Ronald Hogeland (Lexington, Mass: D.C. Heath and Company, 1973. Originally published in 1782); Carroll Smith-Rosenberg, "Sex as Symbol in Victorian Putity; an Ethnohistorical Analysis of Jacksonian America," *Turning Points*, edited by John Demos and Sarane Spence Boocock (Chicago: University of Chicago Press, 1978).

10. Perry Miller, *The New England Mind: the Seventeenth Century* (Cambridge, Mass: Harvard University Press, 1939); Morgan, *op. cit.*

11. Morgan, *op. cit.*

12. Richard Hofstadter, *America at 1750: a Social Portrait* (New York: Alfred Knopf, 1971).

13. Charles Grant, *Democracy in the Connecticut Frontier Town of Kent* (New York: AMS Press, 1961); Hofstadter, *op. cit.*; James Lemon and Gary Nash, "The Distribution of Wealth in Eighteenth-Century America: a Century of Changes in Chester County Pennsylvania, 1693-1802," *Journal of Social History*, Vol. 2, no. 1, 1968, pp. 1-24; Jackson Turner Main, *The Social Structure of Revolutionary America* (Princeton University Press, 1965).

14. Demos, *op. cit.*; Morgan, *op. cit.*

15. Urian Oakes, *A Seasonable Discourse Wherein Sincerity and Delight in the Service of God is Earnestly Pressed Upon Professors of Religion* (Cambridge: n.p., 1682), as quoted in Morgan, *op. cit.*, p. 14.

16. Thomas Shepard, *Works*, compiled by John Albro (Boston: n.p., 1853), as quoted in Morgan, *op. cit.* p. 7.

17. Kenneth Lockridge and Alan Kreider, "The Evolution of Massachusetts Town Government, 1640-1740," *Colonial America: Essays in Politics and Social Development,* edited by Stanley Katz (Boston: Little, Brown and Company, 1971); Michael Zuckerman, "The Social Context of Democracy in Massachusetts," *Colonial America.*

18. Greven, "Family Structure in Seventeenth-Century Andover, Massachusetts"; William Perkins, *The Works of that Famous and Worthy Minister of Christ in the University of Cambridge, Mr. William Perkins,* Vol. 1 (London: n.p., 1612).

19. Hofstader, *America at 1750;* Main, *The Social Structure of Revolutionary America;* Gary Nash, *Class and Society in Early America* (Englewood Cliffs, N.J.: Prentice-Hall, 1970).

20. Miller, *The New England Mind.*

21. Cotton Mather, *Bonifacius (Essays to Do Good)* (Boston: n.p., 1710); as quoted in Mary Ryan, *Womanhood in America: From Colonial Times to the Present* (New York: Franklin Watts, 1975).

22. Demos, *The Little Commonwealth;* Greven, "Family Structure in Seventeenth-Century Andover"; Morgan, *The Puritan Family;* Robert Winthrop, *Life and Letters of John Winthrop,* volume 2 (Boston, n.p., 1869).

23. Hofstadter, *America at 1750;* Main, *The Social Structure of Revolutionary America;* Nash, *Class Society in Early America.*

24. Morgan, *The Puritan Family;* Alden Vaughan, *The Puritan Tradition in American, 1620-1730* (New York: Harper and Row, 1972).

25. Demos, *The Little Commonwealth;* Morgan, *The Puritan Family.*

26. Perkins, *The Works of That Famous and Worthy Minister,* p. 753.

27. Demos, *The Little Commonwealth.*

28. Gordon and Buhle, "Sex and Class in Colonial and Nineteenth Century America"; Elizabeth Pleck, "Sex Roles in Transition: the Historical Perspective" *New Research on Women and Sex Roles,* Dorothy McGuigan, ed., (Ann Arbor, MI: University of Michigan, Center for Continuing Education for Women, 1976); Daniel Scott Smith, "Parental Power and Marriage Patterns: an Analysis of Historical Trends in Hingham, Massachusetts" *The Family in Social-Historical Perspective,* first edition, 1973.)

29. G.J. Barker-Benfield, "Anne Hutchinson and the Puritan Attitude Towards Women" *Feminist Studies,* 1972 (1:2); William Woodward, *Records of Salem Witchcraft,* volume 1 (Roxbury, Mass.: n.p., 1864).

30. Morgan, *The Puritan Family,* p. 142.

31. Demos, *The Little Commonwealth*; Morgan, *the Puritan Family.*

32. Philip Greven, *The Protestant Temperament* (New York: Alfred Knopf, 1977); Morgan, *The Puritan Family.*

33. John Winthrop, *Massachusetts Historical Society Collections,* third series, volume 7, p. 33 (emphasis added) 1838.

34. Demos, *The Little Commonwealth;* Lockridge and Kreider, "The

Evolution of Massachusetts Town Government"; Zuckerman, "The Social Context of Democracy."

35. Lockridge and Kreider, *op. cit.;* Edward Cook, *The Fathers of Towns* (Baltimore: John Hopkins University Press, 1976).

36. Hofstadter, *op. cit.*

37. Zuckerman, "The Social Context of Democracy," p. 230.

38. Kenneth Lockridge, *A New England Town: the First Hundred Years, 1636-1736* (New York: W.W. Norton, 1970).

39. Winthrop, *Life and Letters,* p. 432, as quoted in Miller, *The New England Mind,* p. 426 (emphasis added).

41. Richard Bushman, *From Puritan to Yankee* (New York: W.W. Norton, 1967).

42. Demos, *The Little Commonwealth.*

43. Hofstadter, *op. cit.;* Ryan, *op. cit.*

44. Greven, *Four Generations;* Greven, "Family Structure in Seventeenth-Century Andover."

45. Greven, "Family Structure"; Smith "Parental Power and Marriage Patterns"; Smith-Rosenberg, "Sex as Symbol."

46. Greven, "Family Structure"; Smith, "Parental Power."

47. Greven, *Four Generations;* Hofstadter, *America at 1750;* Main, "the Social Structure of Revolutionary America.*

48. Smith-Rosenberg, "Sex as Symbol."

49. Abbott, *Women in Industry.*

50. Hofstadter, *op. cit.;* Morison, *The Oxford History of the American People.*

51. Grant, *Democracy in The Connecticut Frontier;* Lemon and Nash, "The Distribution of Wealth in Eighteenth-Century America"; Main, *The Social Structure of Revolutionary America;* Perry Miller, *The New England Mind: From Colony to Province* (Cambridge, Mass.: Harvard University Press, 1953).

52. Lockridge and Kreider, "The Evolution of Massachusetts Town Government"; Main, *op. cit.*

53. Mary Ryan, "Femininity and Capitalism in Antebellum America," in *Capitalist Patriarchy and the Case for Socialist Feminism,* Zillah Eisenstein, ed. (New York: Monthly Review Press, 1979).

54. James Henretta, "The Morphology of New England Society in the Colonial Period" in *The Family in History,* Theodore Rabb and Robert Rotberg, ed. (New York: Harper and Row, 1971).

55. Main, *The Social Structure*; Smith-Rosenberg, Sex as Symbol."

56. Elizabeth Pleck, "Two Worlds in One: Work and Family" *Journal of Social History,* winter 1976; Rosalyn Baxandall, Linda Gordon, and Susan Reverby, eds., *America's Working Women* (New York: Random House, 1976).

57. G.J. Barker-Benfield, *The Horrors of the Half Known Life,* p. 305 (New York: Harper and Row, 1976).

58. Edward Jarvis, speech delivered before the Association of Medical Superintendents of American Institutions for the Insane, 1851, as quoted in Barker-Benfield, *The Horrors of the Half-Known Life*, p. 13.

59. Ryan, *op. cit.*

60. Bloch, "American Feminine Ideals in Transition"; Carroll Smith Rosenberg and Charles Rosenberg, "The Female Animal: Medical and Biological Views of Woman and Her Role in Nineteenth Century America" *Journal of American History*, 1973 (60:2:332-356).

61. Henry Wright, *The Empire of the Mother over the Character and Destiny of the Race*, p. 4 (n.p., 1870), as quoted in Ryan, *Womanhood in America*, p. 47.

62. Main, *op. cit.*; Smith-Rosenberg, *op. cit.*

63. G.J. Barker-Benfield, "The Spermatic Economy: A Nineteenth Century View of Sexuality" in *The Family in Social-Historical Perspective*, first edition.

64. Barbara Welter, "The Cult of True Womanhood, 1820-1860," in *The Family in Social-Historical Perspective*, second edition.

65. Edward Jarvis, "Of the Comparative Liability of Males and Females to Insanity, and their Comparative Curability and Mortality when Insane," *American Journal of Insanity*, 1850 (7:142-171).

66. Margaret Coxe, *Claims of the Country on American Females*, p. 13 (Columbus, Ohio: n.p., 184?), as quoted in Ryan, *op. cit.*

67. *Ik Marvel (pseudonym), Reveries of a Bachelor* (New York: Charles Scribner, 1859), 30th edition, as quoted in Barker-Benfield, *The Horrors of the Half-Known Life*, p. 13.

68. Bloch, "American Feminine Ideals in Transition"; Ryan, *Womanhood in America;* Welter, "The Cult of True Womanhood."

69. Barker-Benfield, *op. cit.*, p. 305.

70. *Augustus Kingsley Gardner, Old Wine in New Bottles: Spare Hours of a Student in Paris (n.p., 1855),* p. 110.

71. Barker-Benfield, *op. cit.*, p. 305.

72. John Todd, *The Student's Manual* (Northampton: Hopkins and Bridgman, 1853), p. 150.

73. Nancy Cott, *Bonds of Womanhood* (New Haven: Yale University Press, 1977).

74. Drs. Jordan and Beck, *Happiness or Misery: Being Four Lectures on the Functions and Disorders of the Nervous System and Reproductive Organs* (New York: Barton and Sons, 1861), p. 39, as quoted in Charles Rosenberg, "Sexuality, Class and Role in 19th-Century America" *American Quarterly*, 1973 (25:131-153), p. 144.

75. Barker-Benfield, "The Spermatic Economy."

76. R.J. Culverwell, *Self-Preservation, Manhood, and Causes of its Premature Decline* (New York: n.p., 1830), as quoted in Rosenberg, "Sexuality, Class and Role in 19th-Century America," p. 145.

77. Rosenberg, *op. cit.*, p. 144.

78. Edward Carr, *The New Society* (Boston: Beacon Press 1957); Theodore Lowi, *The End of Liberalism* (New York: W.W. Norton, 1969).

79. Sarah Hale, *Ladies Magazine*, volume 2, January 1829, p. 31-32, as quoted in Cott, *Bonds of Womanhood*, p. 95.

80. Cott, *op. cit.*

81. Samuel Stouffer, *Comunism, Conformity and Civil Liberties* (Garden City, N.Y.: Doubleday, 1955); Robert Lane, *Political Ideology* (N.Y.: The Free Press, 1962).

82. C.E. Ashworth, "Sports as Symbolic Dialogue," *Sports: Readings from a Sociological Perspective,* edited by Eric Dunning (Toronto: University of Toronto Press, 1972).

83. Harry Edwards, *Sociology of Sport* (Homewood, Ill.: Doresey Press, 1973), pp. 63-69.

84. Shaw, *Meat on the Hoof* (New York: St. Martin's Press, 1972), pp. 63, 79, as quoted in Howard Nixon, *Sport and Sociology* (Indianapolis: Bobbs-Merrill, 1976), p. 17.

85. Nixon, *op. cit.*

86. *Klansman's Manual* (n.p., 1925), pp. 9-17, as quoted in David Rothman and Sheila Rothman, *Sources of the American Social Tradition* (New York: Basic Books, 1975), pp. 406-407.

87. *Ibid.,* p. 16, as quoted in Rothman and Rothman, p. 407.

88. *Ibid.*

89. *Ibid.,* p. 17, as quoted in Rothman and Rothman, p. 408.

90. The Cyclops of Texas, "The Seven Symbols of the Klan," *The Imperial Nighthawk,* 26 December 1923, pp. 6-7, as quoted in Rothman and Rothman, p. 409.

91. *Klansman's Manual,* p. 69, as quoted in Rothman and Rothman, p. 409.

92. *Ibid.*

93. Mirra Komarovsky, *Blue Collar Marriage* (New York: Alfred Knopf, 1967); Kathleen McCourt, *Working-Class Women and Grass-Roots Politics* (Bloomington: Indiana University Press, 1977); Lillian Rubin, *Worlds of Pain: Life in a Working-Class Family* (New York: Basic Books, 1976).

94. Richard Centers, *The Psychology of Social Classes* (Princeton: Princeton University Press, 1949); Herbert Hyman, "The Value Systems of Different Classes; a Social Psychological Contribution to the Analysis of Social Stratification," *Class, Status and Power,* Reinhard Bendix and Seymour Lipset, ed. (Glencoe, Ill.: The Free Press, 1953); Richard Sennett and Jonathan Cobb, *The Hidden Injuries of Class* (New York: Alfred Knopf, 1972).

95. Komarovsky, *Blue Collar Marriage;* Rubin, *Worlds of Pain,* Sennett and Cobb, *The Hidden Injuries of Class.*

96. Sennett and Cobb, *op. cit.*

97. McCourt, *Working-Class Women and Grass-Roots Politics.*

98. E.E. LeMasters, *Blue Collar Aristocrats* (Madison: University of Wisconsin Press, 1975); John Lippert, "Sexuality as Consumption" in *For Men Against Sexism,* Jon Snodgrass, ed. (Albion, CA: Times Change Press, 1977); Andy Weisman, "Labor Pains," *For Men Against Sexism.*

99. Herbert Gans, *The Urban Villagers* (New York: The Free Press, 1962); William Foote Whyte, *Street Corner Society* (Chicago: University of Chicago Press, 1955).

100. Whyte, *op. cit.*

101. Gans, *op. cit.*; LeMasters, *op. cit.*

102. Eli Chinoy, "Local Union Leadership," in *Studies in Leadership,* Alvin Gouldner, ed. (New York: Harper and Brothers, 1950).

103. Kenneth Dolbeare and Patricia Dolbeare with Jane Hadley, *American Ideologies* (Chicago: Markham Publishing Company, 1973); John Seeley, R. Alexander Sim and Elizabeth Loosely, *Crestwood Heights* (New York: J. Wiley, 1963); Jack Weller, *Yesterday's People* (Lexington, Ky.: University of Kentucky Press, 1965).

104. Rayna Rapp, "Family and Class in Contemporary America: Notes Toward an Understanding of Ideology," in *The University of Michigan Papers in Women's Studies,* special issue, May 1978; Seeley, Sim and Loosely, *Crestwood Heights.*

105. Rapp, *op. cit.;* Rubin, *op. cit.,* Seeley, Sim and Loosely, *op. cit.*

106. Seeley, Sim and Loosely, *op. cit.*

107. *Ibid.*

108. *Ibid.*

109. Whyte, *op. cit.*

110. Sherry Ortner, "Is Female to Male as Nature is to Culture?" in *Woman, Culture and Society,* Michelle Rosaldo and Louise Lamphere, ed. (Stanford: Stanford University Press, 1974).

111. Jean Baker Miller, *Toward a New Psychology of Women* (Boston: Beacon Press, 1976).

112. Albert Memmi, *Dominated Man* (Boston: Beacon Press, 1968).

THE UNHAPPY MARRIAGE OF PATRIARCHY AND CAPITALISM

Ann Ferguson & Nancy Folbre

Ann Ferguson is currently professor of philosophy at the University of Massachusetts in Amherst. She has been active in the socialist feminist and lesbian feminist communities for a number of years. She is currently a member of the Marxist Philosophers' Group (MAP), the U. Mass Socialist-Feminist Group and a parent in the parent-cooperative alternative Che-Lumumba School.

Nancy Folbre is currently assistant professor of economics at Bowdoin College. In addition to pursuing a continuing interest in the history of women's work in the home she has been developing a theoretical perspective on the relationship between production and reproduction. Much of her research focuses explicitly on the causes and consequences of fertility decline.

In a recent radio interview, an old antique collector expressed his fondness for his collection of antique wringer washing machines and baby carriages. "Them were the days," he mused, "when women were *women* and knew what their jobs were. Now they don't need any of these things, because they don't even raise kids anymore!" Our essay aims to develop two insights of this old patriarch: first, women were easier to control in the old days; second, massive changes in women's role in mothering are indeed central to an understanding of women's oppression.

Our analysis of the relationship between patriarchy and capitalism draws heavily on Heidi Hartmann's work. In our opinion her "Unhappy Marriage of Marxism and Feminism" correctly diagnoses many of the problems which have plagued marxist analyses of women's oppression. By presenting a new analysis of the nature of patriarchy Hartmann provides a viable theoretical middle position for socialist feminists between the reductivist analyses of orthodox marxists (male domination is caused by class domination) and radical feminists (all forms of human domination including those based on class and race are caused by male domination). We agree with Hartmann that this theoretical breakthrough can inform both feminist and socialist strategy and practice. We also agree with Hartmann's general claim that capitalism and patriarchy are separate and semi-autonomous systems in which dominant groups have a material interest in maintaining specific social relations of domination.

Unlike Hartmann, however, we believe that capitalism and patriarchy are wedded in conflict. Their marriage is a truly unhappy one, based upon mutual dependence but weakened by contradictory needs. While capitalist social relations have incorporated many patriarchal forms of domination, they have also weakened some forms of patriarchal control over women. Hartmann and others have failed to appreciate the importance of this contradiction. We attribute this failure to a mistaken tendency to focus exclusively upon women's work in economic production of goods, ignoring what we term sex-affective production: childbearing, childrearing, and the provision of nurturance, affection, and sexual satisfaction. Historical changes in these dimensions of women's work have had an important impact upon the form and the force of women's oppression. The following analysis of these changes suggests some specific strategies for organizing against both patriarchy and capitalism.

HARTMANN'S THEORY OF PATRIARCHY

Hartmann's major contribution to the patriarchy debate lies in her critique of the claim that women's oppression can be explained as the result of class forms of oppression. Marxist analyses tend to emphasize the way in which the larger dynamic of class society structures relations between men and women. Paddy Quick, for instance, explains male dominance as the result of the desire of the ruling class to control the reproduction of labor power.[1] Maria Dalla Costa and Selma James theorize that women's role in housework serves to increase the rate of surplus value.[2] Zaretsky attributes women's oppression under capitalism to the split between the private sphere of the nuclear family and the public sphere of the market.[3] Juliet Mitchell and other neo-freudians see patriarchy as an ideological or cultural phenomenon which reinforces other forms of domination.[4]

Hartmann rejects all these positions because they do not emphasize the way that men as a group benefit from patriarchy. She locates the material base of patriarchy in men's control over women's labor power which she argues is maintained by a) excluding women from access to necessary economically productive resources and b) restricting women's sexuality (Hartmann, p. 15). Hartmann suggests some of men's motives for retaining control over women. "Men exercise their control in receiving personal service work from women, in not having to do housework or rear children, in having access to women's bodies in sex, and in feeling powerful and being powerful" (Hartmann, p.18). She then goes on to list the current elements of patriarchy: "heterosexual marriage (and consequent homophobia), female childbearing and housework, women's economic dependence on men (enforced by arrangements in the labor market), the state, and numerous institutions based on social relations between men—clubs, sports, unions, professions, universities, churches, corporations and armies" (Hartmann, pp. 18-19).

The elements which Hartmann lists are comprehensive. However, the mere listing of these elements is insufficient. First, it suggests that men have a basic urge to control women (an intrinsic urge to domination perhaps?) and will use any tool necessary, (homophobia, housework, restriction of sexual equality, etc.) to achieve this end.

Secondly, it obscures the fact that sexual domination is related to the production and distribution of specific kinds of goods and services. Therefore, it detracts from what we believe is an important insight: *as historical factors change the rewards from and opportunities to control these goods and services, men's motives and abilities to control women vary, and the character and degree of patriarchal domination is modified.*

In describing the persistence of patriarchy in class society, Hartmann overlooks the ways in which the relative importance of the factors which she lists have changed. Though she includes references to social services and mothering she does not integrate a full consideration of these into her analysis. This failing is symptomatic of much contemporary marxist and socialist feminist analysis. While recent efforts have helped widen the definition of production to include the production of use values within the home (housework or domestic labor), the stamp of marxian orthodoxy lingers in the way in which childbearing, childrearing, and the provision of nurturance, affection, and sexual satisfaction are treated.[5]

Most contemporary marxists reject mechanistic models in which the economic base determines the political and ideological superstructure. Still, most marxists affirm that the economic level of society is a particularly important one, and, therefore, the way in which the economic level is defined is crucial.[6] Some marxists exclude the family from the economic level altogether. Bridget O'Laughlin, for instance, describes the organization of family life as a "contingent outcome" of the mode of production *per se*.[7] Others never explicitly exclude the family—they simply ignore it. Marx's own assumptions—products of the nineteenth century —have continued to set the tone: "The maintenance and reproduction of the working class is, and must ever be, a condition of the reproduction of capital. But the capitalist may safely leave its fulfillment to the labourer's instincts of self preservation and propagation."[8].

Long run changes in the size, composition, and stability of the family, as well as the character of social relations there, inevitably affect the production of labor power.[9] Yet most of the literature concerning domestic labor and value theory ignores these factors. The major issue in these debates is whether the use values which wives provide affect the value of their husband's labor power, and thus, the production of surplus value as a whole.[10] "Reproduction of the laborer" is pictured as the physical reproduction of the adult male. The nature of the labor that wives and mothers perform is seldom explored. Furthermore, the labor time which mothers devote to their children—future workers—is never discussed.[11]

Marxist feminists who have expressed an interest in family life *per se* emphasize its noneconomic character. Sex is treated as a psychological, cultural, symbolic category—an element of the ideological level of society. Neo-freudian approaches, for instance, describe the formation of personality in the family, exploring the implications for children, but overlooking the impact of the labor process itself upon women.[12]

In her brilliant and influential essay, "The Traffic in Women," Gayle Rubin argues that every society has a sex gender system which organizes and directs sexuality and creates a sex gender identity.[13] Yet she makes very few references to childbearing and childrearing. The sex gender system, as she describes it, is a system of expectations, rewards, punishments, and role formation. It organizes the labor process as a whole, but has no basis in any particular form of production.

While we agree with many aspects of Rubin's analysis, we believe that her emphasis and her terminology are not quite correct. The sex gender system affects production as a whole, but it has a special relationship to certain specific forms of production. We state our hypothesis in different terms: *Patriarchal relations and the sex gender system form the social context for specific forms of human (typically, female) labor: labor devoted to bearing and rearing children and nurturing adult men.* In order to emphasize the importance of the labor process itself, we utilize the concept of *sex-affective production.*

SEX-AFFECTIVE PRODUCTION

Every human society has ways of organizing childbearing, childrearing, and the fulfillment of human needs for affection, nurturance, and sexual expression. These are sometimes placed under the rubric of human or social reproduction. These terms are not necessarily inaccurate. They have, however, led to a certain amount of confusion. "Reproduction" is a term which Marx used to describe the economic process over time. Human reproduction often refers to a biological process. Social reproduction is a concept that remains uncomfortably vague.

By describing the tasks, alternatively, as a process of production, we mean to emphasize that the term *production*—purposeful human behavior which creates use values—encompasses far more than the production of tangible goods such as food and clothing. The bearing and rearing of children, and the provision of affection, nurturance, and sexual satisfaction, all represent social use values. Human labor devoted to these tasks cannot be placed lower than other forms of labor in conceptual importance.

Sex-affective production is not simply a base on which the superstructure of patriarchy is erected. Any analysis of patriarchy must fully integrate psychological, cultural, political, and a host of other factors which may have an independent influence. However, any analysis of patriarchy *must* include a consideration of the specific forms of labor which women perform, and it cannot pretend that these forms are not labor.

Childbearing cannot be excluded from consideration simply because it includes a biological element. Childbearing has always been subject to a certain amount of social control. Only women can become mothers. But the percentage of women who do become mothers, the age at which they begin to bear children, and the intervals between individual children are socially determined.

Childbearing is inextricably linked with childrearing, partly because of the fact that the breast continues to link mother and child for a significant period after birth. The organization of childrearing as a whole, however, in which women have responsibility not only for small infants, but for direct care and nurturance of all children, is based upon a *social*, not a biological definition of motherhood.

Motherhood itself extends far beyond women's direct responsibilities to children to the care and nurturance of adult men. There are important similarities between the type of nurturance and affection which mothers provide their offspring and the subordination of their own needs to those of their mate. Nancy Chodorow and others argue that the organization of childrearing itself has a tremendous impact on the expressed needs of adults, and one of childrearing's most important effects is the creation of a sex gender identity.[14] Women are socialized toward an "ideal mother" personality which keeps them willing to give more than they receive from men in nurturance and sexual satisfaction.[15]

Although men sometimes engage in sex-affective production, most of its responsibilities and requirements are met by women. This division of labor is not a neutral one, assigning "separate but equal" roles. It is an oppressive one, based upon inequality and reinforced by social relation of domination. Characteristic inequalities include a longer working day with less material and emotional rewards than men, less control over family decisions, and less sexual freedom combined with less sexual satisfaction. Specialization in sex-affective production is also associated with restrictions on options, choices, and remuneration available to women in work outside of the family—restrictions often directly attributed to their presumed or actual mothering role.[16]

Women's oppression in some areas of sex-affective production benefits men directly. But men's desire to benefit directly and immediately from women's labor does not provide a complete explanation for women's oppression. The ways in which children, and therefore, the next generation of society as a whole, benefit from women's work in sex-affective production must also be explored. *While motherhood is an important mechanism for the maintenance of patriarchy, patriarchy is also an important mechanism for the maintenance of motherhood.*[17]

This theoretical claim represents far more than a difference in emphasis between Hartmann's analysis and our own. It generates important differences in our explanation of historical events. In *Capitalism and Women's Work in the Home*, Hartmann argues that the fact that a number of different aspects of housework were not incorporated into capitalist market production is evidence of the persistence of patriarchy.[18] For example, she notes that most laundry continued to be done in the home even though centralized laundry services can wash clothes far more efficiently. She suggests that such inefficient decentralization of washing machines can be explained by a patriarchal desire to keep women in the home.

In making this argument, Hartmann does not address the relationship between housework and childcare. Washing clothes in a washing machine in one's home interferes relatively little with the requirements of mothering. It takes only a few minutes, does not have to be done at any designated time, and requires little thought or attention. If we assume that women remain at home primarily because of their assigned responsibility for the care of infants, then the lack of technical change in some areas of housework appears much less "inefficient."

Repetitive menial work becomes much more meaningful when it is part of a large task providing love and support. This is the point that the antifeminist right has pressed home again and again. Children are sometimes pictured as the reward for housework. As Phyllis Schafley points out, "most women would rather cuddle a baby than a typewriter or factory machine." [19] Of course, many working men might also prefer to cuddle a baby rather than a factory machine, if it weren't for the fact that their sex role identity and economic constraints combine to make it a particularly unlikely choice. Hartmann states that only a theoretical understanding of patriarchy can explain this sexual division of labor. What our analysis adds to this is the claim that the explanation must include not only a reference to the individual male's desires to defend his privileged position, but also an understanding of the *structural* role of the sex-affective production system in directing personal choices and options for men and women.

This distinction proves quite important. While men's desires to keep women at home may not change, women's role in sex-affective production certainly has and will continue to change. Such changes have a tangible impact on the strength of patriarchal control.

Hartmann and others picture the realm of sex-affective production as a relatively constant and unchanging aspect of women's oppression, treating "motherhood" and "sexuality" as relatively abstract, ahistorical categories. [20] In our view, however, the process of sex-affective production is important precisely because of its historical dimensions. Our research in demographic, economic, and cultural history leads us to argue that there have been important historical changes in the realm of sex-affective production.

PATRIARCHY IN PRECAPITALIST AND CAPITALIST MODES OF PRODUCTION

Hartmann's visualization of the nature of patriarchy in precapitalist modes of production, and therefore her picture of the effect of the transition to capitalism, is largely predetermined by her lack of consideration of sex-affective production. In her review of the literature, Hartmann cites the analysis offered by Zaretsky that capitalism created a split between the public work of wage labor (done by men) and the private work of housework and child-bearing (done by women) (Hartmann, p. 5). Emphasizing that the "split" predated the transition to capitalism, she offers no explanation of how it came to be or what factors might widen or narrow it.

We believe that the nature and extent of this "split," which allows men greater control over material and emotional resources, depends upon the nature of women's roles in sex-affective production and the relationship between sex-affective production and other forms of work. While a number of these factors cannot be dealt with here, an analysis of women's work in childbearing and childrearing is particularly central.[21] The number and spacing of children is important, because even in societies in which children over the age of three are cared for by other members of the group, the biological mother tends to care for infants under the age of two. Increases in the number of children born increase the biological mother's responsibilities. Eight children, for example, require at least sixteen years of virtually continuous infant care. Such demands inevitably increase women's specialization in sex-affective production.

Large average family size—high fertility—was an important characteristic of sedentary agricultural societies like those within the precapitalist social formation in Europe.[22] Exploration of this topic is absent from Hartmann's summary of the evidence that the patriarchal peasant family had become the basic production unit in society before the emergence of capitalism.[23]

The etymological origin of the term "patriarchy" is "rule of the fathers." In European precapitalist modes of production the male head of household exercised a considerable degree of control over his children, a control reinforced by legal and economic institutions.[24] By virtue of his control over land, the patriarch could decide when and whom his children would marry, and when and under what conditions they might leave the household. Because children often worked within that household well after they reached physical maturity, their economic contribution to the patriarchal household was particularly significant.

In this context, the relationship between the childrearing component of sex-affective production and the other forms of economic production is quite clear. The time women spent rearing children represented a form of investment in future production within the household, an investment which was particularly important under conditions of high mortality. One might assume, then, that women freely chose to devote most of their energies to childbearing and childrearing. This does not, however, appear to have been the case.

Precapitalist modes of production in Europe and the U.S. were generally characterized by social relations which severely limited women's control over reproductive decisions.[25] Legally, marriage granted the husband a permanent and binding right to sexual intercourse with his wife. Most "folk" methods of contraception depended entirely on the full cooperation of the male. Strong religious sanctions against contraception affected both men and women. Older women and midwives, a group that may have had familiarity with techniques of abortion or been willing to be accomplices to infanticide, were the most common victims of persecution as witches.

Even more importantly, restrictions on forms of work which could be performed outside the household helped to channel women into marriage and childbearing. Within the context of the sexual division of labor women did play an important role in production. Single women, however, were almost always restricted to occupations in which they produced and/or earned less than single men. This reinforced a tendency for a large percentage of women to marry.[26]

Not all forms of patriarchal control over women were relevant to their role in reproduction, but *many were*. It is the connection between these forms of control that suggests a specific link between patriarchal control over children and patriarchal control over women: when and if children are economically advantageous to the male head of household, there is a particularly strong motive to channel women's productive efforts into childbearing and related forms of sex-affective production.

This link between the different forms of patriarchal control is considerably weakened by the transition to capitalism. The economic incentives to high fertility are diminished by the fact that the family loses its viability as a unit of production, the individual patriarch yields control of the means of production to the capitalist class and therefore loses control of his children's labor power, and the sexual division of labor is crosscut (though never eliminated) by a class division of labor.

Hartmann's analysis of the transition to capitalism does not capture these effects. She argues that the threat to patriarchal power posed by the incorporation of women into the wage labor force was countered by a "bargain" struck with male trade unions which agreed to limit women's labor employment opportunities in return for a "family wage" which could support a wife and children on the male wage earner's salary. They lobbied for child labor laws and protection laws for women which would either exclude them from wage labor as competitors to men, or would guarantee that their wages were lower than men's. (Hartmann, p. 21).

There are a number of reasons why this family wage argument is not very convincing. Even if such an implicit bargain did take place, there are good reasons to believe it did not last very long. Capitalists and individual patriarchs both stood to gain from women's oppression, but were competitors for the actual time, energy, and labor of both women and children. The working class as a whole may have benefited from child labor laws. To individual working class fathers, however, these laws meant that his children could not make any contribution to family income—and these laws did not automatically lead to compensatory increases in the money he could take home to support them. Children became true dependents, as the period of time in which they contributed little to their own or the family's support was extended. Despite the fact that many sons and daughters once they reached working ages provided direct economic support to their parents in old age, the economic advantages of a large family were diminished. Many families simply could not afford an additional child.

This weakening of the economic links between the generations is a major reason that the transition to capitalism has been associated with a steady decline in average family size.[27] The pace and timing of fertility decline varies greatly, but it is a virtually ubiquitous result of capitalist development. The average number of children born per family in the U.S., for example, has declined from about seven in 1800 to less than two today (see Table 1).[28] Hartmann makes reference to this decline, but seems to consider it of little significance. We believe it is central. Fertility decline has radically changed the nature of women's work, compressing the period of full-time motherhood into a relatively small portion of the life cycle.

TABLE 1. Fertility Decline in the U.S.*

Year	Total Fertility Rate + 1000		Percentage of Women with 2 Children, Cohorts Based on Women's Year of Birth	Percentage of Women with 5 or More Children, Cohorts Based on Women's Year of Birth
	White Women	Black & Other		
1800	7.04			
1810	6.92			
1820	6.73			
1830	6.55			
1840	6.14			
1850	6.14			
1850	5.42			
1860	5.21			
1870	4.55		12.0	37.1
1880	4.24		13.4	31.1
1890	3.87		16.3	24.5
1900	3.56		19.7	17.5
1910	3.42		22.5	12.7
1920	3.17		25.0	15.3
1930	2.45			
1940	2.10			
1950	3.00			
1960	3.52			
1965	2.79	3.89		
1970	2.39	3.07		
1975	1.71	2.32		

*The total fertility rate is the number of births a 1000 women would have in their lifetime if, at each age they experienced the birth rates occurring in the specified years. In this table, the TFR is divided by 1000 to show the average number of births per woman. The total fertility rate is a "period" measure — it is based upon the age specific birth rates of all women in a given year. "Cohort" measures which trace individual women over time are clearly preferable, but women born after 1940 have not yet reached the end of their childbearing period. The percentage of women with two children, or five plus children, is based on actual cohort data. It is taken from table 1-6, Perspectives on American Fertility, Current Population Reports, Special Studies, Series P-23, no. 70. Total fertility rates 1800-1960 are taken from Ansley F. Coale and Melvin Zelnick, *New Estimates of Fertility and Population in the U.S.*, (Princeton, Princeton University Press, 1963), p. 36, figures for 1965-1975 are from *Statistical Abstract of the U.S.*, 1978, table 80.

TABLE 2. The Female Labor Force as a Percentage of the Female Population *

Year		Percentage
1870		13.8
1880		14.6
1890	(June)	18.9
1900	(June)	20.6
1910	(April)	25.4
1920	(June)	23.7
1930	(April)	24.8
1940		27.4
1950		31.4
1960		34.8
1965		36.7
1970		42.6
1976		46.8
1977		48.

*For 1890-1977 the labor force is defined as those employed or seeking employment, persons 15 years + , 1890-1930; 14 years + , 1940-1966; 16 years + thereafter, as of March except as indicated. Source: Table 655, *Statistical Abstract of the United States*, 1978, and Series D49-62, *Historical Statistics of the United States*. Figures for 1870 and 1880 are based upon Series D75-84 and A91-104 in *Historical Statistics*, on the number of gainfully employed female workers over age 10, number of females in the population. Figures on the percentage of females under age 10 were extrapolated from figures on Percent Distribution of the Population by Age, Table 1-5, Perspectives on Human Fertility / Current Population Reports, Special Studies Series p-23, no. 70.

Changes in the structure of the family and household have increasingly made the very term *family wage* obsolete. Twenty five percent of all households in the U.S. today are headed by women.[29] Only 10 percent of contemporary U.S. families fit the. traditional nuclear family picture, with children at home, father working, mother as full-time homemaker.[30] The number of people in the average household has been drastically diminished. In 1970, 17 percent of all households were comprised of only one person.[31]

The transformation of family and houshold has been accompanied by long-term increases in women's formal labor force participation rates (see Table 2).[32] The family wage has been largely replaced by the two-paycheck family. Hartmann emphasizes that the women who bring home that paycheck continue to devote a tremendous amount of time to housework; time spent performing housework has increased among women who do not work outside the home. But this does not mean that the growth of women's wage labor has not, in the aggregate, diminished women's work in the home. Hartmann herself cites a study which found that women who engage in wage labor perform an average nineteen hours less per week than do full-time houseworkers.[33]

This transformation of the location and content of women's work is significant. It indicates that there has been a decrease in the proportional amount of time which women devote to sex-affective production (which benefits individual men) and an increase in the amount of time they devote to extrafamilial production (which benefits the capitalist class).

This shift has weakened the power that individual men wield over individual women in at least two ways. It has made it possible for women to play their oppressors against each other—using independent employment as a means of backing up demands for more equality and more control over sex-affective production. At the same time, the class division of labor has increasingly provided the capitalist class with paid substitutes for the labor time/attention of their wives (secretaries, nurses, waitresses) and diminished their resistance to progressive social changes in the domain of family life.

These changes might not have been important were it not for the fact that the organized feminist movement has consistently organized against the vulnerable areas of patriarchal control. We have not always been successful, but we have, however slowly and painfully, won important gains, particularly in that domain of oppression which has reinforced women's role in sex-affective production. Most of these victories are a now familiar part of women's history.[34] They include the right to custody of children in case of divorce (once categorically denied to women), control over own property and earnings, right to divorce, legal right to abortion (though economic access remains restricted), rights and access to forms of birth control which can be used with or without male co-operation (though there is as yet none that is both 100 percent safe and reliable), and in some areas, rights to freely express sexual preference. A notable recent gain is legislation in a number of states, such as Massachusetts and Oregon, that defines rape within marriage as a punishable offense.

These gains have not necessarily left women better off in the general, abstract sense. They have certainly been counterbalanced by the genesis of new forms of exploitation of women. Women wage workers have been sexually segregated in low paying occupations and consistently paid less for equal work. But to deny the importance of feminist gains in the area of sex-affective production is to maintain that sex-affective production has never been an important *domain* of women's oppression. It is also to deny that it remains an important struggle today.

Hartmann and others (such as Ewen[35]) recognize the weakening of patriarchal control in the family, but argue that power over women has simply been transferred to other sites. We believe that this claim underestimates the importance of sex-affective production. Many mechanisms of state and corporate control over women are indeed modeled upon forms of oppression of women within the family. Nonetheless, these public patriarchal devices are not as strong as family-based ones. For one thing, they conflict with liberal democratic ideology and are therefore more difficult to legitimate. Furthermore they are not so easily reproduced through childhood socialization.

The force of patriarchy should not be underestimated. The state clearly does reinforce male domination. It has revoked at least one important feminist gain—poor women's right to abortion. The Equal Rights Amendment has been effectively stalled. A great deal of evidence suggests that there have been significant increases in violence against women.[36] But these setbacks do not mean that feminist efforts are being completely neutralized. The increase in male violence may represent a frustrated response to the weakening of forms of male control which were once considered legitimate. The possibility remains that some future political or economic changes will enable men to reestablish traditional levels of control over women's reproductive decisions. It is difficult, however, to imagine what shape such changes might take short of outright fascism.

Hartmann terms the mutual accommodation between patriarchy and capitalism a "vicious circle."[37] We agree that such mutual accommodation persists in some respects. But the oppression of women by the two systems of domination, patriarchy and capitalism, is *not circular*. These systems, in other words, are not in equilibrium. In fact, the conflicts or contradictions between the systems can become foci for both feminist *and* socialist demands.

STRATEGIES FOR CHANGE

Capitalism and patriarchy are not two static interlocking sets of domination relations. They are two complementary systems which are increasingly coming into conflict. Women today have contradictions to face in all aspects of sex-affective production: in *mothering* (expected to defer to men in order to become mothers, yet no longer able to depend on life-long support in this role); in *nurturance* (expected to sacrifice their own interests for the good of their husbands and families yet unable to count on the family's stability); and in *sexuality* (urged to be sexy yet expected to defer their own sexual interests to those of men).

We maintain that these historically developed conflicts in the marriage between capitalism and patriarchy can provide women with important insights into the contradictions of *both* systems. Such conflicts are the source of an increasing dissatisfaction and disaffection with the current state of society. They increase the likelihood that women will become actively involved in radical social change.

Of course not all women will become progressive rebels against the present system. The rise of the New Right as a social movement shows that many women may move in a reactionary direction and hope to reestablish the old "natural" women's role in the home.[38] These hopes may remain in spite of a reality which conflicts with the ideal: women may be divorced and working in wage labor or on welfare and still look to remarriage as the solution to all their problems. However, more women than ever before are likely to find it impossible to see immersion in a family identity as the solution to their problems. Once women question the authority relations in their personal relationships with men, they may move in one of several political directions. They may come to identify primarily with their own interests as women (as an oppressed gender class in patriarchal sex-affective production),[39] becoming feminists opposed to patriarchy in all forms, and thus capitalist patriarchy. A second possibility is that women may become more race or class conscious as they are forced to struggle directly around economic class issues concerning pay, working conditions, or ethnic and racial community problems that also involve class issues (no affordable child care in lower income areas, poor schooling for children, etc.)[40]

These two radicalizing pressures tend to lead more *women* than men toward a *socialist* consciousness. Women may become a new potentially revolutionary force in advanced capitalist societies, not only because of conflicting pressures on women at home and at work, but also because of their historical role in sex-affective production. The same reasoning which Marx applied to his analysis of the revolutionary potential of the working class may be applied to women in capitalist patriarchy. Marx argued that the particular collective social relations of working class life led to the development of radical needs and collective values that challenged the individualist, competitive, profit-oriented needs of capitalism.[41] It is not at all clear that wage labor has had this result. But it does seem that a similar argument can be plausibly made for women.

Women are nurturers: we keep the systems we work in (the family, service jobs in wage labor) together by nurturing. The social relations of our nurturance work account on the one hand for our oppression (sacrificing our own interests for those of men and children), and on the other hand for our potential strength as bearers of a radical culture: we support an ethic of sharing, cooperation, and collective involvement that stands in clear opposition to an ethic based on individualism, competition, and private profit.[42]

What are the implications of these tendencies and possibilities for practical political organizing? Our socialist feminist analysis suggests two key tasks on which organizers should focus. We must continue to inform the left as a whole (the socialist mixed left of men and women, the autonomous women's movement, and nationalist and Third World movements with community bases in this country) with feminist values based on women's historically developed skills of nurturance and collective involvement. We must also continue to build a strong and mass-based autonomous women's movement which provides its own material and social resources for women yet is sensitive to economic and race differences between women.

The task of infusing feminist values into the left as a whole is necessary both to empower women within all segments of the left to be more politically powerful as well as to build conditions for strong coalitions between other segments of the left and the women's movement. This task often requires women in mixed left situations to play the role of moral conscience: to demand egalitarian process and decision making procedures, and to emphasize supportive rather than destructive ways of handling political disagreements within organizations. Political experience suggests that groups that reorganize along these lines are not only more democratic, but also attract larger numbers of women. Another aspect of this task is the development of political coalitions between the women's movement and mixed left groups which emphasize some similar needs in men as well as women (e.g., lesbian feminists uniting with gay liberationists, feminists working with groups organized around demands for full employment, health care, and reduction of the work week (so men as well as women can spend more time with their children).

In order to be successful in infusing feminism into socialism, the women's movement must build a strong and autonomous mass movement which can provide material and social resources across class and race lines. For depth and strength, socialist feminists must find ways of providing support for women to identify their interests with women rather than with their personal duties to men within the family context. This requires the establishment of a self-defined revolutionary *feminist women's culture* which can ideologically and materially support women "outside the patriarchy." Counter-hegemonic cultural and material support networks can provide woman-identified substitutes for patriarchal sex-affective production to give women increased control over their bodies, their labor time, and their sense of self.[43]

There are four key areas around which to organize a strong feminist movement: (1) demands for publicly supported *childcare* and *reproductive rights*; (2) demands for *sexual freedom*, which includes the right to sexual preference (lesbian/gay rights); (3) feminist controlled *cultural* and *ideological production* (important because cultural products affect ends, sense of self, social networks and the production of nurturance and affection, friendship and social kin networks); and (4) the establishment of mutual aid: *economic support systems for women*, from alternative households and women-identified family networks to women's caucuses in trade unions to support feminist concerns in wage labor.

The first area is particularly important because women's immersion in *mothering* is a central factor affecting their freedom to challenge patriarchal controls. Although reduced fertility rates in advanced capitalist societies have lessened women's necessary labor time in childcare, continued struggles for publicly supported childcare and increased reproductive rights are important as a way to give women more autonomy in this area. The demand for publicly supported childcare will also challenge the dominant social definition of motherhood: the patriarchal assumption that children are the private property and hence the private responsibility of parents, especially mothers.

Sexual freedom is important because women need to define themselves as *sexual subjects*, not sexual objects. We have to find ways to combat the commoditization of sexuality which oppresses women (e.g., the fight against pornography which associates sexual pleasure with violence against women) without falling into a puritanism which discredits the right to sexual pleasure as an end in itself. The struggle for lesbian/gay rights is particularly important in the context of a new right movement which explicitly connects its defense of white patriarchal authority and the male dominated nuclear family with an attack on minorities, feminism, gay rights, rights for youth, and sexual freedom in general.[44]

A revolutionary counterhegemonic women's culture requires material support systems which can provide alternatives to patriarchal households and patriarchal relations in wage labor. Examples of new institutions which aim to provide both kinds of support are communal households for women (including single mothers and their children), transition houses for battered women, rape crisis centers, abortion referrals, feminist counseling, parent cooperative child care networks that teach feminist values to children, and women-run cooperative enterprises. As nuclear families increasingly tend to become fragmented, feminists (whether heterosexual or lesbian) must struggle to define new *social* forms of kinship/friendship networks among women that provide alternatives to the nuclear family in meeting nurturance and support needs.

Another important arena in the struggle for economic survival and support for women is trade union organizing. Only 11 percent of women wage workers are members of unions, yet union membership is becoming increasingly essential as more and more women become dependent on wage employment for the majority of their adult lives.[45] Although union leadership has traditionally sidestepped feminist issues (affirmative action, paid maternity leave, sexual harassment on the job, gay rights), a new concern for maintaining and increasing female constituents is forcing some unions to deal with these issues. A strong socialist feminist presence among union organizers can help guarantee sensitivity to sexism and (hopefully) racism.

How can women workers best be mobilized? The disappointing defeat of socialist feminists within the Coalition of Labor Union Women (CLUW) suggests that mass political organizations cannot at this point be radicalized simply by socialist feminists joining their ranks. Rather, what may be more effective are organizations such as Union Wage (in Berkeley) and 9 to 5 (in Boston and New York) which organize women as women and women as workers. This implication is supported by the work of the Red Apple Collective[46] and Cerullo[47] who suggest that the current lack of organizational cohesion in the women's movement in general, and among socialist feminists in particular, can be remedied by the establishment of grassroots groups which establish a constituency by organizing around a single issue. Such groups can then establish informal networks, alliances, and coalitions with other feminist groups around issues of common concern.

In seeking to establish autonomous feminist support networks, socialist feminists must confront several serious problems. While public funds are often an important source of financial assistance, they may also contribute to cooptation. CETA funding for women's centers and transition houses often imposes funding criteria that may undermine the self-help, nonhierarchical structures originally built into such projects. In addition, women who become paid administrators or therapists may acquire a vested interest in bureaucracy. This problem can only be solved by continual struggle, vigilance, criticism/self-criticism sessions, and creative strategies such as regular rotation of "directorships" and other managerial roles.

A second problem facing the existing countercultural women's movement is its race, class, and age/marital/parental composition. Most women who consider themselves members of the alternative women's community are young, white, single, and childless. Many are lesbians. Most grew up in petty bourgeois or professional-managerial type families. As a result, there is a tremendous potential for misunderstanding and conflict. Working class women may feel excluded. White women seldom understand the structure of black and hispanic families. Nonmothers often don't understand the problems of mothers. Lesbian women often feel that straight women don't understand heterosexism. Counter-hegemonic women's networks cannot become a viable alternative for all women unless they can overcome these divisions.

In emphasizing that patriarchy creates a division between men and women as controlling and controlled social gender classes, feminists may mistakenly ignore the equally important fact that patriarchy also reinforces hierarchical control between men and other *men*. Patriarchal oppression of women is used as a social mechanism by men in power to control other *men* as well as women. Batya Weinbaum argues that the challenge to patriarchal relations in a class society comes about in part by a challenge to the rule of the symbolic patriarchal fathers of the ruling class by men and women in subordinate classes.[48] Thus, in past revolutions, women from oppressed classes and races have predominantly chosen to side with the *men* of their class or race against the men (and women) from the dominant class(es) and race(s). White middle class feminists must find creative ways to continue the struggle against patriarchal relations while acknowledging the difference in power and position of men in working class and Third World community contexts.[49]

Concern with broadening the base of the women's movement has motivated many women to organize around issues that are not explicitly feminist, but have the potential to develop a base among minorities and working people. Women working in organizations like the Native American Solidarity Committee and the Puerto Rican Solidarity Committee have done a great deal of consciousness raising among women who were initially exclusively concerned with nationalist issues. The anti-nuclear movement has also enjoyed strong feminist influence. Conversely, the development of women's groups and caucuses within the national subcultures, such as the Third World Women's Alliance and the Native American Women's Organization has pushed women to directly consider issues of race and class privilege.

Such efforts clearly serve as an example for women who have an interest in fighting oppression in all its forms. It is true that much remains to be done. But it is also true that many women have a new and important theoretical understanding of the relationship between sexism, racism, and class oppression. While we face a staggering political agenda, we can also look back on a history of important personal, political, and theoretical gains.

FOOTNOTES

1. Paddy Quick, "The Class Nature of Women's Oppression" (*Review of Radical Political Economics*, vol. 9, no.3, Fall 1977).
2. Maria Dalla Costa and Selma James, *The Power of Women and the Subversion of the Community* (Bristol, England: Falling Wall Press, 1974).
3. Eli Zaretsky, "Capitalism, the Family and Personal Life" (*Socialist Revolution*, January-June, 1973).
4. Juliet Mitchell, *Psychoanalysis and Feminism* (New York: Vintage Books, Random House, 1974).
5. While many socialist feminists, notably Linda Gordon, have written extensively on the topic of birth control, they have not integrated this into a theoretical analysis of production as a whole. As a result, it has been easy for marxists to overlook the significance of their work. There is clearly a growing interest in the theoretical relationship between production and reproduction. This has been a major concern of Claude Meillasoux, in *Femmes, greniers, y capitaux* (not yet in English translation). Meillasoux's argument, however, is confused and often difficult to follow. Our own approach is more directly indebted to a very suggestive analysis in Zillah Eisenstein's introductory essay in *Capitalist Patriarchy and the Case for Socialist Feminism (New York: Monthly Review, 1978).*

6. This is the topic of an on-going debate among marxists, and the litera-ture is far too extensive to review here. Well known contributions include Louis Althusser, *For Marx* (Vintage Books, New York), and E.P. Thompson, *The Poverty of Theory* (Monthly Review Press, New York, 1979).

7. Bridget O'Laughlin, "Production and Reproduction: Meillasoux's Femmes, greniers, y capitaux," (*Critique of Anthropology*), no.8, 1977).

8. Karl Marx, *Capital* (International Publishers, New York, 1967), p.572.

9. For a more complete discussion of this issue see Nancy Folbre, "The Reproduction of Labor Power," unpublished manuscript, Economic Growth Center, Yale University, May, 1980.

10. Maria Dalla Costa and Selma James, *op. cit.* Jean Gardiner, "Women's Domestic Labor," (*New Left Review*, no.83, Jan.-Feb., 1974), Wally Seccombe, "The Housewife and Her Labor under Capi-talism," (*New Left Review*, no.83, Jan.-Feb., 1974).

11. This offers some insights into the reasons why marxists have been reluctant to see childrearing as a labor process. Marx's labor theory of value is built upon the assumption that the value of labor power—unlike the value of other commodities—is *not* determined by the socially neces-sary labor time required to produce it.

12. Juliet Mitchell, *Ibid.*, Nancy Chodorow, *The Reproduction of Mothering* (Stanford University Press, 1979); Ann Oakley, *Sex, Gender and Society* (Harper and Row, New York, 1972).

13. Gayle Rubin, "The Traffic in Women," *Towards an Anthropology of Women* (Monthly Review Press, New York, 1975).

14. The best description of this process is in Nancy Chodorow, *op. cit.* See also Dorothy Dinnerstein, *The Mermaid and the Minotaur* (New York: Harper and Row Publishers, 1976).

15. Ann Ferguson, "Women as a Revolutionary Class" (in Pat Walker, ed., *Labor and Capital*, Boston: South End Press, 1978).

16. *Ibid.*

17. See Nancy Folbre, "Of Patriarchy Born: The Political Economy of Fertility Decisions," Discussion paper #350, Economic Growth Center, Yale University.

18. Heidi Hartmann, *Capitalism and Women's Work in the Home*, PhD. Dissertation, Yale University, 1975, pp.276-330.

19. Phyllis Shafley, *The Power of the Positive Woman,* (Harcourt-Bracc, 1978), p.63.

20. Shulamith Firestone, *The Dialectic of Sex*, (Bantam Books, New York, 1970). Interestingly, Barbara Easton, who offers an analysis of the weakening of patriarchal power somewhat similar to our own, explicitly rejects the notions that these changes are linked to change within the

family. She writes, "...women's mothering has thus far been a constant through history; in order to explain the changes in women's role in the family and in society it is necessary to look to economic and social forces outside the family...". ("Feminism and the Contemporary Family," *Socialist Review*, no.39, vol.8, no.3, May-June, 1978).
21. These factors include the organization of childrearing and, in particular, the role that fathers play. Exploration of the entire area of sex role socialization is clearly crucial, and Margaret Mead's classic *Male and Female*, (William Morrow and Company, Publishers, New York, 1949) remains required reading.
22. D. V. Glass, D. E. C. Eversley, *Population in History*, (Edward Arnold Publishers, Lts., 1965). See, in particular, Carlos Cipolla, "Four Centuries of Italian Demographic Development" and Louis Henry, "The Population of France in the 18th Centruy."
23. Hartmann, "Capitalism, Patriarchy and Job Segregation by Sex," in Eisenstein, *op.cit.*
24. Lutz Berkner, "The Stem Family and the Developmental Cycle of the Peasant Household: an 18th Century Austrian Example," in *The American Family in Social-Historical Perspective*, (ed. M. Gordon, St. Martin's Press, New York, 1973); Lawrence Stone, *The Family, Sex, and Marriage in England, 1500-1800*, (Harper and Row, Publishers, New York, 1977); Edward Shorter, *The Making of the Modern Family* (New York: Basic Books, 1975).
25. Shorter, *Ibid.*, pp.54-78. Shorter's discussion is suggestive but not very thorough. This topic has been almost completely ignored by European social historians. Some new literature on the history of sexuality offers new insights—See, for instance, Randolph Trumbach, "London's Sodomites: Homosexual Behavior and Western Culture in the 18th Century" on what was considered "unnatural sexual behavior" (*Journal of Interdisciplinary History*, vol.11, no.1, Fall, 1977).
26. By 1850, marriage patterns in Western Europe were quite distinct from those other areas. The percentage of never married women was high as 15% and age at marriage was also unusually high. (See J. Hajnal, "European Marriage Patterns in Perspective" in *Population in History*, *op. cit.* Historical demographers seem to agree that marriage rates were higher, and age at marriage lower in the period 1850, but the *timing* of this transition remains unclear. For a further discussion of the relationship between marriage rates and economic opportunities for women, see Nancy Folbre, "Patriarchy in Colonial New England," in *Review of Radical Political Economics*, Summer, 1980.
27. See Folbre, "Of Patriarchy Born: The Political Economy of Fertility Decisions," *op. cit.*
28. Linda Gordon, *Woman's Body, Woman's Right*, (Basic Books, New York, 1976); C. Forster and G. S. Tucker, *Economic Opportunity and*

White American Fertility Ratios, 1800-1860, (New York: Yale University Press, 1972).

29. Walter Guzzardi, Jr., "Demography's Glad Tidings for the Eighties," (*Fortune*, 5 November 1979), p. 102.

30. Alice Rossi, "Who is the Real Family?" (*Ms*, August, 1978). The 15.9% figure for nuclear families—couples without children living with them, or families where the wife works part or full time in wage labor.

31. Frances Kobrin, "The Fall in Household Size and the Rise of the Primary Individual in the U.S.," (*Demography*, vol. 13, no.1, February 1976).

32. *Historical Statistics of the U.S. and Statistical Abstract of the U.S., 1977*, U.S. Department of Commerce, Bureau of the Census.

33. Hartmann, *Capitalism and Women's Work, op. cit.*, p.273. The study cited is Kathryn Walker, "Homemaking Still Takes Time," *Journal of Home Economics*, LXI, October 1969.

34. Eleanor Flexnor, *Century of Struggle* (Cambridge, Massachusetts: Belknap Press of Harvard University Press, 1975).

35. Hartmann, *op. cit.*, Stuart Ewen, *Captains of Consciousness: Advertising and the Social Roots of the Consumer Culture* (McGraw-Hill, New York, 1976).

36. Coleen McGrath, "Crisis of the Domestic Order" (*Socialist Review*, no.43, Jan.-Feb. 1979).

37. Hartmann, "Capitalism, Patriarchy, and Job Segregation by Sex," *op. cit.*, p.208.

38. Linda Gordon and Allen Hunter, "Sex, Family and the New Right," in *Radical America* (Nov./Feb., 1977-78), reprinted by New England Free Press, Somerville, Massachusetts, 1978.

39. cf. Ann Ferguson, "Women as a New Revolutionary Class in the United States," in Pat Walker, ed. *Between Labor and Capital* (Boston: South End Press, 1979).

40. cf. Karen Kollias, "Class Realities: Building a New Power Base for the Women's Movement" in *Quest*, (VI, no.3, Winter 1975) and Bev Fisher, "Race and Class: Beyond Personal Politics," in *Quest* (VIII, no.4, Spring 1977).

41. cf. Agnes Heller, *The Theory of Need in Marx*, (London: Allison and Busby, 1976).

42. cf. Jean Baker Miller, *Toward a New Psychology of Women*, (Boston: Beacon Press, 1976).

43. The idea of a counterhegemonic culture as a centure for resistance to a dominant culutre has been developed in the marxist tradition by Antonio Gramsci, *Prison Notebooks*, Q. Hoare and G. Nowell Smith, eds., (International Publishers, New York, 1973) and by Raymond Williams, *Marxism and Literature*, (Oxford University Press, 1977). Both of these thinkers are concerned with the need for the working class to develop and

sustain its own values in opposition to those of the dominant class, the capitalist class in capitalism. Neither of them considers the possibility that women need to build a countercultural *feminist* culture as a component of the larger culture of resistance. In the U.S. many feminist artists are presently engaged in building such a feminist culture, and many feminist activists (primarily those in social services) think of themselves as building material and social support systems for women.

44. cf. Gordon and Hunter, *op. cit.*

45. Tables 655 and 698, *Statistical Abstract of the U.S.*, 1978.

46. Red Apple Collective, "Socialist-Feminist Women's Unions: Past and Present," (*Socialist Review*, no.38, March/April 1978).

47. Margaret Cerullo, "Autonomy and the Limits of Organization: A Socialist-Feminist Response to Harry Boyte," (*Socialist Review*, no.43, Jan./Feb. 1979).

48. Batya Weinbaum, *The Curious Courtship of Women's Liberation and Socialism*, (Boston: South End Press, 1978).

49. An example of how this issue can come up in practice occurred in the organizing of a *Take Back the Night* march for women against violence against women in Amherst, Mass., Fall 1979. The question of whether the Third World Women's Task Force (a group at the University of Massachusetts) would co-sponsor the march with the Women against Violence against Women group. The issues were (1) should the march condemn racist violence against minorities as a focus of equal importance as violence against women? (2) should the march include men? Socialist feminists suggested a two-part compromise: (1) that the march protest both racist violence and violence against women by focusing on the recent unexplained and unprosecuted death of a Third World area woman (The Seta Rampersad case); (2) that the march be divided into two parts, one of which would be just for women who wanted to march with women and the other of which would include male supporters. In our opinion it is essential that compromises like these continue to be explored as a means to developing alliances between feminists in the autonomous women's movement and Third World and working class women who don't share all of our priorities. (Unfortunately, the suggested compromise was defeated: the first part accepted but the second rejected by the WAVAW group, so the proposed coalition between the two groups did not materialize. As a result, however, there are now some developing networks between socialist feminists and politically active Third World women that we hope will bear fruit in the future.)

REFORM AND/OR REVOLUTION: TO-WARDS A UNIFIED WOMEN'S MOVEMENT

Zillah Eisenstein

Zillah Eisenstein is associate professor of politics at Ithaca College where she teaches feminist and marxist theory. She is editor of Capitalist Patriarchy and the Case for Socialist Feminism and the author of the recently published The Radical Future of Liberal Feminism. She is an active member of the women's movement belonging to CARASA, NOW, and the board of The Task Force for Battered Women, Ithaca, New York.

339

"The Unhappy Marriage of Marxism and Feminism" states that the marriage between marxism and feminism has been an unequal one much in the same way marriage is legally structured as an unequal union between man and woman.* I am in basic agreement with the essay.[1] Marxist analysis has had the upper hand because it is a more fully developed theoretical system than feminism is. Its own history lends it legitimacy whereas the hidden history of feminism puts it on the defensive. As a result, feminists are still in the process of defining the contours of patriarchy as a political system while trying to build a dialectical analysis of it, inclusive of questions of ideology, real historical processes, and consciousness itself.

The more feminists study patriarchy the more we understand that much of its power lies in the ability to mystify the reality of women's oppression. It is no less real than the economic structures of our time, but patriarchy is more deceptively conceptualized and practiced. The mystification of capitalism lies in its exchange system for profit and the correlate concerns with political control. Women's oppression, although a part of these processes, is also part of the more complicated patriarchal arrangements of the family, motherhood, and the sexual division of labor. These arrangements exist to mystify and actualize the potential power women have as reproducers and mothers.[2] These categories of political analysis are not mapped out in classical marxist thought. Therefore, the synthesis of marxist and feminist questions requires

---

*In reviewing this essay for publication I am aware that readers interested in this argument may want to examine my more detailed treatment of it in my publication *The Radical Future of Liberal Feminism* (New York: Longman Inc., 1980) which was written after the completion of this article. I have in mind particularly the discussion of patriarchy, the radical potential of liberal feminism, its ties to radical feminism, and my theory of the capitalist-patriarchal state. My thanks to Beau Grosscup and Miriam Broady for reading and commenting on this article. The discussion of Bella Abzug has appeared in *In These Times*, vol. 3, no. 16, 7-13 March 1979 and much of this article was first delivered at the *Women and Power Conference*, Houston, Texas, 1978.

the transformation of one by the other.[3] A simple marriage will not work.

Because the above points are being analyzed more readily now —at least by socialist feminist women—and because I believe political discussions which are the most productive are those which are connected to the *realities* in which we live—I think we need to move the discussion between marxists and feminists to the realm between liberal feminists and socialist and radical feminists. Although the political reality today can accurately be described as encompassing a high level of feminist consciousness, it is primarily a *liberal* feminist consciousness. We need to better understand exactly what the richness and limitations of this orientation are. The reason to do this is to try and radicalize the liberal feminist movement and at the same time adopt their strategies when they represent real challenges to the state. I will argue later that whether the ERA is passed or not, we can use the struggle to ratify it to mobilize a more radical and socialist feminist movement.

Marxist analysis has taught me to begin with material reality as my starting point and this is defined by what actually exists. Feminism has taught me to understand the daily life struggles within the family and with the state as part of this reality. It has also pushed me to understand that people's consciousness is part of this reality and cannot be ignored or wished away. Hence I want to take Hartmann's commitment to developing a synthesis of marxism and feminism and *use* it to address the political realities of the feminist movement today.[4] I think, as a feminist, there is much more to be *politically* gained by a dialogue between liberal, radical, and socialist feminists than by a dialogue between marxists and feminists.

The unity between these three orientations derives from the concern to understand and dismantle patriarchy. Hence, the best proof of Hartmann's argument of patriarchy as a structural reality of power is to use it as a base for political organizing. What better practical proof can there be that women are a sexual class, than women organizing across different political orientations to build a unified feminist movement. This is the real proof of feminism that no marxist will be able to explain away. Rather than trying to persuade marxists that patriarchy lays the structural base of capitalism, let us radicalize liberal feminists to be able to see the patriarchal and economic class base of liberalism.

If it is true that the structure of patriarchy cuts through all women's lives, however differentiated it may be according to race and economic class, then we need to start working with each other in terms of this continuity in our lives. My argument is then, that, *liberal feminists, who make up the largest part of the visible women's movement as well as women's consciousness today, and radical and socialist feminists have as much in common in terms of the oppression of patriarchy for building a political movement as do socialist feminists and marxists.* If this is true, then we must begin to make the same arguments to liberal feminists about the bourgeois as well as patriarchal bias of liberalism as we have done to marxists about the sex-blind nature of their analysis. In other words, we need to begin political work around day care, medicaid abortions and issues of prochoice, antisterilization abuse,[5] and the ERA, in order to radicalize the women's movement as a whole. Radical and socialist feminists need to become politically active on these issues. Then our presence will have to be dealt with. By focusing on issues which directly relate to women's relation to reproduction and motherhood and hence the hierarchical sexual division of society, and by arguing honestly with each other to better understand the biases of the bourgeois patriarchal state we can uncover the patriarchal dimensions as well as the economic class and racial biases of society. Women, as liberal feminists, once they come to understand the contradiction between liberalism and feminism, through struggling for the equality of opportunity which is unattainable for them, will move to the left *as* feminists. They first need to see that the patriarchal bias of liberalism excludes them from equality with men. The contradictions are becoming more visible as more middle class women work for wages and the double day of work extends to them as well as the working class woman. The bottom line is that the struggle for a feminist society is the groundwork for everthing else, because it dismantles the most implicit, insidious hierarchical relations known to civilization. Once sexual hierarchy is uncovered for what it is, other hierarchical forms in society become clearer as well.

We, therefore, need to think about sexism as a revolutionary issue, but more importantly we must understand that we are not in a revolutionary situation in the United States today. Nor can we accept preexisting definitions of revolution for ourselves. Instead, we need to *rethink* the very issues of reform and revolution and their relationship to each other. We also need to come to terms with the consciousness of women today who, as feminists, demand reform but who, in order to really achieve equality, would need a revolution. What we need at the moment is an understanding of the movement and process of social change taking place in the family and in women's consciousness. If consciousness is part of the process we must deal with, then we must come to terms with the fact that most feminists are liberal in their political demands and radical in terms of what they really want for themselves. We need to develop an understanding of the connections between the individual woman's life and her understanding of political strategy in this society.[6] One way to do this is by dealing with the questions of abortion and the ERA in terms of the progressive issues they represent. Feminist activity then can bridge the gap between the liberal/marxist dichotomy. Such divisions in the end support the state, not us.

As a socialist feminist I think we must open up the dialogue *within* the women's movement itself, particularly within the liberal factions of it. We must begin where most women are—and most women are liberal feminist in their consciousness. Not until we understand why this is so can we build a movement built from their concerns. This is not to say that we should become liberal feminists, but that we must begin to deal with this political reality, in politically intelligent ways, instead of wishing or pretending things were different.

DEFINING LIBERAL FEMINISM

When I use the term liberal feminist, I mean that body of contemporary theory which shares the belief in the supremacy of the individual and the correlate concerns with individual freedom and choice. This belief underlines the demand for women's independence. All feminists, no matter what their particular persuasion is, root their feminism in this (liberal) conception of self.

The liberal feminist picture of the political world as the activity of the governmental realm, the importance of citizenship and the vote, and the property rights of liberalism are redefined to include the equal opportunity for women as well as men. Although pieces of the inequity experienced are understood, they are not understood as a structured reality of power. Hence, the individual is often seen as being able to counter her oppression in individual terms. Patriarchy as a theory of male supremacy involving a structural analysis of power is not understood, although particular (individual) advantages of men over women are. Although woman's economic dependence on men is criticized, this is not understood as an integral aspect of the connecting forms of the sexual division of labor and the economic class system of capitalism. As a result, the realm of power is defined in terms of the politics of the law. Men and women are yet to be made equal before the law and hence the solution to the problem gets defined in terms of creating equal opportunity before the law.

Liberal feminists believe that they can acquire "equality of opportunity" within capitalist patriarchal society. In other words, they know they are unequal but do not see the structural relations of capitalism or patriarchy as the problem. They do not understand the structural and political relationship between the family and the state as problematic for the practice of liberal democracy. Their view of the division between the public and private realms of social activity is the starting point for their analysis. The divisions between these worlds is taken as natural, or necessary. The patriarchal bias of the analysis is that the realm of the family is defined as the women's sphere, the realm of the public world as the man's. Although many of these women want to be given equality of opportunity in the public world they do not see that their particular position in the private world gives historical definition to their particular inequality to men. Liberal feminists often do not understand that the patriarchal ordering of the public/private worlds will have to be restructured in order to equally open opportunity to them. And for this to happen today, capitalism would have to be dismantled as well.

But they do understand that they want their lives to change. They do know that they are tired when they come home from work and still must face the work of the home and the family. They are more and more conscious of the inequities which exist in their lives as they are forced to work both in the public and private worlds of wage labor and the home. More than 50 percent of the women in the United States today work for wages and they are the ones developing a feminist consciousness as their lives become filled with the cross-pressures of both worlds. Much of their consciousness reflects the liberalism of society, but it makes no sense that it should stop here, because liberalism as a system is implicitly patriarchal. Liberal "rights" are structured via the inequalities of man and woman.[7] Hence, liberalism and feminism are at odds with each other given liberalism's unequal sexual base.

The state via the ERA is trying to present a version of liberal feminism which smooths out these contradictions. Hence, as feminists we need to address the patriarchal bias of liberalism and try to show how liberal society is rooted in the inequality between man and woman, the family and the economy, public and private worlds. In so doing, we will uncover the antifeminist dimensions of liberalism. *As a feminist* one has to move beyond liberalism.

Hartmann states that the bourgeois sector of the feminist movement is the sector that is growing. Many of these women are not really bourgeois in my mind, although they are liberals, and I think we must address ourselves to this consciousness. I agree with Hartmann's statement that parts of the movement are being coopted and that feminism is being used against women themselves. More important is that the general consciousness of women is being coopted.

Hartmann says it is logical in these times to turn to marxism as a developed theory of social change to address these issues. I rather think that we must take this tendency and turn it to our own needs; to develop a socialist feminist analysis of liberal feminism. I want to begin such a dialogue here.[8]

THE RADICAL POTENTIAL OF LIBERAL FEMINISM

Liberal feminism which has received the most support by women and by the established power system today needs to be examined most carefully because it shares certain elements (in terms of liberalism) of the dominant ideology of our society. It, however, at the same time lays the basis for a real assault against present inequalities in terms of its feminism and as such must be understood as containing progressive and radical elements for the struggle for women's liberation. To the extent certain liberal *feminist* claims have not been met and cannot be met by the existing society, demands for them uncover the basic contradictions of our society. This is part of the *process* of building a revolutionary feminist consciousness. In this sense, it is important to understand the progressive and radical elements of liberal feminism as well as its limitations.

Today liberal feminism is a mix of several different orientations. Although all liberal feminists adopt the ideas of freedom of choice, individualism, and equality of opportunity, they differ on how self-conscious they are about the patriarchal, economic, and racial bias of these ideas. By differentiating between several different tendencies within liberal feminism itself, I hope to clarify the differences which exist within liberal feminist politics. These tendencies which I label "progressive" and "radical" reflect the different orientations and political understanding of liberal feminists. These two tendencies, which presently coexist within liberal-feminist politics, often lead to an oversimplified and incorrect view of the complexity of liberal feminism and its radical feminist orientation. The equation drawn between liberal feminism and its "progressive," rather than its "radical," faction leads to a much more limiting view of liberal feminism than actually exists. This, of course, is the picture of feminism which the state seeks to legitimize. The purpose, in the end, is to identify the radical feminist tendencies which exist within significant sectors of liberal feminist politics and by doing so clarify the basis for building a revolutionary feminist politics.

The set of ideas, identified as liberal-feminist, has remained strikingly similar in both its nineteenth and twentieth-century formulation. What is interesting to note, however, is that the position this set of ideas holds within the political spectrum of alternatives has changed considerably, especially in relation to the state. Whereas Mary Wollstonecraft, J. S. Mill, Harriet Taylor, and Elizabeth Cady Stanton's feminist demands stood as radically liberal in their day, they stand as part of the established ideology of the state today. Whereas these early feminists were utterly progressive in demanding education, the vote, and property rights for married women, today these formal legal equalities exist. As a result, those who narrowly define women's equality in terms of these citizen rights, believe women have attained equality with men.

The antifeminist traditionalists do not believe in women's equality to begin with. The Right-to-Life Movement cuts through this group and status-quo liberal feminists. Both the antifeminists and the status-quo liberals operate as reactionaries today. Those, like Phyllis Schlafly, who argue against the ERA, believe that

FEMINIST POLITICAL SPECTRUM:

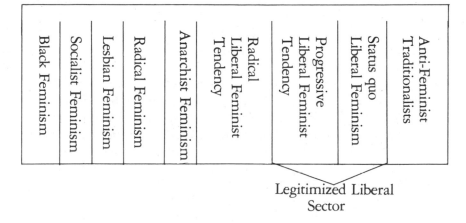

Legitimized Liberal
Sector

woman is already equal to man in the judicial and political sense. It is, Schlafly contends, up to the individual woman whether she takes advantage of the opportunities she has, or not. Such a rendering of liberal feminism is expressed as a defense of the status quo. In this sense, liberal feminism is used to protect the status quo from women's demands. Those adhering to this view make up a much smaller group than the liberal feminists who remain progressive by insisting that their legal reform demands have not yet been met. Their demands for the ERA and other legislation committed to women's equality of opportunity continue to undermine the patriarchal privilege upon which the liberal state is based even though many of these feminists do not fully recognize the radical feminist content of their demands. Therefore, although their politics is potentially subversive to the state, they do not always recognize it as such.

This "progressive-liberal-feminist tendency" within liberal feminism is the aspect of liberal feminism which the state seeks to legitimate, although it does so at the same time it tries to undercut its attack on patriarchal privilege. This orientation within liberal feminism recognizes the struggle for formal equality between men and women within the law as central to women's liberation. This view of liberal feminism accepts liberal rights theory as sufficient for creating women's equality with men with little recognition that "rights" recognize individuals within a structure of sexual, economic, and racial inequality. This version of liberal feminism argues that the present social and political structure can accommodate woman's equality.

The issue which is left unresolved in this view is which men women will be equal to. One hardly believes women are fighting to be equal with coal miners or the male industrial workers in the California plant who were sterilized by the chemicals they work with. The problem is that when these liberal feminists say they want equality with men, they gloss over the fact that men are not equal in the capitalist class structure. This points to the way these feminists see the doctrine of equality of opportunity. They wish to be equal to men in the abstract sense that all men rise according to the amount of initiative, intelligence, and energy they have. However, this notion of abstract equality in actuality does not exist.

What we need to do is take this demand for equal opportunity and use it to show women that there cannot be equal opportunity when there is basic inequality in the economic and sexual structuring of society. Once we recognize that our society is based on the inequality of economic classes and sexual differences, we can take liberal feminist demands and show how they mystify the real relations of power. There is a basic conflict between a liberal (capitalist) society and a feminist one. The two do not mesh easily if one assumes feminist non-hierarchical relations between men and women. As a result, if we show *how* the two contradict each other, we can use the liberal feminist claims themselves to lay the basis for a more revolutionary outlook. In other words, if one wants a feminist society we will need to move further than liberalism (in terms of its capitalist and patriarchal structure) allows. Feminists need to unpack their liberal visions in order to see how they operate in the interests of the state and not women. In the end, women will be less than equal to men in whatever place they occupy until the sexual class structure is addressed.

There are some liberal feminists today who seem to understand this, make radical demands as a result, but who still adopt the liberal theory of politics to structure their feminist strategy for social change. The demands of these women are subversive to the state although their politics often does not make this clear. This "radical liberal feminist" tendency is actually subversive to the state in that it specifically addresses woman's position as a "working mother" in a sexual ghetto and seeks to identify woman's sexual class identity across economic and race lines. Spokeswomen for this viewpoint focus on the exploitation of women in the home, the sexual segregation of women in the work force, unequal pay, the right of women to reproductive choice, and the threat of nuclear energy to the survival of the species. I will argue that this politics led to Bella Abzug's dismissal from Carter's National Advisory Committee on Women. Many liberal feminists today, whether they are what I have termed "progressive" or "radical," understand much more about what women need than a simple review of their legal-liberal politics would lead one to believe they do. Actually, the demands made at the government-funded Houston Women's Conference in 1978 which was attended by a wide spectrum of feminists, not limited to any one segment of the movement but dominated by liberal feminists, have radical implications.

The Houston Report demands: "... as a human right a full voice and role for women in determining the destiny of our world, our nation, our families, and our individual lives."[9] It specifically calls for (1) the elimination of violence in the home and the development of shelters for battered women; (2) support for women's businesses; (3) a solution to child abuse; (4) federally funded non sexist child care; (5) a policy of full employment so that all women who wish and are able to work may do so; (6) the protection of homemakers so that marriage is a partnership; (7) an end to the sexist portrayal of women in the media; (8) establishment of reproductive freedom and the end to involuntary sterilization; (9) a remedy to the double discrimination against minority women; (10) a revision of criminal codes dealing with rape; (11) elimination of discrimination on the basis of sexual preference; (12) the establishment of nonsexist education; (13) an examination of all welfare reform proposals for their specific impact on women.[10] At present, although these demands are part of the consciousness of liberal feminists, they are not developed as a strategy or a theory of women's liberation: they do not challenge the existence of the state but only challenge its ideology, a challenge which is a necessary part of the analysis, but does not comprise the analysis totally. We are left to examine why this list of demands is insufficient and how liberal legal political strategy continues to limit the development of feminism in the United States.

FEMINISM, CAPITALISM, AND PATRIARCHY

We need to note the way that it is *not* in the interest of a capitalist economy to lessen its profits and that this is the cutting edge that shows why the *capitalist* economy cannot provide equality either between men and women or between men. When we look at the fight *against* the ERA we begin to see the issues more clearly. Elinor Langer in *Ms.* magazine states:

> . . . equality for women, coming on top of the decreasing flexibility in hiring and firing of black people that has followed the civil rights movement, would introduce an inelasticity into the labor force that their profit margins cannot bear.''[11]

If men and women had earned equal wages in 1970 it would have cost $96 billion. "If women had earned the same as men and worked the same number of hours, the addition to the payroll would have been 303 billion dollars."[12] The point here is that although a majority of women now work in the labor force we must realize that women are victimized and ghettoized in their jobs. According to 1973 statistics 93 percent of U.S. working women worked for less than $10,000 a year.[13] They most often occupy what have been termed pink collar jobs—waitresses, secretaries, hairdressers, etc.[14] The point here is that the Equal Rights Amendment stands in direct conflict with the role women now play in the labor force *which is* to provide just about the cheapest form of labor available. Capitalism is not based on a structure of equality requiring equal rights. Rather it is organized around the idea of equal rights within a structure of inequality. And what does that mean? The equal right to be unequal?

There is a second important point which needs to be addressed here. The *structure* of power which creates these inequalities is not merely the capitalist class system but the patriarchal structure of male supremacy. What is meant here is the sexual division of labor and society which divides the world into two worlds, one male, one female. The division lays the basis for a structural hierarchy which defines all women as alike. We are first mothers, wives, sisters before we are persons. This system of male supremacy provides society and men with a hierarchical organization which provides control and maintains the sexual reproduction of society. Women as wives and mothers within the family are absolutely necessary to the *smooth* functioning of our society as it presently exists. It is interesting to note that this system of male supremacy frees men from a whole realm of work while at the same time it denies women *equal access* to the labor force and to options outside the home. This is used as a justification for keeping women segregated in low paying, uncreative jobs. It used to be said that women's responsibilities in the home prevented their being able to carry full time "professional" jobs. Today it is said less but women are still effectively excluded, either by their responsibilities in the home or by the structural segregation which exists in the labor force. They work hand in hand to reinforce each other, and the system of higher profits and male privilege.

How does one define equality before the law given these conditions? The point, in sum, is how does one talk about women's equality in a system which by definition is patriarchal and protected by the sexual division of society via the sexual division of labor which divides everything from our dreams to our purposes, to our activity, sexually. Only a small part of this oppressive reality can be found explicitly stated in our legal system. No law says a woman must cook the meals, or dust the house. The law by itself assumes these relations of power and uses them to maintain inequality. But the law does not encompass all the relations of power. *The structure of power needs changing and with it the law.* Changing the law sometimes can put pressure on the structure, but usually these laws are protected with great amounts of power and privilege. There are also those elements of oppression which are extra-legal,[15] and won't be tackled by a legal assault. Put these two points together and a more developed strategy of change is needed, one which recognizes the necessity but also the insufficiency of a legal liberal view of power.

It is this theory of liberal feminism which locates power in the governmental realm rather than in the business world of the Trilateral Commission, the Round Table, and the World Banks, or the intimacy of our home and family life. And this is why liberal feminists do not understand that capitalism today supports women's oppression. This is also why feminists often believe that we can recommend lesbian rights be *given* to us without understanding that the *structure* of heterosexist power will have to be challenged along with male supremacy. Liberal feminists believe that women's "rights" can be recognized without challenging the "right to profit" in our society or the conception of woman as housewife, or the organization of the nuclear family. My question here is whether these expectations reflect an understanding of power in terms of the power relations which exist that negate individual choices and options or whether they are limited by the non-structural liberal theory of power.

It is interesting that Phyllis Schlafly does not say that she believes all women should be mothers but rather that there is nothing in society which says we cannot be anything we want to be. She shares some of the same values that progressive liberal feminists hold. And progressive and radical liberal feminism is in jeopardy to the extent that much of its liberalism serves to defend and protect the status quo even while its feminism is demanding certain changes. By not identifying the full structure of power, liberal feminism assures that women's anger will not be directed at its crucial underpinnings. While defending these aspects of the status quo, it is impossible to meet the feminist demands.

THE ERA AS NECESSARY BUT INSUFFICIENT

Schlafly thinks individuals have the freedom to do what they want if they utilize their individual power—and that society itself does not structurally interfere. This is her basis for rejecting the necessity of the ERA. We do not need it because the individual can have as much freedom/equality as *she* chooses. All we have is the possibility of losing some of our freedom because it (the ERA) might require something of us that we as individuals would not require of ourselves. On the other side stands the progressive liberal feminist position on the ERA. We need it because it will make us equal before the law. It seems to me that although it is important to support the ERA especially now that it is being challenged, it is also important to examine the theory of power implicit in this strategy of social change. It is important to make clear that much of our oppression as women derives from extra-legal realms and as such is not addressed by the sole demand for the ERA.

This is why I think the ERA should be understood as only a first step in building consciousness about the necessity of the destruction of patriarchy and capitalism as systems of power. We need to understand that the ERA presents a false notion that the public sphere (legal, governmental sphere) is where our lives are totally defined. We need to understand that the power relations which define our lives must take into account the economic class and hierarchical sexual spheres of our existence. Then the ERA as a demand for equality can be used to uncover the built in *inequality* of the economic class structure and patriarchal system we live in. In this sense the ERA as a demand for reform lays the basis for *revolutionary* consciousness. The ERA as a reform move will help lay the basis for restructuring the society because *equality* between men and women is not possible under the *power structures* of patriarchy and capitalism. As liberal feminists come to see how their feminism *cannot* be accommodated through liberalism because society as *it exists* cannot supply equality or equality of opportunity between men and women (either economically or sexually or racially) they will move towards a critique of liberalism and hence capitalism. The next step is to understand how capitalism and patriarchy work together. We have moved out of the simple reform/revolution dichotomy and we have become involved in the *process* of change.

Liberalism is not a theory about equality. It is a theory about freedom.[16] Liberal feminism is in the same way, asking for greater freedom for women while at the same time working from *structures* of power that allocate the freedom unequally. We already have freedom with inequality for women. We do not need more of this. We need more freedom with equality. And this requires a new structural organization of our society.

Let us learn from the U.S. feminists of the nineteeth century who were clearly liberal, yet radical for their time. Let us learn from their mistakes. They understood that they were individually, personally powerless but never came to integrate this analysis of their private lives into their political platform. Elizabeth Cady Stanton knew she was oppressed by isolated domestic activity even though she focused her attention on gaining equal representation in the public (state) realm. The problem then as now is that the liberal, legalistic notion of social change only understands power personally in sexual terms, and loses this when it speaks of this power in legal terms. Liberal theory is itself premised on the dichotomy between public and private life.

This is not to say we should abandon the legal struggle for greater equality of opportunity but these struggles must be connected to the process of showing how and why these demands are fought *against* by those in power. We must use this to build consciousness about how women are exploited and oppressed within the structures of capitalism and patriarchy. This is a sexual and racial and economic structure of power. Although the legal structure protects parts of this system, it does not encompass it in its totality. If anything, it mystifies the real system of power by making only parts of it visible. Once you focus on the law, as representative of the system of oppression, you are no longer able to see the total structure. Part of the law's deception is the severing of the private/public realms which cover up the realm of sexual power, and its connection to economic class and racial power. Reform politics' most important contribution to revolutionary struggle is the change of consciousness it brings about by changing the way we think about power relations, as the law becomes demystified.

Given this discussion of power, how does one assess the political importance of the government funded 1978 Houston Women's Conference? How can we try to analyze the conference in relation to the structure of power in society in order to better understand what was accomplished by it? What was its purpose? Was our purpose different than those who funded it?

THE HOUSTON CONFERENCE

The question I continue to ask myself is why did it happen? Why did the government budget $5 million to have a women's convention? My emphasis is not on the $5 million. This is a small amount of money in terms of budgeting government conferences. It works out to be 2^c per woman. The thing that made the women's conference seem as though a lot of money was spent was the way women chose to *use* the money and organize the conference. The $5 million went a long way, given the priorities set by the women organizing it. But why did the government budget the conference in the first place? I do not believe their reason: that they wanted to know what we wanted. I think they already knew that. They have known it for years. Then why? Doesn't it seem strange or politically perplexing that the same President Carter who called for a restrengthening of marriage and the family is the same president who funded the Houston Conference? Maybe not. The same president who led an assault on day care centers and other government funding for abortions, etc., and aid to women and said he had to hear what "the women of the U.S." want. Why? Did we really think he didn't know?

Is it because Carter believed that the reactionary forces (who already are well funded) needed to be countered by a more public hearing of "progressive liberal feminism"? In other words, is it possible that the reactionary statements on women's position are not really helpful to a society which requires that a majority of its women be working mothers? And that public reinforcement is needed for the position of working mothers? By *legitimizing* the women's movement and thereby delegitimizing it as a protest movement has there been a roundabout strenghtening of woman's position in society today as changing, and becoming more flexible when it's not? A platform was sent to the president. But what about its implementation? Do we think something will be done, when it won't?

What about those women who believed it was important to tell Carter and the government what women want? What concept of power do they operate from? Obviously they believe it is government (in the narrowest sense of the term) which decides how the society operates. But this view of policy making seems less valid than ever before in history. During the big oil crises in 1974 and 1979-80, when congress called upon business to produce inventories of how much oil they had in reserve, the oil companies refused to disclose any information. Congress and the president did nothing to enforce their request. Oil prices went up and the oil companies consolidated their control.

Do these women believe that the only reason we don't have what we want for ourselves and our families is because our interests haven't been heard? In other words, is there little understanding here of the real *antagonism* of interests between men and women given the system of patriarchy? There is also little understanding of what the priorities of those who rule are, and that our needs as women, mothers, and workers are in opposition to the needs they perceive for themselves and as a result, for us. Let's even say Carter doesn't know that women need day care, and equal pay, and let's say that the Houston Conference has put this on record. Does this then mean that these needs will be met? I don't think so. Why should those in power, by choice, begin to erode their own base of privilege. True, some needs must be met, but we need to be careful to ask, is this because we need them, or because those in power do.

My point is *not* that the women who took part in the Houston Conference were political lackeys. It is clear that most women who attended felt connected, or reconnected to a large and growing women's movement. It is important, however, to recognize that implicit in the Houston Conference is a re-commitment to the governmental arena (defined in very traditional terms) as a source for implementing change. This contradicts the very nature of their radical demands. We need to ask whether this is a sufficient political strategy or whether we need to link this to an assault against the oppression of women rooted in capitalism and patriarchy.

Understanding power is understanding that those who have it will fight against those who don't because this is part of the dynamic necessary to keep it for themselves. If this is the case, how do you *ask* for equality? or power? You don't. You must organize to take it.

I think it's important to clarify that the meeting in Houston needs to be understood in terms of the question of power. We used the Houston Conference as an opportunity to try and define our goals. But these did not make public the collaboration of capitalism and patriarchy in women's oppression. Why not? Because as a movement we are still being defined too much by the liberal male world. I do not mean to belittle what we have done. Houston was an opportunity, and we must use the opportunities we have. But we must not forget that not being in power, our opportunities are molded for us. That means we must take them, when they come, and remold them to make sure they are shaped according to our needs.

Houston was a beginning. But we need to be clear about what was begun. We need to be ready to *fight* for what we want as we continue to take advantage of the reformist politics of a liberal society. We are feminists—and no matter whether we are liberals, radicals, or socialists—as feminists our commitment is to equality between men and women. In the end we need to understand that for equality to exist between men and women, the structure of patriarchy must be destroyed and for this to happen today we must also dismantle capitalism. Reform is no longer sufficient. But neither is it irrelevant. If we can learn this, then we can win.

Part of winning, at this point is to understand that Carter was actively trying to demobilize the radical faction of the liberal feminist movement and actually laid the basis for Reagan's antifeminism by doing so. The firing of Bella Abzug was part of this tactic.

INTRA-STATE CONFLICT: CARTER & ABZUG

Abzug's firing reflects the high level of internal conflict, which is present within the state, over woman's role in society today. Part of this conflict involves the state's different views on how to salvage the troubled nuclear family. The problem also centers on how the state can demobilize the radical factions of the liberal feminist movement and curtail the growing liberal feminist consciousness among women in the U.S.

Certain "conservative" factions within the state are trying to reassert traditional family values by challenging existing abortion rulings, publicly-funded day care, the ratification of the ERA and homosexual rights. These four policy areas represent the arena for conflict between the conservative right and the center liberals, inside and outside the state apparati. The center liberals, represented by Carter, support the program of stabilizing the family while protecting the image and reality of the working mother. The passage of the ERA is seen as necessary to this strategy. The government's problem is to figure out how to keep the political interpretations of the ERA as narrow as possible, given the conflicts which exist within the state itself between the center and the conservative right. Both the center and the right are trying to contend with the new levels of liberal feminist consciousness in the country. The center liberal faction cannot ignore the conservative right in the state but its representative, Carter, realizes he cannot ignore the liberal feminists any longer without creating further instability for the "family" as a result of their discontent.

Phyllis Schlafly is an example of the conservative faction which does not understand, or want to accept, that her picture of womanhood is outdated, even in terms of the needs of the state. The center liberals know that it is. Elements of the antifeminist backlash do not accept the ideology or practice of the working mother (woman as a secondary wage earner and mother) nor do they understand why elements of the state support it. This is why the antifeminist campaign, supported and led by the "right" both inside and outside the state, is working at cross purposes with the center liberal factions of the state. Antifeminist activity heightens the conflicts which the center liberal dimensions of the state wish to mediate. But the center liberal faction of the state understands that as long as women are to remain in both the family and the waged world, this will be reflected in their liberal demands for equality, and as such must be recognized through the law. Carter's lip-service support of the ERA reflects this recognition.

The right obviously does believe it needs to reassert notions of the traditional family and motherhood by denying many of the feminist gains made for abortion and day care and equal rights. Those of the liberal center know that these gains are also related to women's ability to work and remain in the labor force, and understand that this is a necessity in an economy in which the wages of 46 percent of the jobs are unable to support a family of four. Carter's support of the ERA can be understood and hence reconciled with the huge political mobilization against it when one sees he is trying to preserve motherhood and the family while at the same time maintaining women's position in the waged economy.

If the state through the ERA (and the whole structure of law) can appear to bring satisfaction to liberal feminists, a great victory will be won by the state in its struggle to reassert patriarchal control of the system, by once again demobilizing the activity of liberal feminists by letting them think they have won something, when they have not. That is why the state has been trying to demobilize the feminist movement through the Houston Conference and the ERA. Carter's faction of the state realizes that women's equality before the law is an adjustment which the state has had to make in order to stem the tides of liberal feminist struggle, which otherwise might lead to more radical indictments of society. Carter understands that a law cannot make equality or *by itself* change dominant social relations. Representatives of the state know this although they disagree among themselves on how best to manipulate the pro-ERA feeling of the liberal feminists who believe real equality can be won through the law.

What is important for feminists to realize whether liberal, socialist, anarchist and/or lesbian—is that *the aim of the state is to stabilize the family by conceding women's legal equality through the ERA*. Hence, when we fight for the ERA we must do so with the understanding that it must be connected to other struggles which affect the actual structuring of our everyday lives. Then the passage of the ERA becomes only part of the strategy for the struggle for equality. It becomes a progressive tool we can use in our further struggles, Most important, we will not be fooled by what the state tries to push off as a victory. It rather will be understood as small hurdle passed in the long struggle toward liberation. We cannot let 1980 be 1920 all over again.

What does all this discussion have to do with Bella Abzug's dismissal? Her dismissal was basically Carter's attempt to further

legitimize the narrow legal focus on the ERA rather than the broader view of women's lives which involve questions of the economy, abortion, and homosexuality. Whether Abzug herself was any more progressive than her temporary replacement, Marjorie Bell Chambers, is irrelevant because she had come to represent these broader political issues to the public. Whatever else Marjorie Chambers was, she was not connected with the more radical elements of liberal feminism. The *New York Times* (15 January 1979) reported that she "has been active in the fight for improvements in the economic and legal status of women, she has generally stayed away from the more controversial issues, such as abortion and lesbian rights." Abzug's permanent replacement, Lynda Byrd Robb, further documents this effort. Carter has to reassert his narrow interpretation of the ERA, against pressure from the right within the state. He did it with the dismissal of Abzug.

The ERA is Carter's *indirect* attempt at stabilizing the family by *demobilizing feminist discontentment*. The right liberals in the state disagree and think that the only way to stabilize the family is by fighting abortion and limiting women's choices. Nevertheless, the liberal patriarchal state, even with this level of conflict, is in control here—and is trying hard to keep the feminism of liberal feminism from undermining the supposed stability of the family and hence society. In this sense, Carter's support of the ERA is actually antifeminist if the meaning of feminism has to do with redefining the choices open to women. This is what we must understand. We must understand the motives of the state and, I think, they are trying to keep us in our place as secondary wage earners and as mothers. If we understand this, then we can begin to understand as a women's movement that our feminism can not be met by the patriarchal state which has no commitment to our liberation.

Radical and socialist feminists know this but unless we are part of the liberal feminist struggles with the state we have little ability to fight for this radical political understanding. What becomes very clear is that if we are to be a part of the struggles with the state on questions of the ERA, abortion rights, welfare payments, etc., we need to develop a more coherent feminist theory of the state. Radical feminists, if they discuss the state, equate it with patriarchy itself, but have no particular analysis or strategy as a result. Neither do socialist feminists who equate the state with the ruling capitalist class. The state is rather a complicated blend of the capitalist and

patriarchal social relations in our society. The state functions in relatively autonomous ways as it tries to mediate the conflicts between the economic class needs and the patriarchal requisites of the state.[17] When pushed by reform demands, the patriarchal dimensions of the state become clear. Then liberal feminists can see the patriarchal bias of the state. Once they see this, understanding the economic class dimensions of the state is easier, particularly in these times of the greedy oil companies, subsidization of Chrysler, and Carter's unwillingness to limit corporate profits and hence inflation.

All women share the reality of patriarchy, however differently. We, as feminists, are the only ones who can determine the potential inherent in this for us *politically*—in terms of radicalizing each other and building coalitions within the women's movement and outside of it.

FOOTNOTES

1. See Zillah Eisenstein, "Developing a Theory of Capitalist Patriarchy and Socialist Feminism" in Z. Eisenstein, ed., *Capitalist Patriarchy & the Case for Socialist Feminism* (New York: Monthly Review Press, 1978).
2. See Nancy Chodorow, *The Reproduction of Mothering: Psychoanalysis and the Sociology of Gender* (Berkeley: University of California Press, 1978); Dorothy Dinnerstein, *The Mermaid and the Minotaur, Sexual Arrangements and Human Malaise* (New York: Harper and Row, 1976); Jane Flax, "The Conflict Between Nurturance and Autonomy in Mother-Daughter Relations and Within Feminism," *Feminist Studies*, Vol. 4, no. 2 (June 1978), pp. 171-192; Gayle Rubin, "The Traffic in Women: Notes on the Political Economy of Sex," in Rayna Reiter, *Toward An Anthropology of Women* (New York: Monthly Review Press, 1975).
3. See Zillah Eisenstein, "Some Notes on the Relations of Capitalist Patriarchy," in Z. Eisenstein, *op. cit.*, for a discussion of the transformation of the marxist method.
4. We could as socialist feminists debate among ourselves, or with marxists about particular points in Hartmann's article—like, whether we should call ourselves marxists or socialists. I choose socialist because it is a

more open term, and the unknown dimensions of feminism require this. But I can fight for abortion with anyone who is willing to fight. We don't have to agree on it all. As well, I think it makes sense to speak of our present society as a capitalist patriarchy because patriarchy is the continuous political form in history. Hartmann chooses the term patriarchal capitalism. I don't know why. But it needn't be a source of disunity.

5. See *Women Under Attack: Abortion, Sterilization Abuse, and Reproductive Freedom*, CARASA pamphlet, P.O. Box 124, Cathedral Station, New York, New York 10025.

6. See Nancy Hartsock, "Feminist Theory and the Development of Revolutionary Strategy," in Eisenstein, *op. cit.*

7. This argument can be substantiated through the writings of John Locke, Jean Jacques Rousseau, Mary Wollstonecraft, John Stuart Mill, Harriet Taylor, and Elizabeth Cady Stanton. See Eisenstein, *The Radical Future of Liberal Feminism*, *op. cit.*

8. Much of the following discussion was delivered as the keynote address at a women's conference in Houston, Texas on 4 March 1978. The conference was sponsored by the Women's Group of the First Unitarian Church of Houston. The conference, entitled *Women and Power*, was to focus on how women understand and have understood power. About 250 women attended the conference. Over thirty percent of the audience was over forty-five years old. The audience was mixed racially, ethnically, and in terms of economic class. Most women who attended had children, and also work in the labor force. From the questions asked after this talk it is clear that the audience spanned the reality from welfare women to highly paid engineers. Many, maybe most of the women present, were secretaries, factory and service workers, and mothers, although there were artists and housewives as well. Across all the differences there was an amazing commitment to examine what we are doing as a women's movement and where we are going. It was the most exciting conference I've been to in years because people were really willing to examine the necessity of a revolutionary analysis. This readiness, in part, grew out of their involvement in the IWY conference and then its critique.

9. *An Official Report to the President, the Congress and the People of the United States, March 1978, The Spirit of Houston* (Washington, D.C.: National Commission on the Observance of International Women's Year, 1978), p. 15.

10. *Ibid.*, see the entire report.

11. Elinor Langer, "Why Big Business is Trying to Defeat the ERA," *Ms. Magazine*, Vol. IV, no. 11 (May 1976), p. 66.

12. *Ibid.*, p. 102.

13. Karen Lindsey, "Do Women Have Class," *Liberation*, vol. 20, no. 2 (January-February 1977), p. 18.

14. Louise Kapp Howe, *Pink Collar Workers* (New York: G.P. Putnam's Sons, 1977).

15. See Rosa Luxemburg, "Reform or Revolution" in *Selected Political Writings*, Dick Howard, ed. (New York: Monthly Review Press, 1971) for a discussion of the extra-legal nature of bourgeois domination. I am using this construct to apply to extra-legal patriarchal oppression as well.

16. C. B. MacPherson, *Democratic Theory* (New York: Oxford University Press, 1973).

17. See Ralph Miliband, *Marxism and Politics* (Oxford: Oxford University Press, 1977) and Nicos Poulantzas, *State, Power, Socialism* (London: New Left Review, 1978), for their discussion of the relative autonomy of the state, although neither one discusses the question of autonomy in terms of the needs of patriarchy. Also see, Eisenstein, *The Radical Future of Liberal Feminism*, Chapter 10; and Annette Kuhn and Ann Marie Wolpe, eds., *Feminism and Materialism* (London: Routledge and Kegan Paul, 1978).

SUMMARY AND RESPONSE: CONTINUING THE DISCUSSION

Heidi Hartmann

Each of the essays collected here strives to increase our understanding of gender relations in the current social formation. The critical issues raised in the collection are many: What are the sources of dynamic tension in patriarchal capitalism (one system or two)? Why does patriarchy persist even as forms change? How do we forge a theory and a practice that addresses racism? What is the role of heterosexism in patriarchal capitalism? How can we understand psychological constructs and their role in the perpetuation of racism, patriarchy, and capitalism? How can we attack hierarchy? What are the current openings for action? How do we move people to action? What is the revolutionary role of men? of liberal feminists? I would like to comment on the way these issues are treated by the various authors and to point out what seem to me to be fruitful directions for further thinking and action.

The "Unhappy Marriage" postulates the existence of two separate but interlocking sets of social relations, capitalism and patriarchy, each with a material base, each with its own dynamic. A preliminary analysis of patriarchy, particularly as it exists in capitalist societies, is offered. Several of the other essays in this volume (particularly those by Young, Vogel, Hicks, and Al-Hibri) challenge this view of the current social formation as determined by the operation of two systems and offer various ways to collapse the dualism into one—one system that determines both gender and economic relations in our society. I do not find any of these attempts persuasive, yet. For the time being I find the notion of separate, interrelated systems more useful, not only for understanding our society and the dual (and indeed multiple) motivations of various groups and their shifting alliances, but also for understanding the persistence of patriarchy in socialist societies (I do not agree with those who argue that the USSR, China, and Cuba are not socialist—they may not have the socialism we would like, but they regard themselves as socialist and so do most other folks).

Let me comment on these attempts. Iris Young argues that we must understand patriarchal capitalism (capitalist patriarchy) as one system of which women's oppression is an integral aspect. She defines capitalism as an economic system that, among other things, marginalizes women (via the division of labor) and gives men benefits, and she notes that the development of a capitalism

that is intrinsically patriarchal was the only historical possibility. Young emphasizes the extent to which patriarchal relations shape capitalist economic relations and the concomitant necessity for the marxian view of the economic sphere to be modified. In this sense we need not a dual vision but a "doubled vision" (Joan Kelly's phrase) that sees patriarchy and capitalism operating everywhere simultaneously (not merely in different spheres). This is a useful reminder.

Young suggests the division of labor as a concept which can help us look at all relevant divisions simultaneously (race, sex, and class, for example). Unless we understand, however, how these divisions arise and why (that is, the sources of dynamism in the system) this concept is merely a static, descriptive category, in my opinion. We can imagine a three dimensional matrix in which each cell represents that group of people who are, for example, Black male working class or white female "middle" class, but it is not clear that such a matrix will tell us much about what positions these groups will take in the struggle or what alliances they might make around particular issues. There is no dynamic that causes white females married to white working class males to take a particular, consistent stance. Rather it is overlapping class and gender interests (as well as national and race interests) that interact in changing, fluid ways and influence people's actions. The present configuration of the division of labor is the result of the underlying dynamics of patriarchy and capitalism—it doesn't have its own dynamic.

The point of Young's essay, and indeed of most "unifying" analyses, is to show that feminism is necessarily anti-capitalist because capitalism is inherently patriarchal, and that socialists necessarily fight against patriarchy in their fight against (patriarchal) capitalism. The struggle can thus be a unified one. One problem with the political implications of Young's theoretical framework is that it is not true that struggles are intrinsically both anti-capitalist and anti-patriarchal. There are many examples of socialist movements which did not combat patriarchal relations and of feminist movements which did not challenge capitalist relations. Capitalism and patriarchy are very flexible and adaptable and, to my mind, somewhat autonomous. Unless we can discover a *theoretical* reason for the inherent connection between capitalism and patriarchy (their mere historical convergence is not sufficient), we don't get very far trying to analyze them as one system. It does not seem to me that Young provides that

theoretical connection; she merely asserts it. The common enemy is reduced to the least common denominator (more accurately the intersection of overlapping sets)—white male capitalists. The problem is that although just about everyone else is opposed to this small group they are also frequently in opposition to one another (women against men, black against white, and not necessarily women and minority males against white men—although such alliances will sometimes occur).

Lise Vogel's and Emily Hicks' essays also attempt to offer alternative unified views. Hicks, like Young, posits the necessity to study race, gender, and class simultaneously in the cultural context in which they interact. She proposes that a cultural marxism is capable of doing this. Vogel suggests that the marxist concept of social reproduction can be used to understand women's oppression. Like Young, both authors aim at improving marxist methodology. While both suggest the power these new approaches might have, they stop short of providing analyses using these approaches so we are left wanting to know more about them. Both authors suggest, however, that it is necessary to move beyond a narrowly defined materialist approach. This is a theme which is echoed by several other authors as well, and to which I will return below.

Azizah Al-Hibri also offers a unified view of the world, but she uses radical feminist, not marxist methodology. Her unity of patriarchy and capitalism has a theoretical base—it is the male drive for immortality. In her view both production and reproduction can be instruments to provide men a sense of immortality. In order to gain immortality via reproduction men have to control women (who have access to immortality by having babies). Patriarchy is fundamentally domination, then, and capitalism is an advanced form of that domination, one which elevates production and allows men to gain immortality via production as well (which also requires domination of others). The dynamism in the society comes from men's seeking new and more satisfying ways to dominate and from women's rebelling. The driving force of history is thus the male psyche. While this view of history may be unsatisfying to many marxist feminists because it is so purely psychological, it does have the virtue of internal consistency and provides a clear and unambiguous theoretical link between capitalism and patriarchy that marxist feminists have not been able to discover. The radical feminist approach also solves another problem of marxist feminist theory—what *is* the source of dynamism in patriarchal social relations, if it is *not* a male drive

for power. The "Unhappy Marriage" really provides no satisfactory solution to this problem. The radical feminist approach, of course, leaves unanswered the question of the origins of the male power urge, unless one assumes it is biological.

Harding's essay confronts this issue head-on; the origins of men's urge to dominate lie in our childrearing practices. Like Al-Hibri, she sees that both patriarchy and capitalism are based upon domination (both being based upon dominating men). While Al-Hibri sees capitalism as the offspring of patriarchy, Harding views them as "genetic siblings." Harding is not particularly troubled by the dualism question. Rather her essay addresses a gap she perceives in the theoretical framework suggested in the "Unhappy Marriage." Basing her work upon that by Jane Flax and Nancy Chodorow, she argues that the concept of the material base must be extended to the division of labor by gender which characterized childrearing patterns. In this view, the dynamics of mothering by women only (coupled with women's inferior social position) create men who seek to dominate others. This then provides the theoretical connection between patriarchy and capitalism. Harding's work raises an important political question which must be confronted by the feminist movement—what is the political role of men in the revolution? The long term strategy suggested by Harding's work leads toward working for changes in childrearing, that it become a shared responsibility of social and economic equals. While broadening the concept of what is materialist to include personality structures which grow out of the division of labor is important, and while equalizing childcare responsibilities is valuable in its own right, I am not personally at all convinced that childrearing is the most powerful lever in our efforts to bring about social change.

The essays by Riddiough, Joseph, Ehrlich, and Stewart are also addressed to critical gaps in the theoretical framework provided in the "Unhappy Marriage." Christine Riddiough addresses the interconnection between feminism and gay rights. While she argues for a holistic view of society in which the struggles for feminism and gay liberation are seen to be united, she does not use the feminist analyses of heterosexism that are being developed. In Harding's work, for example, heterosexism can be seen to grow out of the same pattern of childrearing which produces male dominance, and challenges to heterosexism are, therefore, fundamentally anti-patriarchal (challenging, for example, the division of labor by gender).[1] Riddiough's analysis, in

contrast, stresses the challenge of gay liberation to ruling class ideology; by implication, patriarchy is for her important primarily as an ideological support for ruling class hegemony, not something to be destroyed in its own right. Male dominance is for her the dominance of the white male ruling class. In other words, her framework for unity is, like Young's, based on the *intersection* of both interests. Nevertheless Riddiough's stress on the connections between feminism and gay liberation raises a critical issue for marxist feminist theory; in particular the link between patriarchy and heterosexuality needs to be further explored.

Gloria Joseph's essay stresses the necessity for feminist theory to consider racism and for white feminists to recognize their implication in the three-way partnership of patriarchy, capitalism, and racism both as tools and benefactors. The differences in the experiences between Black and white women and between Black and white men must be recognized and must have a central place in any social theory. To speak of women as one category is to be implicitly racist; no theory of male domination can ignore the subordinate position of Black men. In pointing to the solidarity between Black women and men, Joseph is also pointing to the lack of solidarity between Black and white women. Just as men cannot be relied on to liberate women, white women are not likely to liberate Black women because they directly benefit from racial oppression (and generally rely on racially inflated white male incomes).[2] Joseph stresses the need for theory to understand why racism persists and suggests that since neither racism nor sexism can be reduced to purely economic relations we must look beneath economics as well. Thus the theoretical framework in the "Unhappy Marriage" must be substantially altered to encompass racism before it can be relevant to Black people. While I probably differ with Joseph in a few particulars, Joseph's argument seems to me fundamentally incontrovertible and points to an essential direction for further work.

Carol Ehrlich argues that anarchist feminism provides analyses of several important issues not touched on in my essay. One such issue is the hierarchy necessitated by the existence of the state. Anarchism has a developed critique of hierarchy which applies to both capitalist and patriarchal relations. Thus, Ehrlich argues that while marxism and feminism can't be married anarchism and feminism can be. Anarchism goes beyond material base arguments by looking at political power. For example, in the

anarchist feminist view, violence against women, which is surely one of the key elements of patriarchy, is seen as an example of the exercise of power purely for power's sake, rather than primarily as an attempt to solidify men's economic position, via control over women and therefore over their labor power. Ehrlich's essay in this collection does not address the question of where this drive comes from; surely this would be an important next step. She does suggest, however, the need to look at the connections between the psychological and the material.

Katie Stewart's essay examines how people experience hierarchies in their daily lives and how they understand their experiences. Most importantly Stewart argues that people's ideologies cannot be seen as simple reflections of their objective and rational interests. Political strategies must be based as much upon people's understandings of their situations and their ideologies as on their objective material interests. Like Ehrlich she emphasizes the inability to reduce the social and political relations between women and men to the merely economic; relations of dominance and subordination are about more than the control of labor power. Strategies must aim at the full range of "relations and institutions which structure political struggles between women and men, workers and capitalists" (Stewart, p. 303). People's objective conditions are not enough to lead them to act; they must be mobilized as well.

The attempt to broaden and go beyond materialism, represented in the essays by Harding, Hicks, Ehrlich, and Stewart, seems to me to be quite important, particularly in the current political situation. Questions of consciousness, of people's understandings of their situations, of their own psychic investments in their stance toward the world, of the ability to change, are all critical in developing political strategies that can be successful.

The essays by Ferguson and Folbre and by Brown more or less accept the framework offered in "Unhappy Marriage" and attempt to move us forward by looking at how patriarchal relations are currently changing. Ann Ferguson and Nancy Folbre, looking at "changes in the character and degree of patriarchal domination and in the mechanisms of domination" (p. 316), suggest that the most important area for attention is the "sex-affective" work women do in the home, caring for men and children. In general, they argue, women's sex-affective work has decreased while their wage work has increased. Emphasizing the contradiction created by this change, they argue that women can

use their performance of wage work as a lever for change in sex-affective work. They also suggest that the concerns they have developed in sex-affective work give women a basis for developing ways to carry out nurturing tasks collectively. Carol Brown argues that the main change in the form of patriarchy has been the shift from "individual" to "public" patriarchy, that is patriarchal control is exercised less in the private sphere of the home and more in public institutions (for example, the economy-wide use of cheap female labor power and the state provision of benefits to families with dependent children). In looking at that shift, she also focuses on changes in "sex-affective work" (Ferguson and Folbre's term), particularly childrearing and the financial responsibility for children. While there may be strategic openings because of conflict over women's labor power and where it is deployed, as Ferguson and Folbre suggest, Brown warns us that we have to develop strategies that combat emerging patriarchal forms, particularly in the public arena. While contradictions create openings for us, they may also resolve themselves in such a way as to create a new and stronger partnership.

Zillah Eisenstein argues that we should focus our political energies on working with the liberal feminist movement. Strategically, our goal should be to develop a unified women's movement. Liberal feminists, she argues, do not perceive the real limits to the success of strategies aimed at reform of patriarchy. In Eisenstein's view, eliminating patriarchy necessarily entails eliminating capitalism; the women's movement will only be successful if it comes to understand this. The task of marxist feminists is to raise these issues in the women's movement and move it toward this understanding. To do this, we must develop a feminist theory of the state, the entity to which most of the demands of liberal feminists have been posed, that makes clear the role of the state in maintaining patriarchy and the necessary limits on state-based reforms. While I am in agreement with Eisenstein's emphasis on moving the women's movement in more radical directions (and, the consequent need for a marxist feminist theory of the state), I do not find convincing the theoretical reason advanced for doing so (the necessary connection between patriarchy and capitalism via hierarchy).

I find the theoretical questions raised by the essays in this volume equally as important as the strategic issues posed; theory and action progress in tandem. Several of the authors have stressed the need for a major modification of marxist theory in

order to deal with the issues raised by feminism. They are correct in their view that the "Unhappy Marriage" does not argue for such a modification. Rather it attempts to use marxist methodology to analyze patriarchy from a materialist perspective. Our goal in the essay was to retrieve patriarchy from the realm of the purely ideological where it had been consigned by most marxists and many marxist feminists. As such it was an argument addressed primarily to that audience (those who thought patriarchy only ideological), urging them to use their marxism to consider patriarchy as a system of social relations based on men's control of women's labor power, both in the home and in the wider economy. When Amy Bridges and I first began work on this argument I think it is safe to say we felt we were in the minority among marxist feminists in our assertion that patriarchy has equal force with capitalism in the social formation, that gender is as important as class in people's lives. Most argued then that class was dominant.

Now the debate has come full circle. None of the contributors to this volume argues against this view of patriarchy's importance (although there is still some debate about how to address it using marxist theory and there may be some marxists who did not contribute to this volume who would argue that class is more important). But what the attempt to analyze patriarchy fully has brought about is a questioning both of the marxist view of what is material and of the dominance of the "material base" over the "ideological superstructure" in marxist theory generally. Several of the contributors view the framework presented in the "Unhappy Marriage" as too materialist; they put forth ideology, psychology, or culture as either equal with the "base" or part of the base. They do so not to dismiss patriarchy but to better understand it in all its complexity. Patriarchy they say is not merely about the control of female labor power, but about psychic power, personality structures, and so on. I am definitely sympathetic with this view; I think it leads us in the right direction away from a narrowly economistic marxism.

I am not prepared to go along, however, with the thesis that patriarchy is the basis of all hierarchy. In the radical feminist version of this argument a male drive to power is postulated. In the psychoanalytic version, current childrearing arrangements are thought to create dominating individuals who are men. In this view, patriarchy is either the logical precondition for capitalism (Al-Hibri) or at least the genetic sibling (Harding). I remain

unconvinced. Primarily because I see no theoretical basis for a universal male drive for power. Although I recognize that the unconscious is a very powerful element of human personality, I am skeptical that the effects of any childrearing arrangement on personality are so enduring. In addition because other bases, such as racism, for hierarchy exist; in my view these also do not necessarily arise from patriarchy.

Marxist theory may well require some revision in order to encompass fully gender and racial oppression. In particular what some have previously regarded as the material base (and its overwhelming importance) needs modification. Moreover, the study of the interaction of all these phenomena—class, gender, and race, as well as psychology, ideology, and culture—will undoubtedly uncover new social dynamics. The recognition of the importance of gender and racism in the functioning of the capitalist workplace (for example) will undoubtedly change our understanding of capitalism. Nevertheless, while once in the vanguard I may now be in the rearguard beating a hasty retreat from grander theorists.

Of equal importance with these potential modifications of marxist theory is the need to develop a better understanding of racism, its role in patriarchy and capitalism and vice versa, the investment of white women in it, and the consequent differences in the experiences of Black and white women. Such an understanding is essential if we are to transform society as we desire. An understanding of the oppression of lesbians and the links between patriarchy and heterosexism must also be developed. And most fundamentally we must understand the contradictions among social phenomena, the sources of dynamism and the likely directions of change, learning from our inevitable mistakes and keeping on with the struggle.

The essays in this collection move us further toward these goals. Let us continue the debate and the political activity that advances it, learn from our inevitable mistakes, and keep on struggling.

FOOTNOTES

1. Also see Gayle Rubin, "The Traffic in Women," in *Toward an Anthropology of Women,* ed. Rayna Reiter (New York: Monthly Review Press, 1975).
2. See Phyllis Marynick Palmer, "Black Women/White Women: The Dichotomization of Female Identity," paper presented at the annual meeting of the American Studies Association, Minneapolis, Minnesota, September 1979 (revised, George Washington University, 1981).